MINORITY STUDENT RETENTION

The Best of the
Journal of College Student Retention:
Research, Theory, & Practice

Edited by
Alan Seidman

Baywood Publishing Company, Inc.
Amityville, New York

Copyright © 2007 by Baywood Publishing Company, Inc., Amityville, New York

All rights reserved. No part of this book may be reproduced or utilized in any form or by any means, electronic or mechanical, including photo-copying, recording, or by any information storage or retrieval system, without permission in writing from the publisher. Printed in the United States of America on acid-free recycled paper.

Baywood Publishing Company, Inc.
26 Austin Avenue
P.O. Box 337
Amityville, NY 11701
(800) 638-7819
E-mail: baywood@baywood.com
Web site: baywood.com

Library of Congress Catalog Number: 2006101362
ISBN-13: 978-0-89503-331-4 (cloth)
ISBN-10: 0-89503-331-3 (cloth)

Library of Congress Cataloging-in-Publication Data

Minority student retention : the best of the journal of college student retention : research, theory, and practice / edited by Alan Seidman.
    p. cm.
  Includes bibliographical references and index.
  ISBN-13: 978-0-89503-331-4 ((cloth) : alk. paper)
  ISBN-10: 0-89503-331-3 ((cloth) : alk. paper) 1. Minority college students--United States. 2. College attendance--United States. 3. College dropouts--United States. I. Seidman, Alan.

  LC3731.M565 2007
  378.1'6190973--dc22

                                        2006101362

ACC LIBRARY SERVICES
AUSTIN, TX

Dedication

For Brody and his nana Barbara

Contents

SECTION 3   Asian and Asian Pacific Students

SECTION 4   Native American Students

SECTION 5   Biracial Students

SECTION 6   Institutional

Introduction

The book showcases the best minority student articles that have appeared in the *Journal of College Student Retention: Research, Theory & Practice.* By providing these cutting edge articles, colleges, universities, national, state and government policy makers can gain additional insight into this important topic and use the material to enhance minority student retention.

Minority student retention continues to be a major issue in and a vexing problem for the higher education community. Year after year colleges and universities spend vast amounts of money on programs and services to help students persist. Particular interest has been paid to underrepresented groups of students whose retention rates continue to be below those of majority students.

In 1999 the *Journal of College Student Retention: Research, Theory & Practice* was founded to provide a voice to the educational community concerning college student retention issues. The *Journal* continues to be the premier journal devoted solely to the issue of college student retention worldwide.

A panel of well-known retention scholars was assembled to review all *Journal of College Student Retention: Research, Theory & Practice* articles pertaining to minority student retention. The "best of the best" articles which appeared in the *Journal* have been brought together in a coherent whole to provide the educational community with a resource to help minority students persist.

As with the U.S. population, college enrollments are becoming more diverse. College enrollments in 1990 (United States Department of Education, 1998) were made up of 77.5% white students while 19.5% were minority students (numbers do not add to 100% due to international student enrollment). Of the 19.5% minority students, 9% were African American, 5.6% Hispanic, 4% Asian, and .7% American Indian.

By the year 2000 (United States Department of Education, 2000) whites made up 68% of the students enrolled in higher education, and minorities made up 32% of college enrollments. The 32% minority enrollment consists of 13% African Americans, 12% Hispanics, 6% Asians, and 1% American Indians.

According to Seidman (2005):

> Although minority students are entering college at a higher rate than in previous years, they continue to leave at a higher rate than nonminorities. The

1

data is quite revealing. The Consortium for Student Retention Data Exchange (CSRDE) is sponsored by the Center for Institutional Data Exchange and Analysis at The University of Oklahoma, which consists of over five hundred four-year colleges. The CSRDE (2002) data for first-year retention rates of students entering four-year colleges in 1999 reveal the following: for all types of institutions, regardless of selectivity, whites were retained from the first year to the second year at an 80.3% rate; blacks were retained at a 74.7% rate, Hispanic students at a 75.7% rate, and American Indians at a 67.2% rate. Asian students were retained at an 86.9% rate—the highest persistence rate of any ethnic group.

When looking at the CSRDE (2003) six-year graduation rates for students who began college in the fall 1994 semester, we find that for whites 56.9% graduated within six years, compared with 41.7% of black students, 41.7% of Hispanics, and 35.8% of American Indians. Again, Asian students not only persisted at the highest rate but graduated at the highest rate, 61.1%. The correlation between first-year retention rates and six-year graduate rates of ethnic groups is also obvious (p. 8).

So, it is no wonder colleges and universities are concerned with minority student retention and so many pages of the *Journal* have been devoted to minority college student retention issues.

This book is in six sections: African American Students (5 articles), Latino/a Students (2 articles), Asian and Asian Pacific Students (1 article), Native American Students (1 article), Biracial Students (1 article), and Institutional (4 articles) retention efforts. Each topical area is self-explanatory.

From all indications, there is still a continuing need for research and practice to help minority students persist through academic and personal goal attainment. It is the hope of this book to show what is currently being done, raise questions, and stimulate debate and hopefully more research on this ever important topic. This collection of articles showcases what has been and currently is being done, raises questions, and stimulates debate and can serve to clarify future research.

My sincere thanks to my panel of scholars who when asked to review 28 articles, enthusiastically volunteered knowing the importance of this endeavor. I am grateful to Stuart Cohen, president of Baywood Publishing Company, Inc. who encouraged this important project. And finally I would like to thank my wife Barbara for her continued support of my efforts.

REFERENCES

Consortium for Student Retention Data Exchange (CSRDE). (2002). Executive summary 2000-01 CSRDE report. Norman, OK: Center for Institutional Data Exchange and Analysis, The University of Oklahoma.

Consortium for Student Retention Data Exchange (CSRDE). (2003). Executive summary 2001-02 CSRDE report. Norman, OK: Center for Institutional Data Exchange and Analysis, The University of Oklahoma.

Seidman, A. (2005). Minority student retention: Resources for practitioners. In *Minority retention: What works?* (pp. 7-24). G. H. Gaither (ed.), San Francisco, CA: Jossey-Bass.

United States Census Bureau. (2003). *USA Statistics in Brief.* ww.census.gov/statab/www/popart.html.

United States Department of Education. (1998, May). National Center for Education Statistics, Higher Education General Information Survey (HEGIS), "Fall Enrollment in Colleges and Universities" survey; and Integrated Postsecondary Education Data System (IPEDS), "Fall Enrollment" surveys.

United States Department of Education. (2000). NCES, 1999-2000 National Postsecondary Student Aid Study (NPSAS: 2000).

SECTION 1

African-American Students

CHAPTER 1

Correlates of Retention for African-American Males in Community Colleges

Linda Serra Hagedorn, William Maxwell,
and Preston Hampton

The retention rates of African-American men in community colleges are among the lowest of all ethnic groups nationally. This study analyzes organizational data for three cohorts of men in a longitudinal design for three semesters ($N = 202$), and uses logistic regression to identify the factors that best predict retention. The importance of high school grades, age, number of courses, a positive view of personal skills, clear high goals, and the early identification of a college major appear to be salient for this group and offer implications for practice.

Although the civil rights movement of the 1960s remains only a distant memory, issues of equal access to higher education and barriers to desirable employment with higher earnings continue to be a reality for many African Americans. The evidence of unequal opportunities is evident by the staggering proportion (26 percent) of African Americans living below the poverty level (U.S. Census Bureau, 1997). While African Americans make up 12.8 percent of the American population, they comprise 40 percent of the chronically poor (Shinagawa & Jang, 1998). In addition, African Americans have an unemployment rate that is double that of the general population (Shinagawa & Jang, 1998).

The demographic statistics for *male* African Americans are equally dismal. Black men in American society confront formidable challenges to success including lower achievement scores in basic subject areas, higher likelihood of placement in programs for students with learning disabilities, higher likelihood of school suspension, and are the frequent victims of lowered expectations by educational professionals (Reed, 1988). While the number of African-American men enrolled in the nation's colleges and universities has increased slightly during the 1990s, it remains disturbingly low (Reisberg, 1999). African Americans are the only racial group in which females appear to frequently attain greater rewards than males. Cuyjet (1997) commented that "a cursory look around most predominantly white campuses (unless one is standing in a location frequented by the football and basketball athletes) probably reveals the fact that black women attend college in proportionally larger numbers than black men" (p. 5). The proportion of African-American men who graduate from high school, achieve a bachelor's degree or higher, enter the labor force, or become managers or business professionals is lower than the proportion of African-American women who achieve these same milestones (Shinagawa & Jang, 1998).

The reasons for the unique gender differences may be quite complex. Lee (1994) posits that the combination of racial discrimination and lowered socioeconomic status experienced by many African Americans creates a complex array of historical and social interactions that ultimately blend to inhibit success. Majors and Billson (1992) have labeled this phenomenon "subjective cultural realities for black males" (p. 109).

Facts and figures support the commonly accepted nexus between high achievement and higher education, especially for African Americans. The U.S. Census Bureau (1998) indicated the median income of African Americans with only a high school diploma as $18,683, as compared to $31,047 for those with a bachelor's degree. Most would agree that the negative outcomes of un- and under-employment so prevalent among African-American males could be alleviated and reduced with larger scale, more focused efforts in postsecondary education. While the goal may be obvious and simplistic, the avenue to achieving the goal—widespread success in college—is not obvious, direct, nor easily attained.

Community colleges are the predominant entry point for postsecondary instruction for the majority of students of color, including African Americans (Chenoweth, 1998; McCool, 1984; Nora & Rendon, 1990). But the retention of these students remains an important yet perplexing and complicated issue at community colleges, where most students commute, have employment and/or family responsibilities, and are generally poorer than traditional four-year college students (Tinto, Russo, & Kadel, 1994). These students must cope with personal issues such as family or financial problems, lack of child care, and job demands concurrent with the demands of college (Kerka, 1995). Thus, many community college students, especially African-American males, do not achieve their educational goals. Data from the Beginning Postsecondary Student Survey (BPS)–Second Follow-up (National

Center of Education Statistics, 1994) indicates that only 16.6 percent of African Americans who began their education in community colleges in 1989-90 could be traditionally classified as persisters.[1] This finding is consistent with previous research indicating that African Americans are about 22 percent more likely than their white counterparts to leave college prior to goal completion (Carter & Wilson, 1993; Porter, 1990). Among African-American males in community colleges, the retention rate is even more shocking—less than 10 percent (Chenoweth, 1998).

PURPOSE OF THE STUDY

The under-representation of African-American men has serious repercussions not only for the men themselves, but also for our nation as a whole. Whenever a group of individuals is not interacting and achieving at optimum levels, the country is robbed of talent that could enrich the lives of many. We are compelled to question the deplorable retention rates among this important population subsample and to determine factors and subsequent policy to provide academic success. Since the majority of African-American men who begin postsecondary instruction do so at community colleges, it seems intuitive that the identification of factors that promote retention and subsequent success in these institutions is a worthy and important endeavor. Because there has been so little research on this group, the present study was designed not to test a well-elaborated framework of hypotheses but instead to explore the following questions:

- What are the significant factors predicting retention among African-American males in an urban community college?
- Do the factors promoting retention vary with respect to number of semesters enrolled? In other words, do the same factors that promote retention through the first semester also promote retention through the second semester? And what factors will continue to promote retention in a third semester?

CONCEPTUAL FRAMEWORK

A variety of relevant independent variables are suggested in the conceptual literature concerning theories of integration, attrition, and status attainment among community college students.

Integration

The dominant paradigm in retention research posits that academic achievements and social relations with college peers promote learning and retention. Tinto (1975) defined academic integration as identification with, and the degree

---

[1]The classical definition of persister is used—a student who remains at the same institution and completes his goal. Nonpersistence rate does not include students who "stopout" or transfer to another institution.

of achievement (e.g., courses completed) according to, the scholarly standards of an institution. Social integration has been defined as student peer relations consisting of friendship, informal academic discussions and efforts, and shared extra-curricular activities. Theoretically, the student's academic integration and social relations are assumed to influence several attitudes, including college completion goals, which in turn affect retention and persistence in college. Extensive research on four-year colleges has provided substantial support for this theory (Braxton, Sullivan, & Johnson, 1997; Cabrera, Nora, & Casteneda, 1993; Kuh, Schuh, Whitt & Associates, 1991; Pascarella & Terenzini, 1991; Tinto, 1975, 1993, 1998).

Status Attainment and Attrition

Other perspectives place greater emphasis on the social contexts outside the campus, particularly family socioeconomic status and the influence provided by family and friends (Bean, 1980; Hauser & Featherman, 1975; Metzner & Bean, 1987; Sewell, Hauser, & Featherman, 1976). Despite differences in emphasis, these perspectives overlap with integration theory in noting the impact of academic achievement and college completion goals on retention. A considerable amount of research in four-year colleges has provided support for these frameworks (Cabrera, Nora, & Casteneda, 1993; Pascarella & Terenzini, 1991; Tinto, 1993).

In a review of the relevance of these four-year college theories for community college students, Maxwell (1998) concluded that the limited amount of research available on community colleges is inconclusive regarding the impact of social integration on retention. Because the differences between students at four-year and two-year campuses are many, including patterns of residence, ethnicity, gender, parental education and income, and age, there is reason to question the relevance of the four-year theories. Other independent variables in community college research which have also manifested conflicting and inconclusive effects on retention include age of the student, GPA, full/part-time attendance, and day/evening attendance (Brooks-Leonard, 1991; Feldman, 1993; Fischbach, 1990; Grimes, 1997; Pascarella, Smart, & Ethington, 1986; Voorhees, 1987; Webb, 1989),

Several independent variables reported in the community college research literature display a more consistent pattern of relations with student retention, though the number of studies is quite limited and most of them were conducted one or more decades ago. The majority of these few studies did involve multi-racial samples, which included African-American males. Factors found to be positively correlated with retention included high school grades (Feldman, 1993; Fischbach, 1990), number of course credits earned (Grimes, 1997; Webb, 1989), academic self-confidence (Webb, 1989), certainty of major (Webb, 1989), and high educational goals (Feldman, 1993; Pascarella & Chapman, 1983; Voorhees, 1987; Webb, 1989).

After an extensive review of the persistence research on minorities, Nora (1993) concluded that there were no "theoretically based" studies of African-American community college students. However, there has been research comparing male and female African-American students in other kinds of institutions (Allen & Haniff, 1991; Coates, 1987; Plummer, 1995). And, in fact, there have been a few investigations of the outcomes for African-American males in community colleges (Carroll, 1988; Lin & Vogt, 1996; Weis, 1985). Carroll's (1988) findings were consistent with the above studies which reported that high educational goals were positively correlated with retention.

Given the uncertain applicability of four-year college theories to two-year college students, we have followed an exploratory strategy that relies partially on these theories and also on other variables associated with classroom experiences. Using secondary analysis of existing institutional research data we have incorporated theoretically identified variables—such as college completion goals—wherever there were corresponding measures in the data. With respect to the import of classroom experience, Levin and Levin (1991) observed that, due to the usually limited involvement of students with the campus, the classroom is often the only focal point for both academic and social integration. Thus, we elected to include a variety of variables concerning the number of course credit hours and academic achievements (such as GPA) that might be correlates of factors promoting social and academic involvements within the classroom (Nora, 1987).

METHODOLOGY

Sample

The present study took place at a large community college located in a middle-class predominantly blue-collar suburban community on the West Coast. The college was selected because the student population reflected the neighborhood's high ethnic diversity. The largest group of the students are Hispanic/Latino (40.6 percent), about one-eighth of the students are Caucasian/white (16.3 percent), 14 percent are Asian, and 8.8 percent are African American.

The study's sample consisted of 202 African-American male students who began their college experience in the Fall of 1995 ($n = 83$), Fall 1996 ($n = 76$), or Spring 1997 ($n = 43$). For each of the cohorts, data were collected for three consecutive semesters (excluding summer). Thus, we monitored retention through the first, second, and third semesters of enrollment for each of the three cohorts at the community college. We eliminated from the study students who were pursuing neither degrees nor certificates.

Measures

We obtained the student data for this study directly from the Office of Institutional Research at the study site. The majority of the data was collected via Computerized Assessment and Placement Program tests (CAPP), which are routinely administered to incoming students to assist in the determination of appropriate course placement. The CAPP battery used at the study site consisted of three subtests: Assessment and Placement of writing (APW); Assessment and Placement of Reading (APR); and Basic Mathematics Readiness (BMR). In addition, the CAPP queries students on educational background and college plans. Also included in the CAPP were 15 questions added by the Office of Institutional Research concerning varied subjects including planned study, work responsibilities, high school coursework, and self ratings on skills in English and mathematics.

Research Design

Logistic regression was used to analyze the dependent variable because retention in college can be conceived as a binary or dichotomous variable and because this statistic permits the mixing of continuous and categorical variables (Cabrera, Stampen, & Hansen, 1990; Feldman, 1993; Mallette & Cabrera, 1991). To better portray a longitudinal perspective on retention in the sample of African-American men, we designed three logistic regression equations regressing independent variables on the dichotomous outcome of retention. The first equation (Analysis 1) explained retention through semester one, the second equation (Analysis 2) explained retention through semester two, and the last retention equation (Analysis 3) explained retention through semester three.[2] Each equation consisted of four blocks of independent variables. The first block consisted of pre-college factors of social origin and education (i.e., demographics and high school variables). Block two consisted of ability tests administered prior to coursework as well as a scale measuring the self-assessment of ability. Block three consisted of items pertaining to experiences occurring during the semester. Finally, the last block consisted of items and experiences occurring simultaneously, but external to, college. The design allowed us to assess the contribution of each of the variable groups while controlling for the preceding blocks. Table 1 provides specific details on each of the four blocks of independent variables.

In addition to the full models, we derived reduced models using a block-by-block likelihood ratio (LR) backward elimination test. The likelihood ratio test eliminated one variable at a time followed by an estimation of the model by observing the change in the log likelihood.[3] The resulting models were parsimonious versions of the full models (Cabrera, 1994; Nora & Cabrera, 1997; Norusis, 1990).

---

[2]Analysis 3 is predicting enrollment into year 2.

[3]The likelihood ratio is calculated by dividing the likelihood of the reduced mode by that of the full model (Norusis, 1990). The introduction of a reduced model has been used in other postsecondary studies using logistic regression (Cabrera, 1994; Nora & Cabrera, 1997).

Indicators of Goodness of Fit

We analyzed several measures of goodness of fit to assess the overall predictability of each block to each model including the chi square, G^2/df ratio,[4] Cox and Snell R^2,[5] and the PCP[6] (proportion of cases correctly predicted). To interpret the relative importance of the independent variables, we observed the significance levels and calculated the Delta-p statistic[7] where appropriate. Thus, we proceeded via the following steps for each model:

1. Assessment of the block.
2. Assessment of the individual predictors for each equation.
3. Assessment of the reduced model.
4. Comparison across the equation.

RESULTS

Of the 202 men who began their college experience, 75 (36.9 percent) earned credits at the end of semester one. By the end of semester two, 56 (27.6 percent) continued to earn credits in semester two. Semester three retention (beginning of year two) included 69 men (34 percent) from the original sample. The fluctuation in numbers included men who left the college as well as men who "stopped out" for a semester.

Forward Entry of Blocks of Variables

Table 2 provides the results of the block entry of variables for the full model for each of the three analyses. Tables 3a, 3b, and 3c provide parameter estimates (or logistic regression weights, B) and standard errors (S.E.) for each of the independent variables in the equations.

Backward Stepwise Procedure

To facilitate interpretation of the results, we performed the analyses using a backward stepwise procedure. Rather than reproduce all of the parameter estimates for each of the equations, we have included in Table 4 only the final model (after all of the blocks of variables have been considered for entry/removal).[8]

---

[4]According to Stage, ratios of less than 2.5 signify a good fit (1990).

[5]Cabrera (1994) labels this a *"pseudo "R^2"* because it represents the proportion of error variance that an alternative model reduces in relation to a null model" (p. 242).

[6]The PCP compares the probable outcome to the actual outcome. Cabrera (1994) explains that "this measure basically involves a comparison between the number of cases that the model predicted as being either 0...or 1...(i.e., persisted or not persisted) against the total sample size" (pp. 242–243).

[7]The Delta-p statistic was calculated only for those independent variables that were significant predictors of the dependent variable. According to Petersen (1985), the Delta-p statistic provides an estimate of the change in the probability of the dependent variable resulting from a unit change in the predictor variable.

[8]The full analysis can be obtained by contacting the first author.

Table 1. Description of Variables

Block	Variable	Description
Dependent variable	Retention	Dichotomous variable (0 = not retained, 1 = retained) measuring retention. In each of the three equations, retention is defined differently. In equation 1, retention is measured through semester 1. In equation 2, retention is measured through semester 2. In equation 3, retention is measured to semester 3.
Block 1. Pre-college (demographics and high school variables)	Age	Respondent's age in years
	Parent's level of education	1 = advanced degree to 6=less than high school diploma
	Years of English	Number of years of high school English (1 = less than 1 year to 5 = 4 years)
	High School GPA	Self-reported high school GPA (1 = A to 7=below D)
	Highest level of HS math	Highest level of math class completed (1 = none to 8 = Calculus)
	Years of science	Number of years of high school science (0 = none to 4 = 4 years)
Block 2. Ability	Ability scale	Mean score of CAPP's Program subtests in reading, writing, and mathematics. (Alpha = .8069)
	Self-skill rating	The sum of respondent's expressed needs for tutoring, assistance in study skills, math, reading, and writing (Alpha = .8510).
Block 3. College related	Orientation	Dichotomous variable indicating if student attended orientation exercises prior to enrollment (0 = no; 1 = yes)
	Average credit hours	The average number of credit hours enrolled. Analysis 1 = average for semester 1 Analysis 2 = average for 2 semesters Analysis 3 = average for 3 semesters
	Success	The difference between the number of credit hours enrolled and the number of credit hours successfully earned in past semester(s) Analysis 1 = not included Analysis 2 = for semester 1 Analysis 3 = sum for semesters 1 and 2

CUMGPA
Cumulative GPA
Analysis 1 = average for semester 1
Analysis 2 = cumulative average for 2 semesters
Analysis 3 = cumulative average for 3 semesters

Day
Dichotomous variable indicating if student attends college classes during the day (0=evening and/or weekend courses; 1 = day courses)

Voc-ed
Dichotomous variable indicating if student is in a vocational program (0 = no; 1 = yes)

Certainty of Major
Degree of certainty on chosen major (1 = unsure to 3 = very sure)

Study hours
Number of reported hours of studying

Reverse transfer
Dichotomous variable indicating if student had a prior degree.

Stopout
Dichotomous variable indicating if student ceased enrollment for 1 semester;
Analysis 1 = not included
Analysis 2 = student enrolled in semester 2, but earned 0 credit in semester 1.
Analysis 3 = student enrolled in semester 3, but earned 0 credits in semester 1 and/or semester 2.

Block 4 Personal variables (pull factors and self-evaluations)

Work hours
Number of weekly hours of employment while enrolled (1 = none to 6 = more than 40).

Importance to others
Self-rating of importance of completing college to others (1 = not very important to 3 = very important).

Importance to self
Self-rating of importance of completing college to self (1 = not very important to 3 = very important).

Leisure hours
Number of weekly hours reported in leisure activities or getting together with friends (1 = none to 6 = more than 40).

Perceived need for academic assistance
Self-assessed need for assistance in writing, reading, study skills, and mathematics (Alpha = .7740)

Table 2. Analyses by Block for Analysis 1 (Semester 1), Analysis 2 (Semester 2), and Analysis 3 (Semester 3).

	Analysis 1 Semester 1 N = 157	Analysis 2 Semester 2 N = 163	Analysis 3 Semester 3 N = 137
Block 1: Pre-college (demographics and high school variables)			
–2 Log Likelihood	202.797	173.679	170.256
chi square (χ^2), (df)	10.853 (6)	31.93 (6)***	18.78 (6)**
G^2/df ratio,	1.299	1.16	1.27
Cox and Snell R^2,	.067	.178	.128
PCP	61.15%	72.39%	62.04%
Block 2: Ability			
–2 Log Likelihood	195.069	167.912	164.080
chi square (χ^2), (df)	7.728(2)*	5.77 (2)	6.176(2)*
G^2/df ratio,	1.24	1.17	1.24
Cox and Snell R^2,	.112	.206	.167
PCP	68.15%	70.55%	65.69%
Block 3: College related			
–2 Log Likelihood	152.561	117.774	133.465
chi square (χ^2), (df)	42.51(8)***	50.14(9)***	30.62 (10)***
G^2/df ratio,	1.02	0.75	1.03
Cox and Snell R^2,	.322	.417	.446
PCP	73.89%	84.66%	80.29
Block 4: Personal and Pull Factors			
–2 Log Likelihood	149.998	106.975	121.695
chi square (χ^2), (df)	2.563 (4)	10.80(4)*	11.77 (4)*
G^2/df ratio,	0.997	0.844	0.86
Cox and Snell R^2,	.333	.454	.519
PCP	73.89%	84.05	83.21%

For χ^2 analyses *$p < .05$. **$p < .01$. ***$p > .001$.

The Delta-p (Δ_p) statistic is generally calculated for each significant predictor of the dependent variable (Cabrera, 1994). We used the formula recommended by Petersen (1985) to calculate the change in the probability of the dependent variable (retention) for a unit change in each of the significant independent variables in the reduced models (holding all other variables constant):

$$\text{Delta-}p = \exp(L_1)/[1 + \exp(L_1)] - P_0$$

Table 3. Block-by-Block Logistic Regression Weights (B) and Standard Errors (S.E.)
Table 3A: Analysis 1 - End of Semester 1

Block Independent variables	Equation 1	Equation 2	Equation 3	Equation 4
Block 1				
Age	-.0327 (.0402)	-.0306 (.0405)	-.0324 (.0581)	-.0284 (.0603)
Parent level of education	-.2537 (.1217)*	-.2687 (.1269)*	-.3324 (.1587)*	-.3195 (.1627)*
# years of English	.1725 (.1954)	.1353 (.1977)	.2878 (.2286)	.2407 (.2375)
High school GPA	-.1006 (.1444)	-.0523 (.1486)	.0421 (.1841)	.0327 (.1840)
Highest level of high school mathematics	.1136 (.1215)	-.0532 (.1390)	-.1452 (.1651)	-.0996 (.1766)
# years of science	-.0720 (.2108)	-.0483 (.2164)	.1330 (.2606)	.1524 (.2673)
Block 2				
Ability scale		.0780 (.0289)**	.0427 (.0356)	.0355 (.0369)
Self-skill rating		.0357 (.1282)	.0760 (.1553)	.0625 (.1610)
Block 3				
Orientation			-.0661 (.4205)	-.1499 (.4357)
Average credit hours			.2347 (.0562)***	.2379 (.0585)***
Success			Not applicable	Not applicable
CUMGPA			.3313 (.1662)*	.3273 (.1680)
Day			-.3108 (.4746)	-.4203 (.4899)
Voc-ed			-.4059 (.5561)	-.4621 (.5744)
Certainty of major			.2162 (.2081)	.1732 (.2131)
Study-hours			.0033 (.0977)	-.0255 (.1003)
Reverse transfer			1.7165 (1.2226)	1.8312 (1.2587)
Stopout			Not applicable	Not applicable
Block 4				
Work hours				-.0353 (.1477)
Importance to others				-.2708 (.3026)
Importance to self				-.0027 (.4553)
Leisure hours				.2432 (.1944)

*p > .05. **p < .01. ***p < .001.

Table 3B: Analysis 2 - End of Semester 2

Block Independent variables	Equation 1	Equation 2	Equation 3	Equation 4
Block 1				
Age	-.2562 (.0987)**	-.2361 (.0985)*	-.2990 (.1148)**	-.2875 (.1216)*
Parent level of education	-.2642 (.1335)*	-.2607 (.1387)	-.3456 (.1854)	-.4619 (.2068)*
# years of English	.5233 (.3252)	.4695 (.3423)	.7275 (.4880)	.7787 (.5071)
High school GPA	.1665 (.1643)	.2236 (.1696)	.5311 (.2473)*	.6706 (.2732)*
Highest level of high school mathematics	.1168 (.1295)	.0075 (.1485)	-.0541 (.2027)	-.1380 (.2311)
# years of science	.0647 (.2324)	.0721 (.2354)	.3390 (.3052)	.4357 (.3339)
Block 2				
Ability scale		.0599 (.0309)	.0229 (.0416)	.0139 (.0478)
Self-skill rating		-.2276 (.1660)	-.4707 (.2327)*	-.5401 (.2597)*
Block 3				
Orientation			-.4206 (.4898)	-.1901 (.5367)
Average credit hours			.3538 (.0814)***	.4216 (.0963)***
Success			.2291 (.1469)	.3033 (.1725)
CUMGPA			.1464 (.2395)	.1615 (.2557)
Day			-.0158 (.6043)	-.0703 (.6382)
Voc-ed			.7695 (.6657)	.9216 (.7306)
Certainty of major			.6929 (.2519)**	.7687 (.2838)**
Study-hours			.1097 (.1150)	.0845 (.1291)
Reverse transfer			2.1404 (1.7243)	2.1493 (1.7322)
Stopout			Not Applicable	Not Applicable
Block 4				
Work hours				-.2187 (.2018)
Importance to others				.4437 (.4439)
Importance to self				1.7594 (.7052)*
Leisure hours				.2308 (.2341)

$*p > .05.$ $**p < .01.$ $***p < .001.$

Table 3C: Analysis 3—End of Semester 3

Block Independent variables	Equation 1	Equation 2	Equation 3	Equation 4
Block 1				
Age	-.1807 (.0683)**	-.1768 (.0704)*	-.2855 (.1017)**	-.2814 (.1059)**
Parent level of education	-.0693 (.1393)	-.0911 (.1463)	-.0298 (.1698)	-.0834 (.18830)
# years of English	.1844 (.2256)	.1211 (.2346)	.0704 (.2768)	.0400 (.2981)
High school GPA	.2309 (.1662)	.2839 (.1723)	.4371 (.2196)*	.5443 (.2521)*
Highest level of high school mathematics	.1002 (.1279)	-.0301 (.1484)	-.1318 (.1796)	-.2739 (.2059)
# years of science	-.1840 (.2273)	-.1710 (.2314)	-.1227 (.2661)	-.1322 (.2799)
Block 2				
Ability scale		.0714 (.0325)*	.0697 (.0408)	.0877 (.0451)
Self-skill rating		-.1287 (.1429)	-.2247 (.1761)	-.2878 (.2008)
Block 3				
Orientation			-.5739 (.4534)	-.2577 (.4963)
Average credit hours			.2638 (.0788)***	.2898 (.0848)***
Success			.0449 (.0931)	.0805 (.1019)
CUMGPA			.0179 (.2510)	-.0047 (.2671)
Day			-.1416 (.5187)	-.2231 (.5649)
Voc-ed			.5852 (.6550)	.5214 (.7086)
Certainty of major			.6142 (.2350)**	.7277 (.2613)**
Study-hours			.0016 (.1023)	-.0226 (.1160)
Reverse transfer			3.6492 (1.5980)*	3.7293 (1.6249)*
Stopout			.7583 (.9484)	1.1292 (.9877)
Block 4				
Work hours				-.2310 (.2002)
Importance to others				.5955 (.4107)
Importance to self				1.4931 (.5507)**
Leisure hours				.1096 (.2103)

*$p > .05$. **$p < .01$. ***$p < .001$.

Table 4. Reduced Models–Parameter Estimates, Standard Errors, and the Δ_p Statistics

Variable	Analysis 1		Analysis 2		Analysis 3	
	Parameter Estimates (S.E.)	Δ_p	Parameter Estimates (S.E.)	Δ_p	Parameter Estimates (S.E.)	Δ_p
Block 1						
Age	-.3062 (.1426)*	.0545	-.2549 (.1071)*	.1607	-.2730 (.0902)**	.0923
Parent level of education			-.4332 (.1743)*	.1175		
Years of English			.5662 (.3990)			
Block 2						
Ability	.0383 (.0296)		-.0188 (.0358)		.0393 (.0341)	
Block 3						
Success			.2651 (.1289)*	.2900		
Average hours	.2271 (.0521)***	.1870	.3571 (.0694)***	.3124	.2170 (.0677)**	.2141
CUMGPA	.2946 (.1597)					
Certainty of Major			.5984 (.2398)*	.3694	.6652 (.2266)**	.3205
Reverse transfer					3.5152 (1.5538)*	.6312
Block 4						
Importance to self			1.2081 (.5811)*	.4941	.9991 (.4458)*	.3910
Goodness of Fit Measures						
-2 Log Likelihood	159.749		126.497		138.292	
Goodness of Fit	146.022		178.067		146.867	
Cox & Snell R^2	.291		.385		.310	
PCP	71.97		84.05		81.02	

Where:

P_0 = the mean of retention for the specific analysis

L_1 = the parameter estimate (logistic regression weight) for the independent variable in the specific analysis

INTERPRETATIONS OF RESULTS

Assessment of Blocks

For each of the three analysis, the first block of variables (demographics and high school related) explained a large and significant proportion of the variance of the dependent variable, retention. Although the independent variables in the block are beyond the control of the community college, they indicate the importance of pre-college predictors in college outcomes and provide a reminder of the importance of including these variables as controls. Block 2, ability variables measured in college, added little to the predictability of the equation beyond the earlier contribution of the high school achievement measures (which presumably were also related to ability). The strongest set of variables were those of block 3 (college related). The combined effect of the first three blocks explained more than three-fourths of the variance in retention (as defined by the individual equations). Since the college has more control over these factors, important and constructive policies may be implied. Finally, the last block (personal and pull factors) had a small (Analysis 3) or imperceptible effect (Analysis 1 and 2).

Assessment of Individual Predictors

Block One

In all three analyses, being younger was a significant predictor of retention. This contrasts with two previous multi-racial studies (Pascarella, Smart, & Ethington, 1986; Webb, 1989) and Carroll's study of African Americans, all of which found no correlations with age, but is consistent with other studies reviewed earlier which found that younger students were more likely to persist. Various interpretations may be made of this finding. For example, older men may confront more problems in attending the college. Or, it may indicate that for African-American men, family, employment, or other responsibilities that tend to increase with age, are detractors to the community college experience. This finding may indicate the need for more support of older African-American men. Although not tested in this study, it may be that younger men feel more comfortable or better integrated. While many community colleges have adult re-entry programs that stress the needs of older *women*, perhaps this college and others like it should consider expending a more equal effort to accommodate older men with a special emphasis on older men of color.

In retention through semester two (Analysis 2) and through semester three (Analysis 3), high school GPA was a significant predictor, and consistent with previous research (Feldman, 1993; Fischbach, 1990). These findings indicate that as the student progresses in college, his academic preparation—and probably some other correlates of high school GPA, such as motivation and college GPA—become increasingly more important in determining collegiate outcomes. Most likely the effect of high school preparation and correlates becomes more salient as college coursework moves beyond the introductory and into the more advanced.

Block Two

As indicated earlier, we found an absence of significant effects of the ability tests—above and beyond the effects of the control variable of high school GPA—on retention in the first semester. However, for the second semester analysis, the effect of low self-assessment of skills was a significant predictor of non-retention. This is consistent with Webb's (1989) earlier findings of a correlation between academic self-confidence and retention. Therefore, African-American men who feel capable of college-level work tended to complete semester two in greater proportion than those who felt less capable. This finding may underscore the importance of providing academic assistance to those who express a need for it. A full 40 percent of the men in this sample indicated a need for academic assistance in at least one of the five items queried (basic tutoring, study skills, math, reading, and/or writing). It may be useful for academic advisors to extend an invitation to individuals who indicate academic concerns on the CAPP instrument, inviting them to tour or learn more about the academic assistance center. Instructors may also find it appropriate to introduce students to the academic assistance center early in the semester, perhaps during orientation or similar programs.

Block Three

In all three analyses, the number of hours of course enrollment was a positive and significant predictor of retention. Men who attended the college on a full-time basis were more likely to persist. Although the studies cited earlier were in disagreement on the correlation with full-time enrollment, the number of courses attended has usually been found to be related to retention (Brooks-Leonard, 1991; Feldman, 1993; Grimes, 1997; Maxwell, 1998; Voorhees, 1987; Webb, 1989). In the second and third analyses, certainty of major was also a significant predictor of retention, consistent with Webb's (1989) similar finding. Because certainty of major is positively related to college goal commitments, it may be that men who have a specific occupational goal and can pursue it on a more full-time basis are more likely to persist. Community colleges, therefore, should continue to help students identify occupational goals early in their college enrollment and to encourage students to attend full-time whenever possible. Helping students to identify and apply for financial aid may assist some men to focus more exclusively on completing their education. Having sufficient financial means may allow some to attend on a full-time basis rather than appending college to the end of a day at work.

In contrast to several previous studies that have found GPA positively correlated with retention, none of the three analyses found a relationship with cumulative GPA. This is probably due in this case to the introduction of correlated control variables such as high school GPA and motivational measures.

Block Four

In predicting retention through both semesters two and three, men who expressed a high degree of importance (to self) in completing college were found to be more likely to complete the semester. Although this finding was expected and consistent with earlier studies (Pascarella & Chapman, 1983; Voorhees, 1987; Webb, 1989), when combined with the finding of the importance of certainty of major, it further confirms the role of college completion goals ("goal commitment" in the integration literature) for this sample of African-American men. Colleges would, therefore, be well advised to establish activities and experiences that emphasize the need, the importance, and the outcomes of a college degree.

Additional Insights from the Reduced Models

The reduced models simplified the equations by stripping them of variables that did not appear to pertain to this specific sample and by allowing to remain only those variables that explained a significant proportion of the variance of the dependent variable. In many instances, comparing the reduced model to the full model revealed different significant predictor variables. The inconsistency may be explained by an overlap in the full models of multiple independent variables explaining a portion of the variance. Whenever a variable is removed from the equation, its associated explained variance can be attributed to another predictor. Thus, variables that appeared to be non-significant predictors may suddenly emerge as more important in the reduced models. We present these findings with caution because they are based solely on this sample and may not be applicable to other African-American men at other institutions. Yet, we feel that the reduced models can and do provide additional important information. We calculated the delta-p statistic from the reduced models to better understand this study's sample.

The role of age is evident in the reduced models. In predicting retention in semesters two and three, the likelihood of non-retention increases 16 percent and 9.2 percent, respectively, for each additional year in age. From block three, the role of completing courses (success) was a significant predictor for analysis two. In terms of the delta-p statistic, for each credit hour dropped, the likelihood of non-retention increased by 29 percent. For this sample, dropping courses was an indication of possible non-retention. Since the college tracks both courses entered and courses completed, policies to contact individuals after a course is dropped may be an important way to indicate concern and to remind students of the types of available assistance on campus.

Similar to the full models, college related variables (block three) offered many insights. Once again, the importance of full-time enrollment became evident. With each additional credit hour of enrollment, the likelihood of retention through semesters one, two, and three increased by 18.7 percent, 31.2 percent, or 21.4 percent, respectively. The reduced model also indicated that men with a previous college degree were 63 percent more likely to persist through semester three.

Finally, the reduced model underscored the importance of personal goals for retention. Men who reported that college was very important were 49 percent and 39 percent more likely to persist through semesters two and three respectively.

CONCLUSIONS

We did find support for the impact of high school grade point average and college goal commitments, as posited in integration, attrition, and status attainment theories. Also consistent with these theories are the strong correlations with retention of the number of course credit hours (units) and the dropping of course units. The number of course credit hours is useful as a measure of the potential for academic and social involvement of African-American males in the classroom, which is a particularly significant form of involvement in community colleges.

Additional variables that have distinctive manifestations in community colleges were high school preparation, perceptions of the need for academic assistance, and age. Given the greater likelihood that students enrolling in two-year institutions have insufficient preparation and needs for academic assistance, and the special needs of older males, the findings suggest that academic and support services take these factors into account in developing programs and services for African-American males.

Community colleges are important avenues for the success of African-American men. A large portion of the degrees earned by African Americans are at the associate/vocational level (Shinagawa & Jang, 1998). Further, a college degree has positive and important consequences. For example, the U.S. Census Bureau (1998) reported the median earnings of African Americans with a bachelor's degree was $12,364 more than that for only a high school diploma. Finally, African-American men lag behind African-American women in their proportional representation in the ranks of managers and professionals (Shinagawa & Jang, 1998). In short, it is time for community colleges to recognize the potential and the importance of African-American male students and to develop policies specifically aimed at this subpopulation.

REFERENCES

Allen, W. R., & Haniff, N. Z. (1991). Race, gender, and academic performance in U.S. higher education. In W. R. Allen, F. Epps, & N. Z. Haniff (Eds.), *College in black and white* (pp. 95–110). Albany: State University of New York Press.

Bean, J. (1980) Dropouts and turnover: The synthesis and test of a causal model of student attrition. *Research in Higher Education, 12,* 155–187.

Braxton, J. M., Sullivan, A. V. S., & Johnson, R. M. (1997). Appraising Tinto's theory of college student departure. In C. J. Smart (Ed.), *Higher Education: Handbook of theory and research: Vol. 12* (pp. 109–166). New York: Agathon Press.

Brooks-Leonard, C. (1991). Demographic and academic factors associated with first-to-second-term retention in a two-year college. *Community/Junior College, 15,* 57–69.

Cabrera, A. F. (1994). Logistic regression analysis in higher education: An applied perspective. In C. J. Smart (Ed.), *Higher education: Handbook of theory and research: Vol. 10* (pp. 225–256). New York: Agathon Press.

Cabrera, A. F., Nora, A., & Castaneda, M. B. (1993). College persistence: Structural equations modeling test of an integrated model of student retention. *Journal of Higher Education, 64,* 123–139.

Cabrera, A. F., Stampen, J. O., & Hansen, W. L. (1990). Exploring the effects of ability to pay on persistence in college. *The Review of Higher Education, 13,* 303–336.

Carroll, J. (1988). Freshman retention and attrition factors at a predominantly black urban community college. *Journal of College Student Development, 29,* 52–59.

Carter, D. J., & Wilson, R. (1993). *Minorities in higher education. 1992 eleventh status report.* Washington D.C.: American Council on Education, Office of Minorities in Higher Education. (ERIC Reproduction Service No. ED 363 250)

Chenoweth, K. (1998). The road not taken. *Black Issues in Higher Education 14* (26), 24–27.

Coates, D. L. (1987). Gender differences in the structure and support characteristics of black adolescents' social networks. *Sex Roles, 17* (11–12), 667–687.

Cuyjet, M. J. (1997). African American men on college campuses: Their needs and their perceptions. In M. J. Cuyjet (Ed.), *Helping African American men succeed in college* (pp. 5–16). San Francisco: Jossey-Bass Inc.

Feldman, M. J. (1993). Factors associated with one-year retention in a community college. *Research in Higher Education, 34,* 503–512.

Fischbach, R. (1990). *Persistence among full-time students at Illinois Central College.* ERIC Document Reproduction Service No. ED 325 190.

Grimes, S. K. (1997). Underprepared community college students: Characteristics, persistence, and academic success. *Community College Journal of Research and Practice, 21,* 47–56.

Hauser, R. M., & Featherman, D. L. (1975). Socioeconomic achievements of U.S. men, 1962 to 1972. *Science, 185,* 325–331.

Kerka, S. (1995). *Adult learner retention revisited.* Columbus, OH: ERIC Clearinghouse on Adult, Career, and Vocational Education. (ERIC Reproduction Service No. ED 389 880)

Kuh, G., Schuh, J. H., Whitt, E. J., and Associates (1991). *Involving colleges: Successful approaches to fostering student learning and development.* San Francisco: Jossey-Bass.

Lee, C. C. (1994). Adolescent development. *Nurturing young black males: Challenges to agencies, programs, and social policy.* R. B. Mincy. Washington, D.C., Urban Institute Press.

Levin, M. E., & Levin J. R. (1991). A critical examination of academic retention programs for at-risk minority college students. *Journal of College Student Development, 32,* 323–334.

Lin, Y., & Vogt, W. P. (1996). Occupational outcomes for student earning two-year college degrees: Income, status, and equity. *Journal of Higher Education, 67,* 446–475.

Majors, R., & Billson, J. M. (1992). *The dilemma of black manhood in America.* San Francisco: New Lexington Press.

Mallette, B. I., & Cabrera, A. F. (1991). Determinants of withdrawal behavior: An exploratory study. *Research in Higher Education, 32,* 179–194.

Maxwell, W. (1998). Supplemental instruction, learning communities, and students studying together. *Community College Review 26,* 1–18.

McCool, A. C. (1984). Factors influencing Hispanic student retention within the community college. *Community/Junior College Quarterly of Research and Practice, 8* (1–4): 19–37.

Metzner, B. S., & Bean, J. P. (1987). The estimation of a conceptual model of nontraditional undergraduate student attrition. *Research in Higher Education, 27* (1), 15–38.

National Center of Education Statistics (1994). *Beginning Postsecondary Students— Second Follow up,* [CD-ROM]. National Center for Education Statistics, Office of Educational Research and Improvement, U.S. Department of Education.

Nora, A. (1987). Determinants of retention among Chicano college students: A structural model. *Research in Higher Education, 26,* 31–59.

Nora, A. (1993). Two-year colleges and minority students' educational aspirations: Help or hindrance? In C. J. Smart (Ed.), *Higher education: Handbook of theory and research* (Vol. 9, pp. 212–247). New York: Agathon Press.

Nora, A., & Cabrera, A. F. (1997). *Factors affecting the involvement of graduate students in scholarly behavior: A logistic regression analysis.* Paper presented at the annual meeting of the Association for the Study of Higher Education, Albuquerque, New Mexico, November 1997.

Nora, A., & Rendon, L. (1990). Determinants of predisposition to transfer among community college students: A structural model. *Research in Higher Education, 31,* 235–255.

Norusis, M. J. (1990). *SPSS Advanced Statistics Student Guide.* Chicago: SPSS Inc.

Pascarella, E. T., & Chapman, D. W. (1983, Spring). A multi-institutional, path analytic validation of Tinto's Model of College Withdrawal. *American Educational Research Journal, 20,* 87–102.

Pascarella, E. T., & Terenzini, P. T. (1991). *How college affects students.* San Francisco: Jossey-Bass.

Pascarella, E. T., Smart, J. C., & Ethington, C. A. (1986). Long-term persistence of two-year college students. *Research in Higher Education, 24,* 47–71.

Pascarella, E. T., & Terenzini, P. T. (1991). *How college affects students.* San Francisco: Jossey-Bass.

Petersen, T. (1985). A comment on presenting results from logit and probit models. *American Sociological Review, 50,* 130–131.

Plummer, D. L. (1995). Patterns of racial identity development of African American adolescent males and females. *Journal of Black Psychology, 21* (2), 168–180.

Porter, O. F. (1990). *Undergraduate completion and persistence at four-year colleges: Completers, persisters, stopouts, and dropouts.* Washington D.C.: National Institute of Independent Colleges and Universities.

Reed, R. J. (1988) Education and achievement of young Black males. In J. T. Gibbs (Ed.), *Young Black and male in American: An endangered species* (pp. 37–96). Dover, MA: Auburn House Publishing Co.

Reisberg, L. (1999, April 2). In bids to increase minority enrollments, colleges deal with reality and perceptions. *The Chronicle of Higher Education,* p. A49.

Sewell, W. H., Hauser, R. M., & Featherman, D. L. (1976). *Schooling and achievement in American Society.* New York: Academic Press.

Shinagawa, L. H., & Jang, M. (1998). *Atlas of American diversity.* Walnut Creek, CA: AltaMira Press.

Stage, F. K. (1990). LISREL: An introduction and application in higher education. In J. C. Smart (Ed.), *Higher education: Handbook of theory and research* (Vol. 6, pp. 427-466). New York: Agathon Press.

Tinto, V. (1975). Dropout from higher education: A theoretical synthesis of recent research. *Review of Educational Research, 45,* 89–125.

Tinto, V. (1993). *Leaving college: Rethinking the causes and cures of student attrition* (2nd ed.). Chicago: University of Chicago Press.

Tinto, V. (1998). Colleges as communities: Taking research on student persistence seriously. *Review of Higher Education, 21,* 167–177.

Tinto, V., Russo, P., & Kadel. S. (1994). Constructing educational communities: Increasing retention in challenging circumstances. *Community College Journal, 64* (4), 26–29.

U. S. Census Bureau (1997). Income and Poverty Information Staff Report # .301-457-3242 http://www.census.gov/Press-Release/cb98–176.html

U. S. Census Bureau (1998). Table 8. Income by Educational Attainment for Persons 18 Years Old and Over, by Age, Sex, Race, and Hispanic Origin, March, 1998. *Current Population Reports, Educational Attainment in the United States* [On-line], pp. 43–51. Available: http://www.census.gov/prod/www/abs/ed-attn.html

Voorhees, R. A. (1987). Toward building models of community college persistence: A logit analysis. *Research in Higher Education, 26,* 115–129.

Webb, M. (1989) A theoretical model of community college student degree persistence. *Community College Review, 16,* 42–49.

Weis, L. (1985). *Between two worlds: Black students in an urban community college.* Boston: Routledge & Kegan Paul.

CHAPTER 2

Predicting Academic Success and Retention for African-American Women in College

Robert A. Schwartz and Charles M. Washington

This study examined the academic success and retention of 213 first year, female African-American college students at a historically black, private, liberal arts college in the Southeast. The women were surveyed about their preparation and readiness for college during their first weeks on campus. Responses were then compared against actual academic performance and retention during the first year of college.

Since Emancipation, education has the promise of self-improvement and race uplift for African-American women (Perkins, 1985). However African-American women who seek a higher education face many impediments to their success. Some of those impediments include low levels of parental support; low levels of parental education, limited resources to pay for college, low self-confidence, and limited social expectations for Africans Americans (Kunjufu, 1997; Nettles & Gosman, 1986). Despite these problems, a large number of African-American women do succeed in college. But why do some succeed and how can more African-American women be successful?

The purpose of this study was to attempt to determine if specific cognitive, non-cognitive, and demographic variables could predict academic success and retention among African-American females at a historically black, private liberal arts college. If specific variables could be identified as predictors of success and retention, or, conversely, if specific predictors could be found which indicated potential problems, early intervention and other types of assistance could be designed and implemented. The end result would be more women who persisted in college and were satisfied with their experience.

In this study, cognitive variables were defined as variables which "objectively measure intellectual ability and are exhibited by some numerical score, rank, or range" (Johnson, 1993, p. 18). Cognitive variables in other studies have included: the Scholastic Aptitude Test (SAT) scores, high school class rank, high school grade point averages, and American College Test (ACT) scores. Non-cognitive variables were defined as "affective variables . . . psychosocial constructs, subjective in nature, that describe the feelings, perceptions, and/or attitudes one has regarding psychosocial phenomena, which are exhibited by a numerical score, rank, or range" (Johnson, 1993, p. 19). Retention or persistence was used to refer to a student's continued enrollment in college. Bethel College is a pseudonym for a historically African American, private, open admissions, coeducational liberal arts college located in a major city in the South. Founded shortly after the Civil War, Bethel has its roots in the African-American church and maintains a strong relationship in the African-American community.

RELATED LITERATURE

Predicting outcomes for minority students has received increased attention over the last twenty years (Livengood, 1992; Rowser, 1997); in large part, due to the disparities between minority students and their white peers, particularly in majority white institutions (Feagin, Vera, & Imani, 1996; Stith & Russell, 1994). Despite increased concern and research (Hood, 1992; Johnson, 1993), solutions to the problems inherent in race and college success remain elusive. Other studies which have examined the predictive ability of cognitive and non-cognitive variables for academic performance and retention will be discussed briefly. A summary concludes this section.

COGNITIVE PREDICTORS

Previous behaviors in high school have consistently been strong predictors of how well a student will do in college. High school grades appear to be the single best predictor of academic performance, findings which hold true across the board, regardless of ethnicity or race (Amando, 1991; Jacobs, 1985). Bontekoe's (1992) study of 477 freshmen found a stronger correlation between high school and college GPA than between ACT scores and college GPA. Ott (1988) found academic performance highly related to high school academic grade point-average. Connor (1990) found high school grades especially predictive for African-American students. However, Hollingsworth, Walker, and Anderson (1997) argue that their study of 256 African-American students showed that high school performance may not be predictive of college performance.

High school rank has also been a consistent predictor of college grades. Thornell and Jones (1986) compared the predictability of high school performance and ACT scores and showed correlations between high school rank and GPA to be equal to or better than those for the ACT and GPA. Jacobs (1985) compared the predictability of SAT scores to high school rank and found rank was the best single predictor of GPA for both males and females. Hood (1992) and Johnson (1993) found high school rank related to academic performance for African-American males attending a predominately white institution.

Standardized tests like the SAT and ACT, have become essential elements in college admissions, but critics argue the tests are race and gender biased; do not reflect the true ability of certain student populations (Sowa, Thomson & Bennett, 1989); do not predict success uniformly across gender and ethnic groups (Bridgeman & Wendler, 1991; Moffatt, 1993); and add little to prediction equations beyond the use of high school grades or rank (Baron & Norman, 1992; Cowen & Fiori, 1991: Hudson, 1993; Moffatt, 1993; Myers & Pyles, 1992).

NON-COGNITIVE PREDICTORS

Non-cognitive variables provide institutions with a ". . . different way to predict student performance in college" (Kanoy, Wester, & Lata, 1989, p. 65). Interest in these predictors came about as an alternative to traditional measures which did not, by themselves, predict college grades effectively for minority students (Arbona & Novy, 1990). Non-cognitive predictors are effective measures for predicting college success for minority students (Arbona & Novy, 1990; Pickering, Calliotte, & McAuliffe, 1992). Non-cognitive predictors for academic performance include: personality (Brown, 1994), self-responsibility (McConatha, 1990), self-concept (Bloomer, 1991), academic self-concept (Gerardi, 1990; Johnson, 1993), motivation (Livengood, 1992) locus of control (Kanoy et al., 1989), expectations and self-expectancy (Trippi & Stewart, 1989), and self-efficacy (Dole, 1990). Overall, academic self-concept (Gerardi, 1990; House, 1994; Marsh, 1992), and the eight non-cognitive variables found on the Non-Cognitive Questionnaire (NCQ) have received the greatest attention.

Non-cognitive variables can be more effective than standard test scores as predictors for academic success. In a comparison of SAT scores and a non- cognitive variable questionnaire (NCQ) to predict academic performance, Sedlacek and Adams-Gaston (1992) found the non-cognitive variables better predictors than SAT scores. Tracey and Sedlacek (1987) consistently found the NCQ items to be better predictors of academic performance for minority students from SAT scores and more importantly, that the predictive power extends beyond the first year. Positive self-concept and realistic self-appraisal, in particular, have been related to college grades for African-American students.

Non-cognitive variables appear to be useful but less effective than traditional cognitive variables. Arbona and Novy (1990) found that the NCQ was not predictive of college grades for African-American students. Hood (1992) found the expanded version of the NCQ (the NCQ-R) less effective than high school rank in predicting college grades for African-American males. Alexander (1989) found minority students scores on the NCQ not significantly related to first year performance in dental school. Such findings suggest that a combination of cognitive and non-cognitive predictors may be the most effective model for minority students (Alexander, 1989; Pickering, et al., 1992).

RETENTION

Predicting who will stay in college is a challenge. Two of the major authors on college student retention, Astin (1993) and Tinto (1987) content that institutional relationships between the college or university and the student are critical to retention. Further, both contend that a variety of concerns and issues coalesce to influence the decision of a student to stay in school. Clearly, students who make the decision to stay in college beyond the first year are much more likely to graduate. Astin, in particular, has noted the importance of racial homogeneity in the retention of minority students as well as women. As early as 1975, Astin reported that minority students and women were both more likely to become involved and to flourish in institutions which responded to and supported their concerns, specifically historically black institutions and women's colleges.

Other researchers have attempted to examine retention issues on specific variables. Among the results are the finding that standard test scores (SAT, ACT) are suspect for minority students, and are more effective at predicting White students persistence than nontraditional, disadvantaged, and minority students (Hood, 1992; Kim & Sedlacek, 1995). Hood (1992) found high school rank predictive of enrollment status for African-American, Hispanic, and Asian men. Connor (1992) used high school rank, ACT score, first semester grades, and participation in extracurricular activities for African-American freshman at a predominantly White, Southern institution to demonstrate that high school rank was not significant predictor of retention. Overall, the best model for predicting retention for African-American students must consider campus environment and include, in order of importance, first semester grades as an indication of academic integration, non-cognitive, demographic and interactive variables (social integration and commitment), and other cognitive variables models described by Tinto and Astin earlier.

AFRICAN-AMERICAN STUDENTS

Research findings to date offer a variety of cognitive, non-cognitive, demographic, and student-college interaction variables and theories that relate to and explain college success for African-American students (Gold, Burrell, Haynes, & Nardecchia, 1990). Most of have examined college success for African

Americans at predominantly white institutions (Connor, 1990; Feagin, Vera, & Imani, 1996). Recent studies such as Rowser (1997) and Hollingsworth, Walker, and Ryan (1997) have attempted to correlate expectations of African-American freshmen with actual performance. Some students have expectations which exceed their ability or readiness, a gap which can cause greater attrition. There remains a shortage of data available on the prediction of college success of African-American students (Phillip, 1993; Stith & Russell, 1994) particularly at historically African-American institutions. Some have focused on African-American students at historically African-American colleges (Brice, 1993) and at historically African-American, state-supported institutions (Pickens, 1987). Successful performance and persistence of students is also critical for African-American institutions (Martin, 1990; Moline, 1987) as the very existence of the African-American college is threatened.

SUMMARY

High school grades and rank remain significant predictors of academic performance regardless of race. Non-cognitive predictors can improve predictions of academic performance and retention for African-American students over predictions based only on cognitive factors. Academic self-concept and Sedlacek and Brook's (1984) eight non-cognitive variables are useful predictors of academic performance for minority students with some differences related to gender. Academic self-concept consistently emerges as the most reliable and perhaps the single best, non-cognitive predictor of academic success (House, 1994). Demographic and student impact variables, e.g., adjustment and integration or post-enrollment variables, e.g., first year academic performance and faculty-student interactions are useful predictors after college matriculation. Demographic predictors, although helpful, appear to only be indirect variables, useful only in conjunction with other cognitive and non-cognitive variables.

METHOD AND PROCEDURES

Independent Variables

Fourteen independent variables were initially identified including the cognitive variables high school rank and high school grade point average; the eight non-cognitive variables drawn from Tracey and Sedlacek's (1984) NCQ scales and the adjustment variables, personal-emotional adjustment, academic adjustment, social adjustment, and attachment to the college from the Student Adaptation to College Questionnaire (SACQ) (Baker & Siryk, 1989).

Dependent Variables

The dependent variables in the study were academic performance; academic success; and persistence. Academic performance was grade point average at the end of the first semester. Academic success was measured by the categories pass or fail to be determined by the Bethel College academic probation policy which puts a student on probation if they have a cumulative grade point of 1.5 or less at the end of one semester. In this case, probation would be classify a student in the fail category for the study and pass would indicate no probation. Persistence was the continued enrollment of an individual student from the Fall semester to the second semester. Students who did not continue their enrollment in the Spring, 1995-1996 semester were considered non-persisters.

Sample

In the Fall of 1995, 257 freshman female students at a historically black, private, liberal arts institution in the Southwest were asked to participate in a study to predict their academic success and persistence. After excluding women who were not true freshmen students, e.g., transfer students and returning students, as well as those women who chose not to participate, a final set of useable responses from 213 women were analyzed for the study.

Instrumentation

The Non-Cognitive Questionnaire (Tracey & Sedlacek, 1984) is a twenty-three-item questionnaire composed of twenty Likert-type items on college expectations and self-assessment; a categorical item on educational aspirations, and two, open-ended questions on goals and accomplishments. The NCQ measures eight variables important for success in college: knowledge acquired in a field of study; positive self-concept; realistic self-appraisal; preferred long-term goals; understanding of and ability to content with racism; availability of a support person(s); leadership experience, and community service. Tracey and Sedlacek (1984) report test-retest reliabilities from .70 to .94 for each scale, with a median value of .85. Inter-judge agreements on the open-ended items ranged from .83 to 1.00.

The Student Adaptation to College Questionnaire (SACQ) developed by Baker and Siryk (1989), consists of sixty-seven items and has a reported reliability of .90. Students self-report their level of adjustment on each item using a 9-point scale. Higher scale scores represent greater adjustment. The instrument contains four sub-scales: academic adjustment; social adjustment; personal-emotional adjustment; and institutional adjustment. Cronbach alpha coefficients for the SACQ, measuring internal reliability, ranged from .70 for the personal-emotional subscale to the .80 level for the other three subscales.

Data was initially collected on fourteen independent variables. Means and standard deviations were compiled for high school rank, grade point average, the eight NCQ scales, and four SACQ scales. Correlation coefficients were calculated to measure relationships among the independent variables. Dependent variables, academic performance in college and persistence were determined by categories based on actual academic performance and re-enrollment for the spring semester.

Analysis of variance and multiple regression procedures were used to determine relationships between selected cognitive, non-cognitive, and adjustment variables with academic performance. A stepwise multiple regression was used to identify predictor variables for academic performance (Boyer & Sedlacek, 1989; Pickering, Calliotte, & McAuliffe, 1992). The stepwise procedure enters independent variables into the regression equation. Logistic regression analysis allows for multivariate responses in data sets which contain both continuous (grade point) and discrete variables (pass/fail) (O'Gorman & Woolson, 1991). Means and standard deviations for the predictor variables and the criterion variables used in this study are presented in Table 1. (Note: Modifications were made to the original NCQ questionnaire by Bethel College administrators. As a result, final coefficients for seven of the eight non-cognitive NCQ-BC subscales were too low and only availability of a strong support person was retained.)

Table 1. Descriptive Statistics for the Predictor
and Criterion Variables

	Mean	SD
Predictor Variables		
High school rank	51.79	24.30
High school grade point	2.45	.67
Available support person	4.46 (of 9)	.67
Academic adjustment	146.43	24.78
Social adjustment	118.56	23.41
Personal emotional adjust	78.35	21.86
Attachment to college	95.34	19.46
Criterion Variables		
Fall term grades passing	Yes = 173	84%
	No = 33	16%
Enrolled for spring	Yes = 185	91%
	No = 19	09%

RESULTS

Predicting Academic Performance

In response to the research question, to what extent and in what combination, if any, do selected cognitive, non-cognitive, and adjustment variables predict early academic performance among female students at a historically black, institution, the results of the regression analyses for the sample of female students are shown in Table 2.

Academic adjustment and personal emotional attachment were significant adjustment variables, but neither were as important as either rank in high school or high school grades. In the regression analyses used to examine predictor variables for academic performance, cognitive variables like high school grades and rank explained 20 percent of the variance (see Table 3). Five variables did remain in the model, meaning they were significant at some level. The variables were: high school rank; personal emotional adjustment; availability of a strong support person; and social adjustment. These variables accounted for 30 percent of the total variance. High school rank was the best single predictor variable for academic performance as measured by grades.

Predicting Academic Pass/Fail

The prediction of group membership based on academic success or fail, defined as academic probation or not at Bethel, are summarized in Table 4. Three adjustment variables, academic adjustment; personal emotional adjustment, and attachment to the college were significant predictors. Academic adjustment was strongest, followed by personal emotional attachment and

Table 2. Regression Coefficients for
Independent Variables to First Semester
Academic Performance (GPA)

Predictor Variables	r
Cognitive Variables	
High school rank	−.35**
High school grade point average	.38**
Adjustment Variables	
Academic adjustment	.25**
Attachment to the college	.14**
Personal emotional adjustment	.20**

$**p \leq .01$

Table 3. Summary of Significant Predictor Variables for Academic
Performance (First Semester GPA)

Steps/Predictor Variable	Partial R-2	Model R-2	F	p
1 High School Rank	.20	.14	14.84	.0001
2 Personal Emotional Attachment	.04	.18	4.59	.026
3 Availability of a Strong				
Support Person	.02	.27	2.82	.0967
4 High School Grades	.02	.29	2.91	.0915
5 Social Adjustment	.02	.30	2.40	.1253

Table 4. Regression Coefficients for
Variables Related to Academic Pass
(Pass or Success/Fail or Unsuccessful)

Predictor Variables	r
Adjustment	
Academic Adjustment	.24
Personal Emotional Attachment	.17*
Attach to the College	.18***

$*p \leq .05$
$***p \leq .001$

attachment to the college. None of the cognitive variables were predictive in this case, nor was the non-cognitive variable which was retained from the NCQ (1984).

Predicting Persistence

Two variables were significantly correlated with persistence, social adjustment and attachment to the college. Social adjustment was the most significant of the two. Results are shown in Table 5.

DISCUSSION

For new, first year, female students attending a private, historically black liberal arts college, the best combination to predict academic performance and success were high school rank; personal emotional adjustment; availability of a strong support person; high school grade point; and social adjustment. These

Table 5. Regression Coefficients for
Independent Variables to Persistence
(ENROLLMENT STATUS)

Predictor Variables	r
Cognitive	
High School Rank	−.05
High School Grades	.07
Noncognitive	
Available Support Person	.06
Adjustment	
Academic Adjustment	.12
Social Adjustment	.21**
Personal Emotional Adjustment	.14
Attach to College	.16*

$*p \leq .05$
$**p \leq .01$

variables accounted for 30 percent of the total variance. High school rank accounted for 20 percent of the variance by itself.

Academic success for African-American females in this study involved a combination of cognitive, adjustment, and non-cognitive variables. Consistent with Tinto's (1987) integration model, academic success for females was a function of the ability to adjust to the academic environment *and* to receive appropriate and adequate support.

Social adjustment was the best predictor of persistence. Results from the study indicate the importance of social adjustment in predicting persistence or retention for the female students who participated. Social integration, academic integration, and commitment were also factors helpful in predicting early academic performance and success among the female freshmen at Bethel, a population at-risk for both academic success and retention.

College success for African-American first-year women students is a function of the background characteristics students bring to college and their own initial commitment to a college education. Pre-college characteristics are critical for students to be able to successfully integrate themselves into the college environment. This integration or fit, as Astin (1993) has called it, in turn impacts the student's commitment to and their satisfaction with the institution.

A student who has commitment to her educational goals and satisfaction as the result of her interaction with the college is more likely to persist in college. Students are at-risk for academic failure when they are unable to adjust to the various educational demands characteristic of the college experience. Female students who are at-risk for college dropout are often not prepared academically; feel a lack of control over their academic efforts; and may have unrealistic self-appraisal (Baker & Siryk, 1989). Characteristics related to academic adjustment were also the most significant in terms of the overall adjustment of the women at Bethel who participated in the study.

CONCLUSION

The importance of both academic and social adjustment were reinforced in the study. Despite the relative comfort of a historically black college or university (HBCU) like Bethel, issues of social adjustment, personal emotional adjustment, and the identification of a strong support person along with demonstrated academic success in high school, as measured by grades and rank in class, are critical for first-year African-American women. In some areas, the freshmen women were, in fact, different than freshmen men (Washington & Schwartz, in press). Women came better prepared overall but varied from freshmen males on some specific adjustment issues.

In terms of race and new students, it is not enough to provide a homogeneous setting in which racial conflict is minimized. It is also important to insure that students are supported, encouraged, and socially adjusted early in their college career. To be successful, African-American women need to be able to identify a strong support person(s). This variable appeared to be an essential ingredient for the African-American women in this study as they made the transition from home to campus. Strong emphasis on family and relationships in the South may make this finding a regional artifact, more likely to be found among the specific population used in the study. However, we strongly suspect it is generalizable to a broader population of young African-American women in other areas as well.

FURTHER RESEARCH

A number of factors contribute to the success of African-American students. Many of the findings in this study were consistent with other studies. What was strongly suggested in this study was that, in addition to high school rank and grades, adjustment variables like social adaption are important considerations for African-American women, in particular.

It is important to conduct more studies similar to this one on other campuses. Only through replication and dissemination of other studies, specifically focused on African-American women, will we learn more about these students. It is important to better understand the population and as a result, increase the opportunities for success. It is also critical to examine African-American students at historically black institutions, an area of study which appears to have been overlooked in many past studies. We sincerely believe that such racially homogeneous institutions offer minority students a very unique experience and deserve further examination by other researchers. Hopefully other studies at similar institutions will further expand on the findings from this study in the near future.

REFERENCES

Alexander, C. J. (1989). *The use of noncognitive variables for admission into dental school.* [CD-ROM]. Abstract from: ProQuest File: Dissertation Abstracts Item: 8904263.

Amando, C. (1991). *Predictive and differential validation study at the University of Hawai'I at Manoa (Hawaii).* [CD-ROM]. Abstract from: ProQuest File: Dissertation Abstracts Item: 9118026.

Arbona, C., & Novy, D. M. (1990). Noncognitive dimensions as predictors of college success among Black, Mexican-American, and White Students. *Journal of College Student Development, 31* (5), 415-422.

Astin, A. W. (1993). *What matters in college? Four critical years revisited.* San Francisco: Jossey-Bass.

Baker, R. W., & Siryk, M. A. (1989). *SACQ: Student adaptation to college questionnaire manual.* Los Angeles: Western Psychological Services (WPS).

Baron, J., & Norman, M. F. (1992). SATs, achievement tests, and high-school class rank as predictors of college performance. *Educational-and Psychological-Measurement, 52* (4), 1047-1055.

Bloomer, R. H. (1991). *The self-concept and locus-of-control of learning disabled college students.* [CD-ROM]. Abstract from: ProQuest File: Dissertation Abstracts Item: 9119519.

Bontekoe, J. F. (1992). *The ACT as a predictor of college success at Trinity Christian College.* (ERIC Document Reproduction Service No. ED 355 258).

Boyer, S. P., & Sedlacek, W. E. (1989, March). Noncognitive predictors of counseling center use by international students. *Journal of Counseling and Development, 67* (7), 404-407.

Brice, B. E. G. (1993). *A study of persistence of freshman males at two historically Black institutions of higher education.* [CD-ROM]. Abstract from: ProQuest File: Dissertation Abstracts Item: 9312145.

Bridgeman, B., & Wendler, C. (1991). Effects of time-management practices on college grades. *Journal of Educational Psychology, 83* (2), 275-284.

Brown, N. W. (1994, April). Cognitive, interest, and personality variables predicting first-semester GPA. *Psychological Report, 74* (2), 605-606.

Connor, C. A. (1990). *Factors influencing the academic achievement of black and white freshman at the University of Wisconsin-Milwaukee.* [CD-ROM]. Abstract from: ProQuest File: Dissertation Abstracts Item: 9011677.

Connor, R. (1992). *The effect of selected variables on African-American student persistence.* [CD-ROM]. Abstract from: ProQuest File: Dissertation Abstract Item: 9219707.

Cowen, S., & Fiori, S. J. (1991, November). *Appropriateness of the SAT in selecting students for admission to California State University, Hayward.* Paper presented at the annual meeting of the California Educational Research Association, San Diego, CA. (ERIC Document Reproduction Service No. ED 343 934).

Dole, A. A. (1990). *Perceived self-efficacy as a predictor of freshman grade point average for at-risk students and regular-admitted students at the University of Pennsylvania.* [CD-ROM]. Abstract from: ProQuest File: Dissertation Abstracts Item: 8908679.

Feagin, J. R., Vera, H., & Imani, N. (1996). *The agony of education: Black students at white colleges and universities.* New York: Routledge.

Gerardi, S. (1990). Academic self-concept as a predictor of academic success among minority and low-socioeconomic status students. *Journal of College Student Development, 31* (5), 402-407.

Gold, J., Burrell, S., Haynes, C., & Nardecchia, D. (1990). *Student adaptation to college as a predictor of academic success: An exploratory study of Black undergraduate education students.* (Research Report 143). (ERIC Document Reproduction Service No. ED 331 946.)

Hood, D. W. (1992). Academic and noncognitive factors affecting the retention of Black men at a predominantly White university. *Journal of Negro Education, 61* (1), 12-23.

Hollingsworth, K., Walker, R., & Anderson, T. (1997). Using the DEA in the examination of the retention of African American males. *Challenge: A Journal of Research on African American Men, 8* (1), 17-25.

House, D. J. (1994, November). *College grade outcomes and attrition: An exploratory study of noncognitive variables and academic background as predictors.* Paper presented at the Illinois Association for Institutional Research Annual Meeting, Lake Shelbyville, IL. (ERIC Document Reproduction Service No. ED 390 319.)

Hudson, J. B. (1993). The Relationship between tests, course placement, and the academic performance of college freshmen. *NACADA-Journal, 13* (2), 5-14.

Jacobs, L. C. (1985). *GPA prediction procedures and normative data for freshmen.* Indiana Studies in Higher Education Number Fifty-Two, Indiana University, Bureau of Evaluative Studies and Testing, Bloomington, IN. (ERIC Document Reproduction Service No. ED 266 715.)

Johnson, R. (1993). *Factors in the academic success of African American college males.* Unpublished doctoral dissertation, University of South Carolina, Columbia. (CD-ROM). Abstract from: ProQuest File: Dissertation Abstracts Item 9321967, and (ERIC Document Reproduction Service No. ED 364 639).

Kanoy, W. K., Wester, J., & Lata, M. (1989, Spring). Predicting college success of freshmen using traditional, cognitive, psychological measures. *Journal of Research and Development in Education, 22* (3), 133-140.

Kim, S. H., & Sedlacek, W. E. (1995). *Gender differences among incoming African American freshmen on academic and social expectations.* Paper presented at the annual meeting of the American Educational Research Association, San Francisco, CA. (ERIC Document Reproduction Service No. ED 387768.)

Kunjufu, J. (1997). *Black college students' survival guide.* Chicago, IL: African American Images.

Livengood, J. M. (1992). Students' motivational goals and beliefs about effort and ability as they relate to college academic success. *Research in Higher Education, 33* (2), 247-261.

Marsh, H. W. (1992). Content specificity of relations between academic achievement and academic self-concept. *Educational Psychologist, 20,* 102-123.

Martin, O. L. (1990). *The college milieu for the 1990s: Increasing Black student retention rates on white campuses.* Paper Presented at the annual meeting of American Educational Research Association, Boston. (ERIC Document Reproduction Service No. ED 333 091.)

McConatha, J. T. (1990). Assessing the self-responsibility for wellness needs of incoming students. *NASPA Journal, 27* (3), 257-263.

Moffatt, G. K. (1993, February). *The validity of the SAT as a predictor of grade point average for nontraditional college students.* Paper present at the Annual Meeting of the Eastern Educational Research Association, Clearwater Beach, FL. (ERIC Document Reproduction Service No. ED 356 252.)

Moline, A. E. (1987). Financial aid and student persistence. An application of causal modeling. *Research in Higher Education, 26* (2), 130-147.

Myers, R. S., & Pyles, M. R. (1992, November). *Relationships among high school grades, ACT test scores, and college grades.* Paper presented at the annual meeting of the Mid-South Educational Research Association, Knoxville, TN. (ERIC Document Reproduction Service No. ED 353 317.)

Nettles, M. T. & Gosman, E. J. (1986). Comparative and predictive analyses of Black and White students' college achievement and experiences. *Journal of Higher Education, 57,* 289-318.

O'Gorman, T. W., & Woolson, R. F. (1991). Variables selection to discriminate between two groups: Stepwise logistic regression or discriminant analysis? *American Statistician, 45,* 187-193.

Ott, M. D. (1988). An analysis of predictors of early academic dismissal. *Research in Higher Education, 28* (1), 34-48.

Perkins, L. (1985). The impact of the "Cult of True Womanhood" on the education of Black women. *Journal of Social Issues, 39* (3), 17-28.

Phillip, M. L. (1993). Too many institutions still taking a band-aid approach to minority student retention, experts say. *Black Issues in Higher Education, 9* (24), 24-26.

Pickering, J. W., Calliotte, J. A., & McAuliffe, G. J. (1992). The effect of noncognitive factors on freshman academic performance and retention. *Journal of The Freshmen Year Experience, 4* (2), 7-30.

Pickens, E. L. (1987). *An analysis of characteristics influencing the withdrawals of academically eligible Black students in a predominantly Black university: 1981-1984.* [CD-ROM]. Abstract from: ProQuest File: Dissertation Abstracts Item 8267498.

Rowser, J. E. (1997). Do African American student's perceptions of their needs have implications for retention? *Journal of Black Studies, 27* (5), 718-726.

Sedlacek, W. E., & Adams-Gaston, E. (1992). Predicting the academic success of student athletes using SAT and noncognitive variables. *Journal of Counseling and Development, 70* (6), 724-727. (ERIC Document Reproduction Service No. ED 31 501.)

Sedlacek, W. E. & Brooks, G. C. (1976). *Racism in American education: A model for change.* Chicago: Nelson-Hall.

Sowa, C. J., Thomson, M. M., & Bennett, C. T. (1989). Prediction and improvement of academic performance for high-risk Black college students. *Journal of Multicultural Counseling and Development, 17* (1), 14-22.

Stith, P. L., & Russell, F. (1994, May). *Faculty/student interaction: Impact of student retention.* Paper presented at the annual forum of the Association for Institutional Research, New Orleans, LA. (ERIC Document Reproduction Service No. ED 373 650.)

Thornell, J., & Jones, R. (1986, November). *The college admissions equation: ACT scores versus secondary school grade performance.* Paper presented at the annual meeting of the Educational Research Association, Memphis, TN. (ERIC Document Reproduction Service No. ED 278 687.)

Tinto, V. (1987). *Leaving college: Rethinking the causes and cures of student attrition.* Chicago: University of Chicago Press.

Tracey, T. J., & Sedlacek, W. E. (1984). Non-cognitive variables in predicting academic success by race. *Measurement and Evaluation in Guidance, 16* (4), 171-178.

Tracey, T. J., & Sedlacek, W. E. (1986, April). *Prediction of college graduation using noncognitive variables by race.* Paper presented at the annual meeting of American Educational Research Association, San Francisco, CA. (ERIC Document Reproduction Service No. ED 271 513.)

Tracey, T. J., & Sedlacek, W. E. (1987). *A comparison of White and Black student academic success using noncognitive variables: A LISREL analysis* (Research Report 6-87). (ERIC Document Reproduction Service No. ED 294 878.)

Trippi, J., & Stewart, J. B. (1989). The relationship between self-appraisal variables and the college grade performance and persistence of Black freshmen. *Journal of College Student Development, 30* (6), 484-491.

Washington, C. M. & Schwartz, R. A. (in press). African American freshmen students in a historically Black college. *Journal of the Freshman Year Experience.*

Wilson-Sadberry, K. R. (1991). Resilience and persistence of African-American males in postsecondary enrollment. *Education and Urban Society, 24* (1), 87-102.

CHAPTER 3

Retaining Black Students in Engineering: Do Minority Programs Have a Longitudinal Impact?

Jennifer Good, Glennelle Halpin,
and Gerald Halpin

In an effort to assist minority populations who are at risk of attrition in science, mathematics, and engineering programs, university administrators have launched and evaluated minority support programs. One such program implementation and evaluation was completed and reported, which noted trends in academic outcomes of program participants, such as grade point averages and standardized mathematics and science reasoning test scores, with participants' outcomes observably exceeding those of a similar sample of nonprogram participants (Good, Halpin, & Halpin, 1999). As is true with many program evaluations, however, this data only revealed information concerning achievement of the students in the freshman year and did not follow the students' success into subsequent years after program completion. Therefore, the purpose of this study was to examine if an effect on academic achievement occurred throughout the participants' sophomore years of study and if participants in the program were more likely to remain within the College of Engineering as a result of program involvement. The data source for this study was 58 African-American students enrolled in a pre-engineering program at a large land-grant university (34 volunteer program participants and a comparison group of 24). Quarter grade point averages and retention status were collected for both groups throughout their sophomore years. In addition, 12 of these students (six per group) were interviewed concerning their freshman year pre-engineering experiences. Results of this study indicate that, although benefits to academic achievement due to academic support encountered during the freshman year may possibly diminish over time, the effects of engaging in such programs on actual retention remain of significant interest to program administrators and researchers.

The problem of attrition exists in quantitatively-oriented fields and continues to develop as the diversity of the student population of universities increases. Gainen (1995) reported that the greatest attrition among collegiate students occurred between the freshman and sophomore years of study with students who chose to major in science, mathematics, or engineering (S. M. E.). In addition, "among students of color, attrition is much higher" (p. 5) than among White students. In their landmark study, Seymour and Hewitt (1997) explained that "65 percent of students of color entering science or mathematics left their major, compared to 37 percent of white students" (p. 319), and according to their extensive review of the literature, "the question of why students from particular racial or ethnic groups have higher S. M. E. attrition rates than white students has not been satisfactorily answered" (p. 320). What causes this attrition, and how can it be addressed at the university level?

Researchers (MacGuire & Halpin, 1995; McNairy, 1996; Seymour & Hewitt, 1997; White & Shelley, 1996) suggest that some commonalities in experiences exist among African-American students, causing detrimental rates of attrition for this particular population. For instance, McNairy (1996) and Seymour and Hewitt (1997) cite a lack of adequate high school preparation as a deterrent in university science and math programs. White and Shelley (1996) noted that Black students craved a sense of belonging on predominantly White university campuses and stated that often "the ability to identify, create, and maintain supportive learning communities" (p. 32) presented difficulty. Tang (2000) stated that "Blacks are less inclined to enter engineering because of inadequate encouragement and institutional support" (p. 35). Thus, it appears that a combination of cognitive factors, such as inadequate high school preparation and lack of study skills, and noncognitive factors, such as lack of community and identity on college campuses, exacerbate the attrition problem for African-American students.

In order to retain African-American students, administrators in higher education should first consider the academic needs and expectations of these students and then make adjustments at the institutional level in order to meet those needs (Landis, 1995; Wharton, 1992). Administrators in higher education have initiated numerous support programs to foster academic success and encourage a sense of community among African-American students in hopes of retaining them in quantitative majors. Although minority retention programs varied, peer interaction seemed to be a key component in assisting students both cognitively and noncognitively. Three successful minority retention programs described by Carreathers et al. (1996) used peer facilitators in some aspect of the program because "students of color lack peers, faculty role models and mentors" (Seymour & Hewitt, 1997, p. 320). Although many minority engineering programs share common features, "they do not always share common successes" (Torres, 2000, p. 219).

As much as the programs varied, so too did the methods of program evaluation. Giordano (1996) emphasized the importance of varied methods of data collection and formative, ongoing methods of evaluation when completing program evaluations regarding minority retention. Unfortunately, few programs follow the progress of participants' longitudinally to assess if newly acquired skills continue to transfer into future academic careers and coursework. Numerous researchers (Popham, 1993; Posavac & Carey, 1992; Worthen, Sanders, & Fitzpatrick, 1997) stressed the importance of finding appropriate criteria and objectives as an essential aspect of effective evaluation. Thus, when evaluating retention programs, actual retention outcomes should be a central concern of the program evaluation.

In the fall of 1997, a minority engineering program (MEP) was created which considered both the cognitive and noncognitive needs of African-American students. This particular program was comprised of three components designed to help the freshman pre-engineering students meet the demands of science, mathematics, and engineering courses of study: 2-hour tutorial sessions held on Sunday evenings with a weekly dinner, a weekly critical thinking workshop series, and an interactive learning laboratory which students visited for three 1-hour sessions per week. Each student was assigned a mentor, an upperclass division African-American student majoring in engineering, and members of the mentoring staff were available at all program activities. Participants remained in the program throughout their entire freshman years.

An initial evaluation of the program, completed after the first year of program administration, suggested that student achievement was affected by program involvement. Because of the small sample size, the program evaluators analyzed trends in the data, realizing that tests of statistical significance would be inappropriate. Thus, although not significantly different, participants in the program earned observably higher first quarter grade point averages than nonparticipants ($M = 2.53$ as opposed to 2.26). In addition, program participants significantly increased standardized tests in mathematics ($M = 57.41$ to 59.71) and scientific reasoning ($M = 57.73$ to 59.36) from pre- to postintervention. Also, the first quarter grade point averages of students involved in the program exceeded those of their peers in earlier years of study prior to the program's existence (Good, Halpin, & Halpin, 1999). The data regarding various outcomes appeared to be casting in the same positive direction. Although these findings were promising, they were too preliminary to be conclusive. They did not track actual retention status throughout the students' pre-engineering years until they matriculated into the College of Engineering as upperclassmen.

Because a program evaluation yielded positive results on its first implementation, can it be assumed that similar achievement trends will continue for program participants after completing the program? In other words, will the benefits of the program transfer to future years of study and continue to impact grade point averages even after program involvement has ceased? According to Fletcher (1998), first quarter grade point averages are powerful predictors of student success and retention. Therefore, can educators infer that the initial benefit to grade point averages experienced by participants involved in an academic support program will carry over into future quarters and, more important, will this initial bolstering of academic achievement truly have an impact on program retention? Few program evaluations continue to track student achievement after the participants have left a program.

Thus, the purpose of this study was to complete a longitudinal evaluation of this minority engineering program, tracking the retention status of these African-American students as they progressed through their pre-engineering courses of study. Specifically, this report examined if the effect on academic achievement experienced by these students in their first quarters of study continued throughout the participants' sophomore years of study, and if participants in the program were more likely to remain within the College of Engineering than nonparticipants as a result of program involvement. In addition, follow-up interviews of a sample of these students were conducted, which explored potential issues to help understand better why some African-American students continue to pursue an education in engineering and why some do not do so.

PROCEDURES AND ANALYSIS DESIGN

The institutional setting for this study is a large land-grant university in the Southeast. The university enrolls over 20,000 students and houses 12 different colleges, including colleges such as engineering, pharmacy, sciences, and mathematics. Because of an interest in the success of African-American students in quantitative majors, the College of Engineering supported and housed this particular academic support program, which included voluntary involvement in critical thinking workshops, use of mathematic and scientific interactive software, and tutoring sessions.

Participants in this study were 58 African-American students. While 24 of these students opted not to participate in the minority engineering program, the remaining 34 volunteered to take part in the program, making a comparison of similar groups possible. As mentioned earlier, these 34 students were involved in various aspects of the program (critical-thinking workshops, an interactive learning laboratory, or Sunday-evening tutorials) throughout their freshman year of study. With the exception of a few students who returned to the program as upperclass mentors, program involvement ceased for all students in their sophomore years of study.

After students completed their sophomore years of study, quarter and cumulative grade point averages were collected. Program status at the end of the sophomore year was also monitored and recorded into one of three categories: students remaining in the College of Engineering; students leaving the engineering program or the university in poor academic standing (grade point averages < 2.2); and students leaving the engineering program or university in good academic standing (grade point averages > 2.20). To determine if academic achievement and retention differed in the two groups, mean grade point averages throughout the sophomore year of study were compared using t-tests. Cross tabulations to determine the effect of participation in the minority engineering program on status and retention in the College of Engineering were also completed, yielding contingency coefficients as indicators of significance.

In addition, in order to add a qualitative depth to the study, 12 students were selected to complete interviews regarding the students' pre-engineering experiences and choices of major. Using a semi-structured interview protocol, an interviewer solicited responses from one male and one female representative for each of the three categories of program status described earlier (see Appendix). Thus, six program participants and six nonparticipants from each of the three program status categories were interviewed. When all twelve interviews were completed, the interviewees' responses were transcribed, and a content analysis of the responses was completed for each question. The thematic responses were placed in a large grid per individual and question, and the themes were analyzed by gender, participation in the program, and retention status in order to determine if particular patterns occurred for these various groupings.

RESULTS

Grade Outcomes

One of the objectives of the minority engineering program (MEP) is for the participants to have a stronger comprehension of mathematics, science reasoning, and critical thinking skills which will help them to succeed in their programs of study. Inasmuch as the program is designed for mutual reinforcement of the concepts being taught in these different domains, the goal was to increase student understanding within the various domains which might be reflected in grades. Even though the students were no longer involved in the minority engineering program, it was the hope of the program administrators that the skills taught and acquired by participants in their freshman years would help to bolster grades throughout participants' future academic careers. Table 1 indicates the mean quarter and cumulative grade point averages for participants and nonparticipants throughout their sophomore year of study.

Table 1. Means of Quarter and Cumulative Grade Point Averages
for African-American Pre-Engineering Students during the
Sophomore Year of Study

Group	Fall quarter	Winter quarter	Spring quarter	Cumulative
Participants	2.31	2.43	2.44	2.45
Nonparticipants	2.31	2.59	2.35	2.23

As apparent from Table 1, no pattern of mean grade point averages emerged for participants as opposed to nonparticipants. Whereas the mean grade point averages for the participants exceeded those of the nonparticipants during the spring quarter, the mean grade point average for the nonparticipants was higher during the winter quarter, and even though the mean cumulative grade point average appears to be higher for the participants, a series of t tests revealed that no significant differences existed on any of these variables. Thus, these data suggested that no clear impact of the minority engineering program on academic outcomes, such as quarter grades, occurred after program completion. In other words, the effect of the academic support program on grades could possibly be dependent upon current and constant program involvement. Possibly, the constant probing, questioning, and interacting in the tutoring sessions, workshops, and interactive learning laboratory more readily transferred into current courses, but once the interaction ceased, the effect and transfer to coursework ceased as well.

Retention Outcomes

The practical intent of the minority engineering program is to retain students within the College of Engineering by providing them with essential skills which will help them to succeed in their chosen major. If this important objective is achieved, then differences in retention patterns should be apparent for the participants as opposed to the nonparticipants. The students were placed into one of three groups: those who remained within the College of Engineering, those who left engineering (or the university) due to poor academic records, and those who left engineering (or the university) in spite of strong academic standings. Because a grade point average of 2.20 is required for admission into the College of Engineering, this cut-off was used to determine academic standing. Table 2 provides the retention rates at the end of the students' sophomore years of studies by program participants and nonparticipants.

The retention patterns for the two groups were obviously different. Whereas over three-quarters of the program participants remained within the College of Engineering, less than half of the nonparticipants remained. Twenty-four percent more of the nonparticipants left for academic reasons, with grade point averages

Table 2. Program Status and Retention Rates for Black Students
within the College of Engineering

	Status		
	Engineering	Left (GPA < 2.2)	Left (GPA > 2.2)
Participants	26 (76%)	3 (9%)	5 (15%)
Nonparticipants	9 (38%)	8 (33%)	7 (29%)

less than 2.2, with 14 percent more of the nonparticipants also opting to leave in spite of their strong academic standing. A contingency coefficient of .374 indicated that this significance was different at the .01 level. Thus, participation in the minority engineering program appears to have a significant impact on decisions concerning retention within the College of Engineering, the primary thrust of the program and an essential outcome for consideration when evaluating the program.

Interview Responses

Because the retention status of the students participating in the Minority Engineering Program fared notably better than the non-participating comparison group, logical conjectures regarding reasons for this difference needed to be pursued. Possibly, participation in the Minority Engineering Program alone could have accounted for this difference; however, it seemed more reasonable to consider and explore some of the varied factors that students, both MEP participants and nonparticipants, experienced during their pre-engineering years that could have affected their decision to remain in or switch out of their selected courses of study. In order to determine what factors may have impacted Black students regarding their choices of major as engineers, a sampling of twelve students, representing equal numbers of males and females, as well as MEP participants and nonparticipants, were interviewed.

Regarding commitment to engineering and reasons for pursuing engineering, all but one of the interviewees indicated that they were highly or extremely committed to becoming engineers. Their reasons for pursuing engineering varied across the twelve students; however, a clear pattern emerged differentiating the stayers from the switchers. The participants who opted to remain in engineering were familiar with the profession, due to actual exposure to the engineering profession through parents or family friends. In contrast, the switching students admitted to having little knowledge of the engineering profession prior to pursuing the major. Over half of the switchers pursued engineering simply because they were good in mathematics and science. For instance, one individual stated the following: "You know when you are in high school and you don't really know what you want to do? Well, I did engineering because I knew I liked math and science, and I knew it was a good career." Similarly, another student stated that he "really didn't know that much about what actual engineers did." Instead, he "liked the idea of being an engineer." Prior knowledge of the profession and opportunities to talk with engineers appeared to be a factor that differentiated between stayers and switchers, regardless of MEP involvement.

All 12 interviewees experienced some form of academic difficulty during their pre-engineering course of studies, and all 12 interviewees contemplated leaving the pre-engineering major during their freshman years. However, the way the students approached the difficulty at that particular juncture in the program varied, again, by stayers and switchers. Whereas the stayers were determined to get through the program in spite of the academic challenge, the switchers simply tended to leave the program rather than face academic failure. For instance, one of the stayers explained that she decided to remain in engineering for the following reason:

> Because I have a lot of classes already under my belt. I don't want to lose all my credits and start over again. The hardest part I think is like some of the core classes, the physics, and the math, and like the early engineering classes, but after that, I think it gets easier.

Another participant stated that he decided to remain in engineering, in spite of some poor grades early in his academic career, because he had "put so much time working to it." In general, the students who opted to remain in engineering all described an investment to the program once they had survived the initial academic adjustment. In contrast, the switching student cited specific courses and course grades as the primary reason for leaving the pre-engineering program. For instance, one of the switching students stated the following: "After my first quarter, my grades fell substantially, so I went to an easier major." Simply stated, the switching students had not accepted the possibility that the adjustment to the engineering major may coincide with an acceptance of lower grades than they had maintained in high school. As a result, the switchers simply changed majors while the stayers persevered. Again, participation in the Minority Engineering Program did not appear to be a factor when considering the thematic patterns that emerged for these responses.

When asked about involvement in academic support programs, an interesting pattern emerged, this time surrounding the MEP participants versus the nonparticipants. The students who volunteered to participate in the MEP also pursued an average of three additional academic support programs during their pre-engineering courses of study. In contrast, the non-MEP participants did not seek as much outside help through university support programs. Half of the non-MEP students sought help from only one support program, while the other half of the non-MEP students did not pursue any form of academic assistance at all. Although all six of the participants described the MEP as more helpful than the other programs around the campus, this finding still suggested that students who are willing to volunteer to participate in the MEP share a willingness to seek other forms of help as well. Similarly, when asked about support systems, the MEP participants cited a number and variety of systems on which they relied regularly, including parents, mentors, roommates, friends, and classmates; in contrast, the non-MEP participants were more solitary, stating that they relied on either no one or one hometown friend. Essentially, the MEP students appear to reach out to others for assistance more readily. Thus, possibly the findings regarding retention could be clouded by the impact of other academic support programs and systems in addition to the MEP.

One of the most illuminating findings regarding the potential impact of the MEP on students revolves around the students' sense of connectedness to the engineering community during their pre-engineering programs. Whereas four of the six(66 percent) MEP participants stated that they felt as though they belonged to the engineering community, all six of the non-MEP participants stated that they felt disconnected to the engineering community. For instance, when asked if they felt they were part of the engineering community during their freshman year, one student stated the following: "Yeah, well, sort of because I was in the Minority Engineering Program, and I was surrounded by engineers." Another student responded similarly: "In the MEP I did, because there are people like me, pursuing the same goals." And another student stated the following:

> Yeah, I did, I did, I did because, I really did, mainly because I was in MEP, and the majority of the minority students who come here are in engineering, so, you know, I felt like I was part of engineering. I felt like I fit in, just because I was around all the other students like me, you know?

Whereas all of the MEP nonparticipants felt disconnected, the MEP participants actually felt as though they were part of the engineering community as early as their freshman year, and interestingly, they all volunteered the MEP program ast he single factor that made them feel as though they belonged.

Regarding work and study habits, a primary emphasis of the Minority Engineering Program, all 12 of the interviewees felt as though they were not academically prepared when they first entered the university, and 11 of the twelve students (92 percent) indicated that they improved their study habits during their freshman and sophomore year out of necessity to survive academically. No single program or method was cited above others by the students as helping them to improve their study skills at the university.

When asked to compare the pre-engineering courses with other core courses outside of the engineering field, the responses varied per stayers and switchers. All but one of the interviewees stated that the engineering courses were more difficult than non-engineering courses. Specifically, students described the courses as more time-consuming, more demanding, and more open-ended without clear resolutions on problems. In spite of this, the stayers described the engineering courses as more meaningful and practical to them than other core courses, particularly the upper level courses within their majors. In contrast, the switchers described the courses outside of engineering as more meaningful. Again, no differentiation between MEP and non-MEP participants occurred regarding this question.

When asked about ethnicity, all but one of the twelve interviewees stated that ethnicity was not an issue within the engineering program. The only student who expressed any concern stated the following:

> It's hard. It's very difficult, but, like, the Minority Engineering Program, that helped a whole lot. I just don't know if I would still be in engineering without it. You know, just seeing other people like you in engineering. It's very encouraging.

Her statement was the exception. Otherwise, the other interviewees consistently stated that ethnicity was not a distinguishing factor within the pre-engineering program. For instance, one student stated the following: "I really don't think about it as being a minority. I just think about it as trying to be an engineer." Another student noted the following: "I was intimidated because this campus was so huge, not necessarily because I was a minority." When asked if students felt they were treated differently in the pre-engineering program because of their ethnicity, all 12 stated that they were not. For instance one student stated the following: "I don't think I was, especially academically. I don't think it mattered." Other students simply stated that there was "no difference" in their treatment compared to majority students.

In direct contrast to the question regarding ethnicity, every female felt that they had experienced some form of gender discrimination. When asked about being a female in the pre-engineering program, one student stated the following: "Oh man. I felt stupid in physics because all these guys were in there, and they would crack jokes and stuff like that. I felt pretty awkward in that situation." Similarly, when asked how it feels to be a female engineering major, another student replied:

> It's just like, in class you're picked on more, you're called on more, you're looked to more to try and answer questions than maybe the guy next to you, who they think knows it already or something like that, or they automatically think you're not going to do too well in this math course because, you know, you are a female.

And, one student noted that instructors "assumed she wouldn't succeed" because she was a female. Whereas five of the six females interviewed indicated that this was a discouraging issue to face within the pre-engineering program, the other interviewee stated that she accepted the gender difference as a direct challenge:

I like being in a big society where there's a lot of males and very little females. I think it is so much fun. I mean it makes me reach higher. I guess it's expected for females to be a little lower than men, but when it comes to me, I want to be as high as they are.

Her attitude was unique; the other females experienced frustration due to the stereotypes placed upon them.

Finally, regarding pre-engineering experiences, the 12 students had varying suggestions for how to improve the program. Four of the MEP participants had no suggestions at all, while one of the MEP participants suggested expanding the mentoring program and one suggested a supplemental class that would introduce students to various disciplines in engineering. Three (50 percent) of the non-MEP students suggested that advisors needed to make more of an active effort to engage the students in the program in addition to offering both academic support and counseling. Other suggestions from the non-MEP students included setting math and science instructors up in teams that work with the same group of students, slowing the pace of instruction or offering more entry level courses, and offering an introductory course which exposes students to various adjustment issues within the engineering program.

Thus, when considering the various responses solicited through the interviews, it appeared as though the MEP has little impact on certain factors which tend to inhibit success during the freshman year. Instead, a clearer distinction arose between the stayers' and switchers' responses, rather than MEP participants' and nonparticipants' responses. However, some compelling evidence existed regarding the MEP participants' comfort with reaching out for additional assistance and the sense of belonging within the engineering community afforded though the MEP.

DISCUSSION

When considered holistically, some interesting findings can be addressed regarding the longitudinal data on this particular class of freshman pre-engineering students. Although the data regarding mean grade point averages appeared initially discouraging and disconcerting because of its observable decrease after program completion, the data regarding retention patterns was promising. Fletcher (1998) hypothesized that the first quarter of the freshman year is crucial to future success in academic careers, and specifically that first quarter grade point averages act as one of the best predictors of retention. If that is true, then the program participants had an academic advantage over the nonparticipants during the pivotal first quarter of instruction. In addition, Seymour and Hewitt (1997) asserted that Black students experience a sense of ethnic isolation when enrolling in science, mathematics, and engineering programs. Possibly, as suggested by the interview responses, involvement in the minority engineering program negates this sense of isolation. Seymour and Hewitt also stated that many students of color internalize stereotypes and in turn experience self-doubts and a lack of confidence (p. 361). As a result, these students are less likely to seek help. When the academic support program, however, is provided as a constant and natural part of their programs of study, then help is always available without fear or shame of asking questions or being labeled as remedial.

Important future research should attempt to create an evaluation method which quantitatively as well as qualitatively teases out the factors affecting longitudinal retention patterns of Black students, and the relationship of these factors to academic support programs. As evident through this study, retention appears to be affected by program involvement; however, the importance of grades on retention appears to have diminished. What, then, is the cause of the improved retention rates for program participants and how does program involvement achieve this end? This study initially maintained the assumption that academic achievement was directly related to retention issues. Although this hypothesis could have merit, the results of this research seem to suggest that other factors have a greater impact on retention issues than merely academic achievement for Black students. Continued research into minority engineering programs and their effect on minority issues remains imperative:

> Although a significant body of descriptive work offers insight into field switching and stopping out versus dropping out–leaving higher education altogether–the institutional research has largely been short-term and problem-specific and has not addressed the broad spectrum of issues unique to minority students in rigorous science-based majors. (Denes, 2000, p. 317)

White and Shelley (1996) asserted that an "ability to identify, create, and maintain supportive learning communities" (p. 32) most encouraged retention among minorities. Hence, the noncognitive factors provided through involvement in a minority engineering program appear to be as essential to understanding retention as are the cognitive factors of student achievement. Although the longitudinal impact of this minority engineering program on student achievement is questionable, the impact of the program on retention patterns is notable. Future evaluations should continue to discern those other important factors in the noncognitive domain which help to retain Black students in science, mathematics, and engineering disciplines.

APPENDIX

Semi-Structured Interview Protocol

The following questions are based on the landmark study by Seymour and Hewitt (1997) entitled *Talking about Leaving*.

1. Describe how committed you were to the engineering program. What factors affected your level of commitment?

2. Stayers: Why have you chosen to remain within engineering?
   Switchers: Why did you leave engineering?
3. Stayers: Have you ever considered leaving engineering? Why?
   Switchers: When did you first decide to leave engineering? Why?
4. Did you pursue any academic support programs at the university? How helpful were they to your goals as an engineering student?
5. Do/Did you feel like you were a part of the engineering community at the university? Explain.
6. How would you describe your own work and study habits?
7. What strategies for survival did you employ while you were in the College of Engineering?
8. How would you rate the university support for assisting you in academic success during your freshman year? Explain.
9. Describe your support systems (formal systems involving faculty and staff and informal peers) that you rely on regularly. How did you establish these support systems?
10. How would you compare your courses within the pre-engineering and engineering curriculum to those you have taken outside of the engineering curriculum?
11. What advice would you give to a high school student who tells you that they are considering engineering as a college major?
12. How does it feel being a minority at a predominantly White institution? How does it feel being a female? Do you feel you have been treated any differently because of your ethnicity or gender?
13. What changes could the College of Engineering make to better assist the incoming freshman pre-engineering majors in order to encourage them to pursue engineering?

REFERENCES

Carreathers, K. R., Beekmann, L., Coatie, R. M., & Nelson, W. L. (1996). Three exemplary retention programs. In M. J. Barr & M. L. Upcraft (Series Eds.) & I. H. Johnson & A. J. Ottens (Vol. Eds.), *Leveling the playing field: Promoting academic success for students of color: Vol 74. New directions for student services* (pp. 35–52). San Francisco: Jossey-Bass.

Denes, R. (2000). Gaining access: A research and policy agenda. In G. Campbell, Jr, R. Denes, & C. Morrison (Eds.), *Access denied: Race, ethnicity, and the scientific enterprise* (pp. 314–323). New York: Oxford University Press.

Fletcher, J. (1998). *A study of the factors affecting advancement and graduation for engineering students.* Unpublished doctoral dissertation, Auburn University, Auburn, Alabama.

Gainen, J. (1995). Barriers to success in quantitative gatekeeper courses. In R. J. Menges & M. D. Svinicki (Series Eds.) & J. Gainen & E. W. Willemsen (Vol. Eds.), *Fostering student success in quantitative gateway courses: Vol. 61. New directions for teaching and learning* (pp. 5–14). San Francisco: Jossey-Bass.

Giordano, F. G. (1996). Evaluation as empowerment: Using evaluation strategies to improve retention of regularly admitted students of color. In M. J. Barr & M. L. Upcraft (Series Eds.) & I. H. Johnson & A. J. Ottens (Vol. Eds.), *Leveling the playing field: Promoting academic success for students of color: Vol 74. New directions for student services* (pp. 69–78). San Francisco: Jossey-Bass.

Good, J. M., Halpin, G., & Halpin, G. (1999, April). *Retaining minorities in engineering: Assessment of a program prototype.* Paper presented at the Annual Meeting of the American Educational Research Association, Montreal.

Landis, R. B. (1995). *Studying engineering: A road map to a rewarding career.* Los Angeles, CA: Discovery Press.

MacGuire, S., & Halpin, G. (1995, November). *Factors related to persistence in engineering: Results of a qualitative study.* Paper presented at the Annual Meeting of the Mid-South Education Research Association, Biloxi, MS. (ERIC Document Reproduction Service No. ED398052).

McNairy, F. G. (1996). The challenge for higher education: Retaining students of color. In M. J. Barr & M. L. Upcraft (Series Eds.) & I. H. Johnson & A. J. Ottens (Vol. Eds.), *Leveling the playing field: Promoting academic success for students of color: Vol 74. New directions for students services* (pp. 3–14). San Francisco: Jossey-Bass.

Popham, W. J. (1993). *Educational evaluation.* Boston, MA: Allyn and Bacon.

Posavac, E. J., & Carey, R. G. (1992). *Program Evaluation: Methods and case studies.* Englewood Cliffs, NJ: Prentice Hall.

Seymour, E., & Hewitt, N. M. (1997). *Talking about leaving: Why undergraduates leave the sciences.* Boulder, CO: Westview Press.

Tang, J. (2000). *Doing engineering.* New York, NY: Rowman and Littlefield.

Torres, A. (2000). Rethinking the model. In G. Campbell, Jr, R. Denes, & C. Morrison (Eds.), *Access denied: Race, ethnicity, and the scientific enterprise* (pp. 219–221). New York, NY: Oxford University Press.

Wharton, D. E. (1992). *A struggle worthy of note: The engineering and technological education of Black Americans.* Westport, CT: Greenwood Press.

White, C. J., & Shelley, C. (1996). Telling stories: Students and administrators talk about retention. In M. J. Barr & M. L. Upcraft (Series Eds.) & I. H. Johnson & A. J. Ottens (Vol. Eds.), *Leveling the playing field: Promoting academic success for students of color: Vol 74. New directions for students services* (pp. 15–34). San Francisco: Jossey-Bass.

Worthen, B. R., Sanders, J. R., & Fitzpatrick, J. L. (1997). *Program evaluation: Alternative approaches and alternative guidelines.* New York: Longman.

CHAPTER 4

The Retention of Black Male Students in Texas Public Community Colleges

Frank S. Glenn

The purposes of this study were to ascertain which Texas public community colleges have been able to graduate the highest percentages of black males and to analyze the factors contributing to that achievement. An institutional questionnaire was developed, designed to elicit information regarding policies and/or practices directly related to the retention of black male students and mailed to each college in the top and bottom quartiles. On-site case studies were conducted at one institution each from the top and bottom quartiles. The focus of the case studies was to examine the setting, policies, procedures, programs, and culture of each campus for clues concerning their black male retention rate. Data collection was from interviews, observations, and collection of institutional artifacts. This study identified several retention strategies that differentiate institutions in the top quartile of black, male student graduation rate from institutions in the bottom quartile.

The origin of the American community college movement, in its present form, generally has been attributed to William Rainey Harper of the University of Chicago (Monroe, 1972). The impetus for the movement was that further education was needed beyond high school for those aspiring to technical careers, and second that these first two years would provide an additional source of qualified university applicants (Monroe, 1972). Alongside an unparalleled boom in facilities construction, controversy began over the mission and accessibility of community colleges. "Two-year colleges have long been touted as agencies for the democratization of opportunity in higher education" (Lucas, 1996, p. 41). Historically less costly, more numerous, and less restrictive in their admissions, they have sought to make higher education available to virtually everyone.

The question of access has been intensely debated. Some critics argue that open admissions cannot be reconciled with academic standards, and that lowered standards are not consistent with an efficient use of shrinking public finances. Other critics feel that minority students in particular still do not have equal access to higher education. Texas has made an extensive commitment to its state-supported, two-year colleges and currently has 50 community college districts providing geographic accessibility to 95% of the population. Texas community colleges have traditionally offered a wide variety of courses for transfer preparation, certificate or associate degree programs, upgrading of work skills, new technology skills, and personal improvement. They have maintained open enrollment policies and offered a range of remedial courses for the under-prepared student (Facts, 1998). Texas community colleges have attempted to reflect the state's ethnic diversity in their student enrollment, and this has become a subject of intense debate. In the fall of 1997, 70% of all Texas freshman and sophomore students were enrolled in community colleges, and over one-half of those were attending on a part-time basis (Facts, 1998).

One of the measures of student success at community colleges has been graduation rate and/or transfer to a senior college. Nationwide, African-American students have been disproportionately more likely to enroll at community colleges versus four-year institutions, but have tended to earn lower grade point averages and to have higher attrition rates (Ellison & Martin, 1999). African-American students have also exhibited a lower rate of associate degree completion and transfer (Garza, 1994). According to the Texas Higher Education Coordinating Board (1999), the graduation rate of black males in Texas public community colleges is lower than that of their white male counterparts. Some of these institutions, however, have higher rates of black male graduation than do others.

The purposes of this study were to ascertain which Texas public community colleges have been able to graduate the highest percentages of black males and to analyze the factors contributing to such achievement. Specifically, the study attempted to identify the Texas public community colleges with the highest percentages of black male graduations and the features that enhance retention and graduation of black males at community colleges. The following research questions were developed to address the purposes of this study. Which Texas public community colleges have the highest percentages of black male graduates? What are the features that differentiate between community colleges with higher graduation rates and those with lower rates?

Texas does not reap maximum benefits from its public community colleges when students who enroll fail to complete their course of study. Community colleges are heavily vested in both vocational/technical programs and in preparation courses for transfer to a four-year college or university. About two-thirds of all associate degrees are earned by students in job-preparation programs, and about 23% of community college students in this country transfer to a four-year institution (Cohen, 1990). Admission to community colleges is open to all those who graduate from high school, and community colleges tend to serve those with less academic preparation and those of lower socioeconomic status (Dougherty, 1991). Approximately 46% of community college students come from the lowest socioeconomic status quartile (Cohen, 1990). Even so, black students are still disproportionately under-represented (Allen, 1988).

One reason for failure to graduate is inadequate preparation for higher education, and black students often attend high schools characterized by high drop-out rates, student scholastic indifference, and low attendance levels (Orfield, 1988). This may result in a sizeable difference between what was learned in high school and what is required as preparation for college. Remedial courses are designed to help bridge this gap, and nearly half of all mathematics and English classes taught at community colleges are at the remedial level (Cohen, 1990). However, repeating what seems to be high school material may prove discouraging to some students. Also, the cost involved for tuition, books, transportation, lost work-time, child care, and other expenses may rise prohibitively as the time required to graduate increases.

Financial need is a determinant in enrollment and also a factor in attrition. The need to work often forces the student into part-time attendance, and part-time students are more likely than full-time students to leave school (Feldman, 1993). Some students are forced financially into discontinuous enrollment. They drop out of school for a semester or more, until they can afford to enroll again, a process that is referred to as "stop-outs" (Grosset, 1992). Students who have lower scores on the SAT are also more likely to leave, even though the most reliable predictor of retention is the high school GPA (Feldman, 1993). Generally speaking, black students tend to have greater financial needs and to score lower on the SAT, and a greater percentage of black students drop out of school than whites (Feldman, 1993).

Other factors are also associated with student retention. Patterson (1993) noted that students with undefined or unrealistic goals should be referred to career counseling. Definitive goals, concerning a chosen profession and why that field was selected, are positively correlated with educational persistence (Meznek, 1987). Living on campus is also a plus to student retention but is usually more expensive than commuting, especially if the college is nearby. Valez and Javalgi (1987) observed that the combination of living on campus and being involved socially in campus activities increases the probability of degree completion.

Efforts to retain students generally fall into an administrative or a faculty approach. Administrative efforts are policies, procedures, and programs designed to meet the needs of students. Counseling, scheduling, financial aid, payment terms, internships, housing arrangements, and many other programs can enhance retention. For example, many part-time students are negatively affected by the scheduling and the manner in which programs and services are provided by the typical community college (Al-Habeeb, 1990). To enhance retention, services should be interconnected to help create a learning environment (McKeon, 1989). The faculty approach to student retention involves such things as hiring procedures, minority faculty recruitment, and ongoing assessment of teaching effectiveness (Clark & Crawford, 1992). The methods chosen for assessing effectiveness are also important. For example, student evaluation of course content and instruction contributes to the sense of belonging, certainly a factor in retention (Kendrin, 1993).

Although black students were graduating from high school in higher percentages than ever before, the number enrolling in college actually fell about 7% between 1976 and 1985 (Lang, 1992). Lang attributes this, in part, to lower socioeconomic background, decreased quality in educational preparation, rising tuition costs, and a lack of serious investment in equal opportunity by some institutions. Garza (1994) reports that black students are underrepresented among students receiving college degrees, and a review of the literature offers many different programs for the recruitment, retention, and academic success of black students. Halcon (1989) even reports a number of specific successful programs which may be applicable to multiple settings.

During the three-year period of this study, Texas public community colleges awarded academic associate degrees to only 2.4% of the black male students they enrolled as first-time, degree-seeking freshmen (Texas Higher Education Coordinating Board, 1999). According to the American Society for Training and Development, more than 65% of all jobs in this country will require some education beyond high school by the end of the year 2000 (Myran, Zeiss, & Howdyshell, 1995). Therefore, Texas public community colleges need to do a better job of retaining black male students or risk the development of a permanent black economic underclass within the state. A review of the literature has uncovered a lack of research focusing on why some colleges do a better job of black male retention than others.

Some research has shown the problem to be related to personal attributes, such as a lack of positive self-esteem, external locus of control, and low achievement motivation. Other researchers have cited cultural factors as a basic cause of college difficulties for black males. Situational barriers to the retention of black males in college are factors such as poverty, lack of adequate high school preparation, and being a minority student in a predominantly white institution. Certainly, financial problems are a factor in obtaining a college education, and many aspiring black students have limited financial resources.

Many other researchers have focused on institutional barriers to retention, such as a failure to accommodate minority student needs. Alternatives to standardized admission tests, flexibility in tuition payment and course scheduling, and the employment of minority faculty are some of the solutions for barriers cited. Much research has been focused on more specific causes of black male dropouts. The focus of this study was to discover what successful retention policies and/or procedures are used by Texas public community colleges that have the highest black male student retention rates. If indeed these colleges do have unique features that help raise black male graduation rates, then some of these retention strategies may be transferable to community colleges with lower rates.

METHODOLOGY

The phases of this investigation included the determination of graduation rates and the identification of institutions in the top and bottom quartiles, based on graduation rates. In addition, the study included the development and dissemination of an institutional questionnaire, collection of survey data, in-depth case studies of two institutions, and analysis of data.

Determination of Graduation Rates

The initial step in the determination of graduation rates was to obtain data from the Texas Higher Education Coordinating Board (THECB). The data collected and utilized for the calculation of institutional graduation rates included the academic years 1995-96, 1996-97, and 1997-98 for all reporting community colleges. The graduation rate was determined by dividing the enrollment of first-time, black male, degree-seeking freshmen at each Texas public community college, into the number of black male students receiving associate degrees from that institution during the same time period. The time period selected was the most recent three-year statistical report available from the THECB. A total of 61 public two-year institutions were included in this portion of the study. Nine campuses were excluded. Three were excluded because they are specialized and not directly comparable, and six because the THECB data during the target time-period were insufficient to include them.

Identification of Top and Bottom Quartiles

Once a graduation rate had been determined for each of the colleges selected, the institutions were arranged in a list from highest to lowest. The top quartile consisted of the most successful group of institutions in graduating black male students and the bottom quartile, the least successful. The remainder of the investigation focused upon a comparison of these two groups, to determine what, if anything, the more successful institutions were doing to promote black male graduation that the less successful schools were not doing.

Development of Institutional Questionnaire

A questionnaire was developed to identify institutional policies and/or practices that affect the graduation rate, with specific attention directed to the factors that enhance the retention of black male students. The initial questions were developed from a similar study conducted in New Jersey in 1997 (Wellbrock) and from a literature review of common retention practices. The questionnaire was piloted with three community colleges for scope and clarity. Most of the comments received from these reviews concerned the clarity of the questions and/or answering instructions. The validity of the survey instrument was addressed through the use of the questionnaires by other researchers in this same area of education (Donaldson, 1999; Dorsey, 1995; Spradley, 1996; Wellbrock, 1997). Reliability was addressed by using questions that were independent of any specific institution and by conducting the pilot test. In its final form, the questionnaire included both forced-choice and open-ended questions addressing common retention practices, such as counseling, mentoring, tutoring, remedial courses, pre-enrollment, summer catch-up programs, matching course assignments to standard test scores, and follow-up procedures for at-risk students.

Collection of Institutional Data

The questionnaires were mailed to the President of each institution ranked in the top and bottom quartiles by percentage of black male graduation rate. Follow-up telephone calls, letters, and e-mail, were all utilized to enhance the return rate of completed questionnaires. Additional questionnaires were also mailed, at later dates, to some institutions that had been unresponsive to the first mailing. A total of 67% were completed and returned from the top quartile institutions. A total of 47% were completed and returned from the bottom quartile colleges.

Multiple Case Studies

To enhance the data gathered with the institutional questionnaire, on-site qualitative case studies were conducted at one institution each from the top and bottom quartiles in black male graduation rate. A qualitative method was chosen because the questionnaires could not provide the meaning, value, or significance to the students of the various institutional features identified (Meloy, 1994). The qualitative approach permitted the study of the selected institutions in their natural setting (Creswell, 1998) through the observation of, and verbal interaction with, students, staff, and others involved with the college. The case study method was chosen in order to examine the reaction of the individuals under study to their institution's policies and programs that were designed to enhance the retention and graduation of students in general, and of black male students in particular. The case study approach also facilitated a comparison of the retention/graduation practices between one college and another. Both cases were characterized by clear boundaries in place and time (Creswell, 1998), the main campus of each institution, and the time required to collect the desired data. Much contextual material was available to describe the campus setting, and a wide array of information, from a variety of sources, could be gathered to provide an in-depth picture of retention and graduation features. Under study were the perceptions, attitudes, and procedures concerning the retention of black male students to graduation.

Data were gathered from interviews conducted by this researcher over a year's time and from other verbal interactions with students, staff, and others involved with the two colleges. Additional data were gathered through the observation of students, staff, and others as they moved about the campus and interacted with one another. Finally, the method of triangulation involved the utilization of other materials, such as brochures, catalogs, syllabi, and written rules and procedures, to illuminate and reinforce the verbal data and observations.

Case One

Case one is a community college located in a relatively small city (population under 20,000) in a sparsely populated rural Texas county. This college was randomly chosen for study from the top quartile for black male graduation rate during the time periods selected for this research. The campus seems very spacious, but the buildings are concentrated in one area and are within close proximity to one another. Walking distance between buildings appears to be minimal. The physical plant demonstrates a mixture of traditional and modern architecture. Grass and large shade trees are abundant in a somewhat hilly terrain. Parking is apparently ample for both staff and students and is relatively close to the classroom buildings. The campus is located in the city but traffic does not seem to be a problem, even during the rush hours. Inside, the buildings appear clean and well-lighted, with wide hallways and large classrooms. Although most of the buildings are older than 50 years, they look well maintained. The campus also has several newer buildings, probably constructed during the last 15 or 20 years.

The staff members visited had relatively large offices. The cafeteria appears to be spacious, attractively clean and furnished, and the menu included a variety of choices. Many of the staff were seen eating lunch in the cafeteria, even though a variety of commercial eating establishments are near the campus. The bookstore is centrally located on the campus, contains a variety of books and other items, and the employees seem friendly and helpful. The administration building appears spacious and the employees demonstrated efforts to be courteous and helpful. This building is also used for the registration process. The athletic facilities and the student residence halls are older buildings, but appear well maintained. The college has residence hall space for about 350 students including the athletes. The college has other campuses, each much smaller, newer, and more modern in design than the main campus. The black male graduation rates of these campuses are included in the overall rate of the college, but the main campus was selected for this case study because it provides the policy and culture of the whole college.

The college conducted an orientation and registration process for incoming freshman students in July. A group of 50 to 75 students attended this session, many accompanied by parents. The group appeared to be primarily Caucasian, with few minority students evident. In a typical year on this campus, a student body of less than 2000 is 8 to 10% minority, and a substantial number of these are athletes and foreign students. A second session was conducted in August, just prior to the beginning of the fall semester. The orientation ceremony lasted 30 to 45 minutes, with several speakers, each discussing a specific topic. Topics covered a wide range of information important to students and their parents. Religious activities, free lunches, recreation facilities, extracurricular program opportunities, testing, financial aid, counseling, and bookstore policy were all addressed, as well as many other subjects. The overall theme of the speakers was for students to "get involved in the activities of the college, get to know your teachers, and ask for help if you need it." The program concluded with each student meeting with a staff member to complete a preliminary degree plan. This plan is a necessary prerequisite to registration, and each student must see an advisor before every subsequent registration to monitor the plan's progress.

Orientation took place in an auditorium, but registration was conducted in the main hall of the administration building. Numerous staff members were available to keep registration lines short. A number of students in special registration T-shirts circulated among the incoming freshmen and their parents, answering questions, distributing literature on various programs, and directing the flow of registrants. These volunteer aids also acted as group leaders, showing groups of new students about the campus. The entire process seemed to be student friendly, and no evidence of frustration among staff, parents, or students was observed. The new students were given a number of incentives such as doughnuts, candy, and college T-shirts to make the experience more pleasurable. Student identification cards and parking stickers were issued free.

Several of the staff were questioned concerning the attitudes and procedures of the college pertaining to the retention of black male students. The college has no black teachers, but it does have several black administrators in key positions. The Director of Student Support Services said that tutoring is the most important function contributing to retention. The college offers federally funded student support services with free tutoring for low-income first-generation students. Teachers and administrators take a hands-on approach with at-risk students, communicating between faculty, student, and support services staff. Apparently the college has a family tradition, and many of the students have parents and grandparents who attended here also. The Vice President for Student Affairs said that students are pushed to file for graduation. The registrar sends a letter to any student with 45 semester hours or more, requesting them to file for graduation. Even former students with 45 hours or more are contacted and urged to complete their degree plans. Whenever possible, schedules and/or courses are changed to facilitate graduation.

The college also employs an admissions committee, composed of a vice president and various administrators, deans, faculty, and counselors. Any student with a GPA of less than a "C" must interview with this committee before they can enroll for another semester. Many students are assigned a monitor—either a faculty or staff member—who consults with the student's instructors about grades and attendance. No one is assigned more than five students to monitor at any one time. The counselors have various duties, including general, academic, and vocational counseling, as well as counseling the athletes. Each major sport has its own counselor, and many of the athletes are assigned mentors as well. Some counselors serve on the admissions committee and some aid in recruiting through their relationships with the athletes.

Approximately 20 black male students on this campus were interviewed. The interviews took place in various situations, from the cafeteria to the residence hall rooms. Most of the students were chosen on the basis of available opportunity, but a few were recommended by students already interviewed. Almost all interviews took place on the campus. An effort was made to limit these conversations to sophomores (although some freshmen were interviewed), since they had more experience with the school and had already returned once for a new academic year. About one-third of the students were interviewed several times, for clarification and/or additional information. Almost from the start, recurring themes appeared in their answers to such questions as "What do you like most about this college?" A few had experience with another college, but most did not. The themes centered around small classes, helpful teachers, counselors, and a friendly atmosphere on the campus. One young man commented, "The black males who drop out here do so because they don't want to give the effort, not because of the school or the personnel."

Virtually every black male student interviewed mentioned small classes and helpful teachers. "Most faculty come to help the student out, and you can always tell those teachers. They have a positive attitude. Teachers speak to the students and are nice to them, even when things aren't going well. They will stay after class and talk with you, if you have questions or problems." One young black man said that the teachers are "understanding and will help you catch up if you get behind." These comments were typical of those made about the teaching faculty. Several students contrasted this with other colleges, where the classes were large and the teachers always seemed too busy.

Counselors were frequently given as a reason for student satisfaction with the college. Several black male students who were interviewed played varsity sports. They liked the fact that the teams had counselors. They said "different teams may have different needs," and the "counselors know the university programs and requirements and help with selection and transfer." Other students interviewed said that having enough counselors helps a lot. One student said "it's just like in church, when someone takes time for you." Another student provided an overall summary, when he said, "it's the little things that make this a good school. They don't mind helping you out. They don't look at you different."

Case Two

Case two was chosen because this college was in the bottom quartile in percentage of black male graduations for the selected time periods. In some ways, it is almost the opposite of case one. The college serves a densely populated, wealthy district and the main campus resides in a metropolitan area (city with a population over 200,000). The campus has almost 300 residence hall rooms, but it is primarily a commuter school. Classes are conducted in a very large single building, with designated module areas for each academic field. The central area of the building (immediately inside the main entrance) contains the bookstore, cafeteria, fast food restaurant and vending machines, auditorium/theater, counseling, human resources (job placement), registration, cashier, career/transfer services for degree plans and resumes, and a staffed information desk, complete with catalogs, schedules, and brochures.

The halls are wide, and the second floor is a mezzanine on both sides above the first-floor hall. The ceiling is actually a skylight roof. The building is spacious and well lighted. Large parking areas are located in relatively close proximity to the building. The area surrounding the main building and the parking lots is spacious, landscaped, and well lighted. The campus also contains several athletic areas, with small buildings, tennis courts, and a baseball stadium. Classrooms are large, well lighted, and nicely furnished. The central area of the main building has a tile floor and a large fountain. The rest of the building is carpeted, with stuffed, modern chairs distributed in the halls.

The atmosphere was indicative of a commuter school. Some students talked in pairs or trios, with few larger groups. Most students remained as solitary individuals, going to and from class. The students observed were predominantly Caucasian, mixed with Asians, Indians (or Pakistanis), and a few African Americans. The majority of the black students observed were female, with no groups of black students larger than three. The black males interviewed tended to be suspicious of the questions, until they were reassured that this researcher was not connected to the institution. Most were then very cooperative, and three or four appeared to have foreign accents. Students were selected for interviews on the basis of opportunity, as was the process in case one.

The answers received from the black male students concerning why they did or did not like the college tended to be repetitive almost from the start, as was the experience in case one. Although a variety of answers were received concerning why students had chosen this college, the most common reasons given were that the school has cheaper tuition and a good academic reputation. Other common reasons were that the teachers "teach what you need and not a lot of fluff," and the classes are small. Only two repetitive complaints were received about the institution. One was that the halls are too crowded and the lines are too long, since all the classes are in the same building. The second complaint referred to too few campus activities. Being a commuter school, few campus organizations sponsor and/or promote such activities.

Initial attempts to interview staff members were discouraging. The chain of command is apparently more important at this college than in some other educational institutions. However, after the Vice President met with the researcher, everyone else was more than happy to provide information. The institution participates in a federal grant designed to attract minority students to math and science. Among the retention measures employed are counseling, mentoring, teaching assistants, and a summer bridge program designed to reduce the gap between high school and college. The bridge program also facilitates the transfer of courses between this institution and a specific senior college.

The college appears to have a strong orientation program, although it is not mandatory. The program stresses study skills, differences between high school and college course work, and the importance of involvement. All classes have a laboratory, or some other interactive and/or collaborative learning component to encourage involvement. The college also has a learning community program which involves a cohort of the same students taking two or more classes together, linked around a central theme. The staff indicated that research shows this to be effective in retention. Orientation and involvement strategies are based on the assumption that "learning is not a spectator sport." Academic advising attempts to ensure that student expectations equal reality, and that the student understands what he/she is getting into when selecting a course of study.

During the first six weeks of each fall semester, student ambassadors call new students to see how they are doing. The purpose is not to recruit, but to encourage and to answer questions. Also, follow-up calls are made to students who have quit school. The college has joined with a Hispanic organization to conduct a "youth leadership academy." A high percentage of the academy graduates go on to attend the college. The college also does some recruiting outreach in minority neighborhoods, but it is aimed at the poor and not at specific races. However, since black and Hispanic students make up most of the poor who enroll, they are the primary beneficiaries. The staff remarked that the racial mix of the college student body matches the mix of the district population as a whole. This is apparently a source of pride to the institution.

DATA ANALYSIS

Questionnaires

The questionnaire data were scrutinized for detailed, descriptive information regarding institutional policies and/or practices directly related to the retention of black male students. Practices, such as mentoring, tutoring, remedial courses, and pre-enrollment, summer, catch-up programs were anticipated, but features unique to specific institutions were also expected and noted. These descriptive data were compiled and utilized to provide a basis for the qualitative portion of the study. The primary task of analyzing the qualitative data concerned the collapsing of the verbal information collected into distinct categories. For example, reasons given by students for remaining enrolled at a particular college might concern family wishes, economic factors, academic considerations, friends, campus location, or some other classifiable cause. The categorizing of the information collected facilitated an overall interpretation of the institutional perceptions, attitudes, and procedures concerning retention and graduation.

The questionnaire was divided into two parts. The first part concerns institutional practices for the retention of students in general. Table 1 contains a summary of the part 1 questionnaire data. Three strategies seem worth noting in Table 1 when comparing top and bottom quartile institutions. Freshman-only advising programs were conducted by 50% of the top quartile colleges, which rated the student retention value of these programs at 2.60 on a scale of 1 to 3. Only 43% of the bottom quartile schools had similar programs, and they rated their value to retention at only 1.14. Orientation courses for credit were offered by 50% of the top quartile colleges. Only 29% of the bottom quartile institutions did so, even though both groups rated the value to student retention at 2.50 or above. A final comparison worth noting from part 1 concerned staff development. About 60% of both the top and bottom colleges reported conducting staff development programs designed to enhance retention and graduation. However, 57% of the bottom quartile schools included a "preservation of standards" component in their programs, while only 40% of the top quartile institutions did so. All of the colleges in both groups conducted basic skills testing and class placement consistent with test scores. A variety of tests were reported. The top three, in order of their usage, were the TASP, ASSET, and COMPASS. One or more of these three were used by almost every institution. Also, 100% of the colleges in both groups conducted class orientation and tutorial programs, job placement services, work-study programs, and student academic and financial counseling.

Part 2 of the questionnaire concerned retention practices and procedures specifically targeting at-risk groups. Students may be classified as at-risk for a variety of reasons, including cultural, economic, academic, and/or language difficulties. Table 2 summarizes the forced-choice data from part 2 of the questionnaire. What is interesting to note is that only about 70% of both the top and bottom quartile schools specifically identify at-risk students at initial enrollment. However, several noteworthy differences, as seen in Table 2, exist between the two groups of institutions. First, 60% of the top quartile schools maintain required tutorial programs. Only 29% of the bottom quartile schools do so, even though they rate the perceived value to retention of required tutoring at 3.00 on a 1 to 3 scale. Second, 40% of the top quartile schools require certain at-risk students to

Table 1. Comparison of Top and Bottom Quartile Institutions
Concerning General Student Retention Practices

Strategy	Top quartile (TQ) % Yes	Bottom quartile (BQ) % Yes	TQ perceived value to retention (1-3)	BQ perceived value to retention (1-3)
1. Basic skills testing	100	100	2.75	2.71
2. Class placement consistent with test scores	100	100	1.90	2.86
3. Orientation to classes	100	100	2.60	2.71
4. Orientation to extra-curricular activities	70	71	2.38	2.25
5. Freshman only advising	50	43	2.60	1.14
6. Tutorial programs	100	100	2.30	2.71
7. Job placement services	100	100	2.20	2.14
8. Work-study programs	100	100	2.40	2.57
9. Orientation for credit	50	29	2.60	2.50
10. Orientation for minorities only	0	0	—	—
11. Counseling services	100	100	2.70	2.57
12. Staff Development programs for retention enhancement	60	57	2.33	2.25
Preservation of standards urged	40	57	—	—

meet periodically with their advisors. These students might include those on scholastic probation or conditional placement in certain courses. Only 14% of the bottom quartile schools required advisor meetings, even though they also rated the value to retention of this practice at 3.00. Third, 70% of the top quartile schools monitored at-risk student attendance, whereas only 43% of the bottom quartile colleges did so. Finally, 30% of the high retention institutions and 14% of the low retention group targeted minority groups with some specific strategy or strategies

Table 2. Comparison of Top and Bottom Quartile Institutions
Concerning At-Risk Student Retention Practices

Strategy	Top quartile (TQ) % Yes	Bottom quartile (BQ) % Yes	TQ perceived value to retention (1-3)	BQ perceived value to retention (1-3)
1. Math and language developmental courses	100	100	2.00	2.57
2. Required tutorial programs	60	29	1.40	3.00
3. Individual counseling	90	86	2.43	2.80
4. Tracking test scores consistency with placement	80	71	2.62	2.20
5. Required meetings with advisor	40	14	3.00	3.00
6. Attendance monitoring	70	43	2.33	2.00
7. Retention strategies for minority groups only	30	14	3.00	2.00

for retention purposes. The most prevalent targeting criteria were financial problems and/or English language difficulties. No retention policies targeted specific racial groups at any institution reported in this study.

Case Studies

Two qualitative case studies were also conducted to answer Research Question 2. One study was conducted on a campus from the top quartile in black male student graduation and one on a campus from the bottom quartile. The focus of the case studies was to examine the setting, policies, procedures, programs, and culture of each campus for clues concerning each institution's success with black male graduation.

Data were collected from multiple sources, such as observations of and interviews with students, faculty, counselors, administrators, residence hall supervisors, bookstore employees, campus organization leaders, and parents. These data contained descriptions, opinions, perceptions, and other personal information germane to the purpose of the study. The understanding and perception of others is interpretive, rather than quantitative, and necessitates a qualitative analysis. Additional information came from course catalogs, class schedules, school papers, bulletin boards, syllabi, brochures, and various student hand-outs.

A direct comparison between the two case studies was very difficult because the institutions are so different from one another. However, the study first reviews the perceived retention strong points of each case, and then makes such a comparison. The comparison attempts to identify features of case one that enhance the institution's black male graduation rate that are not utilized by case two, which has a lower rate.

Case one is a relatively small, two-year institution located in a city of less than 20,000 people. The researcher was informed that many of the students live on or near the campus, carry a full course load, and plan to graduate from the college. The campus culture appears to be close knit, friendly, and inclusive. The most prevalent reasons expressed by students for continuing to enroll at this institution were small classes, helpful instructors, counselors, and a friendly student body. This college employs several strategies for at-risk student retention. First, the faculty tries to assure incoming students that they are welcome and important to the institution. Second, the college maintains a continuing effort to promote student graduation. Third, the college stresses counseling and tutoring for at-risk students. Finally, an admissions committee is utilized to ensure that any student with less than a "C" average is assigned to a mentor, a tutor, class attendance monitoring, or whatever actions seem necessary to help the student succeed.

Case two is a relatively large community college located in a city of over 200,000 population. The researcher was told that part-time students constitute a sizeable portion of the student body, and that many students are enrolled in courses designed to up-date present job skills or to retrain for other jobs. Many of these students have already earned associate or higher degrees. The overall impression of the campus culture is that most of the students are there to be educated, and not to visit with friends. Most of the students interviewed said their academic goal is to transfer to a four-year college. However, several said they were trying to raise their GPA, or that they were taking job skill courses. The most prevalent answers received from black male students concerning why they continued to enroll at this college were small classes, faculty teaching only what was needed, and cheaper tuition.

This institution also employs several strategies for at-risk student retention. First, the college utilizes counseling, mentoring, teaching assistants, and a summer bridge program to bridge the gap between high school and college. Second, the institution participates in a federal grant program designed to attract minority students to science and math. Third, all classes are directed to include a collaborative or interactive learning component to give students a sense of involvement. Fourth, the college conducts an orientation program that stresses study skills, degree planning, and involvement. Fifth, the college offers a cohort program in which a number of students take several classes together. Sixth, student volunteers call each new student during his/her first semester to answer questions and to offer encouragement. Finally, the institution sponsors several outreach efforts designed to recruit students in poor neighborhoods.

A comparison of the perceived retention strong points in case one and case two reveals several features of case one designed to enhance the graduation rate of at-risk students that are not utilized by case two, which has a lower black male graduation rate. Several of these features could be implemented by virtually any Texas, public community college to enhance the black male graduation rate. These features are as follows:

- an emphasis on freshman orientation to help students feel welcome and important to the college;
- an emphasis on counseling and tutoring services for at-risk students;
- utilization of a committee to ensure that any student with less than a "C" average is assigned to a mentor, a tutor, class attendance monitoring, or whatever actions seem necessary to help the student succeed; and
- a continuing effort to promote student graduations.

Two additional, perceived retention features of case one not noted in case two were a close knit, friendly campus culture and helpful instructors. These features, however, may not necessarily be implemented easily at other institutions.

CONCLUSIONS

If Texas public community colleges are to graduate more black male students, then more successful measures need to be employed to retain black male students in school. Student retention in general, and black male student retention in particular, is a result of many factors, and only a limited number of these factors are under institutional control. However, this study has identified a number of strategies that are presently being utilized by colleges to exert a positive influence on student retention. Several of these strategies are being employed by a substantially greater number of institutions in the top quartile in black male graduation rates than by colleges in the bottom quartile. This suggests a conclusion that colleges with lower rates of black male graduation do not employ as many of these retention strategies, which explains their lower graduation rates. The strategies that differentiate institutions in the top quartile from institutions in the bottom quartile include freshman-only advising, orientation courses for credit, required tutorial programs and meetings with advisors for certain at-risk students, monitoring of at-risk student attendance, and targeting minority groups with specific retention plans.

The research also demonstrated that the most influential institutional strategies concerning the retention of black male students are the measures designed to identify at-risk students at enrollment and to monitor their academic progress. One method of monitoring progress is the admissions committee. This committee meets with every student who has less than a "C" average prior to his/her re-enrollment for another semester. The committee then assigns, for each of these students, whatever measures it deems desirable to enhance the student's chances for success. All of these strategies have been utilized by community colleges with higher rates of black male graduation.

Finally, based upon faculty and black male student comments at an institution in the top quartile, the research shows that a helpful understanding faculty, counseling services that are advertised and utilized, and a friendly inclusive student body are important influences specific to the retention of black male students. A college cannot guarantee a friendly inclusive student body, but it can provide a helpful understanding faculty and advertise its counseling services.

Socioeconomic and cultural factors may influence what institutional leaders feel is necessary to retain black male students, and the environment surrounding the institution may affect what retention measures they deem advisable. For example, a lower socioeconomic environment, as in case one, can influence administrators to more aggressively create and promote retention strategies. Conversely, a higher socioeconomic environment and a suburban culture, as in case two, may tend to have the opposite effect. Hence, the culture and the apparently predominant socioeconomic status of the surrounding community may be a retention factor for black male students.

IMPLICATIONS FOR PRACTICE

Texas public community colleges that seek to enhance their black male student graduation rates should focus more attention on the identification and utilization of retention strategies. Freshman-only advising, orientation for credit, required tutoring, required advisory meetings, and targeting and monitoring of at-risk students are retention strategies that many institutions should consider.

A helpful understanding faculty implies instructors who take the time necessary to work with students and to be available for discussions, questions, and requests outside of class. Many students, especially at-risk students, may not make office appointments. Counseling services are of little value if they are not utilized. Counseling services, such as academic, financial, and personal counseling, are perceived to be important to student retention by both students and institutions. However, often the problem is how to get students to utilize the counselors. Advertising counseling services and convincing students to use such services usually begins at orientation in most colleges. In addition, services need to be continually presented to students on bulletin boards, by instructors and student services staff, and by anyone involved with monitoring at-risk or probationary student progress. Otherwise, many students may not seek help and simply drop out of school. The college cannot provide a friendly student body by institutional decree. The college can, however, provide friendly staff and faculty members as role models to the students, and support student activities that promote inclusiveness.

Some retention strategies require institutional investment. Small classes, available counselors, and low tuition costs are all financial considerations. However, if in the future intensified competition occurs between colleges for the available students, then such opportunities to gain an edge in student retention become increasingly more important. Helpful instructors and courses that cover only needed content are within the power of any institutional faculty. Instructor helpfulness and course content are a matter of attitude and preparation. Finally, the information necessary for the identification of students considered at risk, due to financial problems, minority status, and/or cultural or language difficulties, is available to most colleges at enrollment. What is needed, then, is a program that monitors at-risk student progress and intervenes with counseling and/or mentoring when deemed necessary or desirable.

REFERENCES

Al-Habeeb, A. M. (1990). Equal access to the problem of attrition in a community college: A case study. *Dissertation Abstracts International, 52*(01), 62A.

Allen, W. R. (1988). Black students in U.S. higher education: Toward improved access, adjustment and achievement. *The Urban Review, 20*(3), 165-188.

American Association of Community Colleges (1999). *National community college snapshot: All about community colleges* [On-line]. Available:
http://www.aacc.nche.edu/allaboutcc/snapshot.htm

Clark, S. B., & Crawford, S. L. (1992). An analysis of African-American first-year college student attitudes and attrition rates. *Urban Education, 27*(1), 59-79.

Cohen, A. M. (1990). The case for the community college. *American Journal of Education, 96*(4), 426-442.

Creswell, J. W. (1998). *Qualitative inquiry and research design: Choosing among five traditions.* Thousand Oaks, CA: Sage Publications.

Donaldson, E. L. (1999). *Making transitions work: Navigating the changes.* Calgary, Alberta: Temeron Books.

Dorsey, M. E. (1995). An investigation of variables affecting persistence of African-American males at a Maryland community college. *Dissertation Abstracts International, 57*(06), 2336A.

Dougherty, K. J. (1991). The community college at the crossroads: The need for structural reform. *Harvard Review, 61*(3), 311-336.

Ellison, C. G., & Martin, W. A. (1999). *Race and ethnic relations in the United States.* Los Angeles: Roxbury Publishing.

Facts about Texas community colleges [On-line] (1998, October 15). Texas Association of Community Colleges. Available: http://www.tacc.org/facts.html.

Feldman, M. J. (1993). Factors associated with one-year retention in a community college. *Research in Higher Education, 34*(4), 503-512.

Garza, N. R. (1994). A description and analysis of selected developmental reading programs in Texas colleges. *Dissertation Abstracts International, 55*(06), 1433A.

Grosset, J. M. (1992). A profile of community college stop-outs. *Community College Review, 20*(4), 51-58.

Halcon, J. J. (1989). *Exemplary programs for college-based minority students* (Publication No. 2A180). Boulder, CO: Western Interstate Commission for Higher Education.

Kendrin, L. I. (1993). *Transforming at risk students into powerful learners* (Project R117G10037). Tempe, AZ: Division of Education Leadership and Policy Studies, Arizona State University.

Lang, M. (1992). Barriers to blacks' education achievement in higher education. *Journal of Black Studies, 22*(4), 510-522.

Lucas, C. J. (1996). *Crisis in the academy.* New York: St. Martin's Press.

McKeon, T. K. (1989). Strategies for improving the retention and success of minority students in community college. *Dissertation Abstracts International, 50*(09), 2762A.

Meloy, J. M. (1994). *Writing the qualitative dissertation.* Hillsdale, NJ: Lawrence Erlbaum Associates.

Meznek, J. M. (1987). A national study of student attrition in community colleges. *Dissertation Abstracts International, 48*(11), 2779A.

Monroe, C. (1972). *Profile of the community college.* San Francisco: Jossey-Bass.

Myran, G., Zeiss, T., & Howdyshell, L. (1995). *Community college leadership in the new century: Learning to improve learning.* Washington, DC: Community College Press.

Orfield, G. (1988). Exclusion of the majority: Shrinking college access and public policy in metropolitan Los Angeles. *The Urban Review, 20*(3), 147-163.

Patterson, E. J. (1993). Factors influencing community college students' transfer to a baccalaureate degree program. *Dissertation Abstracts International, 54*(07), 2437A.

Spradley, P. A. (1996). A multiple variable analysis of the persistence of adult African-American male graduates from a baccalaureate degree program. *Dissertation Abstracts International, 57*(07), 2905A.

Texas Higher Education Coordinating Board (1998). *Education Code* (Chapter 130) [On-line]. Austin, TX: Author. Available:
http://www.capitol.state.tx.us/statutes/codes/ED000073/html.

Texas Higher Education Coordinating Board (1999). *Report on graduation/persistence and remediation fall 1995 first time in college (FTIC) cohort.* Austin, TX: Author.

United States Department of Education (1996). *Dropout rates in the United States (based on October 1996 Current Population Surveys),* Washington, DC: National Center for Education Statistics.

Valez, W., & Javalgi, R. (1987). Two year college to four year college: The likelihood of transfer. *American Journal of Education, 96*(1), 81-94.

Wellbrock, R. D. (1997). The retention of black male students in the community college system of New Jersey. *Dissertation Abstracts International, 58*(08), 2978A.

CHAPTER 5

Validating African American Students at Predominantly White Institutions

Sharon L. Holmes, Larry H. Ebbers,
Daniel C. Robinson, and Abel G. Mugenda

The purpose of this chapter is to provide a review of research and theory focusing on factors that have been cited as contributing to the retention and graduation of African-American students attending predominantly White institutions. The authors use recommendations cited in the literature to develop a model for predominantly White institutions to provide African-American students with positive learning experiences. While African-American students are the primary focus of this discussion, the model can be adapted to meet the needs of other minority students in higher education.

The higher education community has struggled for many years with complex issues surrounding African-American students enrolled at predominantly White institutions (Cabrera, Nora, Terenzini, Pascarella, & Hagedorn, 1999). Numerous researchers have provided first-hand information as to why some of these students have not been successful in predominantly White institutions. For example, Fleming (1984), in a comparison study of Black students at predominantly Black and White institutions, found that students on White campuses felt that the campus environment was hostile and unsupportive of their social and cultural needs. Patterson-Stewart, Ritchie, and Sanders (1997), investigating the experiences of recent African-American doctoral graduates at a predominantly White university, found that students had the most difficulty in establishing interpersonal relationships with non-minority members of the academic community as opposed to the academic rigor of their degree programs. Others researchers (Allen, Epps, & Haniff, 1991; Davis, 1994; Davis & Lasane, 1994; Loo & Rolison, 1986; Nettles, 1990; Pasceralla & Terenzini, 1991; Tracey & Sedlacek, 1987; Turner, 1994) have speculated that racial discrimination both in and outside of the classroom, social isolation, alienation, institutional abandonment, lack of congruency between the institution and the student, and interpersonal relationships with faculty, peers, and academic staff all contribute to the unfavorable experiences of minority students (e.g., African American) at predominantly White institutions. Unfortunately, despite this growing literature, the perception remains that predominantly White institutions have not been successful in fully integrating African-American and other minority students into the mainstream of the educational system (Nettles & Perna, 1997).

Over ten years ago, John B. Slaughter's foreword in the NASPA publication *From Survival to Success* (cited in Terrell & Wright, 1988) stated, "the recruitment, retention, and graduation of minority students is the single most pressing problem facing higher education today." To date, the retention and graduation of minority students still remains one of higher education's most pressing concerns as fewer students persist through graduation (Nettles & Perna, 1997; Pound, 1990). Pound (1987) found that over a six-year period African-American students dropped out of college at a rate of 22 percent higher than their White counterparts during the same period.

The purpose of this chapter is to provide a review of research and theory focusing on factors that have been cited as contributing to the retention and graduation rate of African-American students attending predominantly White institutions. The authors used recommendations cited in the literature to develop a model for predominantly White institutions to use in designing programs and services for African-American students.

Concern for African-American students attending White institutions originates from mounting reports of demographic changes that are expected for higher education and the nation. In *One Third of A Nation,* a report by the American Council on Education and the Education Commission of the States (1988), it was predicted that by the year 2010, one-third of all school-age children in America will represent members of ethnic minority groups (African American, American Indian, Asian American, and Hispanic people), and that approximately twenty- two million of the nation's labor force will be minority workers. More specifically, a trend expected to affect higher education institutions will be the decline in qualified replacements for senior-level faculty and staff members nearing retirement (Adams, 1988). If these projections are realized,

African-American students will be one of the minority groups that will be expected to sustain our nation's labor force, including higher education's workforce (Nettles & Perna, 1997).

Since the inception of institutions of higher education in the United States, data have suggested that those who obtain a college education are more likely to increase their potential to achieve social and economic mobility than those who lack a college education (Lin & Vogt, 1996). It is not surprising, therefore, that there is a correlation between the level of one's educational attainment and labor force participation (Pascarella & Terenzini, 1991). What is surprising is the increasing number of retention reports that suggest that African-American students attending predominantly White institutions are having a difficult time persisting in their attempts to obtain a college degree (Nettles, 1990; Porter, 1990). The problem has intensified to the point that if immediate action is not taken to increase the number of African-American students receiving college degrees, especially at the Ph.D. level, the higher education community as well as the nation at large will suffer (Nettles & Perna, 1997). Higher education institutions will suffer because the lack of diversity in the academic community limits the opportunity for people to explore knowledge and gain an understanding of the world from a larger perspective than their own. African Americans will suffer too because they will be unable to take advantage of labor force vacancies, including those in higher education left by retiring faculty and staff. The latter must be considered even though distance education and the use of part-time and non-tenured faculty are gaining popularity as institutions strive to control cost (American Council on Education, 1998). Ultimately, society as a whole will suffer because higher education will have failed in its role to prepare a citizenry that acknowledges and respects the contributions of all of its groups.

Evans, Forney, and Guido-DiBrito's (1998) compilation of theories on student development suggests that people develop most when their environment provides adequate levels of challenge and support of their current belief structures. Challenge is an important element of student development because students who are not exposed to ideologies and philosophies of persons from diverse backgrounds and cultures will not be compelled to review and evaluate their own beliefs for congruency with the larger world in which they must live and contribute. One purpose of education is to provide students the opportunity to extend the boundaries of their familiar settings by exposing them to a world composed of people with opinions and attitudes differing from their own. While they may not espouse those values, behaviors, and opinions, they may develop an appreciation for others and a level of acceptance of differences.

Tinto (1995) maintains that learning communities that stress the use of collaborative teaching strategies build community and instill in students the basic comprehensions needed for responsible citizenship. He stated, "we lecture about citizenship, but we do little to promote teaching and learning environments that themselves could develop in students norms and dispositions of citizenship" (p.11). In order to have an active role in preparing students for effective citizenship, institutions of higher education must first resolve the long-standing problem of successfully integrating African-American and other minority students into all facets of the academic environment.

Why are African-American students having a difficult time adjusting in some White institutions? Is it simply because they are not academically prepared, or are other factors at work within the institutional setting that may impede their success?

Foremost, African Americans in predominantly White institutions have had to couple the normal concerns of first-year students (being away from home for the first time, sharing a room with a stranger, establishing new relationships, etc.) with those of having to adjust in an intellectual and social community that is unprepared to accept their cultural differences (Allen, 1988; Fields, 1991; Jones, 1993; Pound, 1987).

Research studies conducted at Iowa State University, a large predominantly White institution in the Midwest, have consistently identified several factors that contribute to the high attrition rate of African-American students (Curry, 1992; Fields, 1991; Henderson, 1992) (see Table 1). While these findings are consistent with those of leading researchers (Fleming, 1984; Pascarella & Terenzini, 1991; Pound, 1987), they leave out other factors that influence the success of minority students in other college settings.

There is sufficient evidence to validate the premise that some minority students experience difficulty at White institutions because of deficient academic preparation and personal problems related to identity issues (Jones, 1993; Tinto, 1993). There is also a mounting body of evidence to suggest that predominantly

Table 1. Factors that Contribute to the High Attrition Rate of African-American Students Attending Predominately White Institutions

Student Characteristics	Institutional Characteristics
Feeling alienated and isolated	Anglo-European teaching philosophies
Deficient academic preparation	Absence of minority role models
Language barriers	Lack of faculty and peer Involvement
Insufficient financial resources	Hostile and unfriendly campus environment
Low self-esteem/identify issues	Lack of multicultural programs/activities
Family concerns	Low expectations of minority students
Limited exposure to majority group	Institutional abandonment
Poor academic advising in high school	Racial discrimination (subtle and overt)

Sources: Curry, 1992; Dawson, 1989; Fields, 1991; Henderson, 1992.

White institutions may be negligent in providing campus communities that are welcoming and conducive to the learning styles of culturally and ethnically diverse student groups (Curry, 1992; Fleming, 1984).

Lewin's (1936) classic formula, $B = f(P \times E)$, informed the academic community of the importance of the person-environment interaction. The formula suggests that behavior is a function of the interaction of the person and the environment. With regard to African-American students attending predominantly White institutions, this means that because the ethos of the White majority are ingrained in the institutional culture, administrators must prepare the majority group to appreciate the differences that will be inherent with the minority newcomer. If administrators fail to prepare the dominant culture for increases in minorities, especially African-American students, discord will arise and minority students will then be at risk of leaving before completing their degrees; or Worse, the campus environment could become volatile and explosive (Vogt, 1997).

This is not to imply that predominantly White institutions have intentionally created learning communities that are unresponsive to the needs of diverse student groups. But for the most part, these institutions were not created with minority students in mind (Brubacher & Rudy, 1976). During the 1960s when many institutions of higher education witnessed phenomenal growth in minority student enrollment, African-American students and other minority groups were basically expected to "mask" their cultural differences and assimilate or acculturate into the mainstream culture (Anderson, 1988; Jones, 1993; Pound, 1987).

Unfortunately, because of the long and difficult history of race relations in the United States, assimilation and acculturation is difficult for African-American students in White settings. One reason for such difficulties is peer pressure (Dawson, 1989). The Black student who associates with White students in what are typically considered non-Black activities (e.g., skiing, horseback riding, golf, etc.) or who excel academically at the expense of Black group association may be perceived by Black peers as trying to "act or be White" (Fordham & Ogbu, 1986; p.186). Hence, the student may receive pressure from Black peers to discontinue these so-called White behaviors, or be branded as an "oreo" and rejected as a traitor to his or her own cultural group. However, in actuality, what could be occurring is that the student is in the stage of conformity as identified in the Minority Identity Development Model (MID) by Atkinson, Morten, and Sue (1983). Conformity occurs when a student has a preference for values of the dominant culture as opposed to those of his or her own culture. Yet, this conformity does not imply that the student will never seek the company of peers in their own cultural group in the future. Synergistic articulation and awareness is the last stage in the MID. In this stage, the student has resolved internal conflicts about the value systems of the majority and minority group and has begun to incorporate elements of both into his or her personality. Unfortunately, when a student advances to this stage, re-entry into the Black peer group on a White campus may be difficult, if not impossible.

Cultural differences and learning styles make assimilation difficult as well. Katz and Ivey (1977) define culture as "a set of values, beliefs, norms, acceptable practices, traditions, [and] communication patterns that serve as a basis from which individuals operate" (p. 4). The dominant culture in the United States, and, subsequently, the educational system, is European Anglo-Saxon. Learning styles of this group have been characterized as individualistic and competitive. Some minority groups, on the other hand, are characterized as non-competitive collaborative learners. Furthermore, the dominant culture uses the English language as its primary source of written and oral communication, while most minorities are bilingual or have group specific styles of written language and speech (Anderson, 1988; Katz, 1989). For these reasons, minority students experience difficulty adjusting to White campus environments, especially when they try to maintain their cultural traditions within the majority's cultural environment.

Anderson (1988), in *Cognitive Style and Multicultural Populations,* provided the following compilations of world views on cultural and cognitive (learning) style differences in Western (majority) and non-Western (minorities) groups in an effort to communicate the need for a revision of traditional teaching methodologies so that all students benefit from the teaching/learning experience (see Table 2). The model indicates that because of the vast difference in the way both groups communicate and make meaning, it is impossible to generalize the cultural norms and educational practices of one group to all groups of students. When consideration is not given to the needs of all groups within the educational setting, the authors believe Lewin's (1936) person-environment interaction formula $B = f(P \times E)$ can be used to demonstrate the negative effects of the environment upon its members. The low retention rate of African-American students attending predominantly White institutions is a result or function of inadequate planning when combining people with different cultures, values, and learning styles. When members of the dominant culture (including administrators, faculty, staff, and students) have not been prepared to interact with people who are different than they are, the community becomes divisive and intolerance, hostility, frustration, and apathy begin to thrive.

African-American students, particularly, have not adapted well in the current, predominantly White, social and academic community (Curry, 1992; Haro, 1992). Adaptation is very important. Turner (1994) indicated that a key factor to academic success for African-American students is their ability to find a "positive level of comfort" on campus. For many minority students attending predominately White institutions, a positive level of comfort could simply mean becoming involved in the life of the campus community.

Astin's theory of student involvement (1984, 1996) postulated that students who invest their time and energy in the learning process and are involved in the social and academic life of the campus community are more likely to grow and develop, enjoy their college experience, and complete their degree programs than students who are not involved. Involvement includes both in- and out-of-class experiences and assumes that students will take the initiative to participate in the life of the academic community (Pascarella & Terenzini, 1991).

Further examination of the literature indicates that many researchers (Cooper, Healy, & Simpson, 1994; Kuth, Schuh, Whitt & Associates, 1991; Pascarella & Terenzini, 1991; Tinto, 1993) support Astin's theory and have concluded that given the positive level of influence that involvement exerts over a student's academic experience and the long-term personal gains that are realized, a central goal of colleges and universities should be to foster learning communities that maximize student experiences for optimal growth and development.

Rendon's (1994) findings in a study of 132 first-year students enrolled at four different institutions also support the positive effects of student involvement on persistence. Rendon found that traditional students (e.g., White students from families where the precedent of attending college was well established) seemed to benefit most from the institution's activities and organizations because they were comfortable with the established norms of the campus setting and took the initiative to become involved. Rendon indicated that many nontraditional students (e.g., minorities and women) were less likely to become involved without the forward assistance of others and affirmation that they could be successful in college. For these students, Rendon (1994) asserted, "involvement is not easy . . . [hence] validation may be the missing link to involvement, and may be a prerequisite for involvement to occur" (p. 37). Rendon contended that current practices used by colleges and universities for fostering student learning and growth are outdated and fail to recognize the strengths and needs of today's college students. The validation model postulates the following tenets:

1. Validation is an enabling, confirming, and supportive process initiated by in-and out-of-class agents that foster academic and interpersonal development.
2. When validation is present, students feel capable of learning; they experience a feeling of self-worth and feel that they, and everything that they bring to the college experience, are accepted and recognized as valuable.
3. Like involvement, validation is a prerequisite to student development.
4. Validation can occur both in-and out-of-class.
5. Validation suggests a developmental process. It is not a end in itself. The more validation students receive, the richer the academic and interpersonal experience.
6. Validation is most effective when offered early on in the student's college experience, during the first year of college and during the first weeks of class (p. 45).

The model presented by Rendon (1994) identified two categories of "validating agents," out-of-class agents and in-class agents. Out-of-class agents include social group peers, faculty, other members of the academic community, and the student's significant others (e.g., parents and partners). In-class agents are

Table 2. Cognitive Styles and Multicultural Populations

Cultural Grouping of World Views

Non-Western	Western
American Indians	Euro Americans (primarily males)
Mexican Americans	Minorities with high degree of
African Americans	acculturation
Puerto Rican Americans	
Chinese Americans	
Japanese Americans	
Many Euro American females	

Some Fundamental Dimensions of Non-Western vs. Western World View

Non-Western	Western
Emphasize group cooperation	Emphasize individual competition
Achievement as it reflects	Achievement for the individual
Value harmony with nature	Must master and control nature
Time is relative	Adhere to rigid time schedule
Accept affective expression	Limit affective expression
Extended family	Nuclear family
Holistic thinking	Dualistic thinking
Religion permeates culture	Religion distinct from other parts of
Accept world views of other cultures	culture
Socially oriented	Feel their world is superior
	Task oriented

Cognitive Styles Comparison

Field-dependent	Field-independent
Relational/holistic	Analytic
Affective	Non-affective

Characteristics	Characteristics
1. Perceive elements as a part of a total picture	1. Perceive elements as discrete from their background
2. Do best on verbal tasks	2. Do best on analytic tasks
3. Learn material, which has a Human social content and which is characterized by fantasy humor	3. Learn material that is inanimate and impersonal more easily
4. Performance influenced by Authorizing figures expression of confidence or doubt	4. Performance not greatly affected by the opinions of others
5. Style conflicts with traditional school environment	5. Style matches up with most school environments

Table 2. (Cont'd.)

Comparison of Features in the Writing Styles of Holistic vs. Analytical Thinkers

Holistic (Non-Western)	Analytical (Western)
1. Descriptive abstractions	1. Analytic abstraction
2. Word meaning based on content	2. Formal meaning for words
3. Use few synonyms	3. Use many synonyms
4. Use few comparisons	4. Use many forms of generalization comparison
5. Use relational and instructional classification	5. Use hierarchical models of classification
6. Tends to use second person "you," reflects group identity, tends to pull reader in as a part of the writing.	6. Can easily adopt a third person viewpoint in writing and speaking, is objective, reflects separate identity from what is going on

Comparison of Form and Function of Symbolic Imagery between Disparate Cognitive Processes (Speech & Writing)

Non-Western	Western
1. Visual (pictorial thinking)	1. Notions or theoretical statement
2. Thoughts are perceive[d] as . . . living things, holistic thing, doing thing	2. Thought is . . . Mentalistic, devitalized, static
3. Imagery is intensely affective with cultural base	3. Imagery minimizes affective associations
4. Extensive expression of concrete emotional words and heightened use of metaphors	4. De-emphasis on such unless in specialized disciplines or situation
5. Medium is the message	5. Medium communicate the message
6. Medium motivates and socializes	6. Things must be contemplated before they motivate
7. Introduces self into objective analysis of events	7. Removes self

Source: Anderson (1988, pp. 6–7) in *Cognitive Styles and Multicultural Populations.*

faculty, classmates, and teaching or lab assistants. Faculty are represented in both groups of validating agents because researchers have found that this group has one of the strongest impacts on student involvement and persistence both in and outside of the classroom setting (Pascarella & Terenzini, 1991).

The challenge for predominantly White institutions is to foster learning communities that are validating and supportive of all groups of students, particularly minority students (e.g., African Americans) who are at risk of leaving because they are unable to adjust in the current intellectual and social environments found in some White institutions (Cabera, Nora, Terenzini, Pascarella & Hagedorn, 1999; Tinto, 1993).

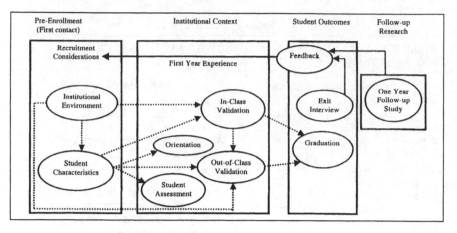

Figure 1. A conceptual model of student involvement through validation.

To assist African-American and other students in overcoming the barriers that have prevented some of them from successfully integrating into the mainstream of the campus culture, administrators, faculty, staff, and students of predominantly White institutions must fully embrace cultural diversity in the academic community. Not because the acknowledgment of diversity is "politically correct," but because cultural diversity is a reality and a simple fact of life in the United States and its educational institutions.

The authors propose a model designed to minimize the barriers that prevent African-American students from succeeding at predominantly White institutions (see Figure 1). The conceptual framework for the model is an adaptation of the Learning Outcomes Model advanced by Terenzini, Springer, Pascerella, and Nora (1995). The Learning Outcomes Model used five sets of interactive to explain influences that affect the students' academic and cognitive development as they proceed through college. The strength of Terenzini's et al., model rest in its use of recent conceptualizations of student development that describe the interplay between and among the sets of influences that impact student outcomes within the institutional setting. We too believe that the college environment exerts a greater influence over minority students success (e.g., retention) than the student's pre-enrollment characteristics.

The proposed model attempts to demonstrate how the college environment, inclusive of faculty and staff, administrators, students, institutional polices and procedures, and academic programs and services, can be re-designed to enhance the total learning experiences of students using the principles of Rendon's (1994) validation model and Astin's (1984) theory of student involvement.

Our model is based on the premise that the success of African-American students at predominantly White institutions is a function of both in- and out-of-class experiences, begins at the point of first contact with the student, can only be achieved if prospective students feel valued and welcomed within the institutional setting at each stage of their academic career, and increases as students become involved in the academic and social life of the academic community.

The model places more emphasis upon the institution's influence over the student's academic outcomes as opposed to the student's pre-enrollment characteristics because extant literature indicates that what happens to students after they enter college has a greater impact on retention than other factors. However, it should be understood that some of the student's pre-enrollment characteristics (level of academic preparedness, prior engagement with Whites, and first-generation vs. second-generation college student) will determine how the student progresses and what types of involvement experiences they may self-engage with. The following is a description of the stages in the model.

STAGE ONE: RECRUITMENT CONSIDERATIONS

Validating Students during Recruitment

Stage one of the model represents the beginning phase in the student-institution relationship. Validation at the recruitment stage involves creating a non-threatening and supportive environment where the prospective student and their outside validating agents (e.g., parents and/or significant others, etc.) can ask questions about the university without feeling intimidates because of his or her cultural group differences. A prospective minority student who feels valued and approved at this point in the enrollment cycle is more likely to begin his or her academic career with a positive attitude about the college or university because they will feel like they belong and matter to the institution. Hence they are more likely to succeed than students who begin but feel as though their presence at the institution does not matter.

We believe outside validating agents (e.g., parents) should be included in the validation through recruitment stage because many African-American and other minority students are first-generation college students, and as such, their parents may not be familiar with what it means for the student to leave the family and familiar surroundings to attend college, especially at an institution out of state and composed of people vastly different than the student's culture group.

The impact of significant others in the persistence of first-year college students is well documented (see Bean & Vesper, 1992; Rendon, 1992). Nora and Cabera (1994) provided evidence to suggest that encouragement and support from significant others (parents, partners, and high school peers) are important influences that students consider when deciding to re-enroll after the first year. Rendon (1992) provided a poignant account of her experiences as a first-generation student attempting to help her family understand her desire to leave the family's cultural enclave to attend a college. Rendon shared how she "faced new academic demands [as she] tried to reconcile [her] new world with [her] old culture" (p. 57). Rendon's academic experience is not an isolated incident. Rendon (1994), in a later work, indicated that "many of today's college students are negotiating the multiple demands of work, family, culture, and school. They are also struggling with adjusting to necessary losses associated with making the transition to college" (p. 49). Hence, Rendon's (1992) validation model advocates for institutions to create validating academic communities that foster events to "bring families together with students (i.e., achievement nights, athletic events, etc.) throughout the year" (p. 50).

The proposed model recognizes the influence that out-of-class validating agents have on the student's decision to attend a selected institution and to re-enroll after the first year. And because attrition is highest at most institutions between the first and second year of enrollment (Tinto, 1993), every effort should be made to minimize non-academic influences that may negatively affect a student's integration (involvement) into the academic community. The sooner influential significant others become actively involved in the student's college experience, the sooner the student will become comfortable with his or her transition away from the family enclave into the university setting.

In the proposed model, administrators recognize that minority students seeking admission have varying academic and social needs than majority group students. Therefore, an effective recruitment program attempts to match the student's academic and social needs with those offered by the institution. It is important for recruiters to be honest with students and explain the institution's strengths and weaknesses as they relate to the prospective students' cultural and ethnic group. Prospective students should be informed of the institution's mission, college requirements, such as various placement tests, expected course loads, institutional programs and services, and activities available for the student's specific ethnic group. We believe by being honest and providing this information during recruitment, the institution will be sending the message to the student that his or her specific needs have been considered and that their success at the institution matters.

The model encourages the use of currently enrolled African-American students to assist in the recruitment of other African-American students. Currently enrolled minority students can provide prospective students with an assessment of the college environment closer to reality than anyone else because they can share personal experiences of what it means to be a minority at the institution.

STAGE TWO: THE FIRST-YEAR EXPERIENCE

Validation Through Orientation

Orientation plays a pivotal role in the student's transition from high school or work into college. It is both exciting and scary and leaves a lasting impression on many students because it is often their first official university course or program.

Yet, in many institutions, orientation programs consist of providing students with a list of "do's and don'ts" and a large number of brochures of how to navigate their way around the campus. Often important information that students need to make a smooth transition during the first weeks of college is learned through trial and error.

Stage two of the model represents programs, services, and activities that new students will encounter during their first year of college. The proposed model advocates for an orientation program that seeks to help the African-American newcomer become integrated into the university community. The orientation programs can provide validation by reinforcing to the students that they matter and will be supported as they proceed toward degree completion. Components of the orientation program should introduce students to current African-American faculty, staff, and students, extra-curricular opportunities available to them, campus-wide grading policies, library services, career planning services to assist them in identifying appropriate degree options, financial aid policies and procedures, and academic support services.

The model stresses the importance of assisting African-American students to establish early connections (become involved) with members of their ethnic group during the orientation period. Extant literature (Pound, 1987; Fleming, 1984; Rendon, 1992; Turner, 1994) indicates that many minority students experience social isolation and alienation on predominantly White campuses because of the lack of a critical mass. Pound (1987) contends that Black faculty and staff are essential to the success of African-American students because they serve as role models, mentors, and informal advisors. Pound indicated that the importance of Black faculty, particularly in the retention of African-American students of White college campuses, "cannot be overemphasized" (p. 36). African-American and other minority students on predominantly White campuses need to see role models that are reflective of their culture group. However, this is not to imply that White faculty and staff cannot serve as role models for African-American students. They have in the past and they will continue to do so.

Student assessment tests such as mathematics and English are generally administered during orientation to determine students' verbal and analytical skills. Ideally, students will have been informed of these tests and corrective measures to be taken during the recruitment stage. Reducing the number of unknown variables that students encounter during the first year of college and the first few weeks of the semester makes the environment more predictable and hence increases the likelihood of the student gaining a positive level of comfort on campus (Turner, 1994). Students needing to improve their verbal and analytical skills should be assigned to developmental sections that emphasize study skills, time management, and reading techniques. Peer tutoring is encouraged because the sooner students begin to interact with other students the sooner they will begin to develop interpersonal relationships.

In-Class Validation

One of the most important in-class validating agents in the student's academic career are faculty (Astin, 1984; Pascarella & Terenzini, 1991). Therefore, professors should be trained in techniques to create a validating classroom environment for African-American students. Such training should orient faculty to the needs, concerns, and strengths of minority students (Rendon, 1994). It is important to validate students early on, during the first month of class, and to continue the process throughout their college years. Faculty trained to validate students show genuine concern when teaching. They are approachable, treat students with respect, and provide meaningful feedback to classroom assignments. Faculty should consider the following precedent to fostering a validating classroom environment:

1. Course content
2. Method of instruction
3. Evaluation and feedback
4. Student-faculty interaction
5. Reward structure

Out-of Class Validation

The institutional context plays a big role in the academic and social adjustment and success of minority students. Pascarella and Terenzini's (1991) review of the past twenty years of research on how college engagement affects student growth and development found two major themes in the literature that were strongly related to how and what students learn in college. These themes represented faculty and peer group interaction (both in and outside of the classroom) and the level of involvement students had in academic and non-academic systems of the institution. Therefore, the model advocates for the university to create a campus environment that validates African-American and other minority students which may be the missing link to involvement for some students (Rendon, 1992). The following factors in particular provide out-of-class validation for African American students:

1. Campus climate
2. Residence halls
3. Work experience
4. Peer interaction
5. Academic advising
6. University recognition
7. Faculty-student interaction outside the classroom
8. Role models of ethnic minority faculty

STAGE THREE: STUDENT OUTCOME

Exit Interviews

Normally exit interviews are conducted by the financial aid office in a university setting to inform students of their financial obligations to the university and outside funding agencies that may have assisted in financing the student's education. Providing African-American and other minority students with exit interviews at the departmental level provides an excellent opportunity to document their experiences for the purposes of evaluating and modifying the department's current retention strategies. Graduating students could be asked to participate in a focus group or complete an open-ended questionnaire that allows them to describe and explain their college experience.

Follow-Up Research

Conduct both qualitative (when possible) and quantitative research on African-American and other minority students at least one year after graduation. Normally, this type of research is generally conducted through the office of institutional research. However, if performed at the departmental level, the benefits could provide meaningful insights for academic departments desiring to assess and evaluate the learning environment and social climate of the department for minority students. The information could also be shared with other university offices responsible for bringing prospective students to campus.

CONCLUSION

This chapter examined factors that have been consistently cited as contributing to the low retention and graduation of African-American students attending predominantly White institutions. Recommendations cited in the literature were used to develop a model that can be used by predominantly White institutions to assist African-American students in achieving their academic goals. The model recognizes the influence that the institutional context (e.g., people, programs, services, policies, etc.) exerts over a student's academic career. Thus, the primary responsibility for creating a validating community rests with faculty, staff, and administrators of the institution. Validation is viewed as a continuous process that is repeatedly used by different agents and at different times throughout the students' college experience, and occurs in a forward motion with institutional validating agents taking the lead. The model also recognizes the influence that outside validating agents may have on a student's decision to attend and remain in college. Thus, we recommend the involvement of outside validating agents (e.g., parents and significant others) in the student's academic career as soon as possible.

The proposed model may not resolve the recruitment, retention, and graduation concerns of all African-American students attending predominantly White institutions. There is no single solution to abate this concern. However, we believe this model may increase the involvement of African-American students in these institutions by fostering a validating and supportive academic community—both of which have been determined to be effective in the retention of minority students in higher education (Astin, 1996; Pascarella & Terenzini, 1991; Rendon, 1992).

REFERENCES

Adams, H. G. (1988). *Tomorrow's professorate: Insuring minority participation through talent development today.* Washington, DC: American Society for Engineering Education. (ERIC Document Reproduction Service No. ED291 273). American Council on Education and Education Commission of the States.

Allen, W. R. (1988). Improving Black student access and achievement in higher education. *The Review of Higher Education, 11,* 403–416.

Allen, W., Epps, E., & Haniff, N. (Eds.). (1991). *College in Black and White: African-American students in predominantly White and historically Black public universities.* Albany, NY: SUNY Press.

American Council on Education and the Education Commission of the States. (1988). *One-third of a nation.* (Report of the commission on minority participation in education and American life). Washington, DC: Author.

American Council on Education. (1998). *Straight talk about college costs and prices.* Washington, DC: National Commission on the Cost of Higher Education.

Anderson, J. A. (1988). Cognitive styles and multicultural populations, *Journal of Teacher Education, 39,* 2–9.

Astin A. W. (1984). Student involvement: A developmental theory for higher education. *Journal of College Student Personnel, 25,* 297–308.

Astin, A. W. (1996). Involvement in learning revisited: Lessons we have learned. *Journal of College Student Development, 37,* 123–134.

Atkinson, D. R., Morten, G., & Sue, D. W. (1983). *Counseling American minorities: A cross-cultural perspective.* (2nd ed.). Dubuque, IA: Brown.

Bean, J. P., & Vespers, N. (1992). *Student dependency theory: An explanation of student retention in college.* Paper presented at the annual meeting of the Association for the Study of Higher Education. Minneapolis, MN.

Brubacher, J. S., & Rudy, W. (1976). *Higher education in transition* (3rd ed.). New York: Harper & Row, Inc.

Cabrera, A. F., Nora, A., Terenzini, P. T., Pascarella, E., & Hagedorn, L. S. (1999). Campus racial climate and adjustment of students to college. *The Journal of College Student Development, 70,* 134–160.

Cooper, D. L., Healy, M. A., & Simpson, J. (1994). Student development through involvement: Specific changes over time: *Journal of College Student Development, 35,* 98–102.

Curry, S. E. (1992). *Experiences of first-year Black students at Iowa State University.* Unpublished master's thesis. Iowa State University, Ames, IA.

Davis, R. D. (1994, November). *Safe havens for African American students: Finding support on a White campus.* Paper presented at the annual meeting of the Association for the Study of Higher Education, Tucson, AZ.

Davis, J. E., & Lasane, T. P. (1994, November). *Campus climate, gender, and achievement of African-American college students.* Paper presented at the annual meeting of the Association for the Study of Higher Education, Tucson, AZ.

Dawson, V. D. (1989). *Involvement of Black students in the residence halls.* Unpublished master's thesis, Iowa State University, Ames, IA.

Evans, N. J., Forney, D. S., & Guido-DiBrito, F. (1998). *Student development in college: Theory, research, and practice.* San Francisco, CA: Jossey-Bass.

Fields, V. (1991). *An investigation into factors affecting academic success associated with on-campus living experiences for African-American undergraduate students at Iowa State University.* Unpublished doctoral dissertation, Iowa State University, Ames. IA.

Fleming, J. E. (1984). *Blacks in college.* San Francisco, CA: Jossey-Bass.

Fordham, S., & Ogbu, J. (1986). Black students' school success: Coping with the "burden of acting White." *The Urban Review, 18,* 176–206.

Haro, R. (1992, January/February). Lessons from practice: What not to do. *Change,* 55–58.

Henderson, V. C. (1992). *Factors affecting success of African-American male graduate students: A grounded theory approach.* Unpublished doctoral dissertation, Iowa State University, Ames, IA.

Jones, Y. (1993). *A study of factors that contribute to the academic achievement of African American freshmen at Iowa State University.* Unpublished master's thesis. Iowa State University, Ames, IA.

Katz, J. H. (1989). The challenge of diversity. In C. Woolbright (Ed.), *valuing diversity on campus: A multicultural approach* (pp. 1–21). (College Unions at Work Monograph No. 11). Bloomington, IN: Association of College Unions-International.

Katz, J. H., & Ivey, A. (1977). White awareness: The frontier of racism awareness training. *Personnel and Guidance Journal, 55,* 484–489.

Kuh, G. D., Schuh, J. H., Whitt, E. J., & Associates. (1991). *Involving colleges: Successful approaches to fostering student learning and development outside the classroom.* San Francisco, CA: Jossey-Bass.

Lewin, K. (1936). *Principles of topological psychology.* New York: McGraw-Hill.

Lin, Y., & Vogt, W. P. (1996). Occupational outcomes for students earning two-year college degrees: Income, status, and equity. *Journal of Higher Education, 64,* 446–475.

Loo, C., & Rolison, G. (1986). Alienation of ethnic minority students at a predominantly White university. *Journal of Higher Education, 57,* 58–77.

National Commission on the Cost of Higher Education (1998). *Straight talk about college costs and prices.* Washington, DC: American Council on Education.

Nettles, M. T. (1990). Success in doctoral programs: Experiences of minority and White students. *American Journal of Education, 98,* 495–522.

Nettles, M. T., & Perna, L. W. (1997). *African American education data book: Volume I. Higher education and adult education.* Washington, DC: Frederick D. Patterson Research Institute of the College Fund/UNCF.

Nora, A., & Cabrera, A. F. (1994). *The role of significant others in the adjustment and persistence of minorities and non-traditional minorities in higher education.* Paper presented at the annual meeting of the Association for the Study of Higher Education. Tucson, AZ.

Pascarella, E. T., & Terenzini, P. T. (1991). *How college affects students.* San Francisco, CA: Jossey-Bass.

Patterson-Stewart, K. E., Richie, M. H., & Sanders, E. T. W. (1997). Interpersonal dynamics of African American persistence in doctoral programs at predominantly White universities. *Journal of College Student Development, 38,* 489–498.

Porter, O. F. (1990). *Undergraduate completion and persistence at four-year colleges and universities.* Washington, DC: The National Institute of Independent Colleges and Universities.

Pound, A. W. (1987). Black student's needs on predominantly White campuses. In D. J. Wright (Ed.), *Responding to the needs of today's minority students* (pp. 23–28). San Francisco, CA: Jossey-Bass.

Rendon, L. I. (1992). From the barrio to the academy: Revelations of a Mexican American "scholarship girl." In L. S. Zwerling and H. B. London (Eds.), *First-generation students: Confronting the cultural issues* (pp. 55–64). San Francisco, CA: Jossey-Bass.

Rendon, L. I. (1994). Validating culturally diverse students: Toward a new model of learning and student development. *Innovative Higher Education, 19,* 33–51.

Slaughter, J. B. (1988). From isolation to mainstream: An institutional commitment. In M. C. Terrell, II and D. J. Wright (Eds.), *From survival to success: Promoting minority student retention* [Monograph]. National Association of Student Personnel Administrators, 9, xi–xv.

Terenzini, P. T., Springer, L., Pascarella, E. T., & Nora, A. (1995). Academic and out-of-class influences on students' intellectual orientations. *The Review of Higher Education, 19,* 23–44.

Tinto, V. (1993). *Leaving college: Rethinking the causes and cures of student attrition* (2nd ed.). Chicago, IL: University of Chicago Press.

Tinto, V. (1995). Learning communities, collaborative learning, and the pedagogy of educational citizenship. *American Association for Higher Education Bulletin,* 11–13.

Tracey, T. J., & Sedlacek, W. E. (1987). Prediction of college graduation using noncognitive variables by race. *Measurement and Evaluation in Guidance, 19,* 177–184.

Turner, C. S. (1994). Guest in someone else's house: students of color. *The Review of Higher Education, 17,* 355–370.

Vogt, W. P. (1997). *Tolerance & education: Learning to live with diversity and difference.* London: Sage.

SECTION 2

Latino/a Students

CHAPTER 6

Leaking Pipeline: Issues Impacting Latino/a College Student Retention

John C. Hernandez and Mark A. Lopez

The continued growth of the Latino college-going population challenges college and university personnel to become better informed on the issues that affect persistence of this diverse group of students. This chapter reviews the current understanding of those personal, environmental, involvement, and socio-cultural factors influencing student retention. Specific recommendations to increase Latino persistence in higher education are included throughout the chapter.

The Latino population grew to 38.8 million in July 2002, an increase of 10% from census; this continued population growth has resulted in Latinos registering as the nation's largest minority group and the number of Latinos could reach 60 million by 2020 (Alonso-Zaldivar, 2003). Latino high-school graduates of all ages go to college at a higher rate than most other major racial or ethnic groups (Rooney, 2002). A larger proportion of Latinos attend college than 20 years ago (Llagas & Synder, 2003). From 1988 to 1998 Latino college enrollment increased by 85%, the highest growth rate among the four major ethnic minority groups (Harvey, 2001). However, there appears to be a leak in the educational pipeline, in spite of this enrollment growth a recent study reported that Latinos trail all other groups in earning undergraduate degrees and summarized that Latinos suffer from a college-persistence problem (Rooney, 2002).

The continued population growth, particularly in regions that previously lacked a Latino presence, has challenged college and university personnel to better understand this diverse group of students. This chapter will attempt to broadly report from the retention literature, those factors that impact the persistence of Latino college students, and provide recommendations for appropriate institutional responses.

DEMOGRAPHIC CHARACTERISTICS

Latinos are a heterogeneous group, which represents a number of different national and ethnic origins, vary by social class, have differing histories, differ in immigration and citizenship status, and live in different regions of this country (Chilman, 1993). Racially, Latinos can be Black, Asian, Indigenous, White/European, or a mixture of these four. Latinos may come from one of 25 Spanish-speaking countries, and variations exist from region to region, often with a mixture of dialects. Given the separate histories and diverse experiences of each major group of Latinos in the United States, it is not uncommon to find that each represents a distinct Latino culture. However, commonalities may exist: many are the first in their family to attend college; may come from low income households where Spanish is the primary spoken language; may be academically under prepared; and may combat feelings of isolation, especially at predominantly White institutions (Justiz & Rendon, 1989).

In terms of ethnic identity, most Latinos generally identify themselves nationally with their family's country of origin (e.g., Mexico, Puerto Rico, El Salvador) while others exhibit a greater preference for a pan-ethnic identity and are more prone to identify with a pan-ethnic term such as "Hispanic" or "Latino" (Jones-Correa & Leal, 1996). An individual may indeed have various overlapping identities that are used consciously and selectively depending on the situation in which they find themselves. Additionally, Jones-Correa and Leal (1996) report that the choice for pan-ethnic identification will vary by national-origin group, by generation, by age, and by level of education.

Latinos are disproportionately enrolled in two-year colleges (Llagas & Synder, 2003). Nationally, about half of all Latinos in higher education are enrolled in two-year colleges and this enrollment figure is even higher in states with larger Latino populations, such as California, where community colleges account for 80% of Latino enrollment in higher education (Lane, 2002). Hispanic Serving Institutions (HSIs) are degree-granting public or private institutions of higher education eligible for Title IV funding in the United States and Puerto Rico in which Latinos comprise 25% or more of the undergraduate full-time-equivalent enrollment. In 1999, Latino enrollment in HSIs accounted for nearly one-half (45%) of the total Latino undergraduate enrollment (Llagas & Synder, 2003).

There are significant differences in educational attainment within the Latino community. Typically, Cubans and "other" Latinos (Central and South American) attain higher college graduation rates than Mexican Americans or Puerto Ricans (Suarez-Orozco & Paez, 2002). Due to the rich heterogeneity of the Latino community, higher education must understand the influx of enrollment in order to serve the vastly growing Latino presence within the academy.

PERSONAL FACTORS

Personal factors are analogous to what is often referred to in the literature as background characteristics or pre-college variables in research studies. These personal factors are useful in understanding how students adjust to college (Cabrera, Castaneda, Nora, & Hengstler, 1992). Flores (1992) conducted an empirical study at two large public universities to determine whether there were notable differences in the characteristics of Latino students who completed the baccalaureate degree compared to Latino students who enrolled but did not complete their degree objective. Flores reported that Latino student persisters' success resulted from prior attributes brought with them to college. Some of the personal factors found in the literature on college student retention include high school grade point average and test scores, academic self-concept, support from the family, and finances.

High School Grade Point Average and Test Scores

Admission to the nation's colleges and universities continues to rely on traditional measurements such as high school grade point average and test scores on college entrance exams. College success is often predicted based on how well a student has performed in high school; however, there is considerable evidence that these traditional measures are not valid for students of color as they might be for White students (Tracey & Sedlacek, 1984, 1985, 1987). Similarly Duran (1994) wrote that evidence exists that test scores may not predict early college grades of Latinos as well as it does for White students.

Mallette and Cabrera (1991) cited several research studies which indicated that pre-college ability and background factors exert no significant direct effects on the retention of Latino students. Gandara and Lopez (1998) researched the extent to which test scores related to college performance on high achieving Latino students. The study found that SAT scores did not predict college GPA, time to completion of a degree, or likelihood of applying to graduate school. Similarly, Hurtado, Carter, and Spuler's (1996) research on Latino student transition reported that academic adjustment to college was not directly related to prior high school grade point average.

Perhaps the strongest criticism of applying these traditional measurements on Latino students is that the information provided has little systematic connection with a students' academic skills or with their motivation to succeed in college

(Duran, 1994). It would appear unwise for college admissions offices to continue to rely exclusively on high school grade point average and test scores because the predictive power of these traditional assessments is modest (Padilla, 1991). Instead, noncognitive variables should be used in higher education admission because research has shown that these variables are better predictors of student success and retention, particularly for students of color (Sedlacek, 1989).

Academic Self-Concept

Sedlacek (1989) reported that a strong academic self-concept is important for students of color at all educational levels. Rodriguez (1996) reported that academic self-concept was significantly related to GPA and that Mexican American students with the same academic background were more likely to achieve higher grades if they had greater confidence in their academic abilities. Astin (1982) also found that academic self-concept was related to persistence in college for students of color in general, and it was related to college grades for African Americans, Puerto Ricans, and Native Americans. In a qualitative research study, Hernandez (2000) reported that successful Latino students who demonstrated a positive mental outlook (described as the belief in and the realization that they possessed the potential to succeed in college) attributed this as the single most important factor that influenced their retention in college.

University personnel have a significant role in validating a student's academic self-concept and should identify ways to encourage the development of an optimistic outlook (Hernandez, 2000). This type of affirmation may be critical for students who believe they are academically underprepared or for first generation Latino students (Rendon, 1994). Academic advisors may want to assess incoming students' level of positive self-concept in order to reinforce this belief in those who possess it, and to facilitate its development among those who lack it (Hernandez, 2000). Sensitizing faculty and staff to contribute to a student's self-worth through words of encouragement, through meaningful interactions, both in and outside of the classroom, and by utilizing constructive critique and feedback of a student's performance (Terrenzini et al., 1994) is recommended.

The Family

Latino family literature is often shaped by discussions of familism, defined as the behavioral manifestations of Latinos that reflect a strong emotional and value commitment to family life (Valdes, 1996; Vega, 1995). Traditional Latino culture is defined as family-oriented given that generally Latinos have strong ties to their family (Rendon & Taylor, 1990). Many Latino students experience the family as a source of emotional security and support (Hernandez, 2002). In Latino culture, the family is often defined broadly and may include single households, combinations of households, and/or all extended relatives (Wilkinson, 1993).

The family plays an important role in Latino life, and the level of its importance does not diminish across generations; it is nearly as important for the third generation as it is for the first generation (Hurtado, Hayes-Bautista, Valdez, & Hernandez, 1992). The report *Latino Persistence in Higher Education* indicated that the family plays a central role in the lives and educational experiences of Latinos (Haro, Rodriguez, & Gonzales, 1994).

Hernandez (2000) reported the importance of the family in the retention of Latino college students. The family was described as a source of support and encouragement; however, the family also placed pressure on the participants in several ways. Pressure was placed by the family's expectations that dropping out of college was not an option. For other students it was a sense of responsibility and a belief that they "owed a debt" to their parents. This was particularly true for students who were the first in their families to attend college. Some expressed it as "their contribution" to the family, particularly after seeing their parents struggle. This pressure served to reinforce their academic motivation and determination while positively influencing their optimistic outlook.

The family and the home environment can be utilized as an effective retention tool by familiarizing Latino parents with the college setting and providing them with an opportunity to meet and develop rapport with college educators and support staff (Hernandez, 2000). In order to gain family support, university personnel should engage parents in programs that assist them to become comfortable and knowledgeable with U.S. higher education. Bilingual and culturally sensitive recruitment materials and parent orientation programs should be developed to familiarize parents with the college setting; to provide opportunities to meet and develop trust and rapport with college faculty and staff; and to better understand the academic rigor that will be placed on their children (Hernandez, 2002).

Finances

Financial assistance is essential to the retention and enrollment of students from low-income backgrounds in higher education (Nora, 2001). Tinto (1993) defined finances as an external force that shapes persistence. Evidence accumulated over the past decade indicates that financial aid does impact student persistence, especially among the economically disadvantaged and students from less affluent families (Tinto 1993). Other research studies have reported the role of finances in determining the persistence or withdrawal of Latino students (Arbona & Novy, 1990; Cabrera, 1992; Hernandez, 2000; Nora, 1990; Padilla, Trevino, Gonzalez, & Trevino, 1997).

The ability to finance a college education remains a major barrier for many Latino students (Nora, 1990). The Latino population has experienced an across-the-board decline in annual income; in the mid 1990s, 30% of all Latinos were considered poor, earning less than $15,569 for a family of four (Goldberg,

1997). It should not seem surprising that Latino students reported higher levels of stress associated with financial matters and indicated that this stress factor negatively impacted their quality of life (Hernandez, 2000; Quintana, Vogel, & Ybarra, 1991). Additionally, Sedlacek, Longerbeam, and Alatorre (2003) reported that Latino college students were more likely to work, to work longer hours, and to drop out of school for financial reasons than non-Latinos.

The issues of financing a college education and its impact on Latino student retention is critical when you consider the national trend of increased student tuition while decreasing financial aid programs. This may result in many Latino students having to work additional hours to defray educational expenses, attending college part-time in order to mitigate college costs, or deferring enrollment in college during the traditional college-age years (Rooney, 2002). Aggressive outreach and educational efforts are needed to educate Latino students and their families about federal and state financial aid programs as well as providing assistance with cumbersome applications. Identification of local and national scholarship programs and providing assistance with scholarship personal statements and essays are critical resources that should be provided by support programs. Additionally, financial planning seminars and materials that are language sensitive should be developed for Latino parents.

ENVIRONMENTAL FACTORS

The influence of the college environment must be considered in order to fully examine Latino college students and their retention. Environmental theory provides the basis from which to understand the relationship between students and the campus environment (Banning, 1989). Conyne and Clack (1981) described an environment as consisting of a physical component, a social component, an institutional component, and an ecological-climate dimension that develops from an interaction of the first three components with each other and with human constituents. Conyne and Clack (1981) also indicated that people are in transaction with their environment and that an individual's environment is heavily influenced by human behavior. "A welcoming campus environment that provides opportunities to incorporate the Latino culture is an important institutional contribution to lowering Latino student stress" (Sedlacek et al., 2003, p. 3).

There are several variables within the institution's scope that can influence student retention. Garland and Grace (1993) wrote that student affairs professionals can no longer "ignore or underestimate the respective influence of the many on- and off-campus variables that simultaneously affect a student" (p. 87). Bean (1982) named such organizational variables (i.e., racial climate, presence of ethnic community, and working on or off campus) which include variables that can be administratively controlled by the institution as well as variables that point to the level of students' involvement in-group values. Astin (1993) referred to the latter as environmental variables, which can positively or negatively impact an institution in its retention efforts. Environmental variables that research has shown to impact Latino student retention include the racial climate of the institution; the presence of an ethnic community; living on-campus, and working and living off-campus.

Racial Climate

The enduring concern is the need for institutions to have an increased comprehension of the causes of racially tense campus environments before taking into account how theses specific incidents affects student's development and ultimately how these incidents influence their retention (Hurtado, 2000). Campus climate will vary from institution to institution, depending on the campuses's demographics, area of expertise/and even institutional type (i.e., Hispanic Serving Institution, Historically Black Colleges & Universities, Tribal Colleges, and Traditional White Institutions). Due to post-secondary diversity, a rise in racial conflict and tension has occurred (Hurtado, Milem, Clayton-Pedersen, & Allen, 1998).

It is possible that students will not adjust academically or socially if the campus racial climate allows these students to feel like outsiders. This feeling of marginality will affect a student's sense of belonging with the institution and can ultimately influence one's intent to persist. Departure is more likely where a sense of marginality exists and when students see themselves located in enclaves (Murguia, Padilla, & Pavel, 1991).

In relation to Latino college students, the campus climate can facilitate Latino students' transition to collegiate life and combat common problems such as feelings of isolation (O'Brien, 1993). According to Helm, Sedlacek, and Prieto (1998), there is a substantial amount of support that campus climate directly relates to the failure or success of students in post-secondary education. A growing area is campus climate due to the diversification of higher education. Numerous studies in the past decade have focused on race-relations on college campuses and campus climate.

In a study of talented Latino students, Hurtado (1994) reported that despite the strong achievement characteristics upon college entry, Latinos continue to experience some degree of discrimination. This study also reported that racial/ethnic tension and experiences of discrimination are more likely to be reported among Latinos at larger campuses. In conjunction with Hurtado's study, institutions must provide a positive and welcoming campus climate for Latinos. As recent demographic data has shown, significant demographic shifts have occurred in enrollment, persistence and graduation rates of non-traditional college students. Colleges and universities must establish and maintain a caring and welcoming environment for all students. Institutions should critically reexamine the initiatives that address diversity and social justice and ensure that these efforts have practical benefits to the campus climate.

Presence of an Ethnic Community

Many students do not feel a sense of belonging with the institution due to a lack of student community. The lack of student community can be defined to include little contact among students outside of class, an apathetic student body, and a place where students do not socialize with one another (Astin, 1993). Tinto (1993) also indicated that students of color may find it especially difficult to settle and become a member of a supportive community within the college environment.

For Latinos, finding a critical mass of students who are like them appears to be important. Hernandez's (2000) research on Latino student retention reported that finding a Latino community on a predominantly White campus had a positive impact on retention. By meeting other Latinos these students were better able to cope with the college environment. Meeting Latinos of similar backgrounds who were succeeding in college was also an important motivating factor. Padilla et al. (1997) reported that in order to overcome the barrier involving a lack of minority presence, the ethnic minority students in their sample first acknowledged the importance of minority support and then searched for the ethnic presence that already existed on campus. The results of these studies support the "repeated observation that the persistence of students of color often hinges upon there being a sufficiently large number of similar types of students on campus with whom to form a viable community" (Tinto, 1993, p. 60).

In the college environment, students need to feel that they matter. Schlossberg, Lynch, and Chickering (1989) developed what has been referred to as a theory of mattering/marginality. According to this concept students must feel that they "matter" if they are to succeed in college. Students need to have a sense of belonging and feel appreciated. If students feel ignored and unaccepted by other students, faculty, or staff, they will feel marginalized and are much less likely to persist in college. Ethnic minority students at predominantly White institutions are particularly susceptible to these feelings of marginality (Moore & Upcraft, 1990).

The fostering of community often occurs within subcommunities, where there are often greater opportunities for involvement. Subcommunities serve as understaffed environments that often foster commitment because students are more involved in campus life (Kuh, Schuh, Whitt, & Associates, 1991). Perhaps Attinasi's (1992) qualitative research provides an understanding of how a specific Latino community made sense of large environments and developed multiple communities while on campus. The students in Attinasi's research study initially found the physical geography of the campus (the students described three geographies: a physical, social, and an academic-cognitive geography) to be large-scale environments in which objects stood separated from each other. The students employed the strategy "getting to know" and "scaling down" to connect themselves in one or more of these geographies. This was accomplished through mentoring relationships with continuing students who showed them the "Inside ropes," and through information sharing with their peers, which resulted in cooperative exploration of the geographies.

Faculty, staff, and administrators can validate the importance of ethnic communities if they understand and recognize the role of these communities, particularly for students who have historically experienced injustice and discrimination. Social scientists have reported that children of Latino ancestry often maintain close ties with their cultural heritage; as such, university personnel should anticipate that when these students enter college they would seek others who share a common culture (Hernandez, 2002). Workshops, seminars, and other staff development training may mitigate an appreciation for the role of ethnic sub-communities in fostering support and a "safe-space" for Latino students.

Working and Living Off Campus

Astin's (1984) research indicated that living and working off-campus could be a detriment to students because the student spends considerable time and energy on nonacademic activities that are usually unrelated to student life. This conceptual framework suggests that off campus commitments decreases the time and energy that a student can devote to studies and other campus activities. Students who work part-time off campus constrain their ability to spend time on campus interacting with other members of the institution, both faculty and student peers (Cabrera, Nora, & Castaneda 1993).

In an empirical study that examined the similarities and differences between Latino and non-Latino college students with respect to retention variables, Canabal (1995) reported that the only variable that affected retention for the two groups is the number of hours of work per week; meaning the more hours a student works during the week, the lower the probability of that student attending college. Although Canabal did not distinguish between working on- or off-campus, the reported findings indicate the negative "pull" that working too many hours per week can have on the persistence of college students. Institutions must attempt to provide additional resources for Latino students who must work to supplement their educational expenses, in order to lower the total number of hours they work while in college. Not only should higher education increase the funding opportunities to underrepresented populations, but also assist them in locating higher paying jobs as well as increasing the number of campus employment opportunities.

INVOLVEMENT FACTORS

Astin (1984), in outlining a developmental theory for higher education, considered involvement to be at the core of his thesis. Involvement theory affirms the belief that students learn best, and are more likely to persist, by becoming involved in the campus community (Morre & Upcraft, 1990). Other research has supported the contention that involvement has a positive relationship with student retention (Astin, 1984; Tinto, 1993). Involvement factors in this chapter are defined as variables that occur within the college environment and focus on the specific ways in which Latino students get involved. Some of the involvement factors found in the literature include faculty-student interactions, the role of mentorship, and participation in student organizations.

Faculty-Student Interaction

The literature strongly supports the positive impact of faculty-student interactions. Students who have contact with faculty outside of the classroom are more likely to persist to graduation, exhibit higher levels of achievement, and be satisfied with college than students not involved with faculty outside of the classroom (Schuh & Kuh, 1984).

In a study of ethnic minority students, Mayo, Murguia, and Padilla (1995) reported that relationships with minority faculty proved to be the most significant dimension of social integration in affecting grade point average. As predicted, having a good relationship with faculty members was an important ingredient to academic success. Another significant indicator linked with academic success was having a quality relationship with a faculty or staff role model. Hernandez (2000) identified having a relationship with faculty or staff as positively influencing Latino student retention. Similarly, Hurtado, Carter, and Spuler (1996) reported that Latino college students who perceive a student-centered faculty and have opportunities for faculty interaction were more likely to adjust to college.

It should be noted that several studies report that nonminority faculty members can also serve as role models for ethnic students and while ethnically matched role models were successful in contributing to academic success so were cross-ethnic role models (Mayo et al., 1995; Padilla & Pavel, 1994). The primary variable seems to be student satisfaction with the level of personal contact with their instructors.

"Programs that facilitate interaction between faculty/staff and students should be encouraged. There are many ways to increase student-faculty interactions, for example: a) incorporate faculty in new student orientation programs; b) create out-of-class opportunities for faculty or staff to interact with students; c) provide financial incentives for faculty to invite students to dinner or lunch or to participate in a campus program such as an athletic or theater event; d) coordinate formal mentoring relationships where students are matched with a faculty or staff member; and e) design living-learning residence halls that house faculty offices or residences" (Hernandez, 2000, pp. 582-583).

Mentorship

Mentoring is a valuable asset for student persistence (Tinto, 1993). "Effective mentoring involves not only the transfer of academic skills, attitudes, and behaviors but a level of interaction, trust, and communication which results in a psychosocial comfort that empowers a student with the knowledge and confidence to grow academically and socially" (Parker-Redmond, 1990, p. 191). In this context, mentoring can provide students with the realization that the university is a place where faculty, staff, and administrators care.

Mentoring addresses several of the causes of student attrition and delayed graduation, including the lack of proper academic preparation for college and the lack of knowledge about or access to social or academic resources (Parker-Redmond, 1990). Minority students are more likely to succeed if they have mentors or role models in their schools (Sedlacek, 1989). In a qualitative study of Latino students at a selective university, Arellano and Padilla (1996) reported that a common theme was the importance of influential individuals outside of their immediate family members. The researchers reported that for many of these students, mentors provided access to information they would not have been privy to, particularly for first-generation college students.

Mentoring programs in both a corporate and university setting show that mentoring can be an effective tool in helping minorities to succeed in unfamiliar settings (Parker-Redmond, 1990). Mentoring programs for Latino students should be developed because mentoring may serve as a retention tool particularly for students who may be at risk of leaving the university before graduation.

Participation in Student Organizations

Cocurricular involvement (including student organization membership) had a number of important positive college and post college effects including encouragement of educational persistence and attainment (Pascarella & Terenzini, 1991). Likewise, Astin (1993) concluded that students who are active in leadership roles in campus organizations are more likely to persist in college and graduate than those who are not. Abrahamowicz (1988) explored the relationship that participation in student organizations has with encouraging broader involvement with the institution, satisfaction with the college experience, and perceptions of college. Abrahamowicz concluded that participation in student organizations seems to lead to greater involvement in the overall college experience, particularly in activities beyond the traditional realm of student organizations.

Hernandez (2000) reported that cocurricular involvement positively impacted the retention of Latino college students. Through cocurricular involvement students had opportunities to make new friends, particularly peers that came from similar cultural and socioeconomic backgrounds; found a caring and supportive community; and were able to break down the larger environment into meaningful wholes. Similarly, Mayo, Murguia, and Padilla (1995) reported that membership in student organizations played a role in the academic success of Mexican American students. Those who participated significantly were more likely to be doing well academically than those who did not participate.

What about the role of ethnic student organizations? Does involvement in ethnic student organizations have a greater impact on retention than involvement in mainstream student groups? Rooney (1985) conducted an exploratory study that provided some descriptive data regarding minority student involvement in student organizations. The study of 927 African American, Asian American, Latino, and Native American students indicated that fewer than one in five students reported being involved in a minority student group, although a total of 70% reported being aware of the existence of their respective student groups. Percentages of awareness was higher in all groups than were percentages of involvement. While a small number of minority students in this study reported involvement in ethnic student organizations, a sizeable number (98%), however, reported involvement in other student groups and had interests beyond the confines of ethnic student organizations. This data seems to support other research studies (Bennett & Okinaka, 1990; Trevino, 1992) which report that Latino students were less likely to belong to an ethnic student organization.

However, it should be noted that for many Latino students, involvement in an ethnic-based student organization positively impacts retention: by aiding student's feelings of comfort at the university (Rooney, 1985); by incorporating, retaining, and nurturing their cultural community as a means of achieving success in college (Padilla et al., 1997); and as a way to stay culturally grounded, particularly at predominantly White institutions (Hernandez, 2000). Furthermore, Latino students who have representative groups to join may feel less socially isolated and less culturally alienated (Fuertes & Sedlacek, 1993; Hernandez, 2002).

Based on this limited amount of research, there seems to be no direct link between Latino student involvement in ethnic student organizations and academic success. The evidence seems to support the overall benefits of involvement in student organizations and activities, albeit in mainstream student groups.

Colleges and universities should ensure that Latino students have multiple options for on-campus involvement opportunities that reflect the many differences in students' background characteristics and level of ethnic or racial identity. Institutions should not assume that a Latino student will automatically want to be involved in a Latino-based student organization. Rather, student affairs practitioners should encourage active participation in a full range of cocurricular activities such as leadership development programs, community/service-learning, student government, pre-professional and honor societies, academic and departmental student clubs, athletics or recreational sports, as well as participation in the fine and performing arts, to name a few. Additionally, institutional support should be provided for the creation and development of Latino student clubs and organizations in order to provide a venue for Latino students who will find a sense of belonging in these type of organizations.

SOCIO-CULTURAL FACTORS

Socio-cultural factors are defined as multiple forces that can shape the personal and environmental experiences of Latino college students and includes various aspects of identity development. Although it is unclear what role ethnic and cultural influences play in the psychosocial development of students of color (Cheatham, 1996), "it is certain that the characteristics that distinguish ethnic minority students from their counterparts must be taken into account in student development conceptualizations" (p. 211). In addition to dealing with issues about racial, ethnic, and gender identity, Latino students may experience their multiple identities within the dimensions of cultural influences, particularly through the influence exerted by their community of origin and their religious or spiritual background.

The following sociocultural factors were identified for consideration: immigrant status, ethnic identity, gender roles, community orientation, and the role of religion.

Immigrant Status

The Latino experience in the United States has been profoundly shaped by immigration. The vast majority of Latinos are either immigrants or the children of immigrants (Suarez-Orozco & Paez, 2002). However, one should not assume that all Latino students come from immigrant households, indeed many Latinos, particularly in the southwest, have been in the United States for generations. In a study which examined the extent of immigrants' participation in U.S. higher education, Rooney (2002) reported that American-born children of Latino immigrants fared·better than their foreign-born Latino peers. Among American-born Latino high school graduates in the 18-to-24-age range, 42% were attending college—a rate similar to that of non-Hispanic White Americans. Only 25% of foreign-born Latinos in this age group were enrolled in an undergraduate institution.

How might the immigrant status of a Latino family influence their educational expectations, particularly as it relates to higher education? What role does education play for "getting ahead"? Do immigrant students outperform their non-immigrant cohorts? If so, does retention influence this phenomenon?

Suarez-Orozco's (1991) ethnographic research among Central American immigrants reported that their adaptive strategies to schooling are quite different from that of minorities with a long history of degradation by the dominant group. Suarez-Orozco also found that Central American immigrants developed a dual frame of reference in which they evaluated their current situation with their anticipated future. There was a clear belief in better opportunities here in the host country than back home and this helped them to face and interpret their current conditions.

Matute-Bianchi's (1991) fieldwork in a California community revealed a relationship between academic performance and students' perceptions of ethnic identities. Matute-Bianchi found that more recent Mexican immigrants, as well as the descendants of Mexican immigrants who maintain a separate identity as *Mexicanos,* tend to persist in school and in many cases outperformed the nonimmigrant Chicano students.

Suarez-Orozco and Matute-Bianchi's studies in part are based on the work of John U. Ogbu (1991) who reported that differences in academic success between minorities can be explained by the nature of their belief system, or their "cultural model" (p. 7). The cultural model guides these groups in understanding how their society works and of their place in that working order. Within the context of education, cultural models coexist with majority and other minority groups' cultural models and as such help provide a framework for interpreting educational events, situations and experiences. According to Ogbu (1991) immigrant minorities tend to interpret economic, political, and social barriers as temporary problems that in time can be overcome. Furthermore, Ogbu believes this group has a positive dual frame of reference that allows them to maintain an optimistic view of their future by comparing their present situation with their former situation "back home" (p. 11).

Although most of these research studies were conducted on elementary and high school students, their results imply that differences exist in educational aspirations and accomplishments of Latino immigrants and native-born Latinos. Additional research is needed to determine if these differences exist among college students. It would be useful to understand what meaning Latino immigrants and native-born Latino students give to their educational expectations and experiences in order to determine if differences exist.

The challenge for institutions to understand the immigrant status of U.S. born and foreign-born Latinos is evident. Many times, the immigrant status of an individual is invisible to the campus community; educators must take a proactive role to further understand the educational experience of U.S.-born as well as foreign-born Latinos.

Ethnic Identity Development

Ethnic identity refers to "one's knowledge of personal ownership or membership in the ethnic group, and the correlated knowledge, understanding, values, behaviors, and proud feelings that are direct implications of that ownership" (Casas & Pytluk, 1995, p. 159). Ethnic identity is an important domain of the self-concept, similar to the multiple social identities that people possess (Bernal, Knight, Garza, Ocampo, & Cota, 1990). Ethnic identity development can help practitioners understand the developmental process of Latino students (Torres, 2003).

Quevedo-Garcia (1987) suggested that a major developmental challenges faced by many Latino college students is the conflict resulting from the need to establish their personal identity within the framework of their ethnic heritage as well as within the more dominant American culture. Casas and Pytluk (1995) mention ethnic identity development as a developing socialization process, that must take into account the effects of interaction with the dominant group; as such, Latino ethnic identity "is defined and formulated not only by their own cultural environment but also by both the dominant cultural group with which it is in contact and the nature of ethnic group/dominant group interaction" (p. 160). In a recent publication, Torres (2003) indicated that the following conditions influenced the starting point of where Latino students situated or placed their identity: their generational status within the United States, the environment of where they grew up, and their self-perception. As such, choosing between assimilation—relinquishing one's cultural identity, or integration—becoming an integral part of the larger society while maintaining one's cultural identity, is shaped by multidimensional factors.

Many Latino students are bilingual and bicultural and may view their identity as both Latino and American. A California study (Hayes-Bautista, Hurtado, Valdez, & Hernandez, 1992) found that by the second and third generation, Latinos saw themselves as "American" while maintaining their Latino identity—they saw no contradiction between the two. Effective adjustment often requires "an acceptance of both worlds as well as skills to live among and interact with both Hispanic and American cultural groups" (Szapocznik, Kurtines, & Fernandez, 1980, p. 354).

Phinney (1993) suggested that the college years are particularly important for identity development. It seems that for many Latino students the development of their ethnic identity is associated with their overall identity development. This may indeed influence their psychosocial development and perhaps impact their college experience in ways, which colleges and universities must take into account. Campuses need to provide adequate services for Latino students who are dealing with such complex issues and practitioners must demonstrate cultural sensitivity when dealing with these concerns.

Gender Roles

Latino culture often transmits a definition of gender-related roles and behaviors. Traditional stereotypes describe men as being strong and in control; while women have been described as submissive and lacking in power (Marin & VanOss-Marin, 1991). However, it is important to note that these male-female relationships have not been fully documented (Marin & VanOss-Marin, 1991).

De Leon (1995) conducted a cross-cultural study that examined gender role identities of male and female college students from four ethnic/racial groups. The researcher reported that "in spite of mixed results, what appears to be fairly consistent in the literature is that there are differences in sex role orientation that can be attributed to race/ethnicity, gender, and social class for the cultural groups included in this study" (p. 247). Current research on gender studies "view Latino families as a relational unit where power between men and women is negotiated . . ." (Hurtado, 1995, p. 56).

Latinas now outnumber Latino men in college; additionally, from 1985 to 1991, the number of bachelor's degrees earned by Latinas grew faster than the number awarded to Latino men (O'Brien, 1993). This suggests that there are gender differences in the college completion rates among Latinos and Latinas (Haro, Rodriguez, & Gonzales, 1994). Does this imply that the educational experiences of Latino men and women differ?

It should be noted that the current trend on feminist research on Latino families has shifted from examining Latinas in their sex roles to studying gendered institutions (Zinn, 1995). This shift recognizes that Latinas are constrained by the social structures of class and race inequalities; "this ubiquitous gender order produces Latino family arrangements that constrain women in particular ways" (p. 182).

Gender differences among Latino men and women is an area that needs additional research in order to understand how differences and similarities impact their collegiate experience. Traditional social science literature often portrays a stereotypical view of gender roles—an experience that may hold true for many Latinos—yet there is evidence that these barriers may not be representative for all. As such it is incumbent that researchers as well as institutions be sensitive to these issues in order to identify and understand the ways in which Latino men and women make meaning of their experiences in college.

Community Orientation

"The college is no longer the only environmental context within which the student functions" (Garland & Grace, 1993, p. 86). This statement is particularly true for Latino college students who often view themselves as representatives of their family and their community (Grossman, 1984); as such community orientation must be considered when examining Latino college student retention. Community can take on multiple meanings and may be defined as more than the physical proximity of where one lives or grew up. "It is not just a collection of people living in proximity, but a kind of extended family connected by self-help organizations, places of worship, neighborhood networks, community centers, business associations, educational centers, and artistic establishments" (Heyck, 1994, p. 162).

Ethnicity can also serve as a way to connect and imagine the concept of community. For many Latinos, "the term 'community' has little meaning without the qualifiers 'Mexican,' 'Puerto Rican,' 'Cuban,' or 'Dominican.' With these adjectives, the term 'community' comes to life. It connotes pride in the barrio and its ethnic heritage, and solidarity in tacking community issues and problems"

(Heyck, 1994, p. 163). For Latinos, these communities bear the regional markings that often shape their lives and their process of thought. Additionally, social scientists have reported that children of Latino ancestry who grow up in Latino communities maintain close ties with their cultural heritage (Wilkinson, 1993).

One aspect of community orientation is involvement in off-campus community organizations. As such it is not uncommon for Latino students to be actively engaged in community service be it as tutors, coaching after school sports, teaching English to recent immigrants, or volunteering at their local church or parish. These are but a few examples of the many ways that Latino students volunteer and stay connected with their communities.

Specifically, first generation college students in particular may be more inclined to sustain and fulfill communal ties and responsibilities (Flacks & Thomas, 1997). For many Latino students, particularly commuter students, membership in external communities may play a vital role in persistence (Cabrera, Castaneda, Nora, & Hengstler, 1992). For persons whose institutional commitments are weak the impact of those communities may make the difference between persistence and departure (Tinto, 1993). However, it is important to note that membership in external communities can result in positive or negative outcomes. When the values of the external communities are supportive to the goals of a college education, they may aid persistence (Cabrera et al., 1992). When they oppose them, the reverse may apply (Tinto, 1993). This occurs because of the ways in which "external obligations limit one's ability to meet the demands of college. Such obligations serve, in effect, to pull one away from participation in local communities of the college" (Tinto, 1993, p. 63). Whether the external obligations of peers and community are an asset or a detriment to Latino students will require further research. However, higher education needs to take into account the importance of Latino college student's community orientation while participating within the academy. Campuses can initiate various events within the community itself to recognize their support or bring the community to the campus by holding social events and college fairs to highlight the institution's services and commitment to the Latino community.

The Role of Religion

The significance of religion to the Latino community cannot be over looked when examining their participation in academe. Minority students in the Phinney and Alipuria (1990) study of ethnic identity rated ethnicity as equal in importance to religion. Religion is often associated with family traditions and cultural celebrations (Heyck, 1994). However, it should also be noted that Latino religious practices and beliefs are not homogeneous; rather they express the great diversity found among Latinos (Heyck, 1994).

Many Latinos, whether they are Catholic, Protestant, followers of the African deities, or members of various sects, believe in some sort of spirituality. As such spiritual matters often weave themselves into the daily lives and decisions made by Latino college students. Being religious or spiritual is not always equivalent with regular church attendance or active participation in religious activities, rather it implies belonging to a religious people (Heyck, 1994). Villafane (1994) in describing the characteristics of "Hispanic spirituality" wrote:

> Hispanic spirituality is the expression of a complex cultural phenomenon. Hispanic spirituality, thus, must be seen as part and parcel of the creative synthesis of the Hispanic value structure and orientation that has emerged from the three root streams that inform its cultural traits and personality. Hispanic spirituality responds to the Spanish, Amerindian, and African makeup of its "soul" (p. 153).

A recent study reported that Latino immigrants who attend church are more likely to do well in school and reverse high dropout rates, particularly in impoverished school districts (Witham, 2003). The report, *Religion Matters* analyzed about 7,000 Latino students and parents and indicated that religion plays an important role for Latinos because it provides important educational opportunities outside of school and because the church environment reinforces the importance of learning and discipline (as cited in Witham, 2003).

The role of religion and spirituality is an area that needs further research in order to understand how spiritual matters are utilized to make meaning of the collegiate experience and whether spirituality and religion impact Latino student success or hinder the retention persistence of this community. Religion and spirituality are often intertwined with cultural and familial affiliations and as such may play a pivotal role in the lives of Latino college students.

CONCLUSION

The leaking educational pipeline that Latino college students are falling through is a growing concern for higher education. The overall growth in the Latino population has led to increased college enrollment, however, post-secondary institutions must address the persistence issues that affect Latino students and respond with effective intervention strategies.

It should be understood that retention is a complex and multidimensional issue, as such, it cannot be quickly or easily understood, and likewise, there are no simple solutions. Latino college students, not unlike other students, experience college in multiple ways and their decisions to sustain their college enrollment is influenced and shaped by a variety of factors.

Latinos are a highly heterogeneous group that defy easy generalizations (Suarez-Orozco & Paez, 2002). Given this heterogeneity and the diverse experiences and distinctive histories of each Latino group in the United States, there are no "cookie-cutter" approaches to increase access and retention rates of the Latino community. Rather, educators must take into account the regional, generational, ethnic, and gender dimension, to name a few, that this population brings with them when they enter our institutions. It is also important to recognize that Latino college student retention begins well before students enter post-secondary education, and is further influenced after enrolling in college.

This chapter examined some of the personal, involvement, environmental, and socio-cultural influences that impact Latino student retention in order to brush the surface of the retention literature and to highlight factors that affect Latino college student's persistence and retention, as well as providing recommendations for higher education institutions. In order to close the retention gap further research on Latino college students is needed to increase our understanding of this leaking educational pipeline.

REFERENCES

Abrahamowicz, D. (1988). College involvement, perceptions, and satisfaction: A study of membership in student organizations. *Journal of College Student Development, 29,* 233-238.

Alonso-Zaldivar, R. (2003, March 11). For millions of Latinos, race is a flexible concept. *The Los Angeles Times,* pp. A1, A15.

Arbona, C., & Novy, D. M. (1990). Noncognitive dimensions as predictors of college success among Black, Mexican-American, and White students. *Journal of College Student Development, 31,* 415-422.

Arellano, A. R., & Padilla, A. M. (1996). Academic invulnerability among a select group of Latino university students. *Hispanic Journal of Behavior Sciences, 18,* 485-507.

Astin, A. W. (1982). *Minorities in American higher education: Recent trends, current prospects, and recommendations.* San Francisco: Jossey-Bass.

Astin, A. W. (1984). Student involvement: A developmental theory for higher education. *Journal of College Student Personnel, 25,* 297-308.

Astin, A. W. (1993). *What matters in college? Four critical years revisited.* San Francisco: Jossey-Bass.

Attinasi, L. C., Jr. (1992). Rethinking the study of the outcomes of college attendance. *Journal of College Student Development, 33,* 61-70.

Banning, J. H. (1989). Impact of college environments on freshmen students. In M. L. Upcraft, J. N. Gardner, & Associates, *The freshman year experience: Helping students survive and succeed in college* (pp. 53-62). San Francisco: Jossey-Bass.

Bean, J. P. (1982). Student attrition, intentions and confidence: Interaction effects in a path model. *Research in Higher Education, 17,* 291-319.

Bennett, C., & Okinaka, A. M. (1990). Factors related to persistence among Asian, Black, Hispanic, and White undergraduates at a predominantly White University: Comparison between first and fourth year cohorts. *The Urban Review, 22*(1), 33-60.

Bernal, M. E., Knight, G. P., Garza, C. A., Ocampo, K. A., & Cota, M. K. (1990). The development of ethnic identity in Mexican American children. *Hispanic Journal of Behavioral Sciences, 12,* 3-24.

Cabrera, A. F. (1992). The role of finances in the persistence process: A structural model. *Research in Higher Education, 33,* 571-594.

Cabrera, A. F., Castaneda, M. B., Nora, A., & Hengstler, D. (1992). The convergence between two theories of college persistence. *Journal of Higher Education, 63,* 143-164.

Cabrera, A. F., Nora, A., & Castaneda, M. B. (1993). College Persistence: Structural equation modeling test of an integrated model of student retention. *Journal of Higher Education, 64,* 123-139.

Canabal, M. E. (1995). Hispanic and non-Hispanic White students attending institutions of higher education in Illinois: Implications for retention. *College Student Journal, 29,* 157-167.

Casas, J. M., & Pytluk, S. D. (1995). Hispanic identity development: Implications for research and practice. In J. G. Ponterotto, J. M. Casas, L. A. Suzuki, & C. M. Alexander (Eds.), *Handbook of multicultural counseling* (pp. 155-180). Thousand Oaks, CA: Sage.

Cheatham, H. E. (1996). Identity development in a pluralistic society. In F. K. Stage, G. L. Anaya, J. P. Bean, D. Hossler, & G. D. Kuh (Eds.), *College students: The evolving nature of research* (pp. 205-216). Needham Heights, MA: Simon & Schuster Custom Publishing.

Chilman, C. S. (1993). Hispanic families in the United States. In H. P. McAdoo (Ed.), *Family ethnicity: Strength in diversity* (pp. 141-163). Newbury Park, CA: Sage.

Conyne, R. K., & Clack, R. J. (1981). *Environmental assessment and design: A new tool for the applied behavioral scientist.* New York: Praeger.

De Leon, B. (1995). Sex role identity among college students. In A. M. Padilla (Ed.), *Hispanic psychology: Critical issues in theory and research* (pp. 245-256). Thousand Oaks, CA: Sage.

Duran, R. (1994). Hispanic student achievement. In M. J. Justiz, R. Wilson, & L. G. Bjork (Eds.), *Minorities in higher education* (pp. 151-172). Phoenix, AZ: Oryx Press.

Flacks, R., & Thomas, S. L. (1997). *College students in the nineties: Report on a project in progress.* Unpublished manuscript, University of California at Santa Barbara.

Flores, J. L. (April, 1992). *Persisting Hispanic American college students: Characteristics that lead to baccalaureate degree completion.* Paper presented at the annual meeting of the American Educational Research Association, San Francisco, CA. (ERIC Document Reproduction Service No. ED 345 609).

Fuertes, J. N., & Sedlacek, W. E. (1993). Barriers to the leadership development of Hispanics in higher education. *NASPA Journal, 30,* 277-283.

Gandara, P., & Lopez, E. (1998). Latino students and college entrance exams: How much do they really count? *Hispanic Journal of Behavioral Sciences, 20,* 17-38.

Garland, P. H., & Grace, T. W. (1993). *New perspectives for student affairs professionals: Evolving realities, responsibilities and roles.* ASHE-ERIC Higher Education Report No. 7. Washington, DC: The George Washington University, School of Education and Human Development.

Goldberg, C. (January 30, 1997). *Hispanic households struggle as poorest of U.S. poor.* [On-line]. Available 187-L@CMSA.BERKELEY.EDU

Grossman, H. (1984). *Educating Hispanic students.* Springfield, IL: Charles C. Thomas.

Haro, R. P., Rodriguez, G., Jr., & Gonzales, J. L., Jr. (1994). *Latino persistence in higher education: A 1994 survey of University of California and California State University Chicano/Latino students.* San Francisco: Latino Issues Forum.

Harvey, W. B. (2001). *Eighteenth annual status report on minorities in higher education.* Washington, DC: American Council on Education.

Hayes-Bautista, D. E., Hurtado, A., Valdez, R. B., & Hernandez, A. C. R. (1992). *No longer a minority: Latinos and social policy in California.* Los Angeles: UCLA Chicano Studies Research Center.

Helm, E. G., Sedlacek, W. E., & Prieto, D. O. (1998). The relationship between attitudes toward diversity and overall satisfaction of university students by race. *Journal of College Counseling, 1,* 111-120.

Hernandez, J. C. (2000). Understanding the retention of Latino college students. *Journal of College Student Development, 41,* 575-588.

Hernandez, J. C. (2002). A qualitative exploration of the first-year experience of Latino college students. *NASPA Journal, 40,* 69-84.

Heyck, D. L. (1994). *Barrios and borderlands: Cultures of Latinos and Latinas in the United States.* New York: Routledge.

Hurtado, A. (1995). Variations, combinations, and evaluations: Latino families in the United States. In R. E. Zambrana (Ed.), *Understanding Latino families: Scholarship, policy, and practice* (pp. 40-61). Thousand Oaks, CA: Sage.

Hurtado, A., Hayes-Bautista, D. E., Valdez, R. B., & Hernandez, A. C. R. (1992). *Redefining California: Latino social engagement in a multicultural society.* Los Angeles: UCLA Chicano Studies Research Center.

Hurtado, S. (1994). The institutional climate for talented Latino students. *Research in Higher Education, 35,* 210-241.

Hurtado, S. (2000). The campus racial climate. In C. Turner, M. Garcia, A. Nora, & L. I. Rendon (Eds.), *Racial and ethnic diversity in higher education* (pp. 485-506). Needham Heights, MA: Simon & Schuster Custom Publishing.

Hurtado, S., Carter, D. F., & Spuler, A. (1996). Latino student transition to college: Assessing difficulties and factors in successful college adjustment. *Research in Higher Education, 37,* 135-157.

Hurtado, S., Milem, J. F., Clayton-Pedersen, A. R., & Allen, W. R. (1998). Enhancing campus climates for racial/ethnic diversity: Educational policy and practice. *The Review of Higher Education, 21,* 279-302.

Jones-Correa, M., & Leal, D. L. (1996). Becoming "Hispanic": Secondary panethnic identification among Latin American-origin populations in the United States. *Hispanic Journal of Behavioral Sciences, 18,* 214-254.

Justiz, M. J., & Rendon, L. I. (1989). Hispanic students. In M. L. Upcraft, J. N. Gardner, & Associates, *The freshman year experience: Helping students survive and succeed in college* (pp. 261-276). San Francisco: Jossey-Bass.

Kuh, G. D., Schuh, J. H., Whitt, E. J., & Associates (1991). *Involving colleges.* San Francisco: Jossey-Bass.

Lane, K. (2002). Special report: Hispanic focus—Taking it to the next level. *Black Issues in Higher Education, 19,* 18-21.

Llagas, C., & Synder, T. D. (2003). *Status and trends in the education of Hispanics.* Washington, DC: U.S. Department of Education, National Center for Education Statistics.

Mallette, B. I., & Cabrera, A. F. (1991). Determinants of withdrawal behavior: An exploratory study. *Research in Higher Education, 32,* 179-194.

Marin, G., & VanOss-Marin, B. (1991). *Research with Hispanic populations* (Applied Social Science Research Methods Series, vol. 23). Newbury Park, CA: Sage.

Matute-Bianchi, M. E. (1991). Situational ethnicity and patterns of school performance among immigrant and nonimmigrant Mexican-descent students. In M. A. Gibson &

J. U. Ogbu (Eds.), *Minority status and schooling: A comparative study of immigrant and involuntary minorities* (pp. 205-247). New York: Garland Publishing.

Mayo, J. R., Murguia, E., & Padilla, R. V. (1995). Social integration and academic performance among minority university students. *Journal of College Student Development, 36,* 542-552.

Moore, L. V., & Upcraft, M. L. (1990). Theory in student affairs: Evolving perspectives. In L. Moore (Ed.), *Evolving theoretical perspectives on students* (New Directions for Student Services No. 51) (pp. 25-36). San Francisco: Jossey-Bass.

Murguia, E., Padilla, R. V., & Pavel, M. (1991). Ethnicity and the concept of social integration in Tinto's model of institutional departure. *Journal of College Student Development, 32,* 433-439.

Nora, A. (1990). Campus-based aid programs as determinants of retention among Hispanic community college students. *Journal of Higher Education, 61,* 312-331.

Nora, A. (2001). How minority students finance their higher education. *ERIC Clearinghouse on Urban Education, EDO UD-01-0.*

O'Brien, E. (1993). *Latinos in higher education* (Research Briefs, Vol. 4, No. 4). Washington, DC: American Council on Education.

Ogbu, J. U. (1991). Immigrant and involuntary minorities in comparative perspectives. In M. A. Gibson & J. U. Ogbu (Eds.), *Minority status and schooling: A comparative study of immigrant and involuntary minorities* (pp. 3-33). New York: Garland Publishing.

Padilla, R. V. (1991). Assessing heuristic knowledge to enhance college students' success. In G. D. Keller, J. R. Deneen, & R. J. Magallan (Eds.), *Assessment and access: Hispanics in higher education* (pp. 81-92). Albany: State University of New York Press.

Padilla, R. V., & Pavel, D. M. (1994). Using qualitative research to assess advising. *The Review of Higher Education, 17,* 143-159.

Padilla, R. V., Trevino, J., Gonzalez, K., & Trevino, J. (1997). Developing local models of minority student success in college. *Journal of College Student Development, 38,* 125-135.

Parker-Redmond, S. (1990). Mentoring and cultural diversity in academic settings. *American Behavioral Scientist, 34,* 188-200.

Pascarella, E. T., & Terenzini, P. T. (1991). *How college affects students.* San Francisco: Jossey-Bass.

Phinney, J. S. (1993). A three-stage model of ethnic identity development in adolescence. In M. E. Bernal and G. P. Knight (Eds.), *Ethnic identity: Formation and transmission among Hispanics and other minorities* (pp. 61-79). Albany: State University of New York Press.

Phinney, J. S., & Alipuria, L. L. (1990). Ethnic identity in college students from four ethnic groups. *Journal of Adolescence, 13,* 171-183.

Quevedo-Garcia, E. L. (1987). Facilitating the development of Hispanic college students. In D. J. Wright (Ed.), *Responding to the needs of today's minority students* (pp. 49-63). San Francisco: Jossey-Bass.

Quintana, S. M., Vogel, M. C., & Ybarra, V. C. (1991). Meta-analysis of Latino students' adjustment in higher education. *Hispanic Journal of Behavioral Science, 13,* 155-168.

Rendon, L. I. (1994). Validating culturally diverse students: Toward a new model of learning and student development. *Innovative Higher Education, 19,* 33-51.

Rendon, L. I., & Taylor, M. T. (1990). Hispanic students: Action for access. *Community, Technical, and Junior College Journal, 60*(3), 18-23.

Rodriguez, N. (1996). Predicting the academic success of Mexican American and White college students. *Hispanic Journal of Behavioral Sciences, 18*, 329-342.

Rooney, G. D. (1985). Minority students' involvement in minority student organizations: An exploratory study. *Journal of College Student Personnel, 26*, 450-456.

Rooney, M. (2002, September 6). *Report on Latino-American students notes high college-enrollment rate, lower graduation rate.* Retrieved September 9, 2002 from http://chronicle.com/daily/2002/09/2002090604n.htm

Schlossberg, N. K., Lynch, A. Q., & Chickering, A. W, (1989). *Improving higher education environments for adults: Response programs and services from entry to departure.* San Francisco: Jossey-Bass.

Schuh, J. H., & Kuh, G. D. (1984). Faculty interaction with students in residence halls. *Journal of College Student Development, 25*, 519-528.

Sedlacek, W. E. (1989). Noncognitive indicators of student success. *Journal of College Admissions, 1*(125), 2-9.

Sedlacek, W. E., Longerbeam, S. L., & Alatorre, H. A. (2003). *In their own voices: What do the data on Latino students mean to them?* (Research Report #5-02). College Park, MD: University of Maryland Counseling Center.

Suarez-Orozco, M. M. (1991). Immigrant adaptation to schooling: A Hispanic case. In M. A. Gibson & J. U. Ogbu (Eds.), *Minority status and schooling: A comparative study of immigrant and involuntary minorities* (pp. 37-61). New York: Garland Publishing.

Suarez-Orozco, M. M., & Paez, M. M. (2002). Introduction: The research agenda. In M. M. Suarez-Orozco & M. M. Paez (Eds.), *Latinos: Remaking America* (pp. 1-37). Berkeley, CA: University of California Press.

Szapocznik, J., Kurtines, W., & Fernandez, T. (1980). Bicultural involvement and adjustment in Hispanic-American youth. *International Journal of Intercultural Relationships, 4*, 353-365.

Terenzini, P. T., Rendon, L. I., Upcraft, M. L., Millar, S. B., Allison, K. W., Gregg, P. L., & Romero, J. (1994). The transition to college: Diverse students, diverse stories. *Research in Higher Education, 35*, 57-73.

Tinto, V. (1993). *Leaving college: Rethinking the causes and cures of student attrition* (2nd ed.). Chicago: University of Chicago Press.

Torres, V. (2003). Influences on ethnic identity development of Latino college students in the first two years of college. *Journal of College Student Development, 44*, 532-547.

Tracey, T. J., & Sedlacek, W. E. (1984). Noncognitive variables in predicting academic success by race. *Measurement and Evaluation in Counseling and Development, 16*, 171-178.

Tracey, T. J., & Sedlacek, W. E. (1985). The relationship of noncognitive variables to academic success: A longitudinal comparison by race. *Journal of College Student Personnel, 26*, 405-410.

Tracey, T. J., & Sedlacek, W. E. (1987). Prediction of college graduation using noncognitive variables by race. *Measurement and Evaluation in Counseling and Development, 19*, 177-184.

Trevino, J. G. (1992). *Participating in ethnic/racial student organizations.* Unpublished doctoral dissertation, University of California, Los Angeles.

Valdes, G. (1996). *Con respeto: Bridging the distances between culturally diverse families and schools: An ethnographic portrait.* New York: Teachers College Press.

Vega, W. A. (1995). The study of Latino families: A point of departure. In R. E. Zambrana (Ed.), *Understanding Latino families: Scholarship, policy, and practice* (pp. 3-17). Thousand Oaks, CA: Sage.

Villafane, E. (1994). The liberating spirit: Toward a Hispanic American Pentecostal social ethic. In D. L. Heyck (Ed.), *Barrios and borderlands: Cultures of Latinos and Latinas in the United States* (pp. 152-158). New York: Routledge.

Witham, L. (2003). *Churchgoing Hispanics do better at school, study finds.* Retrieved on January 30, 2003 from http://www.washtimes.com/national/20030128-30457960.htm

Wilkinson, D. (1993). Family ethnicity in America. In H. P. McAdoo (Ed.), *Family ethnicity: Strength in diversity* (pp. 15-59). Newbury Park, CA: Sage.

Zinn, M. B. (1995). Social science theorizing for Latino families in the age of diversity. In R. E. Zambrana (Ed.), *Understanding Latino families: Scholarship, policy, and practice* (pp. 177-189). Thousand Oaks, CA: Sage.

CHAPTER 7

Stopping Out and Persisting: Experiences of Latino Undergraduates

Martha Zurita

[Students] who come from households where, you know, their parents are college educated and they have good jobs and if [the students] ever need something, they would always have somewhere to go and someone to turn to for that little extra money. . . . It made me feel like I really have to stay [enrolled] here [at the university] and I really have to work hard because I want to be at that point. I want to be able to one day provide for my kids or if they ever needed something like that—they could always turn to me.

Armando, Latino stopout

This study examines the experiences that 10 Latino recent undergraduate students reported having at a large midwestern university. Five persisted through graduation, and five stopped out. Both groups described similar home environments, a lack of social integration, and feelings of academic unpreparedness. Differences among groups were academic difficulties, home-to-school transition, high school segregation, anticipatory socialization, first contact with the university, and education and career goals. The study's implications suggest several approaches to increasing Latino persistence.

From 1990 to 2000, the Latino population grew by a significant rate (58%) and became the nation's largest "minority" group. This tremendous growth and significant-sized population has major implications across all sectors of society. Despite their increasing presence in the U.S. landscape, however, their educational attainment levels are relatively low. In 2001, for example, Latinos were well behind other groups in terms of their high school completion rates. While 93% of Whites ages 25 to 29 had completed high school, a mere 63% of Latinos had done so (NCES, 2002). A more dismal picture is painted when examining the college graduation rates. In 2001, one of every three (33.0%) Whites ages 25 to 29 held at least a bachelor's degree. Approximately one of every nine (11.1%) Latinos had similar educational attainment levels (NCES, 2002). Clearly, for a population growing so rapidly, Latinos are not being educated at rates necessary for an economically healthy nation, particularly at the higher education level.

Although the school dropout problem starts much earlier, this chapter focuses on retention through college of Latino undergraduates. Literature on Latino attrition points primarily to financial difficulties (Arbona & Novy, 1991; Haro, 1983; Olivas, 1986a) and academic issues (Chacón, Cohen, & Strover, 1986; Fields, 1988; Fiske, 1988; Justiz, 1994; Ramirez, 1987; Rendón & Nora, 1988). One large research university took direct action to reverse this trend by providing race-based, need-based scholarship for high-achieving students of color, still, between the fall of 1993 when these recipients were enrolled and the fall of 1994, approximately 20% withdrew—35% were Latino. There seemed to be no apparent explanations for this pattern, since the two main reasons for Latino attrition (financial and academic issues) were, for the most part, eliminated. Although this pattern was manifest in varying degrees for all racial/ethnic groups who were recipients, this study examines the Latino withdrawals.

Based on interviews with students, I compare the experiences of five Latino students who stopped out[1] from a large research university with five Latino students who graduated from the same university after continuous enrollment from entrance to graduation. In addition to focusing on reasons for the withdrawal of the stop-out group, this study describes the contemporary experiences of Latino college students, as reported by these 10, and the impact that differences between their home culture and university culture has on their academic achievement.

Research Context

The literature focusing on Latino students reports four primary factors in their attrition: academic, financial, personal, and institutional issues. As a result of the Latino population's lower educational and occupational levels as a group, the financial burden of college is a larger problem for Latino families (Arbona & Novy, 1991; Haro, 1983; Olivas, 1986b). In 1999, while 49.3% of non-Hispanic white full-time, year-round workers earned $35,000 or more annually, 23.3% of Latino full-time, year-round workers earned similar amounts (Therrien &

---

[1] Not to be confused with a "drop-out," a "stop-out" is someone who has left the college or university and has either transferred to another institution or returned to the same one (Astin, 1977). Stopping out is discussed in greater detail during the section on methodology.

Ramirez, 2000). Countering these findings, however, is Tinto's (1987) report on all college students that financial difficulties for college students in general are "not significant in and of themselves" (p. 80).

Tinto (1987) also sees low academic achievement as weighing relatively less in withdrawal decisions. "Less than 15 percent of all institutional departures on the national average take the form of academic dismissal," he observed (p. 53). However, this figure does not account for those who have reason to believe that they are failing academically and withdraw, even though the university has taken no action against them. Again, Tinto's findings [based on American undergraduates as a group] are contradicted by ethnic-specific studies. Ramírez (1987) and Rendón and Nora (1988) report that poor academic performance is an important factor in the attrition of Latinos. In addition, Smedley, Myers, and Harrell (1993) found that "conflicts between academic expectations and questions about readiness to compete academically are an important additional source of academic vulnerability for [minority] students," which includes African-American and Latino students. As such, academic issues manifest themselves not only in actual grades, but also in additional stress.

The third factor impacting Latino college students is personal difficulties, such as those related to their family and/or to their lack of career and educational goals (Chacón et al., 1986; Fields, 1988; Fiske, 1988). Such circumstances are a source of stress for students and also form barriers to integration into the college culture (Tinto, 1987). Experiencing additional stress as a result of their family obligations not only impairs students' abilities to persevere toward graduation but also does not allow students to become completely disassociated from their home community, a situation that Tinto (1987) identifies as imperative for integration into the college environment and college success. Again, researchers of ethnic populations argue that complete disassociation from family is not necessary for integration (Hurtado & Carter, 1997; Hurtado, Carter, & Spuler, 1996) and disagree with Tinto's overall concept of integration as it applies to students of color at predominantly white colleges (Tierney, 1992).

The lack of strong educational and career goals, often a function of family background, is another barrier to retention because "the higher the level of one's educational or occupational goals, the greater the likelihood of college completion" (Tinto, 1987, p. 40). Similarly, Astin (1975) finds that first-year students who drop out usually have low aspirations. Ramírez (1987) reports that many Latino college students do not have compatible, well-established personal and career goals which they will pursue throughout their college years. Many Latinos also do not have clear educational goals, illustrated by the fact that many Latinos' first contact with the university or college is the post-acceptance freshmen orientation program (Ramírez, 1987). As a result, they are more likely to experience mismatches between themselves and the universities since they have often already agreed to attend the universities without even visiting the campus (Tinto, 1987).

The final major category of difficulties experienced by Latino college students is institution-related issues, such as student integration into the college culture. Hurtado and Carter's (1997) findings suggest that the college environment has more to do with the transition to college than with students' background characteristics. The general research consensus is that student-faculty and student-student interactions are crucial for student integration and college persistence (Davis & Murrell, 1993). Student-student interactions outside of the classroom, for example, have been found to have a strong relationship with students' sense of belonging in college, particularly during the second year (Hurtado & Carter, 1997). Latinos may face difficulties with student-student interactions because some view themselves as having relatively fewer options than Caucasian students, particularly at predominantly white institutions (Fiske, 1988). Similarly, many Latinos do not interact with faculty outside of the classroom (McJamerson & Larke, 1989) and consequently do not receive the benefits that result from student-faculty contact. As a result of lower levels of student-faculty and student-student interactions, Latinos experience fewer opportunities to become integrated into the college culture.

Institutional factors contribute to the students' perceptions that the university is a hostile environment, thus resulting in increased feelings of isolation (Justiz, 1994) that interfere with their academic and personal achievement. Although such feelings may be subjective—a function of how these students perceive and interpret the university—and not how the university may actually be structured, Tinto (1987) points out this reality: "What one thinks is real, has real consequences" (p. 127).

The previous bodies of research have helped further our understanding of the factors involved in Latino attrition. What has been missing from the literature, however, has been the actual voices of the Latino college students describing in their own words their experiences in American colleges and universities in recent years, which this study attempts to provide.

Methodology

The university selected for the study is its state's flagship public university. It is a major research university with a history of more than 125 years. The university is highly selective and academically challenging. According to the university, the "average student" in a typical freshman class was in the top 10% of his or her graduating class and scored in the top 10% of those taking the national ACT and SAT college entrance exams. At the time of the study, the university had a total population of approximately 36,000 students, approximately 2% of whom were Latino. Many of the Latino and African-American students attending the university are residents of a major city and its neighboring suburbs less than 130 miles away.

The relationship between the university and its Latino students has been a mixed bag, in that it ebbs and flows with time. In the early 1990s when the participants were enrolled, the university experienced a particularly tumultuous time with Latino students. The students presented the administration with a list of needs after very public demonstrations of their frustration with the university. The students' requests were centered around an improved environment for Latinos such as culturally-sensitive policies and practices, more Latino faculty, and improved recruitment and retention of Latino students.

The participants in this study were 10 Latino recent undergraduate students. They were also recipients of the University Scholars Program (USP), a pseudonym. Started in the mid-1980s, USP is a need-based scholarship program created to increase the number of African-American, Latino, and/or Native American students at the university. The program has been successfully increasing diversity on campus: it began with 110 freshmen and it currently averages over 500 freshmen scholars. Only students from the target groups who are residents of the state are eligible. The academic criteria for eligibility are: a) a composite ACT score of at least 24 or a combined verbal and quantitative SAT score of 1080 or more; b) a ranking in the upper half of the applicant's high school graduating class; and c) meeting the university's general admission criteria, such as taking mandated sequences of high school courses. The university takes an active role in identifying qualified students by their ACT/SAT scores and encourages them to apply by making them aware that they are eligible for the USP scholarship. The USP meets the students' demonstrated financial needs for a maximum of four years, which includes tuition, fees, room and board, books, and transportation. As a result, students' financial background is not a factor in receiving the scholarship, but it plays a major role in the amount of assistance the students receive, as the scholarship is intended to supplement family resources. Those students who do not have a demonstrated financial need receive a minimum award of $1,000 for the first and second years.

The scholarship program is a relatively large program with more than 1,000 recipients enrolled during the fall of 1993. Of these students, 194 recipients who were enrolled in the fall of 1993 but not in the fall of 1994—approximately 20% of their total scholarship recipients. Of the 194 students not enrolled during the fall of 1994, approximately 35% were Latino. I made attempts to contact all of these students by mail and telephone; but partly because of address changes, only five students responded. I interviewed these five—two women and three men—during the spring of 1997. I contacted by mail scholarship recipients who had graduated after being enrolled in both fall 1993 and fall 1994 and interviewed the first five to respond positively. By coincidence, two of the first five were women and three were men.

The term "stop-out" refers to students who have not maintained continuous enrollment in college. Astin (1977) defines stop-outs as "those who leave college but intend to return to complete their degrees" (p. 107). For the purposes of this study, a stop-out is someone who has left the university and either transferred to another university or returned to the same university at least once, although he or she may have not been enrolled at the time of the interview. Only one of the stop-outs interviewed had actually transferred to another university; the other four had returned to the original university. Again, the "stop-out" category contained students who were enrolled in the fall semester of 1993 but not in the fall of 1994. The category of "persisters" refers to "all students who complete a degree program within a specified time" (Astin, 1977, p. 107). Another important criterion for persisters in this study was that the students must have been continuously enrolled from the first semester of their first year until their last semester (either fall 1993 or fall 1994). I included continuous enrollment as a criterion because the literature indicates that being continuously enrolled increases the likelihood that a student will graduate from college (Astin, 1975; Tinto, 1987).

Once the sample was established, I collected data using one-time semi-structured, in-person interviews. As Fontana and Frey (1994) state, "The question must be asked person-to-person if we want it to be answered fully" (p. 374). Interviews were divided into five major areas drawn from the literature focusing on Latino students: a) differences between students' home and school cultures; b) financial issues; c) academic issues; d) institutional issues; and e) personal issues. The interviews, all tape-recorded with the students' permission, were approximately 60 to 75 minutes long. Each interviewee was assigned a pseudonym when the tape was transcribed. I conducted the interviews on the university campus, at other university campuses, and in students' homes.

I chose interviewing as the main method of data collection because it is "one of the . . . most powerful ways we use to try to understand our fellow human beings" (Fontana & Frey, 1994, p. 361). Furthermore, since much of the Latino retention research utilizes approaches such as surveys, I wanted to give students the opportunity to tell their stories. As Fontana and Frey (1994) state,

> To learn about people we must remember to treat them as people, and they will uncover their lives to us. As long as many researchers continue to treat respondents as unimportant, faceless individuals whose only contribution is to fill one more boxed response, the answers we, as researchers, will get will be commensurable with the questions we ask and with the way we ask them (p. 374).

A limitation of the study was that participants were asked to remember and analyze past events. This retrospection can be viewed as a limitation because the participants may have forgotten events, particularly those that cast an unfavorable light upon them. If this was the case, the prepared questions may have helped minimize lapses in memory. On the other hand, asking students to reflect on past events apparently enabled them to analyze events thoroughly and, as a result, to evaluate more accurately whether or not certain events influenced their overall college experiences.

Another limitation was the selection process. The participants who stopped out were the only five to respond and the persisters were the first to respond positively to my requests for interview. By selecting the first respondents, the process could have eliminated those students who had hesitation about participating, for whatever reason, and those students who had relocated and could not be contacted or did not have sufficient time to respond. Due to the selection process, the stories collected may be skewed.

As a result of the small number of students used in the sample, the study is not generalizable to the larger population of Latino college students. But this fact does not render its findings unimportant. This study's conclusions can offer insight into the current experiences of Latino college students and offer new directions for further investigation.

FINDINGS

I group the findings into two major categories: similarities of and differences between the two groups. Similar factors include: a) the students' home cultures; b) students' perceptions of the dominant university culture; c) financial issues; d) parental support; and e) feelings of being academically unprepared. The differences are: a) home-to-school transitions; b) characteristics of their high schools; c) anticipatory socialization; d) students' initial goals; and e) first contact with the university.

Similarities

Home Culture vs. University Culture

By and large, students' home cultures from both groups were very similar (see Table 1). Most of the students were from two-parent homes, with the exceptions of Iris, a female persister whose mother was widowed, and Jaime, a stop-out whose parents were divorced. Jaime's parents divorced when he was in early high school; his mother, who was Mexican American, was the custodial parent until her death while he was in graduate school. Of the 20 parents in the combined groups, 18 had been born in Mexico, Puerto Rico, or Colombia with the majority (14) born in Mexico. Two students, Michael, a persister, and Jaime, a stop-out, had Caucasian fathers. Seven students were the first generation in their families to be born and/or raised in the United States.

In both groups, approximately half of the students came from homes where their parents were laborers. Three students had at least one parent who was employed in a semi-skilled position, such as in the secretarial and law enforcement fields. The educational attainment of most parents was very low. Both parents of five students had completed less than high school diplomas in their homelands of Mexico or Puerto Rico. Two students had one parent with an elementary school education. Both parents of two students had received high school diplomas,

Table 1. Description of Sample

	Ethnicity[a]	Home language	Parental education levels[b]	Parental occupation[b]	Siblings[c]/birth order	Gen. American
Stop-Outs						
Mariposa	Mexican American	English/Spanish	Some Jr. college/3rd grade (Mexico)	Secretary/Butcher	Three/Third oldest	2nd
Alicia	Mexican American	Spanish	6th grade (Mexico) (Both)	Homemaker/Laborer	Three/Second oldest	1st
Armando	Chicano	Spanish	3rd grade (Mexico) (Both)	Factory workers (Both)	Six/Oldest	1st
Jaime	Mexican American/Caucasian	English	U.S. HS diplomas (Both)	Deceased/Supervisor at steel mill	Three/Oldest	3rd
David	Mexican American	Spanish	6th grade/Voc. Ed. (Mexico)	Homemaker/Laborer	Three/Oldest	1st
Persisters						
Iris	Mexican American	Spanish	6th grade (Mexico) (Both)	Factory worker/Deceased	Six/Youngest	1st
Elisa	Mexican American	Spanish	Elementary school (Mexico) (Both)	Homemaker/Cook	Four/Oldest	1st
Javier	Colombian American	English/Spanish	HS school (Colombia) (Both)	Homemaker/Welding technician	Five/Youngest	1st
Michael	Mexican American/Caucasian	English	Associate/bachelors degrees	Insurance agent/Gov. employee	One/Youngest	4th
Martin	Puerto Rican	Spanish	6th grade/4th grade (Puerto Rico)	Homemaker/Law enforcement	Three/Youngest	1st

[a]Ethnicity as reported by students. All, except one, of the Mexican American students self-identified as Mexicans; but for the purposes of this study, I refer to them as Mexican Americans to distinguish them from Mexican nationals. One student identified himself as "Chicano." [b]Reported "Mother/Father." [c]The students' number of siblings.

although one set of parents did so in the United States and the other in Colombia. On the other end of the spectrum, two parents had attended either technical or junior colleges but did not receive certificates. Michael, a persister, had a Caucasian father who had graduated from college with a bachelor's degree (the only parent who had done so), while his Mexican American mother received an associate's degree.

With the exception of Michael, whose home culture seemed to be fairly typically "American," the home cultures of the other nine students reflected the cultures of Mexico, Puerto Rico, or Colombia, with influences from American culture. Spanish was the primary language used in these homes, particularly in conversations between the students and their parents. The foods in the homes strongly reflected the countries of origin, with an admixture of more typical U.S. cuisine. All 10 students described themselves by referencing their country/island of descent: Mexican, Mexican American, Chicano, Puerto Rican, and Colombian American. All students reported having strong ties to their home cultures.

I asked the students to describe the dominant student culture at the university so that their perceptions of the university were clearly on the record; as Tinto (1987) noted, "Perhaps . . . most important is the implied notion that departure hinges upon the individual's perception of his/her experiences of higher education" (p. 127). If students perceived that university life was centered around one group, regardless of whether it really was, then such perceptions could have had very real consequences for these students' integration into the university. And since Latino students tend to have more negative perceptions of the campus climate than Whites (Hurtado, 1992), it is crucial to fully understand students' perceptions of their college experiences.

All of the interviewees described the dominant university culture as White, suburban, middle-class students with college-educated parents, which was very different from their descriptions of their own homes. This simple description pinpointed differences of race/ethnicity, social class, parental educational attainment levels, and primary home language between most of the Latino students' home cultures and the university culture. These four differences are neither small nor inconsequential.

The students described a variety of differences between their own home cultures and that of the dominant university culture. In addition to the obvious non-ethnic, 'bland" foods served in the dormitories and campus town that some students "never really ate before [coming to campus]," the language spoken on campus was "different"—and not just English versus Spanish. Some students identified the English spoken on campus as "academic English," "sorority girl" or "valley girl" English, and "non-dialectical English." One student noted that Caucasian students did not "speak dialectical English . . . like minorities do." They also identified other differences: campus culture was "very competitive," "individualistic," and "superficial." Furthermore, six students perceived that the campus was "very segregated . . . [people] associat[e] only with people who are like them."

Integration into Campus Culture

Tinto (1987) argues that thorough integration into the university culture prevents students from being distracted by potentially interruptive factors, such as issues at home. Certain characteristics of colleges have been found to play roles in students' adjustment to college, such as college size (Chickering & Reisser, 1993, as cited in Hurtado et al., 1996, p. 138). Also, the higher the selectivity of the college, the more likely Latinos are to experience difficulty in their transition to college (Hurtado & Carter, 1997; Hurtado et al., 1996).

In both groups—persisters and stop-outs—a majority of students felt that they were not integrated into the larger university culture, although most felt that they were integrated into the Latino culture on campus. Mariposa, a stop-out, recalled her experiences as a student:

> When I'm by myself—like in class—I do feel out of place because I'm . . . the only one that's Mexican or brown, and I'm just—like—isolated. And [Caucasians] all talk amongst themselves. They'll share notes, even if they don't know each other. . . . I'll talk and they'll answer me, if I ask them a question, but they don't include me in the conversation.

It is important to note, however, that Hurtado, Carter, and Spuler (1996) found that Latino students who interacted frequently with other racial/ethnic groups were not significantly more likely to demonstrate higher levels of college adjustment.

Both formal and informal mechanisms within university communities aid in the integration of students into the university culture. Some of these mechanisms include fraternities, sororities, student unions, intramural sports, and religious organizations. At the time of the study, there were only three predominantly Latina/o Greek-lettered organizations on campus: one sorority, one fraternity, and one coed fraternity. I raise this issue, not to suggest that Latino students could not join other fraternities and sororities but because, due to the segregation these students noticed on campus, the low presence of Latino fraternities and sororities is one of the realities they must deal with. Not surprisingly, only one student in the sample belonged to a fraternity. Although he was a stop-out, his membership in the fraternity did not contribute to his dismissal from the university, as he had joined the organization after being readmitted. The low numbers of such organizations is problematic because "students who belonged to religious organizations and sororities and fraternities had a significantly stronger sense of belonging than did nonmembers in the second year" (Hurtado & Carter, 1997, p. 335). This finding indicates that early membership have lasting effects on students' sense of belonging.

Financial Issues

Although financial problems influence low Latino retention rates (Arbona & Novy, 1991; Haro, 1983; Olivas, 1986b), that was not the case with these Latino need-based scholarship recipients. This is not to suggest that the students did not experience financial difficulties within their home environments because many students did experience financial difficulties within their homes that created additional stress. However, the students did not feel the "economic pinch" of not having enough financial aid funds to pay for a semester of school, forcing them to withdraw. In fact, the participants recognized that their Latino peers who were not USP recipients had significant financial difficulties simply getting to pay for tuition and books; difficulties that the participants did not have because they had received the university scholarship.

Rather, financial issues as related to college for them were part of their perception that money and social class were important aspects of fitting comfortably into the university culture. Because most came from working-class homes, the large majority of interviewees felt out of place on campus. In fact, when I asked them to list any advantages or disadvantages they faced in college as a result of their home cultures, the majority of the students identified social class and finances as disadvantages. Mariposa stated,

> Most of the students—they come to college and it's expensive and they're just—like—"This is the most wonderful place." . . . I don't find that among my friends [who are Latinos]. . . . [The financially well off students] sort of make me feel like I'm the different one, like they're the norm and [those from financially modest backgrounds are] the . . . outsiders.

Feeling like "outsiders" on campus does not facilitate the students' integration on campus, further hampering their retention (Tinto, 1987). It is important to note that feelings of financial marginality are not confined to Latinos; many students have perceptions as a result of belonging to a disadvantaged social class. Still, Latinos as a group tend to experience greater rates of poverty. For example, in 1999, while only 7.7% of non-Hispanic Whites lived in poverty, 22.8% of Latinos lived below the poverty level (Therrien & Ramírez, 2000). This dynamic becomes even more apparent in examining the overall financial and educational backgrounds of the interviewees' parents and their ability to offer support to their college-bound children.

Parental Support

All of the students interviewed, like most students attending the university, lived on campus. Five students' homes were located in a major city 130 miles away. Four students' homes were located in various suburbs of that city; on average, their homes were two hours away from campus. The tenth student, Michael, lived in a small, rural town less than one hour away from campus. Thus, nine of the students could have attended one of many colleges and universities in the metropolitan area. The fact that the students chose to attend a school farther away from their homes and families raised the issue of parental support. Martin, a persister, explained:

> [My parents] were supportive of me going to college, but at first, they weren't supportive of me going away to school—just because they didn't see any reason why I would have to leave home . . . to go to school. They figured that [two other universities located in the city] were great enough schools and "why did you have to go somewhere to school when you have all these good schools here?" . . . I think it was a cultural thing. Because when I think about a lot of my friends who had Latino parents, or even my relatives—like they wouldn't want their kids to go anywhere other than to stay home . . . it was a cultural thing. . . . The one thing I noticed was among some people on my [dorm] floor that were . . . Anglo-American; their parents would visit a lot. They would come down on weekends and if [the university sponsored events], like Mom's Day, Dad's Day, they would come down and bring their kids food. Like my parents never came down.

It is important to examine Martin's observation that his parents' reactions to going away to college or even their lack of visits were "cultural thing[s]." This may be the case to a certain degree; however, it is also important to note that their reactions may be due to their social class. Overall, the participants' parents had low educational attainment levels and had never attended college. As such, a lack of understanding of college and all of its many facets may have prevented them from fully supporting their students' decisions.

Martin's description of students whose parents supported their decision to attend college but not of their decision to go away applied to three students in each group. The consequences for them included a lack of financial and emotional support, unnecessary feelings of guilt and disappointment, and many visits home. Such results can have negative impacts on student retention, particularly because Hurtado, Carter, and Spuler (1996) found that "for academically talented Latino students who attend college full time, maintaining family relationships and support is among the most important aspects of transition that facilitates their adjustment to college" (Hurtado & Carter, 1997, pp. 328-329).

Six of the 10 students commented that their parents did not come to campus to visit them, in marked contrast to the parents of Caucasian students. The students explained this lack of visits by their parents' irregular work hours or not understanding English well enough to participate in university events. Again, these are basic reasons provided by the students, whereas the lack of parental visits may have stemmed from social class issues versus simply cultural issues. Some students admitted feeling jealous of Caucasian students as a result. Iris, a persister, said:

> My mom did not want me to go away [to school], so she wasn't that happy or supportive. She wasn't interested in my grades or anything, which was mostly due to her unfamiliarity with the American educational system. Like other parents would be interested in their kids' grades, but not my mom. She didn't look out for my grades; and when I got straight A's, I would have to show them to her. . . . It was disappointing because, in a sense, I was robbed. I wasn't commended when I would make Dean's List, which was

not an easy thing to do. But yet, she didn't pay attention to that. My [older] brothers and sisters weren't really supportive either. . . . It's just like I picked that path and so . . . that was that. It was my choice. No big deal.

Three of the six students experiencing a lack of parental support due to attending a college away from home were the oldest children; the other three had older siblings who attended college, but the siblings had chosen schools closer to home. In essence, these six were the first children in their families to "leave home" to attend school. Furthermore, five of the six played major roles in assisting with or sometimes managing parents' business affairs—for instance, paying bills, writing checks for those parents who did not know how to write English, and verbally communicating with such agencies as the Social Security Administration. So, in addition to being the first child to leave home to attend college, many students had significant roles in their families creating a reliance on them from other members, which may have made their leaving more detrimental to the family structure.

Academic Issues

Although the students were scholarship recipients and had performed well in high school and on standardized college entrance examinations, the reality was that they were not as academically prepared when compared to their peers. Again, the USP criteria for eligibility were as follows: a composite ACT score of 24 or higher or a combined verbal and quantitative score of 1080 on the SAT and rank in the top upper half of their high school graduation class. Compared to the average freshman student, the ACT/SAT scores required for USP eligibility were relatively low; approximately 60% of the 1998 freshmen class had a minimum composite ACT score of 27 and almost 65% scored at least 1200 on the SAT. Furthermore, 49% of the same freshmen class was in the top 10% of their high school class. Students who barely met the criteria for USP were clearly academically unprepared to compete at level with many of their classmates.

As such, it is not surprising that almost all of the participants in the study felt academically unprepared to compete at the university, although they had been top of their respective high school class and received a four-year scholarship. Students vividly described feelings of being academically unprepared in comparison to peers. Alicia, a stop-out, reported:

> Once I came here and all these people were like, "Oh, I got a 35 on my ACT," and I'm like, "Oh, my God!" I'm thinking, "Oh, I was all happy about my grade." It intimidated me a lot. They were saying, "I already had, like, 24 hours earned through AP and all that." And I'm thinking, "What are you talking about?"

Martin, a persister, also communicated feeling out of place academically:

> Sometimes in your class, you just meet these people who they have, like, 20 advance hours of AP credit and they did a senior thesis in high school. And they're talking about it and the whole time you're thinking, "I didn't do any of that stuff." . . . The longest paper I wrote in high school was five pages long.

Whether these feelings of being underprepared were actually justified, they could have potentially had negative consequences for the students, affecting their self-esteem and increasing stress and pressure levels (Smedley et al., 1993) (see discussion below). Furthermore, feeling out of place academically can impact student-student interactions, which Hurtado and Carter (1997) found have a strong relationship to students' sense of belonging.

Differences

Although both persisters and stop-outs expressed feelings of being academically unprepared, academic difficulties were the most significant difference between the two. Of the five students who stopped out, four did so because the university dismissed them for not meeting grade point average minimums. Mariposa, the fifth, who withdrew after her freshman year, was on academic probation at the time. After returning to the university for approximately two years, she again withdrew voluntarily. The remaining four students had already been on academic probation for at least one semester before being dismissed. Alicia was dismissed her sophomore year. David and Jaime were dismissed after their first year, while Armando was dismissed as a second-year freshman. The university had dismissed all three male stop-outs a second time after being readmitted according to their number of credit hours, they were all sophomores.

Although this pattern of academic dismissal cannot be statistically generalized outside the group of interviewees, the academic difficulty experienced by the stop-outs is consistent with literature focusing on Latino retention. Ramírez (1987) and Rendón and Nora (1988) report that poor academic performance is a very important factor in the attrition of Latinos. Similarly, Hurtado, Carter, and Spuler (1996) found that high school grade point average was not directly related to the academic adjustment of scholarship students in their sample. Again, this may be an ethnic-specific finding, since both Tinto (1987) and Astin (1975) (in their national samples) found that high school performance was a strong predictor of college performance.

The five persisting students performed so well that fears of academic dismissal never entered their college experiences. None of the students had ever been placed on probation nor had their grade point averages ever been close to the minimums for their respective colleges. In fact, four of the five persisters have attended either graduate school and/or law school at Big Ten universities; only one of the stop-outs attended graduate school and chose a smaller, less selective university.

The four academically dismissed students primarily blamed themselves, rather than analyzing a complex of factors that may have been involved in their academic dismissal. David, for example, stated that he was dropped by the university "because of what I didn't do. Not because they said, 'Get out of here,' but because I didn't make the grade." Others cited such reasons as not appreciating and valuing their scholarships, not studying enough, not being aggressive enough with professors, not taking the initiative and using university services, and not integrating into the university culture. A simple functionalist perspective that explores only student characteristics, however, does not provide a completely satisfactory explanation. My findings suggest that the interaction of several variables provide a more comprehensive explanation.

Home-to-School Transition

As stated, the students' home cultures were largely similar: working-class poorly educated parents who retained the ethnic culture of their homeland in the household. The home cultures of three students—persisters Michael, Javier, and Martin—had home cultures that deviated in at least some respects. Javier's parents were both born and raised in Colombia and Martin's parents were both born and raised in Puerto Rico. Both Javier's and Martin's families were, however, middle-to upper-middle class and all of their older sisters had attended college before them. Michael was unique among the interviewees in describing his home culture as 'American' because he was removed from his Mexican heritage. I hypothesize that the transition of these three students from their home culture to the university culture was not as stressful as that of all five of the stop-outs.

Michael, a fourth-generation American with a Mexican American mother and an Irish American father, described his home as "American" in language, foods, and traditions. They spoke English in the home. His mother had spoken Spanish as a young child but had forgotten it in growing up. A family traditional food was "pizza every Friday." He saw that "the Mexican culture gets diluted a bit every generation" in his family and terms his home culture as "probably . . . fairly normal to American culture." In addition, his parents were the only ones that received degrees; his mother had an associate's and his father a bachelor's. Michael's description of his home-to-school transition was also different from that of the other students. He reported no feelings of social isolation, lack of parental support, feelings of guilt for displeasing his parents, or homesickness for food, traditions, language, and music.

In contrast, Jaime, a stop-out, was also the son of a Caucasian father and Mexican mother. His parents had divorced when he was in early high school, he lived with his mother from that point until her death while he was in graduate school, and classified himself as "'Mexican' since we adhere to most of those traditions." While living with his mother, he spoke Spanish at home. It seems probable that the mixture of American and Mexican home culture made Jaime's transition to college life more difficult than Michael's; in fact, Jaime reported experiencing 'cultural shock' when moving on campus.

Martin and Javier, two more persisters, also differed from the stop-out students by being middle class. Their mothers were homemakers; Martin's father was in law enforcement and Javier's father was a welding technician. Both students were the youngest children whose older sisters had finished college. Two of Martin's three sisters, a nurse and a lawyer, pooled their finances with their father's to establish a few small but successful family businesses, which elevated their family's social class. Javier's three oldest sisters also successfully graduated from college (one was a medical doctor), were financially well off, and helped Javier's parents financially, although his father's job provided a stable income. Significantly, Javier, Martin, and Michael were the only students who did not say they felt out of place at the university due to their family's financial status.

High School Segregation

One important issue revealed through interviews was racial/ethnic segregation in high schools. Two persisters had attended high school in the suburbs, two in the city, and one in a rural town. Three of the stop-outs attended urban high schools, and two suburban schools. Four out of five in each group attended public schools. However, the degrees of racial/ethnic segregation within the high schools (Chapa & Valencia, 1993; Donato, Menchaca, & Valencia, 1991; Frankenberg, Lee, & Orfield, 2003; Valencia, 1991), as identified in the interviews, was a major difference between persisters and stop-outs. I asked the students to estimate the racial composition of their high schools, so these descriptions are personal perceptions, not actual statistics. In almost all of the cases, however, the students reported that their high schools were overwhelmingly comprised of either racial/ethnic minorities or Caucasians that an exact percentage breakdown was unnecessary. For example, Alicia estimated that her high school student body was 99% Latino.

Racially/ethnically segregated schools are defined as schools in which Latinos and African Americans collectively constitute a majority (50-100%) (Frankenberg et al., 2003). Segregated schools tend to give their students a lower quality education due to lower quality teachers, lack of supplies, and low funding (Donato et al., 1991). All five stop-outs attended high schools where Latino and African Americans constituted the majority of the student population. Of the five persisters, only two students attended schools in which the majority of the students were Latino and African American, while in the remaining three high schools students of color were a clear minority.

In addition to the academic handicaps of lower teacher quality, supplies, and funding in segregated schools (Donato et al., 1991) must be added the social limitation of moving from a daily environment where the majority of the students are Latino and Black to an environment where fewer than 5% are—the profile at the university granting these scholarships. Armando, a stop-out, recalled visiting the campus and thinking, "Wow! There's a lot of White people here!" Similarly, Alicia, another stop-out, stated, "My high school . . . was 99 percent Hispanic and I think [the high concentration of Latinos] sheltered me more because I was not open [to other cultures]. . . . [If] I could have [attended] a different [high] school . . . I think [the transition to college] would have been easier."

Anticipatory Socialization

Tinto (1987) has identified "anticipatory socialization" as an aid to student persistence in college (p. 97). By this phrase, he means that parents who have attended college can help their student become oriented to college and benefit from their parent's experiences in college. As already mentioned, only Michael had a parent who had graduated from a four-year institution. His were also the only parents in the sample to accompany their student to freshman orientation, although they let him attend the events on his own. When he showed them his class schedule, "My dad wasn't too pleased with it. He kind of knew that it wasn't the best cut one, so then we went back and changed it." This example illustrates a direct benefit from a parent's expertise with college culture. In contrast, David, a stop-out, lamented, "It would have helped if I knew—if someone told me, 'Watch out for this class' or 'Don't slack here because it'll affect over here.'"

However, to broaden the possible range of anticipatory socialization, I also asked interviewees about older siblings who were college attenders. Only one stop-out, Alicia, had an older sibling in college, and this sister was only a year ahead of her; thus, the benefits were quite limited. Of the remaining stop-outs, all four were the first in their families to attend college. Of the five persisters, in contrast, only Elisa was the first in her family to attend college. Michael's father and older brother had attended a four-year college, while Iris, Martin, and Javier were the third, fourth, and sixth, respectively, to attend a university. These three were also the youngest siblings in their families. It seems reasonable to hypothesize that students who graduated and were continuously enrolled had benefited from their older siblings' college experiences; as a consequence, they were more knowledgeable about how to succeed in college. Javier, in fact, identified his birth order and his college-bound sisters as an advantage in his own educational expertise:

> When I was younger, my sisters were going through college, so I got to see or either learn from a lot of the mistakes that they made. Or see some of the things or how hard they worked, in essence. So it had a lot of influence on what I wanted to do or what I wanted to achieve at a younger age. . . . A lot of [students] that were my age were always the oldest or if not, the second oldest, whereas I'm the youngest.

Latino college students are far from being the only group disadvantaged by being first-generation college students, regardless of race/ethnicity. But the problem is intensified for Latinos because such large numbers of them are first-generation Americans and have parents who had very limited education in their homelands. Both factors intensify the lack of anticipatory socialization for Latinos.

Initial Goals

The literature on Latino retention finds a direct correlation between specific student goals and retention, a finding that the interviews fully supported. Fields (1988) reported that Latinos experience difficulty in college as a result of a lack of strong educational and career goals. Ramírez (1987) stated that many Latino college students lacked compatible (between student goals and institutional goals), well-established personal and career goals to guide them in their college years. Tinto (1987) agreed that "the higher the level of one's educational or occupational goals, the greater the likelihood of college completion" (p. 40).

The students who stopped out had relatively lower goals than the persisters. Three stop-outs—David, Jaime, and Mariposa—had entered college with the goal of graduating in either four years or an undetermined time period; specifically, they had no clear career goals. The fourth student, Alicia, aspired to be an engineer solely based on the advice of her sister who was one year older, although she did not know what an engineer was or did:

> When I first began college, I came here thinking, "I'm going to be an engineer and that's it." That's all I wanted to do because my sister told me to. . . . And then I took some [engineering] class and I'm thinking, "No. This is too weird." . . . It's weird because when [my sister] told me, "You should [major in engineering]," I'm thinking, "Okay. I will." It's not like I said, "Oh. Will I be able to do that?" I never doubted myself for anything because that's the way I was in high school. I never doubted myself.

The fifth stop-out, Armando, aspired to be a chemist and included graduate school as part of his goal but knew about graduate school only because his teaching assistants were graduate students. Since he had not fully discussed graduate school with his teaching assistants, Armando had very limited knowledge about the process involved.

In contrast to the students who stopped out, four of the five persisters had careers as their primary goals, as opposed to simply desiring to complete their undergraduate education. Furthermore, they had clearer ideas of what those careers entailed. They planned to be a teacher, financial analyst, and lawyer, in direct contrast with Alicia and Armando who did not know what an engineer did or the process of becoming a chemist. Although this study did not fully cover the issue, it is possible that siblings who attended college before the students may have helped persisters set job-related initial goals, especially if the siblings were older and academically successful.

groups fit into a White, middle-class model of education is not working
1992). As Verdugo (1986) writes, "That Hispanics face considerat
tional difficulties has perplexed many individuals. Attempts at finding
have been well intentioned but less than satisfying because the targe
Hispanics themselves rather than the educational system" (p. 343).

From this study, specific recommendations have come forth. First,
stated that the university should be commended for initiating and
a race-based, need-based scholarship to increase student diversity, p
during these times of anti-affirmative action sentiment. The unive
continue to fund this and similar programs, especially during these
conservative and financially-difficult times for publicly-funded entities
earlier, this program has been successful in increasing the pool of talen
African American, and Native American undergraduate students o
The university, however, must improve its support of these students
maximize the return on their financial investment, which will assist in e
its importance to the university and the state.

The findings indicated that there is much room to improve the exister
The first recommendation is that the university systematically exa
Latino students and ask the important question, "Who are our Latino
This is a recommendation that may prove beneficial if applied to
groups. Through a freshman survey, for example, the university coul
the percentage of Latino students who are first generation college stuc
from segregated schools, have parents with low educational attainmer
have well-established personal and career goals. Using this data, the
could tailor programs and services to meet the actual needs of student

The university must re-evaluate its expectations of USP recipien
the criteria for eligibility were very low when compared to the
"typical" student. But being "scholarship recipients," these student
sufficiently informed of programs available to academically "at-risl
perhaps because of assumptions on the part of university administratc
that these "scholarship recipients" would not require such programs.
made to feel as though they were very high achievers, which they ma'
in their high schools and some clearly were at the university as wel
knowing that the typical student at the university would be more ac
prepared, it was the university's responsibility to provide the USP st
sufficient tutoring, if necessary, and other types of academic program
support. Assuming that these students would not require additional
virtue of being scholarship students was irresponsible, particularly k
the eligibility criteria were relatively low.

A major difference between the stop-outs and persisters was tha
stop-outs attended segregated high schools. The stop-outs came fror
different school settings; where Latino and African American student
the majority in their high schools, they became a clear minority at the

must be qualitative studies that allow students
encing, how they perceive the college enviror
experiences.

I see a strong need for research on the r
Since an important difference between the two
persisters had older siblings who attended co
socialization on retention mandates further exar
because immigration activities occur among pec
attainment levels. As such, more teenagers a
parents who can provide anticipatory socializ
partially filled, at least for younger siblings, by

In conclusion, the Latino population within
tremendous rate (Llagas & Snyder, 2003). By
Latinos will number 98 million and thus will co
total population. Yet, to date, Latinos have no
parity with other groups. If Latinos continue
economic, and intellectual consequences will b
The goal of increasing the numbers of Latino
make it through graduation—is an urgent one.

REFERENCES

Arbona, C., & Novy, D. M. (1991). Hispanic colleg
differences? *Journal of College Student Developm*

Astin, A. (1968). *The college environment.* Washi
Education.

Astin, A. (1975). *Preventing students from dropping c*

Astin, A. (1977). *Four critical years: Effects of*
knowledge. San Francisco: Jossey-Bass.

Chacón, M. E., Cohen, E. G., & Strover, S. (1986).
progress in higher education. In Olivas, 1986a, pp.

Chapa, J., & Valencia, R. R. (1993). Latino popula
teristics, and educational stagnation: An examinatio
of Behavioral Science, 15(2), 165-187.

Chickering, A. W., & Reisser, L. (1993). *Education*
Bass.

Davis, T. M., & Murrell, P. H. (1993). *Turning teachin*
responsibility in the collegiate experience. ASH
No. 8. Washington, DC: George Washington Un
Human Development.

Donato, R., Menchaca, M., & Valencia, R. R. (1991
integration of Chicano students: Problems and pr
Chicano school failure and success: Research a
(pp. 27-64). Basingstoke, UK: Burgess Science Pres

First Contact with University

Astin (1968) and Tinto (1987) both pointed to a positive correlation between not visiting campus before registration and later stopping out. My findings paralleled this literature. The earliest any of the five stop-out students visited the campus for the first time was during their senior year. The first visit to the campus for three students in the stop-out group, Jaime, Armando, and David, was the university's summer orientation program. Mariposa, Jaime, Armando, and David accepted the scholarship before visiting the campus.

In contrast, only two of the persisters, Elisa and Martin, visited the university for the first time during the summer orientation program after accepting the scholarship. Iris, Michael, and Javier all had some familiarity with the campus before accepting the scholarship as results of visiting siblings who had attended the university. Although it is not conclusive, it seems probable that the stop-outs may have experienced greater mismatches between themselves and the university because they had fuzzier information about it (Hurtado & Carter, 1997).

CONCLUSION

Both groups of students interviewed for this study had exceeded academic criteria for admission to the university and were relieved of many of their financial concerns as related to school costs, two of the major barriers identified in the literature as major impediments to Latino retention. Nonetheless, some of these students did withdraw from college, even if only temporarily. If students so talented continue to falter, then those who are relatively marginal or less prepared are truly at risk of non-completion.

Recommendations

The big lesson from the 2000 Census is that the fabric of the country is changing and it is increasingly become more colorful. Several facts have come to light. The Latino population has grown tremendously from 1990 to 2000, which accounts for much of the national growth during that time period. As a group, Latinos are a much younger population than other U.S. groups with a median age of 26.6 compared to 30.6 for Blacks and 38.6 for Whites (Llagas & Snyder, 2003). As such, Latinos are over-represented in the school-age population and are projected to grow. In the year 2020, it is projected that Latinos under 18 will constitute 23% of their age group, which will be a 58% growth (Llagas & Snyder, 2003).

These Latino elementary and secondary school students will grow up to become the pool of college students in future years. Our nation is dependent upon colleges and universities to supply an educated workforce necessary for advancement and a critical citizenry necessary for democracy. As such, colleges and universities must understand how to better recruit, retain, and graduate Latino students, as well as other students of color. Clearly, attempting to make these diverse non-White groups fit into a White, middle-class model of education is not working (Tierney, 1992). As Verdugo (1986) writes, "That Hispanics face considerable educational difficulties has perplexed many individuals. Attempts at finding solutions have been well intentioned but less than satisfying because the target has been Hispanics themselves rather than the educational system" (p. 343).

From this study, specific recommendations have come forth. First, it must be stated that the university should be commended for initiating and continuing a race-based, need-based scholarship to increase student diversity, particularly during these times of anti-affirmative action sentiment. The university must continue to fund this and similar programs, especially during these politically conservative and financially-difficult times for publicly-funded entities. As stated earlier, this program has been successful in increasing the pool of talented Latino, African American, and Native American undergraduate students on campus. The university, however, must improve its support of these students in order to maximize the return on their financial investment, which will assist in establishing its importance to the university and the state.

The findings indicated that there is much room to improve the existent program. The first recommendation is that the university systematically examine their Latino students and ask the important question, "Who are our Latino students?" This is a recommendation that may prove beneficial if applied to all student groups. Through a freshman survey, for example, the university could ascertain the percentage of Latino students who are first generation college students, come from segregated schools, have parents with low educational attainment levels, or have well-established personal and career goals. Using this data, the university could tailor programs and services to meet the actual needs of students.

The university must re-evaluate its expectations of USP recipients. Clearly, the criteria for eligibility were very low when compared to the university's "typical" student. But being "scholarship recipients," these students were not sufficiently informed of programs available to academically "at-risk" students, perhaps because of assumptions on the part of university administrators and staff that these "scholarship recipients" would not require such programs. They were made to feel as though they were very high achievers, which they may have been in their high schools and some clearly were at the university as well. However, knowing that the typical student at the university would be more academically prepared, it was the university's responsibility to provide the USP students with sufficient tutoring, if necessary, and other types of academic programs and social support. Assuming that these students would not require additional support by virtue of being scholarship students was irresponsible, particularly knowing that the eligibility criteria were relatively low.

A major difference between the stop-outs and persisters was that all of the stop-outs attended segregated high schools. The stop-outs came from extremely different school settings; where Latino and African American students were once the majority in their high schools, they became a clear minority at the university.

Such stark difference between environments can clearly be very difficult for students. In addition to the social difficulties of such racially different environments, there are significant resource, preparation, and achievement disparities between non-segregated and segregated schools, which would impact students' performances at the university. Since the university recruits students from segregated high schools, it has the responsibility to ensure that these students transition smoothly to a campus that is clearly opposite from their high schools, particularly with the impacts of segregation on student outcomes clearly documented. Creating diversity on campus cannot and must not stop with having Latino students enroll for the first semester of classes. The university must demonstrate its commitment to diversity and to these students by acting accordingly and providing the students with the support and services necessary to retain them. Such programs would include social support and services, as well as academic and general counseling.

Since many of the students did not visit campus until after they accepted admission and their scholarships, the university should take a proactive role in ensuring that these students visit the campus before accepting the scholarship. Since many of these students were first generation college students, they may not have understood the importance and role of having a good match between themselves and their selected college. As such, many chose to attend the university because of its outstanding academic reputation and the four-year scholarship they were offered. They never spoke of considering whether there was a good match between the university and themselves. By mandating that students attend a two-day orientation on campus *before* accepting the scholarship, the university can reduce the number of students who withdraw as a result of factors stemming from mismatches.

The university must take a proactive stance on the recruitment and retention of Latino faculty and students. Several participants of the study suggested this recommendation. As Armando stated, "[With Latino professors] it's easier to feel at home. . . . sometimes, I feel like the white professors really don't know what I'm going through." Latino faculty may help ease the cultural conflict between their homes and campus experienced by Latino students because Latino faculty may have had similar experiences during their academic careers. The recruitment and retention of Latino faculty, as well as faculty-student contact, is of utmost importance because the literature points to student-faculty contact as significant to student retention (Tinto, 1987).

Recommendations for Further Research

I begin this section by calling for researchers to allow Latino college students to tell their own experiences. As researchers, we utilize old studies to inform new ones. Yet some of the studies done on Latino persistence used in this study are up to 30 years old. Times change constantly, and so do students, their experiences, and their perceptions. Paralleling the invaluable quantitative research must be qualitative studies that allow students to describe what they are experiencing, how they perceive the college environment, and the impact of various experiences.

I see a strong need for research on the role of anticipatory socialization. Since an important difference between the two groups in this study was that the persisters had older siblings who attended college, the impact of anticipatory socialization on retention mandates further examination. This point is imperative because immigration activities occur among people of color with low educational attainment levels. As such, more teenagers are reaching college age without parents who can provide anticipatory socialization; still, this function can be partially filled, at least for younger siblings, by older ones.

In conclusion, the Latino population within the United States is growing at a tremendous rate (Llagas & Snyder, 2003). By the year 2050, it is projected that Latinos will number 98 million and thus will constitute one-fourth of the nation's total population. Yet, to date, Latinos have not been able to reach educational parity with other groups. If Latinos continue to be undereducated, the social, economic, and intellectual consequences will be dire for the nation as a whole. The goal of increasing the numbers of Latinos who make it to college—and make it through graduation—is an urgent one.

REFERENCES

Arbona, C., & Novy, D. M. (1991). Hispanic college students: Are there within-group differences? *Journal of College Student Development, 32*(4), 90-100.

Astin, A. (1968). *The college environment.* Washington, DC: American Council on Education.

Astin, A. (1975). *Preventing students from dropping out.* San Francisco: Jossey-Bass.

Astin, A. (1977). *Four critical years: Effects of college on beliefs, attitudes, and knowledge.* San Francisco: Jossey-Bass.

Chacón, M. E., Cohen, E. G., & Strover, S. (1986). Chicanas and Chicanos: Barriers to progress in higher education. In Olivas, 1986a, pp. 296-324.

Chapa, J., & Valencia, R. R. (1993). Latino population growth, demographic characteristics, and educational stagnation: An examination of recent trends. *Hispanic Journal of Behavioral Science, 15*(2), 165-187.

Chickering, A. W., & Reisser, L. (1993). *Education and identity.* San Francisco: Jossey-Bass.

Davis, T. M., & Murrell, P. H. (1993). *Turning teaching into learning: The role of student responsibility in the collegiate experience.* ASHE-ERIC Higher Education Report No. 8. Washington, DC: George Washington University, School of Education and Human Development.

Donato, R., Menchaca, M., & Valencia, R. R. (1991). Segregation, desegregation, and integration of Chicano students: Problems and prospects. In R. R. Valencia (Ed.), *Chicano school failure and success: Research and policy agendas for the 1990s* (pp. 27-64). Basingstoke, UK: Burgess Science Press.

Enchautegui, M. E. (1995). *Policy implications of Latino poverty.* Washington, DC: Urban Institute.

Fields, C. (1988, May-June). The Hispanic pipeline: Narrow, leaking, and needing repair. *Change: The Magazine of Higher Learning, 20*(3), 20-27.

Fiske, E. (1988, May-June). The undergraduate Hispanic experience: A case of juggling two cultures. *Change: The Magazine of Higher Learning, 20*(3), 28-33.

Fontana, A., & Frey, J. H. (1994). Interviewing: The art of science. In N. K. Denzin & Y. S. Lincoln (Eds.), *Handbook of qualitative research* (pp. 361-376). Thousand Oaks, CA: Sage.

Frankenberg, E., Lee, C., & Orfield, G. (2003). *A multiracial society with segregated schools: Are we losing the dream?* Cambridge, MA: Civil Rights Project of Harvard University. Available online at: http://www.civilrightsproject.harvard.edu/research/reseg03/AreWeLosingtheDream.pdf

Haro, C. M. (1983). Chicanos and higher education: A review of selected literature. *Aztlan, 14*(1), 35-78.

Hurtado, S. (1992). Campus racial climate: Contexts of conflict. *Journal of Higher Education, 63,* 539-569.

Hurtado, S., & Carter, D. F. (1997, October). Effects of college transition and perceptions of the campus racial climate on Latino college students' sense of belonging. *Sociology of Education, 70,* 324-345.

Hurtado, S., Carter, D. F., & Spuler, A. (1996). Latino transition to college: Assessing difficulties and factors in successful college adjustment. *Research in Higher Education, 37*(2), 135-157.

Justiz, M. J. (1994). Demographic trends and the challenges to American higher education. In M. J. Justiz, R. Wilson, & L. G. Björk (Eds.), *Minorities in higher education* (pp. 1-21). Phoenix, AZ: American Council on Education and Oryx Press.

Llagas, C., & Snyder, T. D. (2003). *Status and trends in the education of Hispanics.* Washington, DC: U.S. Government Printing Office.

McJamerson, E. M., & Larke, P. J. (1989, March). *Data-driven retention research: Using institutional research to inform institutional practice.* Paper presented at the meeting of the American Educational Research Association, San Francisco.

National Center for Education Statistics (NCES). (2002). *The condition of education, 2002.* Washington, DC: U.S. Government Printing Office.

Olivas, M. A. (Ed.). (1986a). *Latino college students.* New York: Teachers College Press.

Olivas, M. A. (1986b). Research on Latino college students: A theoretical framework and inquiry. In Olivas, 1986b, pp. 1-25.

Ramírez, G. M. (1987, March). *Retention of the Latino student: Student affirmative action at CSULB.* Paper presented at the meeting of the National Association for Bilingual Education, Denver, CO.

Rendón, L. I., & Nora, A. (1988). Hispanic students: Stopping the leaks in the pipeline. *Educational Record, 68*(4), 79-85.

Smedley, B. D., Myers, H. F., & Harrell, S. P. (1993). Minority-status stresses and the college adjustment of ethnic minority freshmen. *Journal of Higher Education, 64*(4), 434-452.

Therrien, M., & Ramírez, R. R. (2000). *The Hispanic population in the United States. Population characteristics.* Washington, DC: U.S. Census Bureau.

Tierney, W. G. (1992). An anthropological analysis of student participation in college. *Journal of Higher Education, 63*(6), 603-618.

Tinto, V. (1987). *Leaving college: Rethinking the causes and cures of student attrition.* Chicago: University of Chicago Press.

Valencia, R. R. (1991). The plight of Chicano students: An overview of schooling conditions and outcomes. In R. R. Valencia (Ed.), *Chicano school failure and success: Research and policy agendas for the 1990s* (pp. 3-26). Basingstoke, UK: Burgess Science Press.

Verdugo, R. P. (1986a). Educational stratification and Hispanics. In Olivas, 1986a, pp. 325-347.

SECTION 3

Asian and Asian Pacific Students

CHAPTER 8

Issues of College Persistence between Asian and Asian Pacific American Students

Theresa Ling Yeh

This chapter offers an exploration of the Asian Pacific American (APA) ethnic groups that show high rates of departure, and presents strategies and approaches to improving their persistence and graduation rates. A detailed examination of the APA population is presented to identify the subgroups that are underrepresented in higher education and who suffer from high dropout rates. Subsequently, several traditional retention theories are reviewed to determine how they apply to these APA subgroups. Specific barriers to college persistence for these students also are examined. Finally, the chapter presents strategies and programs designed to improve APA's persistence rates.

The past decade has seen a proliferation of research on college student retention and persistence that examines the plight of underrepresented populations within higher education. However, rarely does the literature include Asian or Asian Pacific Americans (APAs) in this category. When the research includes this population, often the numbers are so small that meaningful analysis is not possible (Porter, 1990). Indeed, at first glance, it appears that students of Asian descent are very successful in higher education, and that they persist and graduate at rates even higher than White students (Chan & Hune, 1995). However, a closer examination of specific ethnic groups within the APA populations reveal the existence of subgroups of students who demonstrate very low college attendance and persistence rates. Contrary to common belief, these students experience considerable difficulty in the college environment, and face a high risk of leaving college before completing their degree. The purpose of this chapter is to offer a deeper exploration of the Asian Pacific American ethnic groups that show high rates of departure, and to present strategies and approaches to improving their persistence and graduation rates.

To begin, a more detailed examination of the APA population must take place, in order to identify the subgroups that are underrepresented in higher education and who suffer from high dropout rates. Subsequently, several traditional retention theories will be reviewed to determine how they apply to these APA subgroups. Specific barriers to college persistence for these students will also be examined. Finally, the chapter will outline strategies and programs that might improve APA's persistence rates.

COLLEGE-GOING RATES FOR ASIAN PACIFIC AMERICANS

Since the late 1970s, the American media has portrayed APAs as a "model minority." As such, most attention on this population has been devoted to the phenomenon that students of Asian descent appear to perform exceptionally well in academics. In seeming support of this argument, research indicates that in 1997, APAs represented approximately 4% of the U.S. population, but made up approximately 6% of all college students (Hune, 2002). When educators hear these statistics, it is no wonder that they do not consider Asian Pacific Americans to be an "underrepresented" group in higher education, nor a group that needs to be concerned about college persistence. However, a more detailed analysis of the data reveals that these conclusions do not acknowledge the complexity of the situation. For example, Bennett and Debarros (1998) indicate that high school completion rates vary significantly between APA ethnic groups (from 31% for Hmong to 88% for Japanese Americans in 1990). In addition, while 58.4% of Asian Indians in the United States had completed a bachelor's degree, only about 5% of Laotian and Cambodian students and 2.9% of Hmong in the United States were college graduates in 1990 (Siu, 1996). Interestingly, Kiang (1992) also notes that while Asian Pacific Americans are most often portrayed as high-achieving Ivy-league students, in fact 40% of APA's enrolled in higher education actually attend two-year colleges, and 82% attend public institutions.

In order to create a more accurate picture of the academic performance and needs of APA students, researchers argue that data on these populations must be disaggregated by criteria such as ethnicity, English proficiency, and generation in the United States (Educational Testing Service, 1997; Hune, 2002; Kim & Yeh, 2002; Pang, 1995). Admittedly, this type of analysis can prove quite difficult, because there is a small number of APA college students in the United States. As a result, many educational reports leave this group out entirely (NCES, 2001; Porter, 1990). However, these subgroup analyses are necessary to fully uncover and understand the complex factors affecting the college persistence and educational success of this population.

Fifty-seven distinct ethnic groups fell under the category of "Asian Pacific Islander" in the 1990 census. With respect to ethnicity, most research on Asian Pacific American college students focuses on those of East Asian descent (Chinese, Japanese, and Korean), because of their significant numbers and longer history. in the United States. While Filipinos Americans also comprise a large percentage of the APA population, they are often left out of the picture (Siu, 1996). Research on Southeast Asian college students is quite sparse, presumably because so few of them enroll in higher educational institutions. However, the studies that have disaggregated data by ethnicity show that certain APA ethnic subgroups have lower educational attainment as well as higher rates of poverty and illiteracy than other groups. For example, a study published by the Educational Testing Service (1997) found that while Asian Americans as a homogenous group seem to excel in school, in actuality high school dropout rates were approximately 46% for Filipinos, 50% for Southeast Asians, and 60% for Samoans. Additionally, Kiang's (1992) study of an urban public institution with a high percentage of Southeast Asian students revealed that only 14% of their APA students had graduated at the end of five years.

English proficiency is another critical factor that is overlooked when examining the success of APA students. Numerous studies on ESL (English-as-a-Second-Language) learners indicate that students who have limited English proficiency experience significant language barriers and are subsequently at a greater risk of leaving college prior to graduation (Ignash, 1992; Pang, 1995; Siu, 1996; Suzuki, 2002). In addition, the National Center for Education Statistics (2001) states that "assignment to remedial reading in college is associated with additional remediation and a lower likelihood of degree completion." Data from the California State University (CSU) system indicate that a staggering 63.5% of Asian American, 51.4% of Pacific Islander, and 53.8% of Filipino freshmen required English remediation instruction in the Fall of 2001 (CSU, 2001). Current CSU academic policy states that those students who do not successfully complete remediation courses in their freshman year must leave the university. Since such a high percentage of APA students find themselves in this rather precarious situation, it is imperative that retention efforts target this subgroup as well.

Pang (1995) also indicates that "an important variable to consider when teaching or doing research with Asian Pacific American students is place of birth—U.S. born or immigrant" (p. 413). This distinction is necessary to consider, because a group's circumstances or cause for immigration essentially dictates the educational and income level, employment status, and educational aspirations of a family once they arrive in this country. For instance, immigrants who come to the United States to seek a better education and economic future are more likely to persist in college than involuntary refugees who may not have had any formal schooling in their lifetime. Another distinct yet related factor is foreign versus resident student status. Hune (2002) argues that Asian foreign students should be considered a separate group from APAs because they have markedly different characteristics and needs. Because foreign students come to the United States with the specific goal of attaining an education, they are more motivated to complete a degree. To illustrate, Hune (2002) reports that Asian foreign students earned 18% of all U.S. doctoral degrees in 1997, while Asian Pacific Americans earned only 3% of all doctorates. In other words, combining foreign student data with APA data can significantly skew results.

These multiple intra-group differences have dramatic implications when determining whether or not APAs are indeed underrepresented in higher education. When critical variables are not taken into account, it appears as though APAs are well-represented and persisting in college. However, there are subgroups of students who are significantly underrepresented and at risk of departure, and currently invisible to most retention researchers and student affairs professionals. The research thus far has suggested that, in general, East Asians and Asian Indians have demonstrated higher proportions of educational persistence and completion, and were more likely to have been educated before immigrating to the United States. On the contrary, Southeast Asians (e.g., Vietnamese, Cambodian, Hmong, Laotian, Burmese) and Pacific Islanders (e.g., Native Hawaiians, Tongans, Samoans, Guamanians, Micronesians) are more likely to be refugees or involuntary immigrants who may not have had exposure to education, even in their own countries. Given these factors, it can be argued that Southeast Asians and Pacific Islanders are indeed underrepresented populations in higher education. Therefore, the remainder of this chapter will focus on these two groups, even though some of the issues and problems that will be discussed later are applicable to all Asian Pacific American groups.

REVIEW OF RELEVANT LITERATURE

A review of the theoretical and empirical literature on the retention of APAs has revealed very minimal results. Tinto's (1993) widely-used interactionalist theory of college student departure briefly addresses retention programs for students of color, but reminds the reader that not all students of color are disadvantaged, and not all disadvantaged students are students of color. He even points out that some "racial minorities (Asian Americans and Cuban Americans, among others) have higher rates of educational success than do groups commonly classified as belonging to the racial majority" (p. 181), implying that they may not need as much assistance as others. Over the years, Tinto's theory has been heavily studied and sometimes critiqued, with respect to its applicability to minority students (Braxton, 2000; Kuh & Love, 2000; Rendon, Jalomo, & Nora, 2000; Tierney, 2000). Additionally, new research and theories on the retention and persistence of minority college students have continued to increase tremendously. However, the vast majority of these studies focus on African-American and Latino students. Unfortunately, the little research that does mention Asian-American students often perpetuates the model minority stereotype by highlighting their high degrees of persistence in the aggregate, but ignoring the Asian-American subgroups that are underrepresented and underperforming (Brawer, 1996; Mow & Nettles, 1990).

Upon closer investigation, it appears that the research on APA educational issues is more plentiful for elementary and secondary school students. In fact, a number of studies and publications specifically address the existence of Asian Pacific American youth who exhibit educational risk factors (Asian American/Pacific Islanders in Philanthropy, 1997; Bempechat & Omori, 1990; Dao, 1991; Dolly, Blaine, & Power, 1989; Ima & Rumbaut, 1995; Peters, 1988; Siu, 1996). In addition, numerous articles examine the APA students' experience on campus, related to topics such as the model minority stereotype, racial identity, and the use of academic and counseling services. However, a literature search on the academic persistence or retention of APA college students generated four relevant results. Upon narrowing the search by ethnicity, refugee status, and language ability, several more studies were discovered.

Kiang (1992) conducted a qualitative study of the college experiences of Asian immigrant and refugee students at an urban public institution, and how these experiences impacted student persistence. From his findings, he identified several dimensions of their cultural and historical background that created obstacles for them in the college setting, including: 1) being Southeast Asian; 2) being refugees; 3) being new immigrants; and 4) being racial minorities. Another qualitative case study was conducted on two first-generation college students who were identified as gifted, one of whom was a Vietnamese-American (Olenchak & Hebert, 2002). The study described the struggles these students faced in college, and also identified four areas that significantly influenced the quality of their college experience: 1) family and educational background; 2) cultural influences; 3) university peer relationships; and 4) university academic experiences. One study specifically examined retention factors for Hawaiian students at four community colleges on Oahu, and found slight differences for students from liberal arts majors and vocational-technical majors (Makuakane-Drechsel & Hagedorn, 2000). Lee (1997) analyzed the educational participation of Hmong women, and focused on economic, racial, and gender barriers. Tsuchida (1982) described the academic retention efforts of a program at the University of Minnesota, to support the Indochinese students at their institution. Yeh (2002) presented a range of educational risk factors for Asian-American college students at the individual, family, institutional, and community levels, and provided some suggestions for colleges and universities to address these factors.

In reviewing this literature, it is clear that a handful of scholars are working to identify the educational obstacles that subgroups of APA college students face. However, these barriers and issues have not been systematically analyzed with respect to theories of college retention and persistence. The following section will attempt to begin this exploration.

ISSUES SPECIFIC TO UNDERREPRESENTED
ASIAN PACIFIC AMERICANS

Several issues specific to underrepresented Asian Pacific Americans are discussed in this section of the chapter. They help frame the later discussion.

Minority Retention Theories

In order to better understand the persistence behavior of underrepresented Asian Pacific American college students, we must first examine the factors that place minority students at greater risk of departure, as well as theories about improving their persistence. There are numerous empirical and theoretical investigations of the circumstances that lead students of color to leave college early. Noel, Levitz, and Saluri (1985) identified several groups of students who could be considered at risk for dropping out, including low income students, academically underprepared students, students with uncertain academic goals, returning learners, and commuters. Mow and Nettles (1990), in their comprehensive review of minority retention literature and research, found that academic preparation, SAT scores, high school GPA, socioeconomic status, educational aspirations, noncognitive variables (i.e., attitude, coping, self-concept), motivation, commitment to the institution, social integration, quality of campus life, presence of racism, and institutional fit could all act as predictors of academic performance. From a cultural perspective, Kuh and Love (2000) present eight propositions that attempt to explain premature student departure. Specifically, they argue that: a) student's culture of origin mediates the importance attached to obtaining a college degree (proposition 2); b) the probability of persistence is inversely related to the cultural distance between a student's culture of origin and the cultures of immersion (proposition 4); and c) the amount of time a student spends in one's culture of origin after matriculating is positively related to cultural stress and reduces their chances of persistence (proposition 6). A study of the influences of in- and out-of-class experiences on the learning and retention of culturally diverse students suggested that academic and interpersonal validation is critical to the success of nontraditional students (Rendon, 1994). The researcher found that validation empowered students to trust their learning abilities and gave them a sense of self-value, whereas lack of validation or invalidation made them feel "silenced, subordinate, and crippled" (p. 44). Furthermore, she argues that students who do not receive any validation inside or outside of class experience the greatest challenges. While it is safe to assume that almost none of these findings and theories were developed with Asian Pacific American students in mind, there is growing evidence that underrepresented Asian Pacific American students face many of the same obstacles and barriers that other underrepresented minority students encounter.

Challenges for Asian Pacific Americans

As outlined earlier, a main premise of this chapter is that Southeast Asians and Pacific Islanders are underrepresented populations in higher education. Their main challenges will be divided into individual/contextual factors and institutional factors, which are discussed below.

Individual/Contextual Factors

A majority of Southeast Asians (mainly Vietnamese, Cambodian, Laotian, and Hmong) who immigrated to the United States after 1975, came as refugees or former political prisoners (Ranard & Pfleger, 1993; Siu, 1996). The families of Pacific-Islander students may have moved to the mainland many years ago, or may still live in the islands. In either case, while most Pacific Islanders are U.S. citizens by birth, they face many of the same challenges that immigrants face. Thus, a majority of the issues described below are either an indirect or direct result of conditions and circumstances in their homeland.

Academic Underpreparedness

Southeast Asian immigrants are often academically underprepared to some degree. This could be due to the fact that they came to the United States as adolescents with little education from their homeland, and/or that they currently live in low-income neighborhoods and attend low-performing schools. In addition, Pacific-Islander students who grew up on the islands may also have attended schools that have a less rigorous curriculum than schools on the mainland. Moore and Carpenter (1985) affirm that these factors place students at a significant disadvantage in college.

First-Generation Status

The Southeast-Asian and Pacific-Islander students who do enroll in college are almost always the first generation in their family to do so. As such, their families are not able to support them academically, and may not understand what they are experiencing emotionally. Additionally, some families may place less value on education because it does not play a large role in their traditional culture, while others place tremendous pressure on students to succeed because they will be the first students to have the opportunity to go to college (Pang, 1995). Rendon, Jalomo, and Nora (2000) state that first-generation status is characteristic of many students who have difficulty transitioning to and adjusting to college.

Language/ESL Issues

Since most Southeast Asians and some Pacific Islanders do not speak English as a primary language, they struggle with language issues when they arrive in the mainland United States. Many ESL programs at the K-12 level are geared toward Spanish-speakers, and thus APA students do not receive adequate preparation at the secondary level. This results in high need for remediation courses when they reach college (Suzuki, 2002). Additionally, Kiang (1992) found that many immigrant and refugee students experience academic and social difficulty because of their language barrier. For instance, many students are afraid to speak up or ask questions in class because they are afraid of being ridiculed. Additionally, they have trouble taking notes, understanding their teachers, and completing reading assignments because of their limited English abilities. This type of academic environment is clearly invalidating and alienating for students, and as such, places them at risk of dropping out (Rendon, 1994).

Low-Income Background

Numerous studies indicate that large proportions of Southeast Asians and Pacific Islanders live in poverty. Thus, college students from these backgrounds are usually expected to work from 15 to 50 hours per week to help support their families, in addition to attending classes (Kiang, 1992). They also face financial struggles to pay for college tuition, books, and fees. Additionally, because they cannot afford to live on-campus, they spend a great deal of time commuting from home. For these and many other reasons, low-income students as well as commuter students have both been determined to be at high risk of attrition from college (Stewart, Merrill, & Saluri, 1985; Tinto, 1993; Valverde, 1985).

Other Family Demands

APA students from immigrant and low-income families often have parents who work two or three jobs to support the family. Thus, these students are often required to take care of their younger siblings, take care of household duties, as well as translate for parents and other family members who do not speak English. In addition, young women from some ethnic groups are encouraged to leave college early, in order to marry and have children. According to Kuh and Love (2000), these students need to spend most of their non-class time operating in their culture of origin, which reduces their likelihood of persistence.

Cultural Adjustment

As newly-arrived residents from Southeast Asia or the Pacific Islands, these students also face significant cultural adjustment challenges when they attend college in the mainland United States. Students from extremely remote, rural, or island settings may have a particularly difficult experience. For example, many students from the Pacific Islands may have a hard time adjusting to non-tropical climates as well as the faster pace of life (J. Tuleda, personal communication, June 12, 2003). These students were also raised to value modesty, and are unlikely to be aggressive or vocal about asserting their needs. Since most of them have never left their families before, they also have difficulty coping with the extreme distance from their family support system (the flights may take over 24 hours). As another example, many Hmong people had not had exposure to electricity or running water until leaving their country. Kuh and Love (2000) would argue that these students may leave college prematurely because the cultural distance between their culture of origin is so far from the culture of immersion.

Institutional/Environmental Factors

Many theorists cite the need for institutions to acknowledge their part in contributing to student retention and persistence. There are several institutional factors that significantly affect APA students.

Marginalization on Campus

Since the numbers of Pacific Islanders, Cambodians, Hmong, and Laotians are so small on most college campuses, the few students who do attend feel quite alienated from the rest of the students on campus. Not unlike the experience of many Native American college students, they are invisible and forgotten populations in the community. Moreover, Kim and Yeh (2002) document that some of the more wealthy Asian Americans will try to distance themselves from the less educated and poorer Asian American groups. Rendon, Jalomo, and Nora (2000) cite that "students who feel afraid or out of place in the mainstream college culture" have difficulty adjusting to and becoming involved in college.

Racism/Discrimination on Campus

Suzuki (2002) highlights the increasing occurrence of racism, discrimination, and violence against Asian Pacific Americans on college campuses across the country. What is most disappointing is that racist statements have come from not only other students, but from faculty as well. Kim and Yeh (2002) also reported that Asian-Pacific American students exhibited higher levels of distress from being threatened, racially insulted, and excluded from activities than did African American, Hispanic, and white students. Nora and Cabrera (1996) found that perceptions of discrimination and prejudice negatively affect minority student adjustment to college and damage their cognitive and affective development.

Cultural Barriers

Cultural differences can create barriers that negatively impact the academic performance and psychosocial adjustment of APA students. Particularly for students who were raised in the Pacific Islands and other Asian countries, mainland U.S. classroom expectations are difficult to adjust to. More specifically, students find it hard to switch from a traditional teacher-focused classroom to a student-centered classroom that encourages participation. Since they were taught to respect the wisdom of their elders, these students are very reluctant to share their opinions, disagree with the readings, or challenge their professors (R. Nelson, personal communication, June 15, 2003). As a result, their academic experience suffers. In addition, there is ample evidence in the psychology literature stating that APA students underutilize counseling services, and tend to keep their problems to themselves. Sometimes this behavior is due to negative cultural beliefs about counseling, but other times it is because counseling and advising centers do not tailor their services to APA populations. Regardless of the reason, this underutilization has been shown to lead to higher incidences of depression and even suicidal ideation (Sue & Sue, 1999). Additionally, the inability to seek help for problems is a negative internal force that affects college persistence (Anderson, 1985).

Model Minority Stereotype

Suzuki (2002) and many other researchers have demonstrated the harmful consequences of the model minority stereotype. First and foremost, the false perception that APA are all well-adjusted and high-achieving has led student service and outreach programs to overlook the issues and needs of these students, and even exclude them from receiving services or benefits. This type of systemic and institutional neglect has very damaging effects for underrepresented APA students. Additionally, the model minority stereotype places unrealistic academic expectations on students, who sometimes feel so much pressure that they are forced to drop out of college. Similarly, this stereotype can inhibit students from admitting their emotional and academic problems, and thus from seeking assistance.

Citizenship Status and Financial Aid

An unusual issue for some Pacific Islanders also involves financial aid. While most U.S.-affiliated islands in the Pacific are eligible for Federal financial aid, islands that are affiliated with France or Britain are not eligible for this assistance (R. Nelson, personal communication, June 15, 2003). Moreover, students who do receive financial aid rarely receive enough to cover their expenses, because their travel costs are extremely high and because their families earn very low salaries. These students do not have access to most private scholarships because they are rarely advertised in the islands, and they do not have access to state scholarships, because they live in U.S. territories. As a result, many of these students must hold full-time jobs while taking a full load of college credits, which can negatively affect their financial aid as well as their academic performance.

STRATEGIES FOR IMPROVING PERSISTENCE

Given the numerous barriers that underrepresented APA students clearly face, colleges and universities must begin to acknowledge their needs and concerns, and create strategies for improving the retention of APAs. There are extremely few programs and services targeted specifically for APAs, and institutions that have larger percentages of these students (especially those students who demonstrate high risk factors) should develop programs to serve these groups. Other colleges and universities can add to or modify their existing services to accommodate this population. In her model of academic validation, Rendon (1994) presents a list of criteria for fostering a validating classroom, as well as a therapeutic learning community. She also stresses the active role that higher education institutions must play in developing this kind of positive environment, in order to improve student satisfaction and persistence. Some suggestions for creating such a community are reviewed below.

Student Services

• Increase outreach to underrepresented APA in admissions recruitment as well as when advertising programs and services on campus. Many college admissions and outreach offices target African-American, Latino and Native-American students, but tend to exclude all Asian Pacific American students, even if they are from underrepresented ethnic groups or come from low-income backgrounds. This type of unequal treatment only serves to further alienate these students from other students of color, as well as perpetuate the model minority stereotype. Include eligible APA students in retention programs for underrepresented minorities. Many campuses offer services and programs for other minority groups, such as ethnic-specific advising groups, tutoring programs, counseling/peer support groups, peer and faculty mentoring programs, and leadership development programs. However, these types of programs are not usually available for underrepresented APA students. While many campuses do have ethnic-specific cultural organizations, these groups are mostly student-run rather than staff-supported. Additionally, they are usually culturally/socially focused as opposed to being academically focused. Although research suggests that social support groups are a vital part of improving student retention, students still need to maintain their academics in order to persist to graduation. Again, due to the widespread belief that Asian Pacific American students are all academically successful, many student affairs personnel believe that cultural groups provide sufficient support to meet the needs of this population. As a result, these students do not receive the academic support or guidance that other students of color may receive, and are left feeling isolated and unsure about where to find resources and assistance for their problems.

• Provide more culturally sensitive counseling services. To their credit, many campus counseling centers have finally recognized the need to hire

African-American and Latino professionals, in order to reach out to students from these communities and provide more culturally sensitive psychological services. These efforts have greatly improved the quality of care delivered to these student populations. However, as cited in Suzuki's (2002) anecdotal account, many centers still do not see the need to provide this same service to Asian Pacific American students. Since much of the counseling research demonstrates that APA students do indeed suffer from psychological pressure and other individual and environmental risk factors, colleges and universities need to make an effort to serve this population as well.

• Offer more comprehensive ESL programs and services. Many researchers cite the need for increasing and improving programs for English language learners, many of whom are Asian Pacific Americans (Hunter & Ratliffe, 1991; Ignash, 1992; Ima & Rumbaut, 1995). Because there is a whole field of study concerning ESL education, this chapter will not attempt to prescribe in-depth strategies for improving these services. However, studies of the California State University 23-campus system as well as community colleges nationwide clearly demonstrate the need for providing tutorial and study skills support, academic advising, and ESL content courses (Ignash, 1992; Suzuki, 2002). These services can assist students in completing their remediation courses and moving on to successfully function in regular classes. In addition to these academic services, Ignash (1992) discusses the need for support programs (particularly at the community college level) to help students with cultural adjustment issues, self-esteem, learning to speak up in class, asking for help, and negotiating with administrative offices and social agencies.

Institutional Practices and Policies

• Gather disaggregated statistics on APAs. While many institutions may resist this idea because it may require additional resources, there is increasing evidence to suggest that aggregated data on this population simply does not provide accurate results. In order to gain a more thorough understanding of APA students, institutions should collect ethnic-specific data in addition to race-specific data. Furthermore, Hune (2002) indicates that separating Asian foreign students from Asian Pacific Americans will also result in more useful analyses.

• Diversify and better train the student affairs staff. Suzuki (2002) recommends that institutions recruit more APA staff to work across all student affairs divisions. In addition, they need to provide extensive and ongoing staff training (as opposed to one-day, once-a-year training) about the issues and needs of all underrepresented student populations, as well as strategies for working with them.

• Improve the campus climate. Colleges and universities must continue to make the campus climate welcoming for all underrepresented students, including Asian Pacific Americans. Many studies suggest that APA students feel particularly excluded and alienated in college, because they are neither accepted by the majority population, nor by other minority groups. Hune (2002) reports that chilly climate, racial and ethnic stereotyping by faculty, staff and other students, language bias and discrimination, and hate crimes are all serious obstacles for APA college students. As such, universities must increase their efforts to monitor racial harassment incidents, establish policies and practices for improving the campus climate, and commit to implementing those practices.

• Conduct empirical research on the needs of underrepresented APA students. In their discussion of minority student retention theory, Rendon, Jalomo, and Nora (2000) indicate that "especially fertile territory is research on American Indians, Asians, Pacific Islanders, Filipinos . . . and immigrant students from Asia and Central and South America" (p, 130). In order to better understand how to retain these students, more information must be gathered and used to inform program design.

CONCLUSIONS/IMPLICATIONS

Pursuing the recommendations listed above would go a long way toward improving the retention and persistence of underrepresented APA college students. However, university administrators and staff must first fully recognize the struggles and needs of this population, before successful implementation of these programs and policies can occur. It is always harmful to generalize across entire populations; in the case of Asian Pacific Americans, educators have assumed their unwavering success for too long. Indeed, the Educational Testing Service (1997) states that "the stereotype of Asian American academic success appears to have led to official neglect of the development of programs and services for such students" (p. 2). It is hoped that when the specific efforts mentioned above are combined with more traditional retention strategies (Noel, Levitz, & Saluri, 1985; Seidman, 2002; Tinto, 1993), educators and administrators can move toward a more comprehensive methodology for working with underrepresented APA students.

REFERENCES

Anderson, E. (1985). Forces influencing student persistence and achievement. In L. Noel, R. Levitz, & D. Saluri (Eds.), *Increasing student retention.* San Francisco: Jossey-Bass.

Asian American/Pacific Islanders in Philanthropy. (1997). *An invisible crisis: The educational needs of Asian Pacific American youth.* [Report]. New York: Author.

Bempechat, J., & Omori, M. C. (1990). *Meeting the educational needs of Southeast Asian children* (ERIC/CUE Digest No. 68). New York: ERIC Clearinghouse on Urban Education.

Bennett, C. E., & Debarros, K. A. (1998). The Asian and Pacific Islander population. In U.S. Census Bureau, *The official statistics.* Washington, DC: U.S. Government Printing Office.

Brawer, F. B. (1996). *Retention-attrition in the nineties* (ERIC Digest). Los Angles: ERIC Clearinghouse for Community Colleges. (ERIC Document Reproduction Service No. ED 393 510.)

Braxton, J. M. (Ed.). (2000). *Reworking the student departure puzzle.* Nashville: Vanderbilt University Press.

California State University Analytic Studies (2002). *Fall 2001 Regularly admitted first-time freshman remediation systemwide.* [On-line]. Available: www.asd.calstate.edu/remediation01/remediation/2001-ftrnr023.htm

Chan, K., & Hune, S. (1995). Racialization and panethnicity: From Asians in America to Asian Americans. In W. Hawley & A. Jackson (Eds.), *Toward a common destiny: Improving race and ethnic relations in America* (pp. 205-233). San Francisco: Jossey-Bass.

Dao, M. (1991). Designing assessment procedures for educationally at-risk South Asian American students. *Journal of Learning Disabilities, 24,* 594-601, 629.

Dolly, J. P., Blaine, D. D., & Power, K. M. (1989). Educationally at-risk Pacific and Asian students in a traditional academic program. *Journal of Instructional Psychology, 16,* 155-163.

Educational Testing Service. (1997). *Stereotyping shortchanges Asian American students.* [On-line]. Available: modelminority.com/modules.php

Hune, S. (2002). Demographics and diversity of Asian American college students. In M. K. McEwen, C. M. Kodama, A. N. Alvarez, S. Lee, & C. Liang (Vol. Eds.), *New Directions for Student Services: Vol. 97. Working with Asian American College Students* (pp. 11-20). San Francisco: Jossey-Bass.

Hunter, R. L., & Ratliffe, S. A. (1991, July). *A community volunteer program for supporting second language students who may be academically at-risk.* Paper presented at the Speech Communication Association Summer Conference, Huntington Beach, CA. (ERIC Document Reproduction Service No. ED 331 565.)

Ignash, J. M. (1992). *ESL population and program patterns in community colleges* (ERIC Digest). Los Angeles: ERIC Clearinghouse for Junior Colleges. (ERIC Document Reproduction Service No. ED 353 022.)

Ima, K., & Rumbaut, R. G. (1995). Southeast Asian refugees in American schools: A comparison of fluent-English-proficient and limited-English-proficient students. In D. T. Nakanishi & T. Y. Nishida (Eds.), *The Asian American educational experience: A source book for teachers and students.* New York: Routledge.

Kiang, P. N. (1992). Issues of curriculum and community for first-generation Asian Americans in college. *New Directions for Community Colleges, 80,* 97-112.

Kim, A., & Yeh, C. J. (2002). *Stereotypes of Asian American students* (ERIC Digest). New York: ERIC Clearinghouse on Urban Education. (ERIC Document Reproduction Service No. ED 462 510.)

Kuh, G. D., & Love, P. G. (2000). A cultural perspective on student departure. In J. M. Braxton (Ed.), *Reworking the student departure puzzle* (pp. 127-156). Nashville: Vanderbilt University Press.

Lee, S. J. (1997). The road to college: Hmong American women's pursuit of higher education. *Harvard Educational Review, 67*(4), 803-827.

Makuakane-Drechsel, T., & Hagedorn, L. S. (2000). Correlates of retention among Asian Pacific Americans in community colleges: The case for Hawaiian students. *Community College Journal of Research and Practice, 24,* 639-655.

Moore, W., Jr., & Carpenter, L. C. (1985). Academically underprepared students. In L. Noel, R. Levitz, & D. Saluri (Eds.), *Increasing student retention.* San Francisco: Jossey-Bass.

Mow, S. L., & Nettles, M. T. (1990). Minority student access to, and persistence and performance in, college: A review of the trends and research literature. In J. C. Smart (Ed.), *Higher education: Handbook of theory and research* (Vol. 6, pp. 35-105). New York: Agathon Press.

National Center for Education Statistics (NCES). (2001). *The condition of education, 2001: Remediation and degree completion.* NCES 2001-072. Washington, DC: U.S. Department of Education, Office of Educational Research and Improvement.

Noel, L., Levitz, R., & Saluri, D. (1985). *Increasing student retention.* San Francisco: Jossey-Bass.

Nora, A., & Cabrera, A. (1996). The role of perceptions in prejudice and discrimination and adjustment of minority students to college. *Journal of Higher Education, 67*(2), 119-148.

Olenchak, F. R., & Hebert, T. P. (2002). Endangered academic talent: Lessons learned from gifted first-generation college males. *Journal of College Student Development, 43*(2), 195-212.

Pang, V. O. (1995). Asian Pacific American students: A diverse and complex population. In J. A. Banks (Ed.), *Handbook of research on multicultural education* (pp. 412-424). New York: Macmillan.

Peters, H. A. (1988). A study of Southeast Asian youth in Philadelphia: A final report. Philadelphia: Institute for the Study of Human Issues. (ERIC Document Reproduction Service No. ED 299 371.)

Porter, O. F. (1990). *Undergraduate completion and persistence at four-year colleges and universities.* Washington, DC: National Institute of Independent Colleges and Universities.

Ranard, D., & Pfleger, M. (1993). Language and literacy education for southeast Asian refugees (ERIC Digest). Washington, DC: National Clearinghouse for ESL Literacy Education. (ERIC Document Reproduction Service No. ED 365 170.)

Rendon, L. I. (1994). Validating culturally diverse students: Toward a new model of learning and student development. *Innovative Higher Education, 19*(1), 33-51.

Rendon, L. I., Jalomo, R. E., & Nora, A. (2000). Theoretical considerations in the study of minority student retention in higher education. In J. M. Braxton (Ed.), *Reworking the student departure puzzle* (pp. 127-156). Nashville: Vanderbilt University Press.

Seidman, A. (2002). *A retention formula for student success.* [On-line]. Available: www.collegeways.com/docs/retentionformula2002-A_files

Siu, S. F. (1996). *Asian American students at risk: A literature review* (Report No. 8). Baltimore: Center for Research on the Education of Students Placed at Risk, Johns Hopkins University. (ERIC Document Reproduction Service No. ED 404 406.)

Stewart, S. S., Merrill, M. C., & Saluri, D. (1985). In L. Noel, R. Levitz, & D. Saluri (Eds.), *Increasing student retention.* San Francisco: Jossey-Bass.

Sue, D. W., & Sue, D. (1999). *Counseling the culturally different.* New York: Wiley.

Suzuki, B. (2002). Revisiting the model minority stereotype. In M. K. McEwen, C. M. Kodama, A. N. Alvarez, S. Lee, & C. Liang (Vol. Eds.), *New Directions for Student Services: Vol. 97. Working with Asian American College Students* (pp. 21-32). San Francisco: Jossey-Bass.

Tierney, W. G. (2000). Power, identity, and the dilemma of college student departure. In J. M. Braxton (Ed.), *Reworking the student departure puzzle* (pp. 127-156). Nashville: Vanderbilt University Press.

Tinto, V. (1993). *Leaving college* (2nd ed.). Chicago: University of Chicago Press.

Tsuchida, N. (1982). Support services and academic retention programs for Indochinese students at the University of Minnesota. *Alternative Higher Education, 6*(3), 160-171.

Valverde, L. A. (1985). Low-income students. In L. Noel, R. Levitz, & D. Saluri (Eds.), *Increasing student retention.* San Francisco: Jossey-Bass.

Yeh, T. L. (2002). Asian American students who are educationally at risk. In M. K. McEwen, C. M. Kodama, A. N. Alvarez, S. Lee, & C. Liang (Vol. Eds.), *New Directions for Student Services: Vol. 9 7. Working with Asian American College Students* (pp. 61-71). San Francisco: Jossey-Bass.

SECTION 4

Native American Students

CHAPTER 9

The Retention/Intervention Study of Native American Undergraduates at the University of New Mexico*

Mary Jiron Belgarde and Richard K. LoRé

Student service programs act as key resources to help students persist in school until graduation. However, some critics question whether service programs aimed at specific ethnic populations contribute sufficiently toward their persistence. Tinto (1975) argues that the stronger one is integrated into the institution, the more likely he/she will graduate from college. Thus, Native students' use of Native and non-Native student service programs is likely to effect the strength of their integration. The chapter presents study findings to explain how Native undergraduates used mainstream and Native programs to support their persistence to graduation at the University of New Mexico. It reports the students' levels of involvement, satisfaction of the services received, and why some students didn't use them. It also includes stop-out information and reasons for stopping out. Finally, the authors discuss how the findings and conclusions may be viewed in light of Native philosophy and views on education.

*Throughout history and in much of the literature, many different terms have been used to describe this group of people: American Indians, Native Americans, First Nations People, and Indigenous populations, for example. In this chapter we use the terms of Native American and American Indians interchangeably to reflect the institutional designation of students and the names of programs serving them.

INTRODUCTION

In this chapter we present some findings of a research study that examined the personal and institutional factors that affect the retention of American Indian undergraduates at the University of New Mexico during the academic period between Fall 1990 and Fall 1996. The purpose of this study was to examine how the Native American Studies Academic and Retention and Intervention (NASARI) Program affected the persistence, retention, and graduation rates of American Indian undergraduate students enrolled at the University of New Mexico. It also sought to identify personal and institutional factors outside of NASARI that may have affected the persistence, retention, and graduation rates. Two research questions were addressed: 1) How did the pilot NASARI affect the persistence, retention, and graduation rates of American Indian undergraduate students? and 2) What were the personal and institutional factors affecting retention of American Indian undergraduate students?

We provide the reader with some background information about American Indians in higher education, and describe the demographic characteristics of this Native student population in our state and university. We then describe the study and present some of the findings related to their prior academic experiences and the use of and quality of services received from three different groups (the NASARI program, other Native and non-Native programs). We also include stop-out information and their reasons for stopping out. Finally, we summarize the findings and share how the findings should be understood in light of local Native philosophy and views of education.

REVIEW OF THE LITERATURE

American Indians have been attending higher education institutions since the mid-17th century (Wright, 1985, 1991, 1992). They continue to register the lowest admission, retention, and graduation rates among students enrolled in public and private colleges (Fox, 1982; McNamara, 1982; Pavel, 1987; Tierney, 1993; Wright, 1991, 1992; Wright & Tierney, 1991). Some researchers who have studied American Indian college student performance and persistence have found that socioeconomic status, type of high school, high school grade point average, parental educational level, parental attitudes and support, and financial aid yield the highest predictive power for college performance and completion (Fox, 1982; Grits, 1991; Jeanotte, 1981; McNamara, 1982). Others have found that their study habits and attitudes, achievement motivation, career maturity, and social and cultural factors also yield positive outcomes (Hoover & Jacobs, 1992; Huffman, Sill, & Brokenleg, 1986; Rindone, 1988; Sawyer, 1981; West, 1988).

Other studies have found structural and normative characteristics within institutions to be mediating variables to student outcomes. Support programs, such as tutoring, counseling, and culturally based programs (Native American Studies, Native American advisory, pre-college preparatory and orientation programs), were found to enhance American Indian student performance and persistence (Barnhardt, 1994; Edgewater, 1981; Fuchs & Havighurst, 1972; Kleinfeld & Kohout, 1974; Patton & Edington, 1973; Pavel & Padilla, 1993; Pepion, 1991; Perechi, 1994; White, 1991; Whitehorse, 1992; Wright, 1992). The University of New Mexico has offered many of these types of services since the mid 1950s (e.g., academic and social orientation program for incoming students; tutoring and counseling through the American Indian Program Office) and Indian student persistence and graduation rates appear to have improved considerably. Yet, these students still lag behind White and other minority students (Jojola & Alcantara, 1996).

In some studies, students socialized to the Indian tradition appear to have a better chance for achievement in college than their non-traditional counterparts (Barnhardt, 1994; Belgarde, 1992; Hobson, 1994; Huffman, Sill, & Brokenleg, 1986; Jaimes, 1982; Kirkness & Barnhardt, 1991; Lin, LaCounte, & Eder, 1988; LoRé, 1998; Rindone, 1988; Wright, 1992; Wright & Tierney, 1991). These studies, along with our own research, suggest that the strength students receive from their cultural heritage and families seem to matter. For example, since college completion in some Indian communities is unusual but considered admirable, traditional students receive respect, encouragement, and emotional support from extended family, clan, and tribal members. Jaimes cites a U.S. Office of Education study which found that the most successful Indian college students were not the ones who came from the most acculturated environments, but were from homes where no English was spoken and where traditional Indian roots were firmly established. Jaimes suggests that these students succeed because they have a positive self-image both as Indians and participants within the dominant society. LaFromboise (1988) examined the use of traditional values as additional coping mechanisms among Indian college women. She found that American Indian students who live in two cultures learn bicultural competence skills. Students learn appropriate behavioral norms of both cultures and apply this knowledge and skill to succeed. These researchers suggest that traditional cultural identity and heritage fosters a strong sense of personal self-identity and confidence among Indian students and in turn positively influences academic achievement.

Approximately 35 tribal colleges have been developed on or near reservations in the United States and Canada. These institutions attract many students who desire to remain at home while going to school. They also provide many different levels of education, from short-term certificates to master's of arts degree programs. The tribal colleges are highly successful because they are guided by tribal leaders, local businesses, industry, government, organizations, and families. They determine and design the programs that benefit the local communities. They offer programs that embed language and culture into the curriculum, provide Native faculty and support programs (American Indian Higher Education Consortium & The Institute for Higher Education Policy, 2001; Belgarde, 1993; Machamer, 2000; Wright, 1992; Wright & Tierney, 1991).

BACKGROUND INFORMATION

At the University of New Mexico (UNM), when American Indian students are compared to White and other minority counterparts, they have the lowest retention to the third semester of all beginning freshmen. Except for the foreign students, the American Indian students generally have the lowest retention rates of all students (Official Enrollment Reports, 1990-1998, Institutional Research Reports, 1990-1998; Jojola, 1992; Jojola & Alcantara, 1996; Martinez, 1998; Montoya, 1999). Many programs have been developed to meet their unique needs.

During the period between 1990-1996, the New Mexico State Legislature appropriated a substantial amount of money from the general fund to the University of New Mexico (UNM) to create a Native American higher education academic and intervention and retention pilot project program at the Native American Studies Center.[1] The project was to assist Native American students to stay enrolled in the University. The project was to identify academic problem areas for Native students and assist them in solving those problems; provide computer literacy and reference training; conduct research, publish finding, and hold education, curricular, and policy symposia. The grant was to assist students attain undergraduate degrees, seek advanced degrees, pursue rewarding and productive careers, and to serve their communities.

The Legislators asked the UNM Office of the Provost to examine whether the Native American Studies Academic Retention and Intervention Project had a positive effect on the retention of American Indian students and how it did so. The Provost's Office and the Native American Studies Program had a vested interest in the research and granted a research study team cooperation and support for the study for the same period.

DESCRIPTION OF
THE UNIVERSITY COMMUNITY

At the time of the study, The University of New Mexico, a large comprehensive Research I institution, enjoyed a student population of approximately 26,000 students. The University has one main campus and three branch campuses located in Gallup, Santa Fe, and Taos. The main campus is geographically located in

[1] Native American state legislators, such as Senator Leonard Tsosie, were instrumental in securing the legislation for this initiative.

the north-central part of New Mexico and in the city of Albuquerque of nearly 500,000 people. The University can be best described as commuter campuses. The University offers bachelor's, master's, doctoral, and professional degrees in the Colleges of Architecture, Arts and Sciences, Business, Dental Hygiene, Education, Engineering, Fine Arts, Miscellaneous Allied Health, Law, Medicine, Nursing, Pharmacy, Public Administration, Undergraduate Studies, and University Studies (University of New Mexico, 1989-1991, 1991-1993, 1993-1995, 1995-1997, 1997-1999, 1999-2001, 2001-2003). Montoya (1999) reported that American Indians made up about 10% of the state's total population and that half of the Indian population was in its mid-20s or younger. The university has been extremely diverse in its ethnic composition. During the time of the study, the student body composition was 52% White, 33% Hispanic, 3% Black, 4% Asian, 4% Native, and 3% other (Institutional Research Reports, 1996). The institution also attracted many part-time students completing degrees at night, on weekends, and during the summer months. Some of the local students completed some of their basic core courses at a local proximate two-year institution called the Albuquerque Technical Vocational Institute and transferred to the main campus, but for the most part, most students began their programs on the main campus.

The University and Southwestern tribes established formal relationship agreements in the early 1920s when a few students lived in the Albuquerque Indian Boarding School dormitories and attended the University of New Mexico. The first formal Native support program commenced in the mid-1950s (Jojola, 1996). The University currently engages in formal written agreements between university and tribal officials, referred to as Memoranda of Understanding, to clarify how the organizations will help students remain in school to graduation completion.

NATIVE STUDENT POPULATION

Most of the Native students attending the University of New Mexico come from the 19 Pueblo and two Apache (Mescalero and Jicarilla) tribes, and the large Navajo Nation (Belgarde, 2001). A few Native students from out-of-state areas also attend. Pueblo, Apache, and Navajo nations still maintain their Native languages, traditions, and culture to a large extent (Martinez, 1998; Sando, 1998). Some of the Native students also emanate from urban areas, such as Albuquerque. Students who live in urban areas continue to return to their home communities to participate in cultural traditions. While some students from both the reservations and urban communities neither speak their Native languages nor practice traditional activities, most do; and attending an institution such as the UNM allows many to live on the reservation and participate in Native culture while going to school (Linthicum, 2001).

STUDY DESIGN

The researchers drew from Tinto's (1975) general theory of persistence in higher education to explain why students persist in college. His model asserts that students enter higher education with a variety of personal attributes (gender, culture), precollege experiences (grade-point averages, academic and social attainments), and family background (social economic status, parental educational level), each of which has direct and indirect impact upon performance in college. These factors influence the initial commitment students make to their career goal and to the institution. Once in college, students participate in the academic and social systems of the organization. The degree to which they are integrated into these systems affects their level of commitment. Tinto (1975) argues that the more they are integrated into the academic and social systems, the higher is their level of commitment to the institution, and hence the more probable is college completion.

METHODOLOGY

The research team sought to answer the research questions through a quantitative and qualitative research design. To answer the first question, the research team analyzed quantitative data from the Office of Institutional Research at UNM and from responses to a telephone survey of Native Americans who had attended or were attending UNM at the time of data collection. Specifically, the research team looked for effects of student participation in the NASARI project on the outcome variables of cumulative UNM grade-point-average (GPA), cumulative credit hours attempted at UNM, cumulative credit hours earned at UNM and elsewhere, and degrees awarded. These outcome variables were compared for groups of participants and non-participants in the program across four different cohorts of American Indian students enrolled at UNM from Fall 1990 (when the program began) to Fall 1996. The first cohort included all American Indian students enrolled at UNM ($N = 3466$). The second cohort included all American Indian students beginning their first semester at UNM ($N = 1918$). The third group included all American Indian students who began at UNM as freshmen ($N = 690$). The fourth cohort included all American Indian students who began as freshmen at UNM in 1990 and graduated ($N = 25$). To address the second question, qualitative analyses were conducted on responses to a telephone questionnaire containing 33 items, administered to a comparative sample ($N = 183$) of participant (88) and non-participant (95) students by trained interviewers. The formal telephone interviews had the explicit research goal of probing academic and social integration. Interviewers asked students to describe their academic and social experiences at the University of New Mexico; how the Native American Studies retention program helped them integrate into the academic and social systems; and whether there was anything within the institution that prevented them from academically or socially integrating. The formal interviews lasted approximately 30 to 40 minutes.

DESCRIPTION OF THE RESEARCH TEAM

Approximately 20 graduate and undergraduate students comprised a majority of the research team. A Native faculty member in the College of Education trained and supervised the research team leaders and members. The research team members helped to develop the study design, construct and field test the questionnaire, and gather and analyze data. Four team leaders supervised and trained others with regard to the theoretical framework, questionnaire development, and telephone interviews. The team leaders and interviewers were highly selected graduate and former undergraduate students at the University of New Mexico and had familiarity with the university system. Many of the interviewers were from the American Indian communities in New Mexico and knowledgeable about being a Native undergraduate student at the University. They were thoroughly informed about the overall goals of the project and trained in completing telephone interviews. All interviewers were supervised by a team leader and/or the principal investigator. American Indian team members familiar with American Indian student populations were employed as trackers to locate former undergraduate students. In some cases, they attempted to locate the students through other data sources (e.g., New Mexico Voter Registration and old university phone books; trackers' friends and family in Indian communities). Data entry personnel were trained as telephone interviewers and thoroughly familiar with the questionnaire. They were also trained to enter the data on Microsoft Access database management program. The data analysts were recommended by College of Education faculty, and had taken numerous graduate courses in statistics and/or in qualitative analyses. Some had prior experience in writing statistical programs on SPSS. All of the data analysts were trained specifically regarding the purpose of the project, the theoretical framework, and the questionnaire.

THE INSTRUMENT

The first portion of the questionnaire elicited demographic data (e.g., gender, number of dependents, tribal affiliation, age, and parental education) and pre-college information (e.g., high school type, ratings of high school academic preparation, study skills, whether students had a career goal and major at time of UNM entry). The second section of the questionnaire examined matriculation, current enrollment, and graduation information; identified faculty or staff who helped them to reach their career goals; courses unprepared for, developmental courses taken, and whether they were required; highest degree goal; and stop-out information. The third through fifth sections of the questionnaire examined the frequency and quality of services received through the Native American Studies

Program, other Native services, and the overall university, date when they began using each of these services, and why they didn't use any or more of these services provided. Finally, the sixth section measured cultural knowledge and ethnic loyalty constructs; how Indian culture helped or hindered their staying in school; and how services may be improved to help Indian students.

THE SAMPLE

From a population of 3,466 current and former American Indian students, a sample of 200 students was drawn. An Enrollment Research Analyst from the Registrar's Office generated an unduplicated list of names of American Indian undergraduate students who attended the University of New Mexico main campus between Fall 1990 and Fall 1996 ($N = 3466$). The Native American Studies Program provided the research team with a list of undergraduate students who participated in their retention efforts ($N = 502$). From both lists research team members located and asked students to participate in the study. A sample of convenience occurred due to the high mobility of college students. However, an effort was made to stratify the sample to reflect gender and program utilization (use/non-use of retention services). One hundred eighty-three of 200 students (92%) were surveyed via the telephone questionnaire. Forty-eight percent were students who participated in the Native American Studies Retention/Intervention Project and 52% were non-participants.

QUANTITATIVE DATA ANALYSIS

The team conducted quantitative analyses at four levels. The first level yielded descriptive statistics of the demographic variables and academic performance of all American Indian students enrolled during the period under study. The descriptive statistics for variables such as gender, tribe, and full- and part-time status were computed in aggregate form to describe the whole American Indian population ($N = 3466$), the sample population, and quantitative questionnaire items. Then, means and standard deviation for credits completed and grade-point-averages were computed. The second stage of quantitative analyses identified the retention proportions of students. For example, the numbers and percentages of students enrolled in school at the end of the third semester were compared between the sample population and the random sample and subsequently, the academic performance among NAS participating and non-participating students. Academic performance was determined by credits and grades completed. Finally, the statistics identified the academic pace for all students who graduated from UNM during this particular period—how long it took these students to graduate once they matriculated into UNM.

QUANTITATIVE DATA FINDINGS

Table 1 reveals the descriptive data for the student cohorts enrolled at UNM from Fall 1990-Fall 1996. Table 2 shows the comparisons of outcome variables of grade-point-averages, mean hours attempted, and mean cumulative hours earned for participant and non-participant students.

Analysis of the data on Table 2 show that there were no significant differences between participants and non-participants on the outcome variable of mean grade-point-averages. There were statistically significant differences between participants and non-participants on the outcome variables of mean cumulative hours attempted at UNM and mean cumulative hours earned at UNM and elsewhere. Participants attempted and completed more cumulative credit hours than non-participants

QUALITATIVE DATA ANALYSIS

Research team members used two different methods to qualitatively examine emerging relationships in an iterative fashion. First, they accounted for the frequency of conceptual relations reported among the students. Second, they employed data source and technique triangulation (Fetterman, 1989; Miles & Huberman, 1984). Data source triangulation involved comparing different sources of data about the same phenomenon, during different phases of the fieldwork, points in the temporal cycles in the setting, and from different participants.

Table 1. Descriptive Statistics for Cohorts of American Indians
Enrolled, Fall 1990 to Fall 1996

Fall 1990-Fall 1996	Number of students	Number of participants in NASARI	Number of non-participants in NASARI
All American Indian students enrolled in UNM	3466	502 (15%)	2,964 (85%)
Students entering UNM Fall 1990 or after	1918	262 (14%)	1,655 (86%)
Students entering UNM as beginning freshmen	690	107 (16%)	583 (84%)
Students entering UNM as beginning freshmen and graduated	25	7 (28%)	18 (72%)

Table 1. Comparison of NASARI Participants to Non-Participants on Outcome Variables

Fall 1990-Fall 1996	Mean cumulative grade-point-average	Mean cumulative hours attempted (UNM)	Mean cumulative hours earned (UNM and elsewhere)
All American Indian students enrolled in UNM	Participants = 2.39 Non-participants = 2.37	Participants = 61* Non-participants = 48	Participants = 76* Non-participants = 65
Students entering UNM Fall 1990 or after	Participants = 2.34 Non-participants = 2.26	Participants = 47* Non-participants = 32	Participants = 65* Non-participants = 50
Students entering UNM as beginning freshmen	Participants = 2.21 Non-participants = 2.11	Participants = 48* Non-participants = 36	Participants = 46* Non-participants = 34
Students entering UNM as beginning freshmen and graduated	Participants = 3.02 Non-participants = 2.65	Participants = 139* Non-participants = 100	Participants = 151* Non-participants = 103

*$p < .05$ level of significance.

Technique triangulation involved using such different techniques as archival documents and formal interviews (Fetterman, 1989; Hammersley & Atkinson, 1983). In counting the frequency of relationship occurrences, they noted how many times two or more relations occurred at the same time among the various participants, such as similarity of problems. Thus, they elicited a number of themes that were reinforced, abandoned, or reconfigured as the weight of the data suggested persistence of particular patterns.

DESCRIPTIVE INFORMATION QUALITATIVE INTERVIEW

Sample

The interview sample consisted of 183 students, including both students who had participated in the Native programs and those who were non-participants. Representing approximately 35 different tribes, 35.5% were males and 64.5% were females. Thirty-nine percent were Pueblo, 36% were Navajo, 7% were a combination of tribes (in New Mexico and elsewhere), and 17% were from out-of-state tribal nations. Of the Pueblo students, 49% were participants and 51% were non-participants. Of the Navajo students, 62% were participants and 38% were non-participants.

High School Preparation

Of the total questionnaire sample, most (73%) of the students had attended public high schools. Seventy-one percent of the participants and 76% of the non-participants attended public high schools. Fewer percentages of survey students attended other types of high schools.

High School Rating

Many of the students rated their high school preparation from poor to fair: 17% of the participants and 21% of the non-participants rated them poor; 31% of the participants and 27% of the non-participants rated them as fair. Only 19% of the participants and 9% of the non-participants rated them as very good to excellent.

Study Skills Rating

The students were also requested to rate their study skills in five areas: reading comprehension, test-taking, note-taking, writing skills, and organization and time management (Table 3).

At the time of their matriculation, NAS participants and non-participants perceived themselves about even on reading, test-taking, note-taking, writing, and

Table 3. Skills/Actions of Participants and Non-NAS Participants
at Time of Matriculation

Type of preparation/rating	NAS Participant		Non-NAS Participant	
	N	%	N	%
Reading				
Poor = 1	5	6	6	6
Fair = 2	21	24	18	19
Good = 3	34	38	33	35
Very good = 4	22	25	21	23
Excellent = 5	6	7	16	17
Total	88	100	94	100
Mean score	3.03		3.24	
Test-taking				
Poor = 1	9	10	11	12
Fair = 2	34	38	16	17
Good = 3	26	29	43	46
Very good = 4	19	22	18	19
Excellent = 5	1	1	6	6
Total	89	100	94	100
Mean score	2.65		2.91	
Note-taking				
Poor = 1	12	13	13	14
Fair = 2	16	18	20	21
Good = 3	34	39	36	38
Very good = 4	21	24	20	21
Excellent = 5	5	6	5	6
Total	88	100	94	100
Mean score	2.90		2.83	
Writing				
Poor = 1	14	16	6	6
Fair = 2	22	25	23	24
Good = 3	29	33	30	32
Very good = 4	17	19	25	27
Excellent = 5	7	8	10	11
Total	89	100	94	100
Mean score	2.79		3.11	
Organization and Time Management				
Poor = 1	12	13	17	18
Fair = 2	37	42	24	25
Good = 3	24	27	30	32
Very good = 4	12	13	15	16
Excellent = 5	4	5	8	9
Total	89	100	94	100
Mean score	2.54		2.71	

organization and time management skills. Using an alpha of .05, ANOVA analyses revealed that there were no statistically significant mean score differences between the groups on any of the five skills measured. Test-taking skills ($p = .079$) and writing skills ($p = .057$) came close to being significant, favoring non-NAS participants. Non-NAS participants tended to have higher means (though not statistically significantly higher) than NAS participants on all items, with the exception of note-taking. Both groups thought they were strongest in reading skill (rating it between good and very good), and least strong in organization and time management skills (rating them between fair and good).

Unprepared Courses

Table 4 shows that most students felt that they were not prepared for some college courses. Many students felt unprepared in math and English. Smaller percentages cited weaknesses in the science and the social science areas.

Table 4. Course Preparation and Developmental Course Enrollment

	NAS participants		Non-NAS participants	
Survey questions/responses	N	%	N	%
Did you feel unprepared for any courses?				
Yes	65	73	68	72
No	24	27	26	28
Total	89	100	94	100
Did you take developmental courses?				
Yes	35	40	42	45
No	53	60	51	55
Total	88	100	93	100
Were you required to take developmental courses?				
Yes	25	28	23	25
No	64	72	71	75
Total	89	100	94	100
Did you matriculate having a career goal?				
Yes	66	76	74	79
No	19	22	19	20
Unsure	2	2	1	1
Total	87	100	94	100

Developmental Courses

Forty percent of participants and 45% of the non-participants completed developmental courses (see Table 4). The developmental courses were defined as having a special course number (100 or lower), pre-college or academic skill course designations and do not count toward course requirements. These courses are recommended and sometimes required by various university colleges if any of the ACT or SAT test scores, grades, or amount of credits received in high school are perceived as weak. More participants than non-participants completed developmental courses in English and math. More non-participants than participants completed developmental courses in science. Of those who completed developmental courses, only 28% of the participants and 25% of the non-participants were required to take them. This may suggest that these students were willing to take additional classes to succeed in college.

Career Goals

Most students had career goals in mind when they entered the University of New Mexico. More participants than non-participants had a staff or faculty member advise them on how to reach their career goals. However, chi-square tests revealed no significant differences between participants and non-participants regarding these two items.

Chi square analyses revealed that there were no statistically significant associations between group membership and positive or negative answers on the course preparation and developmental course enrollment survey questions. There was also no statistically significant association between group membership and responses to the career goal question.

Given these descriptive statistics on the sample, it is interesting to see how often NAS participants used the services available to them and how they rated the services.

Participation in the Legislative Funded Program

The NASARI Project included nine different services: 1) computer pod and staff; 2) books, articles, and videos; 3) research library and research staff; 4) academic advisement; 5) financial advisement, including emergency funds; 6) tutoring; 7) Native American Studies courses; 8) lectures and symposia; and 9) social events and a Center that students could regard as a "home away from home."

Table 5 reveals the mean number of times that students participated in the NASARI Program each semester and how students rated the quality of services provided by these programs. Participants used the computer pod, library, tutoring, book, and media more frequently than other aspects of the legislatively funded program. However, they also frequently participated in social events provided

Table 5. NAS Program or Service Participation and Ratings

NAS program or service	Frequency of use (per semester)		Rating of program	
	N (%)	Mean	N (%)	Mean
NAS Computer Prod	88 (99%)	27.98	66 (74%)	4.02
NAS Books, Media	87 (98%)	9.10	46 (52%)	3.89
NAS Library	88 (99%)	11.98	43 (48%)	4.09
NAS Academic Advisement	88 (99%)	3.52	30 (34%)	3.83
NAS Financial Aid	88 (99%)	1.19	32 (36%)	3.81
NAS Tutoring	88 (99%)	10.69	28 (31%)	4.04
NAS Courses	87 (98%)	0.67	28 (31%)	4.00
NAS Lectures, Symposia	87 (98%)	1.87	35 (39%)	3.83
NAS Social Events	87 (98%)	17.90	47 (53%)	4.23

by the Native American Studies Program. When asked to rate the quality of Native American Studies services received on a Likert-type scale (1 = Poor to 5 = Excellent), most students rated the NASARI programs as good to very good.

The most frequently used NAS facility was the computer pod, with NAS students using it nearly twice a week per semester. Social events sponsored by NAS were the next most attended, each NAS student attended an average of over one of these social events per week per semester. The tutoring program was used by all NAS students an average of almost 11 times per semester, and the NAS library was visited an average of 12 times per semester per student. The highest rated NAS services or programs were the social events, library, tutoring, computer pod, and courses, all with ratings of 4.0 or above (ratings of very good to excellent).

Other Native American Support Programs

Table 6 reveals the levels of participation in 11 other Native American support programs at UNM and the mean quality of service rating for participants and non-participants. Students could choose to participate in the following student

Table 6. Other Native Programs at UNM:
Mean Use and Quality Ratings

Programs or services	NAS participants (N = 89)			Non-NAS participants (N = 94)		
	N	Mean use	Mean rating	N	Mean use	Mean rating
1. NA Program, College of Engineering	25	20.8	3.8	7	12.3	3.9
2. American Indian Student Services	52	23.8	3.7	28	13.4	3.5
3. Native American Outreach	7	12.3	4.5	4	1.8	2.5
4. NA College Enrichment Program	10	7.5	3.9*	2	5.0	1.7
5. AI Financial Aid Representative	15	3.7	3.1	3	1.7	2.7
6. AI Librarian in Center for SW Research	26	11.0	3.9	9	11.6	4.0
7. KIVA Indian Club	26	17.5	3.7	8	9.0	3.3
8. AI Science and Engineering Science	26	21.8	3.6	12	20.4	3.7
9. AI Business Association	8	26.3	4.3	4	27.0	3.5
10. NA Health Professional Organization	12	6.8	3.3	1	3.0	4.0
11. Native American Faculty	30	10.5	4.0	12	20.9	4.2
12. Southwest Indian Law Clinic	12	1.9	4.0	5	7.6	3.3
13. Singing Wire/KUNM	32	15.9	4.3	14	9.6	4.3

*$p < .05$ level of significance.

organizations: KIVA Indian Club, American Indian Science & Engineering Society (AISES), American Indian Business Association (AIBA), and the Native American Health Professional Association. They could have accessed help from Indian representatives located in recruitment (Native American Outreach) and financial aid offices, the library (Center for Southwest Research), first year retention program (Native American Component of College Enrichment Program), Southwest Indian Law Clinic, and the Native American Program in the College of Engineering (NAPCOE). Finally, they could have taken courses or assisted in some way by Native faculty or been part of the listening audience for a radio program called the "Singing Wire." More participants were involved in many of these programs, two to three time more than non-participants. Except for their participation in two Native organizations (AISES and AIBA) the mean use of service was usually twice as high for participants than for non-participants. Participants rated the quality of services higher only on seven programs. Non-participants clarified why they did not take advantage of these same programs. "I thought that the services were for full-bloods," "I thought that the services were for reservation students," or "I thought that the services were for Navajo students."

Table 6 reveals a statistically significant group mean quality rating difference on the Native American College Enrichment Program. NAS Participants rated the program greater than non-NAS Participants. Otherwise, there were no significant group mean differences in use of programs or ratings of programs.

General Services for All Students

Many other support programs are available through the university. The researchers investigated whether students received help from these programs and asked them to rate the quality of services provided (Table 7). The programs included: academic advisement from a department or college; financial aid counseling, emergency loan services; counseling assistance; career services; CIRT computer pods; general library services; student activities center; religious organizations; fraternity/sorority organizations; intramural programs; leisure services; child care center; and housing assistance. Student support from the Student Services, Upward Bound, or Handicapped Services programs could have also been received. The NAS participants used the CIRT computer pods, library, religious organizations, and the child care center more frequently than other general services. Non-participants used the student activities center, leisure services, and intramural activities more than the NAS participants. Neither group used all of the resources available. If they used these services, they rated the quality as good to very good.

ANOVA analyses revealed no statistically significant mean group differences in either the use of general university programs or services or in the ratings of any of the general university programs or services.

Stop-Out Information

Most respondents had stopped out of this university for at least one semester (67% NAS, 43% non-NAS) (Table 8). Sixty-seven percent of the participants and 75% of the non-participants had stopped out for one semester or more. Of those who stopped out, some students in both categories stopped out four or more times.

Although one-third of NAS participants did not stop out for a semester or more compared with one-fourth of non-NAS participants, chi-square analysis showed no statistically significant association between group membership and stopping out status (see Table 9).

There was no statistically significant mean difference on frequency of stopping out between NAS participants and non-NAS participants. Their reasons for

Table 7. General University Programs:
Mean Use Times per Semester and Quality Ratings

Programs or services	NAS participants (N = 89)			Non-NAS participants (N = 94)		
	N	Mean use	Mean rating	N	Mean use	Mean rating
1. Academic Advisement	78	14.3	3.2	64	3.4	3.1
2. Financial Aide Counseling, Loan	53	4.1	2.9	47	2.7	4.3
3. Counseling Assistance	22	6.2	3.0	15	4.3	3.4
4. Career Services	18	6.6	3.0	13	3.2	3.1
5. CIRT Pod (Computer Facility)	63	43.0	3.4	40	23.0	3.3
6. General Library Services	86	40.0	4.1	77	32.0	3.5
7. Student Activities Center	37	30.6	4.0	26	58.5	3.0
8. Religious Organizations	11	32.0	4.2	8	12.5	3.6
9. Fraternity/Sorority Organizations	4	38.3	3.3	4	53.5	3.0
10. Intramural Programs	8	20.4	4.0	9	123.0	3.6
11. Leisure Services	17	57.6	3.9	20	67.3	3.8
12. Child Care Center	4	80.8	4.0	4	68.0	3.5
13. Housing Assistance	11	15.5	2.7	11	35.6	2.6
14. Student Services, Upward Bound, or Handicapped Services	10	12.9	3.4	9	16.7	4.0

stopping out were mixed. Economic and family issues were reasons they stopped-out. Of those who stopped-out, 69% of the participants and 43% of the non-participants stopped-out for economic reasons and 30% of the participants and 18% of the non-participants cited academic reasons for stopping out. Some of the reasons included, "feeling financial[ly] overwhelmed," and "money problems." Some of the family-related causes included "my son was born," "I had to take care of family responsibilities" and "to care for my parents." When students were asked how the university could have assisted them at that time, students in both categories specifically mentioned "better communication" to clarify policies, procedures, and/or potential resources as the possible ways in which the institution

Table 8. Stopping Out

	NAS participants		Non-NAS participants	
Survey questions	N	%	N	%
Have you ever stopped for a semester or more?				
Yes	60	67	70	75
No	29	33	24	25
Total	89	100	94	100

Table 9. Stopping Out Frequency *t*-Test Results

Group	N	Mean	SD	df	t	p
NAS Participants	89	.99	1.11	181	1.003	.317
Non-NAS Participants	94	1.15	1.05			

could have mitigated their personal situations. Participant students also cited culturally-related courses, support programs, Native faculty, and Native philosophy as ways of supporting and encouraging them to stay in school. Non-participants cited financial help and advisement as support mechanisms.

SUMMARY OF THE FINDINGS

The findings reported in this chapter revealed that the American Indian students who participated in the NASARI Program attempted and accumulated more credits than those students who did not participate. Their prior academic backgrounds had a strong influence on their academic performance at UNM. Most of the students surveyed ($N = 183$) attended public high schools and didn't feel that their secondary schools prepared them well for college. At the time of student matriculation, NAS participants and non-NAS participants rated themselves about even on reading, test-taking, note-taking, writing, and organization and time management. ANOVA analyses reveled that there were no statistically significant differences on mean score differences between the two groups on any of the five skills measured.

Although statistically significant differences did not occur between the two groups, most students felt that they were not prepared for some college courses.

NAS participants and non-NAS participants took developmental courses, were not necessarily required to take them, and most students entered UNM with career goals at time of matriculation.

The intent of NASARI was to support the academic retention in Native American higher education at a large four-year public research institution. Jojola (1996) argues that the model that was used to justify the program was based on the examination of 22,000 individual academic records of Native American students who attended the UNM system from 1973 to 1984. Research then showed that students took twice as long to complete a degree than their non-Native peers principally because they failed to declare a degree objective or changed it numerous times over the course of their studies. Thus, the academic intervention program was designed as an integrated process model and incorporated an academic planning and advisement component. The advisors were to use admissions and performance data to help students declare their majors and to plan their courses of studies. The concept met with limited success due to the slow access of information from the various student affairs offices. The study participants did not use the advisement component nor rate the quality of those services as high as other components of the program.

A second major component offered a state-of-the-art computer facility where students could access information through the Internet and complete research papers and other course requirements. Trained librarians were available to assist participants in the research process. This component was highly successful for participants because they had knowledge of its availability and access to its resources. They gave the quality of services high marks.

A third component provided an information and materials resource collection. Jojola (1996) states that it is more than a collection of topical materials. It represented an access to "voices" by Native scholars and non-traditional native scholars. NAS also provided lectures and symposia from Native scholars and leaders. These resources were open to Native and non-Native patrons. The participants in this study used the library, attended lectures and symposia, and rated the quality of services favorably.

Participants and non-participants took advantage of academic and social support programs when needed or desired. The computer pods, library and other research resources, as well as, other social programs (intramural, leisure services, Native cultural activities, Native radio program) were used by both groups. Students rated these services positively.

Most students stopped out for one or two semesters. The reasons for stopping out were mixed for both groups. But, economic and family situations seemed to be the primary causes. Fewer participants and non-participants cited academic reasons for stopping out. In retrospect, non-participants wished that they had participated in the NAS retention program and would have if they had a clearer understanding of program offerings.

CONCLUSIONS

We have attempted to understand the retention of American Indian students at the University of New Mexico through Tinto's (1988) model of persistence in higher education. Several threads emerge regarding the performance and persistence of American Indian students. We can conclude from this study that the students who attend UNM emanate from strong cultural communities and participate in numerous and ongoing culturally related activities and that they participate in two cultures—the dominant mainstream culture and Indian culture. Many of these students are not prepared for college and in ways not necessarily academic. In this study, for example, students who participate in Native and non-Native university support programs fare better than non-participants only with regard to credits attempted and credits completed. The study shows that students who minimally participate or who did not participate in the academic and social programs provided by the university may have time constraints, other commitments, and may be unaware of how these programs could help them. Nevertheless, Native students stop out for many reasons. Many students place family and community values (e.g., meeting the needs of their family and participation in ceremonies/other traditional activities) ahead of individual needs—completing their college education in a timely manner. And it is our opinion that while the university can help retain students with various programs, unless these programs help bridge an understanding between value systems, then these programs will not necessarily succeed.

DISCUSSION

We have noticed that change in one of the retention paradigms is occurring; more and more individuals are committing themselves to "life-long learning" experiences. Some may attend school for a short while because they are interested in a particular course, learning from a particular instructor, and/or because they want to strengthen their skills for work. Many students from the dominant population are staying in school longer as well. At UNM, one data source indicated that it took a student from the dominant population, 6.8 years to graduate with a four-year degree. It took American Indian students 8.2 years to graduate (Institutional Report, 1996). The Commission on Higher Education Report (1999-2000) states that only 10% of the students at any of the New Mexico universities have completed their degree in four years

Tinto's (2000a, 2000b, 2000c) more recent work indicates that support programs, such as NASARI, have had little long-term impact on retention problems. He states that some support programs do little to change the quality of academic experiences for students, especially during the first year. He argues that too many people blame student affairs personnel for admitting and not retaining students. Strong faculty involvement, he maintains, is the secret to successful retention programs. Yet faculty in this instance cannot be held responsible to operate in two distinct worlds.

Nevertheless, Tinto (1993, 1996, 2000a, 2000b, 2000c) suggests that academic innovations need faculty involvement particularly at commuter campuses where classrooms and laboratories might be the only place where students engage with others. Students, he argues, need stronger educational environments during their first year, perhaps within the first month of school. He suggests that institutions consider offering "learning communities" where block scheduling for cohorts of students works well even for those large classes that have small study groups that meet 2-3 times per week and 4-6 hours at a time. Such communities enhance student to student and student to teacher interactions. A learning community may be linked together by themes called "connected learning." In one example, the courses in human biology, psychology, and sociology were joined to explore "why humans behave the way they do." Another type of learning community, called "shared learning," allows faculty members to restructure their courses to include team teaching and other group activities. In learning communities with connected learning themes, students are actively involved in co-constructing knowledge rather than listening to lectures. In this way many courses can be linked together with "service learning"—a form of community interaction. In learning communities, students learn more and with other students and in the process, they form social groups, enjoy co-constructing knowledge, and build bridges between academia and their social environments.

Today, UNM has added other support programs that are known to work, such as summer bridge programs for first-year and transfer students. The bridge programs incorporate the learning community model suggested by Tinto (2000a, 2000b) and supported by many Native faculty. UNM continues to promote student participation in Native programs while also offering academic, financial, and career support. The university, however, operates as a commuter campus. Many students are on campus for only brief periods of time to attend class and access, in a limited way, academic and other resources.

The commuter campus is both an advantage and a disadvantage, perhaps grist of another article. Yet, cultural differences and value orientations weigh heavily on student retention. What appears to be missing from these efforts are clear lines of communication between tribal and university officials to develop the type of academic programs suitable for Native students and in support of community needs. The summer bridge programs and the learning community initiatives are developed primarily for incoming students. There are too many upper-division students who have started and stopped their education over a long period of time. They, too, could benefit from meaningful relationships with faculty and students. In another study of American Indian students in the College of Education (Belgarde, Mitchell, & Arquero, 2003) we found that for far too many students, many of their courses were outdated. And, this might be true of others enrolled in the various colleges as well.

These data and Tinto's 1988 model does not capture how Native American philosophy and its ontological and pedagogical view of education influences a Native student's perspective of a formal college education. For example, in writing about Navajo philosophy and education, Benally (1994) states that Navajos are endowed with minds, physical bodies, and emotions. These endowments subject the people to the natural laws and orders of the physical world where they must learn the skills and knowledge that will enable them to survive and understand their relation to all other phenomena. Navajos, therefore, must develop the mind and skills for survival, learn to appreciate positive relationships, and understand and relate to one's home environment. This form of collective understanding is in keeping with Pueblo philosophy as well and can be associated with Native American philosophy as a whole (LoRé, 1998).

According to Cajete (1994), a Pueblo scholar and philosopher, there is a direct relationship between nature and learning. One learns by studying and observing nature and then relating that understanding to the human experience. Benally (1994) posits that when one is firmly grounded in spiritual teachings and traditional wisdom founded upon such an understanding, a person finds strength and stability. This is the basis for learning and living and what he also calls the "first basic principle of learning." Built upon this foundation, individuals are then better able to weigh decisions against traditional values whenever choices are to be made. Benally (1994) refers to this process as "that which gives direction to life." Cajete (1994) defines this first basic lesson as "finding face," or finding the ways to happiness.

To both scholars, there are subtle and overt differences in how learning and knowledge is perceived in Western and Native American traditions. In the Western tradition, the emphasis is to separate secular and sacred knowledge. This is a process that separates the individual from the collective purpose. In the Native American tradition however, life experiences and knowledge gained from those experiences benefit the person through the whole of the community (Cajete, 1994). And in Native American thought life is seen as a process that is guided by principles where ". . . knowledge, learning and life itself are sacred and are interwoven [as] parts of a whole." They are not segmented or compartmentalized but "are holistic principles that determine the quality of each other" (Benally, 1994, p. 23).

Native philosophy approaches learning by recognizing that connections are found by doing and experiencing through a spiritual-centered epistemology. "Learning is always a creative act. Education is an art of process, participation, and making connections. Learning is a growth and life process: and Life and Nature are always relationships in process" (Cajete, 1994, p. 24).

According to Cajete (1994), the ideal purpose of education is to help students "find face, heart, and foundation." Finding face, or finding the way to happiness (the first basic lesson), is seen as a process by which a student discovers who they are as human beings. They discover their innate characteristics and then find ways to express their potentialities. Finding one's heart is finding those inner passions that motivate and inspire one to do good things. The third purpose of education is seen as helping to guide the student in his/her search for a "foundation." This is where the student discovers his/her vocation, which in turn gives him/her the opportunity to fully express him/herself and his/her truth. These propositions are orienting foundations, which are held together in harmony and balance by the notion of Spiritual Ecology—the interplay that exists between the physical and spiritual worlds of existence. Spiritual Ecology then, as it relates to educational philosophy, is both a foundational process and a field through which traditional approaches to education occur. Many college students then, are developing personal strengths for the good of the community.

American Indian epistemology has historically approached education in a holistic social context that then helps to develop the importance of each individual as a contributing member of the group. Learning is seen as a unifying whole when gained from first-hand experience and then placed into context with other experiences. It is learned through participation and developing relationships with the whole of nature. Knowledge is explored and transmitted through ritual, ceremony, art, and appropriate technology. The purpose of education and learning for Native Americans then is to increase awareness and to develop one's innate human potentials and relate it back to the community.

In a 2002 high school graduation ceremony at the Santa Fe Indian School, Native leaders encouraged Native students to pursue their dreams, become doctors, lawyers, engineers, etc., and to return home to help their own people. Many of UNM's college students have been pursuing these dreams as well but without explicitly understanding the ramifications of how their Native philosophy and views of education might affect their relationships with families and community. In addition, many Native students, particularly those coming from traditional families, have had to become conscious of how they express this new knowledge. We have observed others who have become so articulate and polished, for example, that when they speak to their community and family members they feel unappreciated, disrespected, or rejected. One student said, "At home I have to speak my native language which is Navajo. I can not go back with the impression that I have been white-washed. The community will immediately shut me out." Even accomplished Indian academics and respected members of their communities find it difficult. We should help community members understand this dilemma. Tribal leaders and families must bear some of this responsibility to help students feel welcome and respected for the sacrifices that they have made and the risks they have taken in order for them to complete their college degree.

What does this mean to those of us in Indian Education and for those of us who have been fighting for decades to make universities and curricula relevant to the needs of our students? As Native American educators, we understand the cultural dynamics of our communities; particularly Navajo and Pueblo traditions, where the group and the community have warrant over self-achievement and personal gain. This translates into a psychology of learning and a perspective on what makes knowledge relevant verses what is perceived to be of value in a compart- mentalized materialistic culture. Native students may be telling us something— courses are dichotomized, knowledge is fractured and both are not relevant to their ontological outlook of holism and integrated thinking. And while universities may be structured for an urban and corporate environment, students can still relate this knowledge to the benefit of the communities.

What does this research suggest to other institutions enrolling Native American students? The services provided NASARI, other Native programs, and general support services offered to Native students are important ones. The data show that students who used these services generally rated them well. The Native services, in particular, are important offerings to many Native students. The importance of offering these types of services depends on the context of the Native students enrolled. It cannot be said enough that our students come from highly embedded cultural communities and this is not always true of the other Native students enrolled in other higher education institutions. We encourage other institutions to collaborate with tribes to strengthen the academic and student service related programs. We also encourage other institutions to learn from the models offered by tribal colleges. Indian educators at these sites have found ways to retain students in meaningful ways. This research tells us that universities must broaden its perspectives, recognize and value an ancient way of thinking that has survived for centuries. Community-based learning, holistic and integrated learning experi- ences linked with relevant knowledge is the key to retention. Native students are telling us this but in a language and in a manner that we in academia are perhaps, unprepared to accept.

REFERENCES

American Indian Higher Education Consortium & The Institute for Education Policy (2001). *Building strong communities: Tribal colleges as engaged institutions.* Alexandria, VA: American Indian Higher Education Consortium.

Barnhardt, C. (1994). *Life on the other side: Alaska Native teacher education students and the University of Fairbanks.* Ph.D. Dissertation, University of British Columbia.

Belgarde, M. J. (1992). *The performance and persistence of American Indian undergraduate students at Stanford University.* An Unpublished Dissertation, Stanford University.

Belgarde, M. J. (2001). *Responding to American Indian language and culture issues in the southwest: An American Indian professor's story.* Unpublished manuscript.

Belgarde, M. J., Mitchell, R., & Arquero, A. (2003, Summer). "What Do We Have to Do to Create Culturally-Responsive Programs?: The Challenge of Transforming American Indian teacher education," Indigenous perspectives of teacher education: Beyond perceived border. *Action in Teacher Education, XXIV*(2), 42-54.

Belgarde, W. L. (1993). Indian control and the management of dependencies: The case of tribal community colleges. Ph.D. Dissertation. Stanford, CA: Stanford University.

Benally, H. (1994). Navajo philosophy of learning and pedagogy. *Journal of American Indian Education, XII*(1), 23-31.

Cajete, G. (1994). *Look to the mountain: An ecology of indigenous education.* Durango, CO: Kivalki Press.

Cajete, G. (1999). *A people's ecology: Explorations in sustainable living.* Santa Fe, NM: Clearlight Publishing.

Edgewater, I. L. (1981). Stress and the Navajo university student. *Journal of American Indian Education, 20*(3), 25-31.

Fetterman, D. (1989). *Ethnography step by step.* Newbury Park, CA: Sage.

Fox, M. J. T. (1982). *American Indian student in higher education: Factors related to their under-graduate college entrance.* Ph.D. Dissertation, University of Arizona.

Fries, J. E. (1987). *The American Indian in higher education, 1975-76 to 1984-85,* National Center for Education Statistics, U.S. Department of Education, Washington, DC: U.S. Government Printing Office.

Fuchs, E., & Havighurst, I. (1972). *To live on this earth: American Indian education.* Albuquerque, NM: University of New Mexico Press.

Grits, J. (1991). Financial aid and the Indian college student. In Montana State University, *Opening the Montana Pipeline: American Indian in Higher Education* (pp. 54-62). Sacramento, CA: Tribal College Press.

Guyette, S., & Heth, C. (1984). Higher Education for American Indians in the 1980s. *Integrated Education, 22,* 21-30.

Hammersley, M., & Atkinson, P. (1983). *Ethnography: Principles in practice.* New York: Tavistock.

Hobson, B.T. (1994). *Cultural values and persistence among Comanche college students.* Ph.D. Dissertation, University of Oklahoma.

Hoover, J. J., & Jacobs, C. C. (1992). A Survey of American Indian College Students: Perceptions Toward Their Study Skill/College Life, *Journal of American Indian Education, 32*(1), 21-29.

Huffman, T. E., Sill, M. L., & Brokenleg, M. (1986, January). College achievement among Sioux and White South Dakota students. *Journal of American Indian Education,* 32-38.

Jaimes, M. A. (1982). Higher educational needs of Indian students. *Integrated Education, XIX,* 1-2, 7-12.

Jeanotte, L. D. (1981). A study of the contributing factors relating to why American Indian students drop out of or graduate from educational programs at the university of North Dakota. Ph.D. Dissertation, University of North Dakota.

Jojola, T. (1992). *Continuation data for UNM Native American students, report to the legislative committee on American Indian affairs.* An unpublished document. Albuquerque, NM: University of New Mexico.

Jojola, T. (1996). Personal communication. Albuquerque, NM: University of New Mexico.

Jojola, T., & Alcantara, D. (1996). *Native American Studies Report to the Legislative Committee on American Indian Affairs.* An unpublished document. Albuquerque, NM: University of New Mexico.

Kirkness, V. J., & Barnhardt, R. J. (1991, May). First nations and higher education: The four r's—Respect, relevance, reciprocity, responsibility. *Journal of American Indian Education, 30*(3), 1-15.

Kleinfeld, J. S., & Kohout, K. L. (1974). Increasing the college success of Alaska Natives. *Journal of American Indian Education, 13*(3), 27-31.

LaFromboise, T. D. (1988). *Cultural and cognitive considerations in the coping of American Indian women in higher education.* Stanford, CA: Stanford University, School of Education.

Lin, R. L., LaCounte, D., & Eder, J. (1988). A study of Native American students in a predominantly White college. *Journal of American Indian Education, 27*(3), 8-15.

Linthicum, L. (2001). "Leading Double Lives": "Urban Indians" move to Albuquerque for jobs and school, but for many the reservation is still home," Albuquerque Journal, April 29, 2001.

LoRé, R. (1998). *Art as development theory: The spiritual ecology of learning and the affluence of traditional Native American education.* Unpublished dissertation. University of New Mexico.

Machamer, A. M. (2000). *Along the red road: Tribally controlled colleges and student development.* Ph.D. Dissertation, University of California, Los Angeles.

Martinez, G. (1998). *Living conditions for Pueblo Indians of New Mexico.* Personal Communication, April 1998.

McNamara, P. P. (1982). *American Indians in American higher education: A summary of findings and recommendations.* Los Angeles: Higher Education Research Institute.

Miles, M. B., & Huberman, A. M. (1984). *Qualitative data analysis: A sourcebook of new methods.* Beverly Hills, CA: Sage.

Montoya, S. (1999). Making the circle a circle. *Black Issues in Higher Education, 16*(16), September 30.

Patton, W., & Edington, E. D. (1973). Factors related to the persistence of Indian students at college level. *Journal of American Indian Education, 12*(3), 19-23.

Pavel, D. M. (1987). A qualitative study of Native American attrition at an elite, private institution. An unpublished manuscript. Tempe: Arizona State University, College of Education, Program in Higher Education.

Pavel, D. M., & Padilla, R. V. (1993). American Indian and Alaska Native post-secondary departure: An example of assessing a mainstream model using national longitudinal data. *Journal of American Indian Education, 32*(2), 1-23.

Pepion, K. (1991). Psycho-social adjustment of American Indian college students: A study of Indian student stress and coping. In *Montana State University, Opening the Montana Pipeline: American Indian in Higher Education* (pp. 63-75). Sacramento, CA: Tribal College Press.

Perechi, R. O. (1994). *Participants' perceptions of mentoring in the American Indian teacher corp program at the University of Oklahoma.* Ph.D. Dissertation, University of Oklahoma.

Rindone, P. (1988). Achievement motivation and academic achievement of Native American students. *Journal of American Indian Education,* October, 1-8.

Sando, J. S. (1998). *Pueblo nations: Eight centuries of Pueblo Indian History.* Santa Fe, NM: Clearlight.

Sawyer, T. M. (1981). Indian students' study habits and attitudes. *Journal of American Indian Education, 20*(3), 13-17.

Tierney, W. G. (1993). The college experience of Native Americans: A critical analysis. In L. Weis & M. Fine (Eds.), *Beyond silenced voices.* Albany: State University of New York Press, 309-323.

Tinto, V. (1975, Winter). Dropout from higher education: A theoretical synthesis of recent research. *Review of Educational Research, 45*(1), 89-125.

Tinto, V. (1988). Stages of student departure: Reflections on the longitudinal character of student leaving. *Journal of Higher Education, 59*(4), 439-455.

Tinto, V. (1993). *Leaving college: Rethinking the causes and cures of student attrition* (2nd ed.). Chicago: The University of Chicago Press.

Tinto, V. (1996, Fall). Reconstructing the first year of college. *Planning for Higher Education, 25,* 1-6.

Tinto, V. (2000a). *Student success and the construction of involving educational communities.* Handout, New Mexico Student Persistence/Retention Summit, Las Cruces, NM, February 25-26, 2000.

Tinto, V. (2000b). *Learning better together: Learning communities on student success in higher education.* Handout, New Mexico Student Persistence/Retention Summit, Las Cruces, NM, February 25-26, 2000.

Tinto, V. (2000c). *The assessment of student retention programs.* Handout, New Mexico Student Persistence/Retention Summit, Las Cruces, NM, February 25-26, 2000.

University of New Mexico (1989-1991). *The University of New Mexico Catalog, 1989-1991.* Albuquerque, NM: University of New Mexico.

University of New Mexico (1919-1993). *The University of New Mexico Catalog, 1991-1993.* Albuquerque, NM: University of New Mexico.

University of New Mexico (1993-1995). *The University of New Mexico Catalog, 1993-1995.* Albuquerque, NM: University of New Mexico.

University of New Mexico (1995). Fall Enrollment Report, Institutional Research Office, p. 9. Albuquerque, NM.

University of New Mexico (1995-1997). *The University of New Mexico Catalog, 1995-1997.* Albuquerque, NM: University of New Mexico.

University of New Mexico (1997-1999). *The University of New Mexico Catalog, 1997-1999.* Albuquerque, NM: University of New Mexico.

University of New Mexico (1999-2001). *The University of New Mexico Catalog, 1999-2001.* Albuquerque, NM: University of New Mexico.

West, D. K. (1988). Comparisons of career maturity and its relationship with academic performance. *Journal of American Indian Education,* May, 1-7.

White, C. J. (1991). Institutional racism and campus climate. In Montana State University, *Opening the Montana Pipeline: American Indian in Higher Education* (pp. 33-45). Sacramento, CA: Tribal College Press.

Whitehorse, D. M. (1992). *Cultural identification and institutional character: Retention factors for American Indian students in higher education.* Ph.D. Dissertation, Flagstaff: Northern Arizona University.

Wright, B. (1985). Programming success: Special student services and the American Indian college student. *Journal of American Indian Education, 24,* 1-7.

Wright, B. (1991). The roles of Native American studies programs: Building stature in the 1990's. In *Montana State University, Opening the Montana Pipeline: American Indian in Higher Education* (pp. 93-100). Sacramento, CA: Tribal College Press.

Wright, B. (1992). *American Indian and Alaska Native higher education: Toward a new century of academic achievement and cultural integrity.* Commissioned paper, The Indian Nations At Risk Task Force, U.S. Department of Education.

Wright, B., & Tierney, W. G. (1991). American Indians in higher education. *Change, 23*(2), 11-18.

SECTION 5

Biracial Students

CHAPTER 10

Identifying Interventions to Improve The Retention of Biracial Students: A Case Study

Nicole Sands and John H. Schuh

Biracial students represent a growing number of students on many campuses and an increasingly significant segment of the population of the United States. Nevertheless, this group of students rarely has been studied with respect as to how their experiences affect persistence at colleges and universities. This case study reports on the experiences of biracial students at one institution. It also analyzes their racial identity development and presents recommendations designed to improve their persistence to graduation framed by Tinto's theory of academic departure. Recommendations for additional study are presented.

A growing segment of the increasingly diverse racial composition of the United States is that of biracial citizens. Biracial citizens were not counted during the 1990 decennial census, but a category for this group of people was created for the 2000 census. The U.S. Census Bureau reported that 6,826,228 individuals were identified as being of more than one race in the 2000 census (U.S. Census Bureau, 2000a). That biracial individuals are being recognized as a separate and distinct group of citizens is not surprising. In the 2000 census 126 counties had more than 10,000 citizens of two or more races (U.S. Census Bureau, 2001). All states except North Dakota, Wyoming, and New Hampshire had at least 10,000 citizens of two or more races in their populations (U.S. Census Bureau, 2000b). According to one federal educational report, 31 states had received requests to include "biracial" as a category of students. Due to the high number of requests, including a category for biracial students is planned for the future (National Center for Education Statistics, 1998).

Following the Civil Rights Movement of the 1960s, the enrollment of students of color in colleges and universities increased dramatically. With the increase of these students came concerns about inequities in the education of students of color (Hurtado, Milem, Clayton-Pedersen, & Allen, 1999). The experiences of students of color have not been as robust as those of white students, particularly in the areas of "support systems" and the availability of "role models and mentors" notes Hoard (1989, p. 72). Consequently, many assert that campuses have much work to do before developing comparative experiences for minority students (Cabrera, Nora, Terenzini, Pascarella, & Hagedorn, 1999; Cuyjet, 1997; Gloria, Robinson Kurpius, Hamilton, & Wilson, 1999). Cheatham (1991, p. 33) concluded that "retention and graduation rates are uneven and unenviable" when comparing students of color with white students. Indeed, authors have identified discrepancies in retention and graduation rates for students of color compared with their white counterparts (Gonzalez, 2000-2001; Ybarra, 2000-2001).

Graduation rates may be linked to the fit between students and their institution. Institutional fit includes issues associated with "social and economic character-istics," "levels of adjustment in predominantly white institutions," and "academic success" (Allen, 1991, p. 5). Allen (1991) asserts that black students are likely to have greater adjustment problems and consequently lower graduation rates than white students. He also indicates that black students have to put substantial effort in adjusting to the culture of historically white campuses before they can succeed socially and academically. Finally, Allen (1991) states that students of color may not have a peer group, with whom to associate, which also may contribute to adjustment challenges. "For instance, many of these (black) students often find it necessary to create their own social and cultural networks given their exclusion [self- and/or otherwise-imposed] from the wider university community" (p. 5). Problems concerning "isolation, alienation, and lack of support" (p. 5) are often the most serious for black students.

This study had three purposes. One was to learn about the non-academic experiences of biracial undergraduate students at Plains State University (PSU [a pseudonym]). A second purpose was to explore how the racial identity forma-tion of biracial students was affected by their experiences at PSU. Understanding more about the experiences of these students can be used to develop specific recommendations to develop institutional initiatives to improve their retention at the University, the third purpose of this study.

While there is substantial research on the challenges faced by students of one race (Allen, Epps, & Haniff, 1991; Cabrera, Nora, Terenzini, Pascarella, & Hagedorn, 1999; Cuyjet, 1997; Gloria, Robinson Kurpius, Hamilton, & Wilson, 1999), very little inquiry has been conducted on students of two or more races.

This study was conducted to begin to fill this void in research. For the purpose of this study, biracial citizens are defined as those who result from the coupling between two distinctly different racial persons (Herring, 1995). Because the number of mixed-race births has been increasing substantially since the late 1960s, it is incumbent on institutions of higher education to prepare for an ever-increasing number of students who cannot claim a single racial background since it is likely that such students will attend institutions of higher education in the future.

THEORETICAL FRAMEWORKS

Two theoretical frameworks are used in this study. First, Root's (1996) concept of "border crossings" is used to help understand the individual change that biracial persons undergo in their life's journeys. A border crossing is defined as a biracial person's ability to cross prescribed racial borders. "These border crossings are neither motivated by attempts to hide nor to denigrate some ethnic or racial heritage" but, rather, "the process of connecting to ourselves and others" (Root, 1996, p. xxii).

The other theoretical framework that informed this study was Tinto's (1998) theory of institutional departure that asserts the following about persistence to graduation: "The more academically and socially involved individuals are—that is the more they interact with other students and faculty—the more likely they are to persist" (p. 168). In the case of biracial students it is hypothesized that social and academic connections would be harder to establish for biracial students than for white students, as is the case for minority students of a single race. Tinto's work can be useful in informing a study such as this one, since the students may be challenged to establish those social connections that will affirm their place in their college and lead ultimately to graduation.

METHODOLOGY

Qualitative methodology is employed in this study. The experiences of biracial students are the focus of the study, and PSU is defined as a single case. The dimensions of this case are consistent with what Merriam (1998) describes as the special features of case studies. These features are particularistic, meaning that the case focuses on a particular phenomenon: descriptive, indicating that the product is a rich, thick description of the phenomenon under study; and heuristic, indicating that the case illuminates the reader's understanding of the phenomenon under study (pp. 29-30).

Data Sources

This case study is concerned with learning more about the experiences of biracial students at Plains State University (a Midwestern, Research I, land-grant institution of over 25,000 students). Criterion and snowball sampling (Patton, 1990) are used in this study. Two biracial undergraduate students at PSU who were known to the senior investigator were identified as potential data sources since they met the criteria established for data sources (undergraduate biracial students at PSU). Each agreed to participate in the study. After they were interviewed they were asked who else they knew who could contribute to the study. They were helpful in identifying other data sources, and this snowball selection process continued until the point of saturation was reached. Saturation was defined as an interviewee not contributing anything new to the data pool. Ultimately six students were interviewed for this study (see Table 1).

Data Collection

Semi-structured individual interviews were conducted with each of the participants. The interview questions were open-ended to allow the students to elaborate on their personal experiences. Probing questions were asked, when appropriate to further develop and clarify the information received. All of the interviews were tape-recorded. PSU human subjects regulations were followed rigorously.

During the first interview, introductory information (year in school, major, housing accommodations, and ethnic background) was gathered along with information concerning the students' non-academic experiences. The second interview was used to gather information pertaining to each student's racial identity development.

Table 1. Six Students Interviewed

Name	Gender	Year in school	Major	Housing	Race
Ayenna	Female	Sophomore	History	Off campus	African American & Caucasian
Carlo	Male	Sophomore	Undecided	Greek system	Hispanic & Caucasian
Dan	Male	Sophomore	Engineering	On campus	Asian & Caucasian
Kiara	Female	Junior	Psychology	Off campus	African American & Caucasian
Raun	Male	Junior	Engineering	Off campus	Asian & Caucasian
Taye	Male	Freshman	Engineering	On campus	African American & Hispanic

Data Analysis

The interview tape recordings were transcribed within 48 hours of each interview. The constant comparative method (Glaser & Strauss, 1967) of data analysis was utilized to identify themes, patterns, and trends revealed by the data.

Establishing Trustworthiness

Lincoln and Guba's (1994) approach to establishing trustworthiness was employed in this study to ensure that it had sufficient rigor. Several strategies contributed to establishing trustworthiness.

Prolonged Engagement and Participant Review

The interviewer initially was engaged with each participant for more than an hour. The second interview was conducted with each participant and included time in which the transcript of the first interview was reviewed for accuracy. This also served as a form of member checking. Participants were provided an opportunity to correct any errors in the transcript and to clarify their answers to the questions as they wished. A third contact was made with each participant through electronic mail. The corrected transcript was sent electronically to the participants to make sure that the corrected transcript was accurate. Again, participants were allowed to make corrections or additions to the transcript.

Peer Debriefing

Two peer debriefers assisted the senior investigator during this inquiry. One of them was a graduate student and the other was a biracial college graduate. The debriefers assisted the senior investigator in developing alternative interpretations of the data, but had no direct contact with the subjects.

Audit Trail

A complete audit trail was developed including tape recordings, interview notes, interview transcripts, and other notes kept for inspection.

RESULTS

Results related to the purposes of this study will be presented in this section of the report. This section is divided into two distinct subject areas: student non-academic experiences and racial identity development.

Student Non-Academic Experiences

The first purpose of this study was to learn about the non-academic experiences of biracial students at Plains State University. Exploring the impact of the campus environment on the students' racial development was the second purpose of this study. Initial interview questions asked to assess non-academic experiences of the participants include the following:

- Why did you choose to attend Plains State University?
- Describe the demographics of the community that you grew up in.
- Describe the racial diversity at PSU.
- Compare the racial diversity at PSU to that of your high school.
- What campus and community activities are you involved with?
- Have you been involved in activities or programs sponsored by the Office of Minority Student Affairs?

Perceived Diversity

Before enrolling, Carlo (all respondent names are pseudonyms) thought that PSU was a diverse institution. Once he arrived on campus, he realized that "my (his) high school was a lot more diverse." Kiara noticed as she attended classes that "I (she) might be the only black student in a huge auditorium, or maybe one of two or three other minority students that would be around." Although Kiara may have felt like one of a few minority students in her classes, she noted that there is some diversity on campus, but not "a wide amount."

Others indicated that PSU was segregated into narrow racial groups. Ayenna felt that the Plains State community is "polarized and very cliquey." This environment makes it difficult for a biracial student to find a group of people with whom to associate. Ayenna shares, "It's crazy here. I mean, it's so polarized and very cliquey, it's sort of like high school, it's very racially divided you know. The international folks hang out, the blacks hang out, the whites hang out . . . I don't really get into clique things, and being mixed . . . I sort of feel like there is this imperative to fit in with them (black community) and since I don't . . . they treat me like a step child."

Although the students' perceptions indicated that they did not find much diversity on the Plains State campus, the amount of perceived diversity on campus was far greater than the perceived diversity in each of the student's high schools, except for Carlo.

Friends in College

The students in this study selected their high school friends and college friends based on different criteria. This selection may be because each student's high school was not very diverse and forming friendships was based on what potential friends were available, often including non-minority students.

Some of the students reported that their preferences for friends had changed since high school. Several students reported that this change resulted because even though Plains State University was not a particularly diverse institution, it was more diverse than the population the students had encountered in their high school.

Kiara shared that her preference in friends has "changed in a lot of ways." She felt that her choice in friends had changed because she had more opportunities to interact with minority students. Ayenna preferred to associate with friends who are "older and international." She chose this group because she felt that older and international students did not put as much emphasis on her racial composition. The students selected their friends upon criteria that were not available in their high school environments, most notably a greater variety of students.

Dating Relationships

Five out of six of the students stated that they did not care about the race of the person whom they were dating. Raun also said that he did not care about what race his significant other would be, but that his mother would care. Kiara seemed to prefer to date African Americans because "it's just the people that I (she) met right away" when she arrived on campus.

Services for Biracial Students

At the time of this study, there were no specific programs in place at PSU for biracial students. Some of the students felt that having a student organization on campus for biracial and multiracial students would be desirable. Few felt that an organization would not be needed. Kiara reported that "offering services specifically for biracial students on their adjustments" might be helpful.

While some students felt that a biracial organization or network would be a good idea, other students indicated that they might not participate. Dan reported that he would not necessarily use the services, but possibly would assist with planning for a group. Ayenna indicated that the services would be useful "maybe for some biracial people" but not her. She felt that a group would have been more useful in high school, but that she is "beyond all of it" by now.

The students who reported that they would not use or need any services for biracial students were not opposed to having them available on campus. Dan's interest in helping with a group and Ayenna's sense that some students may need such services, perhaps at an earlier stage of their college career, suggest that additional services are needed at Plains State.

Involvement with the Office of Minority Student Affairs

Although the amount of campus and community involvement varied greatly from student to student, a majority of the students were not involved in any activities that were created specifically for minority students. The services provided through the Office of Minority Student Affairs (the Office) do not address issues specifically focusing on biracial students. The services are geared toward ethnic minorities in general. Programs offered through the Office include academic, programmatic, and of team-building initiatives.

When the participants were asked if they were involved in any programs or activities sponsored by the Office, four reported that they had not been involved in these initiatives. Both Carlo and Taye noted involvement with an academic program sponsored by the Office. However, Carlo was only involved with this program during his freshman year. When asked about continuing his involvement, Carlo responded, "I kind of wish that I would participate more in that (Office of Minority Student Affairs programs), but I don't feel like I fit in sometimes." Kiara has not been involved with the Office either. Her lack of involvement stemmed from the fact that "I (she) wasn't aware of it (the office)." Lastly, Dan chose not to participate in programs through the Office of Minority Student Affairs because "it seems to emphasize the fact that you're different somehow." Although the reasons varied from student to student, a majority chose not to affiliate themselves with the Office of Minority Student Affairs.

Racial Identity Development

The second purpose of this study was to examine the racial identity development of the participants. Self-identification and others' perceptions of the student's racial identity are discussed. To assess the racial identity development of the participants, the following questions were asked:

- What do you choose as your race when filling out a standardized form?
- Are others curious about your ethnic background?
- How do you prefer to be known (ethnicity-wise)?
- How do you identify with each part of your ethnic background?

Self-Identification

Each of the students had different experiences when asked to identity their racial composition. When students complete a standardized form such as an application for admission, a choice has to be made regarding their race. When faced with five rigid categories (African American, Caucasian, Asian, American Indian, Hispanic), the participants reported that they responded in several different ways.

For some of the participants choosing one race on applications or other forms was not an issue. The reason for being comfortable choosing one race may be related to the perceptions of others. Kiara reported that she preferred to simply choose "African American" when faced with rigid racial categories. She stated, "You know I don't have strong issues with that. I do sometimes question whether that's right . . . there's really nothing else to pick." Raun also selected one category but wished for another choice. "I wish you could check two boxes for white and Asian, but normally I'll check Asian Pacific Islander." Ayenna preferred to choose

African American because she has "always just put black." She explained, "I say that I'm black because . . . for lack of anything else to do. But it would be silly for me to put that I'm white. I mean it's silly for me to put that I'm black, but that's what I've been taught to do." Based on the information provided by these students, their willingness to select a single race on standardized forms was a result of life-long habits and limited selection choices.

Some students who are unhappy with the choices available may deliberately choose to fill many blanks or fill in the "other" choice when it is available. When asked how he categorizes himself on forms where racial identity is required, Taye responded, "I probably filled in a bunch of them." I then asked Taye how he likes to be identified racially. He also reported, "I like to be identified by my last name." Dan indicated that he usually "put(s) other" but that he would prefer to select "Amerasian" when reporting his race on a form.

Although Ayenna chose "African American" on forms, she had strong feelings about the "other" choice available on some forms. "It sounds like something you would pick up at the goodwill or something . . . other is growth sounding . . . it doesn't even sound right." Even though the "other" selection is becoming popular on standardized forms, it appears that it is not well liked or is regarded as a completely inadequate choice.

Others' Perceptions of the Students' Racial Identity

The most significant experiences in the student's careers at PSU centered on repetitive questioning about the students' racial backgrounds. Each had been questioned about their racial composition. Often, they were mistaken for a member of a racial group of which they were not a part.

Dan felt that others were simply "curious." He shared that people often mistake him for Hispanic. Kiara has had similar experiences in that others often will comment on her features, "you've got such pretty hair . . . you're skin's so pretty . . . you have to be mixed with something." She is often mistaken for "Jamaican or Puerto Rican or even Indian." Taye shared that when he first arrived on PSU's campus the African Americans on campus "just assumed that I was African American, so . . . I would hang out with them." As the Hispanic students on campus "found out that my (his) mom was from Panama" they assumed that he was one of them. Ayenna reported being questioned frequently about her racial heritage. She indicated that "a lot of people think I'm Latina."

When Raun told others at PSU that he is "half Japanese," they reacted as if it was not a real surprise to find out that he is biracial. However, as he was growing up he felt that some of his friends were "surprised to find out that I'm half Asian." He felt this was because "maybe they haven't been around people who are (biracial)." Carlo indicated that he had received different responses from Caucasian and Latino students when he shared his racial composition.

"White people really think I'm joking." The Latino community was receptive to having him as one of their own.

For these students, others created their own perceptions of the students' racial composition. Often, this perception did not include biracialness, but rather a single ethnic identity to which the student did not belong. Biracial students may have a more difficult time fitting into specific racial and peer groups if they are not perceived as belonging to the specific group.

CONCLUSIONS

Each student in this study has developed a sense of biracial identity. Despite the frequent inquiries by outsiders, the students had few negative thoughts about being biracial. The most overwhelmingly negative experience was that some biracial students may be excluded from a racial group of which they are a member and may have some degree of difficulty in finding a peer group.

Comparison with Literature

In comparing the findings of this inquiry with Chickering and Reisser's (1993) theory of racial identity development and Cross's (1971) theory of Nigrescene, it is clear that the biracial identity development of these students differs from mono-racial identity development reported in the literature. As suggested by Williams (1999) biracial students experience identity development with a sense of "simultaneity." Williams' idea of "simultaneity" suggests that biracial students may experience more than one stage of a racial identity theory at the same time. This idea of a simultaneous racial development stage is supported by Wardle (1992) who observed, "a biracial child must not select a traditional group to avoid role confusion" (p. 8). The previous theories provide a new insight into understanding how biracial students may develop their racial identity. To further explore the racial identity development of biracial college students, Root's border crossings will be examined.

Crossing

Two of the students appear to be handling their biracialness by utilizing the "multiple perspectives" border crossing. Dan and Raun each seem concerned with addressing both aspects of their race. These students are placed in this category because they do not seem to emphasize one half of their racial composition more than the other. They also seem comfortable with their minority status and sympathetic to the needs of other minority students.

Kiara and Carlo are "situational" in their border crossing. The need to display one part of their ethnicity over another depends on where they are and with whom. These experiences seem deliberate in some instances and a way to connect with their minority half in other instances. For both Kiara and Carlo, their skin color aids in their ability to utilize the "situational" border crossings. Kiara, by appearance, looks African American and it does not seem surprising that the African American community would accept her.

Carlo, on the other hand, appears to be Caucasian. It is because of Carlo's skin color that he has had such difficulty finding a niche on campus and feels the need to live a double life. Carlo affiliates himself with his predominantly Caucasian fraternity brothers, and other Latino students on campus. However, these two distinct groups do not cross paths. Carlo is either with one group or the other, thus, creating his double life.

Taye and Ayenna display the characteristics of individuals who are in a "multiracial" border crossing. They do not see the need to identify specifically with their racial composition.

SPECIFIC RECOMMENDATIONS
FOR PRACTICE

The third purpose of this study was to identify recommendations for practice at PSU. The framework of Weick (1984) who recommends that in trying to create social change attempting a number of initiatives is preferable to a large, complex project is used.

1. Expanded Racial Categories on Admission Applications

To assist in making biracial students feel welcome on college campuses, the first measure that should be employed is the creation of an admission application that allows students to choose more than one race. If the racial categorization questions do not allow students to accurately depict their racial identity, the institution has, in a sense, already alienated them before they have arrived on campus.

Furthermore, if institutions do not have systems in place to track students by more than one race, biracial students may be alienated from preferred racial affiliations. For example, if a Latino and Asian biracial student is tracked as a Latino student for University data collection purposes, this student may experience greater difficulty in gaining access to the Asian community. In discussing reasons why students leave college, Tinto (1993) notes that some students "may experience difficulty in making contact with other persons and establishing competent membership in the communities of the college." Oftentimes for these students "isolation is a primary cause of departure" (p. 176).

2. Development of Programs and Services

To aid in biracial student development on college campuses, initiatives to assist biracial students in becoming involved in some facet of the institutional life should be created.

Mentoring programs may be of great value to not only minority students, but also biracial students. Hoard (1989) feels that mentoring programs are valuable in increasing student involvement on campuses. Furthermore, "without a viable support network student achievement will suffer and the problem of student retention will be exacerbated" (p. 72).

Allen and Haniff (1991) noticed that "quality of life at the institution" (p. 108) can affect a student's academic performance. "Quality of life" includes "relationships with faculty, and friend-support networks" (p. 109). Gloria, Robinson Kurpius, Hamilton, & Wilson (1999) also notice a link between institutional involvement and persistence particularly in the areas of "social support, comprised of support from family and friends and perceived mentoring" (p. 265).

Services that may be useful include a mentoring program, a racial exploration class or workshop, and a social organization created specifically for biracial and multiracial students. Although not every biracial student may need assistance in developing a healthy biracial identity, simply having services available would allow biracial students the opportunity to meet others who are biracial and may even enhance the awareness of multiracial issues campus-wide. Tinto (1993) summarizes the importance of involvement when stating that "long-term intervention programs" to decrease student departure should include measures "to further involve students in the life of the institution" (pp. 176-177).

3. Learning Community

A learning community created specifically for biracial students may be beneficial for first year students at PSU. A residential peer group may help biracial students feel more comfortable in their new surroundings. This learning community would provide the opportunity for biracial students to explore their race and learn what services and programs are available for biracial students and students of specific racial groups. "Regardless of how we choose to define success in college—whether it is a statistical measure of persistence and retention, or gains in critical thinking and writing abilities that show up as positive outcomes on student learning assessments—we now have compelling evidence to suggest that creating learning communities on campus leads to greater student success in college" (Shapiro & Levine, 1999, pp. 14-15).

RECOMMENDATIONS FOR FUTURE RESEARCH

Future research on the academic experiences of multiracial college students is warranted. Not only is this a rapidly growing population in the United States, it is a population that will not disappear as racial groups become more fluid and interracial relationships become more prolific. Because of the potential magnitude, biracial and multiracial student academic experiences would be an important area for future research initiatives.

Beyond what has been reported in this study, comparing biracial students of similar backgrounds (e.g., African American and Caucasian with Hispanic and Caucasian) may provide insight into how members of various groups adjust to college and develop racial identity. Such a study would also assist in discovering if students who are biracial with two minority backgrounds have different racial development issues than biracial students who are partly Caucasian. This study would assist in discovering innovative means to assist the biracial college student persist and graduate.

An additional area of research is to examine biracial student's persistence in undergraduate programs. This study would be able to compare and contrast the persistence and commitment to undergraduate biracial students to that of other minority groups and the majority culture. Results of this study would be useful in determining what efforts must be made on campuses to ensure that all students are encouraged to persevere and obtain their degrees.

REFERENCES

Allen, W. (1991). Introduction. In W. Allen, E. G. Epps, & N. Z. Haniff (Eds.), *College in black and white: African American students in predominantly white and in historically Black public universities* (pp. 1-16). Albany, NY: SUNY Press.

Allen, W., & Haniff, N. Z. (1991). Race, gender, and academic performance in U.S. higher education. In W. Allen, E. G. Epps, & N. Z. Haniff (Eds.), *College in black and white: African American students in predominantly white and in historically Black public universities* (pp. 95-110). Albany, NY: SUNY Press.

Allen, W., Epps, E. G., & Haniff, N. Z. (1991). *College in black and white: African American students in predominantly white and in historically Black public universities.* Albany, NY: SUNY Press.

Cabrera, A. F., Nora, A., Terenzini, P. T., Pascarella, E., & Hagedorn, L. S. (1999). Campus racial climate and the adjustment of students to college. *Journal of Higher Education, 70*, 134-156.

Cheatham, H. E. (1991). Identity development in a pluralistic society. In Author (Ed.), *Cultural pluralism on campus* (pp. 23-38). Alexandria, VA: AACD.

Chickering, A. W., & Reisser, L. (1993). *Education and identity* (2nd ed.). San Francisco: Jossey-Bass.

Cross, W. E., Jr. (1971). Toward a psychology of black liberation: The Negro-to-black conversion experience. *Black World, 20*, 13-27.

Cuyjet, M. J. (1997). African American men on college campuses: their needs and their perceptions. In Author (Ed.), *Helping African American men succeed in college* (pp. 5-16). New Directions for Student Services Sourcebook 80. San Francisco: Jossey-Bass.

Glaser, B. G., & Strauss, A. L. (1967). *The discovery of grounded theory: Strategies for qualitative research.* Chicago: Aldine Publishing Company.

Gloria, A. M., Robinson Kurpius, S. E., Hamilton, K. D., & Wilson, M. S. (1999). African American students' persistence at a predominantly white university: Influence of social support, university comfort, and self-beliefs. *Journal of College Student Development, 40*, 257-268.

Gonzalez, K. P. (2000-2001). Toward a theory of minority student participation in predominately white colleges and universities. *Journal of College Student Retention, 2*(1), 69-91.

Herring, R. D. (1995). Developing biracial ethnic identity: A review of the increasing dilemma. *Journal of Multicultural Counseling and Development, 23,* 29-38.

Hoard, D. W. (1989). Models of community resources for the enhancement of black student retention. In J. N. Niba & R. Norman (Eds.), *Recruitment and retention of black students in higher education* (pp. 71-88). Lanham, MD: University Press of America.

Hurtado, S., Milem, J., Clayton-Pedersen, A., & Allen, W. (1999). Enacting diverse learning environments: Improving the climate for racial/ethnic diversity in higher education. *Higher Education Report, 26*(8).

Lincoln, Y. S., & Guba, E. G. (1994). But is it rigorous? Trustworthiness and authenticity in naturalistic evaluation. In J. S. Stark & A. Thomas (Eds.), *Assessment and program evaluation* (pp. 651-658). Needham Heights, MA: Simon & Schuster.

Merriam, S. B. (1998). *Qualitative research and case study applications in education.* San Francisco: Jossey-Bass.

National Center for Education Statistics (1998). *State survey on racial and ethnic classifications* (NCES 98-034). Washington,, DC: US Department of Education,

Patton, M. Q. (1990). *Qualitative evaluation and research methods* (2nd ed.). Newbury Park, CA: Sage.

Root, M. P. (1996). *The multiracial experience: Racial borders as the new frontier.* Newbury Park, CA: Sage.

Shapiro, N. S., & Levins, J. H. (1999). *Creating learning communities: A practical guide to winning support, organizing for change, and implementing programs.* San Francisco, CA: Jossey-Bass.

Tinto, V. (1998). Colleges as communities: Taking research on student persistence seriously. *The Review of Higher Education, 21,* 167-177.

Tinto, V. (1993). *Leaving college: Rethinking the causes and cures of student attrition* (2nd ed.). Chicago, IL: University of Chicago Press.

U.S. Census Bureau (2000a). *Census 2000 Summary File* (On-line). Washington, DC: Author. Available:
http://factfinder.census.gov/bf/_lang_vt_name=Dec_2000_SFI_U_QTP3_geo_id=01000 US.html

U.S. Census Bureau (2000b). *Mapping census 2000: The geography of U.S. diversity. Two or more races.* Washington, DC: Author.

U.S. Census Bureau (2001). *Ranking tables for counties by race alone, race alone or in combination, and two or more races population.* Washington, DC: Author.

Wardle, F. (1992). *Biracial identity: An ecological and developmental model.* (University Microfilms No. ED 385 376).

Weick, K. E. (1984). Small wins. *American Psychologist, 39*(1), 40-49.

Williams, C. B. (1999). Claiming a biracial identity: Resisting social constructions of race and culture. *Journal of Counseling and Development, 77,* 32-35.

Ybarra, R. (2000-2001). Latino students and Anglo-mainstream instructors: A study of classroom communication. *Journal of College Student Retention, 2*(2), 161-171.

SECTION 6

Institutional

CHAPTER 11

Institutional Commitment to Diversity and Multiculturalism Through Institutional Transformation: A Case Study of Olivet College

Evon Walters

Olivet College is a private, residential liberal arts college in central Michigan that enrolls approximately 900 students. The College was founded in 1844 by abolitionists and was the first college in the nation, by charter, to open to women and people of color. Yet, over the last two decades Olivet College failed to acknowledge changing demographics and problems of intergroup relations. In 1992, a racial brawl involving White and African-American students put the college into crisis. The incident launched the college into a process of reassessment and redefinition that resulted in a major institutional transformation. Diversity was a major part of this initiative. As a result of its success in infusing multiculturalism into its structure, Olivet College was recently selected by the Association of American Colleges and Universities as a Model Institution for its diversity initiatives. Additionally, it was selected as one of 35 institutions out of 675 nationwide to participate in President Clinton's initiative on race and was spotlighted by the American Council on Education for its exemplary work in infusing diversity across the campus. This chapter presents all aspects of Olivet College's diversity initiative including mission, curriculum, co-curriculum, students, faculty, and staff. These strategies are applicable not only to small private liberal arts colleges, but to other institutions of learning as they attempt to create an action plan that addresses the challenge of diversity/multiculturalism in the higher education system.

Given the high failure rate of students of color in American higher education over the past two decades, the issues surrounding their performance and retention are becoming increasingly complex. This chapter looks at the connections between multiculturalism and diversity and minority student performance and retention. The chapter presents a case study of Olivet College, highlighting its successful yet challenging model of institutional commitment towards multiculturalism and minority student success. It examines the contemporary debate on multiculturalism within the United States from the liberal and conservative perspective. It also defines multiculturalism as an institutionalized entity within a college setting. The model of multiculturalism presented in this chapter stresses the importance of a multi-faceted/holistic approach to multiculturalism in addressing the developmental characteristics of a college or university and the needs of minority students.

The Controversy Surrounding Multiculturalism

For the past two decades, raging debate over multiculturalism and diversity has permeated virtually every facet of education (Kuh & MacKay, 1989). The debate has attracted the attention of many scholars, both liberals and conservatives (Asante, 1991; D'Souza, 1991; Glazer, 1991; Schlesinger, 1991; Torres, 1999). Their positions range from the assertion that the multicultural's Philosophy is one that seeks to explore and validate a more in-depth and holistic examination of the role of the education system in attempting to provide accessibility to quality education for all children. This is opposed to the current system that marginalizes the experiences of people of color (Banks, 1996; Foster & Herzog, 1994; Gates, 1992; Neito, 1996). This philosophy is in contrast to the conservatist notion of a self-segregating movement that can potentially dilute academic standards and freedom of speech in an institution that supposedly should have free reign (Auster, 1994; Bloom, 1987).

In higher education, these controversial issues include but are not limited to the following: 1) affirmative action; 2) institutional mission; 3) curriculum and faculty development; and 4) recruitment, retention, and admissions policies of faculty, staff, and students. The backlash from conservatives has come from many angles. Some conservatives claim that these well-intentioned multicultural efforts have actually accomplished the opposite intent by heightening the divisive tensions on campus, compromising academic integrity, and quieting the democratic voice of all.

Despite these various assertions, the central question remains: is the American educational system (specifically higher education) doing its best in providing quality education for all students? The position of this chapter is no. Higher education administrators must challenge their institutions to improve the quality of life experiences for students, faculty, and administrators of color. Person (1990) and Simpson and Frost (1993) support this assertion by stipulating that American institutions of higher learning have failed to keep up with shifting demographics and that Blacks and other people of color remain underrepresented in the academy at all levels. Unfortunately, the dialogue on diversity and multicultural- ism in America for the past two decades has been characterized by intellectual battles and patronage, in which all factions (trustees, presidents, provost, faculty, and administrators) verbally express commitment to and responsibility for this area of institutional development. While these public expressions represent the fashion- able and politically correct thing to say, there is often little evidence of a clear understanding of multiculturalism or its effective implementation. It is distressing to see the constant scapegoating of students by institutions who view them as the only group required to become more sensitive and culturally aware. This is most evident when institutions are faced with the challenge of responding to inappro- priate racist behavior within the residential halls, cafeteria, or classrooms. Administrators are quick to seek out short-term solutions while ignoring the factors that precipitated a racial incident. They should instead consider the fol- lowing questions: were appropriate structures in place? is this the first time? if yes, what has the institution done to combat this problem?

Defining Multiculturalism

Given the on-going debate on multiculturalism, a definition has been difficult to conceptualize (Arthur & Shapiro, 1995). This is compounded by the rhetorical political stance held by various constituents within higher education. Gitlin (1995) describes this stance as vague enough to appease many interests. For the purposes of this chapter, multiculturalism, as it relates to higher education, is defined within the context of organizational elements and structures that shape and form an institution. These elements may include mission, curricula, policies, campus norms, rituals, and staffing (Tierney, 1994; Walters, 1996). This chapter adapts Neito's (1996) definition of multicultural education which views multicultural education as a comprehensive movement that embraces the belief that gender, ethnic, racial, and cultural diversity should be acknowledged within every aspect of the institutional environment. It should permeate the curriculum and the pedagogi- cal strategies used by teachers. It refers to the fact that higher education institutions must acknowledge and be sensitized to various issues of its diverse student/faculty consumer pool. This sensitivity must be expressed in a holistic and comprehensive manner.

AN INSTITUTIONAL MODEL OF MULTICULTURALISM

What Constitutes Institutional Commitment

Lester (1994), in *The Future of White Men and Other Diversity Dilemmas*, dis- cusses the institutional approach to multiculturalism as a self-sustaining change process which occurs in stages. Change occurs when all new programs and policies are automatically scrutinized for their impact on institutional direction. Rakhsha (1996) takes this process further by sharing some insights by noted multicultural expert Pope-Davis:

> It is important to distinguish between multiculturalism and diversity . . . . For some institutions diversity has come to mean the fulfillment of a quota requirement. In other words, in some institutions diversity has become a matter of numbers . . . . Multiculturalism goes beyond incorporation of people with diverse backgrounds . . . . It is important for institutions to ask what changes must occur if we commit ourselves to become culturally aware and diverse . . . . One of the significant issues regarding diversification of our academic institutions is the issue of responsibility . . . . The responsibility to diversify should be shared among all the members of the academic community including students, staff, faculty members and administrators . . . . It is of significant importance for members with more power, such as tenured faculty and especially administrators, to assume a larger portion of this responsibility. Such members usually have the means and power available to them to investigate and implement organizational changes (1996, p. 1).

Lester (1994) asserts that the transformational process should not depend on the energies and leadership of specific individuals. In higher education, this dependency is most visible in minority student unrest or in professionals who have specific responsibility for minority/multicultural affairs. The well intentioned but sporadic programs of these dedicated professionals and students do not meet Lester's criteria.

Institutional commitment and not student activism must guide the direction in which an institution is going. This commitment, along with the leadership from faculty and administration, is viewed by Smith (1989) as an important catalyst that will create and reinforce mechanisms for accessing and monitoring progress. Although it was student unrest that initiated the transformation efforts, its stability came primarily on the collaborative efforts of senior administrators, faculty, staff and students.

OLIVET COLLEGE: A CASE STUDY OF INSTITUTIONAL COMMITMENT TO MULTICULTURALISM

The Historical and Institutional Context

Olivet College, a private liberal arts college in central Michigan that enrolls approximately 900 students, was founded in 1844 by abolitionists and was the first college in the nation chartered to accept women and people of color. Yet eight years ago, Olivet was rocked by a troubling racial disturbance on campus and resulting negative media attention. In response, Olivet undertook a process of self-analysis that led to a reaffirmation of its commitment to its founding principles and to a comprehensive strategy for promoting diversity and multiculturalism throughout the institution. Since that time, Olivet College has been selected by the Association of American Colleges and Universities as a model institution for its diversity initiatives, was chosen as one of 35 campuses nationwide to participate in President Clinton's initiative on race, and spotlighted by the American Council on Education for its exemplary work in infusing diversity across the institution.

How was Olivet able to move beyond the common tactic of evasion and damage control to transform itself as an institution? Although the answers are particular to this college and its history, Olivet's story may be useful to other educational institutions grappling with the same issues. The project described below began in 1997 when I first considered joining Olivet's education department as a faculty member and has continued since I became director of the Office of International Education. At the time, Olivet was already deeply engaged in an institutional transformation process that embraced diversity and multiculturalism. What follows is what I have learned.

Despite its historic commitment to integration and tolerance, in the past two decades Olivet, like so many American institutions, had not acknowledged changes in its demographics and their effect on intergroup relations. The number of African-American students had increased (reaching 9 percent of the total student body in 1992), most of them hailing from inner-city Detroit and Chicago, while the White students came primarily from neighboring rural towns. Before coming to Olivet, each group had little or no previous experience with the other. On April 1, 1992, a racial incident involving three male students (two White and one African American) served as the catalyst for the enormous institutional changes that were to follow. Some of the African-American students, understandably distraught, sought the counsel of their parents, who in turn contacted the media. The subsequent media presence put the unprepared college into a crisis that led to a dramatic decrease in minority enrollment and the immediate firing of the president and the resignation of the succeeding acting president.

Although it took a hostile incident to get its full attention, the administration was forced to respond in a comprehensive and purposeful manner. It began in an ambitious and challenging interrogation of these issues by drafting a mission statement in December of 1993. The entire campus community was invited to participate in defining the college's institutional vision through a number of open forums. The resulting declaration stated that "We aspire to provide a campus-wide academic culture such that our students will come to understand the need to serve others as well as themselves, to celebrate both the wealth of human diversity and the bond of human similarity."

From this mission statement, in consultation with faculty, staff, students, alumni, and trustees, the new president quickly developed a set of six institutional priorities and objectives that incorporated a multicultural agenda. The objectives were: to build an academically distinctive and purposeful institution grounded in the College's new vision; to prepare all students at the College to participate effectively in a diverse society; to strengthen and extend the relationships between the College and its external communities; to promote the continuing development of positive student peer cultures consistent with the College's new vision; to promote the continuing development of roles and responsibilities of all employees consistent with the College's new vision; and to strengthen the fiscal health and operating effectiveness of the College.

The president worked with faculty, staff, students, and board members to develop strategies for meeting these objectives. Strategies included: articulating Olivet's long-standing commitment to diversity in all appropriate institutional planning documents and statements of institutional direction; developing a core group of faculty, staff, students, and administrators to serve as an ongoing resource for the campus regarding diversity programming and education; promoting campus-wide responsibility for enriching the climate for diversity on the campus; building specific attention to diversity issues into the curriculum; and providing multiple opportunities for individuals to learn about and validate their group identities and to share those identities with the entire campus.

Through this inclusive process, Olivet's administration solicited points of view that otherwise would not have been represented (secretaries, lower to mid-level staff personnel), encouraged a climate in which diverse groups could feel themselves an integral part of the college, and recognized the role of community in the learning and retention of students, faculty, and staff. At the same time, the various open and closed forums allowed all campus constituencies to acknowledge and address differences in views and agendas within and among themselves. To gain some much-needed objectivity, outside consultants were included in some sessions. One session, for instance, included the nationally renowned Ann Austin from Michigan State University, Arthur Chickering from the University of Vermont, and John Dolton from Florida State, whose continuing participation at Olivet College has been part of a national research effort sponsored by the Kellogg Foundation. As one faculty member noted, "The stage was set, and there was a clear sense of direction as to what the campus wanted to accomplish. The mere presence of these consultants set a foundation for openly sharing issues that all felt impacted us as an institution."

A multi-pronged strategic action plan was developed by faculty and administrators. A major element of this plan was launching new recruiting initiatives. As mentioned above, between 1992 and 1994 African-American enrollment numbers decreased significantly at Olivet College as African-American students no longer felt comfortable attending a place portrayed by the media as racist, unsafe, and insensitive to their needs. Knowing that these concerns were being addressed systemically and that appropriate measures were being taken to meet them, in 1995 the Office of Multicultural Affairs, in collaboration with the Office of Admissions and the Office of Youth Outreach Programs, began a new recruiting strategy. The goal was to develop long term relationships with youth-serving organizations that would increase the post-secondary educational opportunities of less-privileged and inner-city children. Olivet also established a partnership with a community youth organization in Chicago, the Ada S. McKinley Community Services. In the spring of 1996, 48 students from that organization visited the college, during which they were exposed to college life and the idea that attending college was a realistic goal. They met with the admissions staff and other college officials to learn about college requirements and expectations, talked with current Olivet student leaders about what it was like to be a student at the college, toured the campus, and ate lunch and dinner in the dining hall. Of those 48 visitors, 30 enrolled as students in the fall of 1997, demonstrating that such recruiting initiatives could attract students of color who might otherwise not have considered attending this institution.

Taking its cue from multiculturalism's emphasis on understanding students' unique learning needs, (Neito, 1996; Sleeter & Grant, 1993) Olivet College maximized on its students to faculty ratio of 16 to 1 by devising a multi-faceted plan to increase the individualized attention given to all its students, a factor especially important to the success of African-American and economically disadvantaged students. Michigan's Department of Equity awarded a grant to Olivet to create an innovative Student Support Services Project that would strengthen existing academic support services. A collaborative program among several departments, the Student Support Services Project fostered academic success by promoting student involvement in curricular and co-curricular programs. The project resulted in the creation of the Academic Resource Center, an individualized learning center that provides free assistance to students wanting to improve their academic skills. Additionally, it assists faculty and administrators in monitoring students' academic progress. The Center also provides academic counseling, orientation for new students, a peer tutoring program, portfolio advising, services for students with learning disabilities, and instruction in study skills and time management. It also works closely with the Communication Center and Mathematics Center, which offer peer assistance in math, reading, writing, listening, and speaking.

Yet Olivet's multicultural commitment did not stop at individualized add-on services, as important as those are, but extended to the entire curriculum. The college's academic program was revised to take a more holistic approach to student development by including as part of its curriculum and requirements the development of important life skills as well as intellectual skills. This approach is supported by research that links student involvement on campus in various capacities—i.e., student leadership roles to positive learning outcomes (Astin, 1984; Pascarella & Terenzini, 1991). This approach is reflected in the General Education component of the curriculum, which consists of 11 required core courses designed to link the learning of skills and content to multiple perspectives, to promote intellectual inquiry, and to inspire life-long learning within and beyond the classroom. Of the 16 required Learning Outcomes, students must demonstrate to graduate, at least three—interpersonal skills, working with others, and awareness and sensitivity to issues of diversity directly relate to the college's multicultural goals. The new curriculum also incorporates service learning and collaborative learning techniques that complement traditional lectures with an assortment of active-learning pedagogies such as oral presentations, service learning, learning communities, small group work, field research, and class portfolios. These methods reflect multicultural education's philosophy that multiple conceptions of learning afford students opportunities to illustrate talents that might otherwise have been ignored and enhance the participation of all students in the learning process (Sleeter, 1996).

The General Education component of the curriculum begins with each entering student enrolling in a three-credit semester course titled the First Year Experience. The course, taught by administrators and faculty from across the institution, centers on transitional issues and engages students in activities that strengthen and affirm their role as participating members of the campus community. Because an important objective of the course is developing positive peer relationships, it places students in group situations in which they work collaboratively on numerous projects with peers from different races, cultures, ethnicities, and philosophies. The course introduces students to Olivet College's environment as well as to its academic and social standards and expectations, aids them in defining their goals for learning, helps them to explore how to pursue the goals, and assesses their progress.

All entering students take Self and Community, another General Education requirement. This is a year-long interdisciplinary freshman seminar that presents multiple perspectives on diversity within the United States. Issues include race, gender, sexual orientation, religion, and class. As in any seminar, the group dynamic requires student accountability and participation, and class discussion is enriched by dialogue and by both personal and textual references. The process includes learning to actively listen, to discuss appropriately, to ask significant questions, and to understand that class discussions are not intended to change personal opinions but to understand different viewpoints. In one section, for instance, students spent three class sessions discussing the controversial topic of affirmative action. They first examined their own views, liberal and conservative perspectives, and the influence of the media and then explored the historical and socioeconomic nuances of the subject. This allowed students from different backgrounds to examine their conscious and unconscious beliefs, myths, and stereotypes.

Assessment of student learning in these courses takes various forms, notably student presentations, reaction papers, and Identity Narratives. Identity Narratives are formalized student assessment papers in which each student reflects on how his or her own experience relates to the issues discussed in the course. In these Narratives, students respond to the points of view expressed by their peers and on the content and format of the course. Sharing these narratives with the other members of the class helps students identify areas of discomfort and creates a learning environment conductive to full student participation.

Sophomores take another General Education requirement, a course titled Civilization Studies, that also examines diversity-related issues, this time from a historical and global perspective. This two-semester course engages and familiarizes the student with global issues and their impact on different countries and cultures. It includes an analysis of major political, environmental, and economic events of this past century and how they have influenced our society today. Students in this class learn more about other cultural traditions, norms, and values from an historical and sociological perspective that extends beyond the boundaries of the United States.

Juniors are required to take a 300-level capstone General Education course in their major that includes an in-depth exploration of at least two areas of diversity, including race, class, gender, ethnicity, religion, and bio-diversity. The course may also take a global or international perspective and encourages an integrative and interdisciplinary approach.

This series of classes reinforces one of Olivet's other guiding principles, the recognition that knowledge changes and that learning is not a one-time thing. Issues discussed in a given class might be influenced by any number of current political, social, and economic factors, and students discover that they must engage in life-long learning if they are to keep abreast of issues that affect themselves and others. The same principle is applied to course development. Faculty committees for each of the courses meet during the semester and over the summer to evaluate and revise courses in response to feedback from student surveys and faculty comments to revise the course.

At the heart of the College's new initiatives is its Portfolio program, a formalized mentoring system intended to improve the quality of learning and teaching for every student. It supports the notion of holistic learning where students are viewed as maturing intellectually, physically, psychologically, socially, ethically, spiritually, and aesthetically (NASPA, 1987, p. 11). It includes a one-credit course taken every semester that allows students to work one-on-one or in a small group setting with a faculty member on some critical area of their education. This system reflects multicultural education's philosophy of empowering students to develop decision-making skills (Banks, 1997; Ramsey, 1998; Sleeter & Grant, 1993). Included are such activities as drafting an academic plan that identifies students' academic goals, making an informed choice about an academic major, improving skill areas such as writing and researching, serving internships to meet a graduation requirement, and developing Portfolio exhibits that demonstrate one or more of the required Learning Outcomes. Students are required to satisfy 16 learning outcomes. Evaluation of these learning outcomes are conducted by the Portfolio team, chosen by the students reviewing and providing feedback on each exhibit. Exhibits such as a research paper highlighting writing skills can serve as marketing tools in seeking a job or admission to graduate school. The Portfolio program is a mentoring process in which students form long-term relationships with their mentors and are empowered to identify and build upon their academic and professional strengths. Neito (1999) describes this critical pedagogy and empowerment as one in which teacher and student engage in learning as a mutual encounter. During their first two years, students work with their faculty mentor; once they have declared a major, they are joined by an academic advisor from the major department and by a career/professional advisor to form a Portfolio team that helps students refine their academic and career plans and their Graduation Portfolio. The career/professional advisor may be a faculty, staff, or a profession within the profession of the student's interests. This continuing feedback from the Portfolio team improves the educational process for every student and is critical to the matriculation and retention of minority students.

Olivet College's curricular initiative mirrors the paradigmatic shift in American education from a focus on teaching to a focus on learning, a retreat from the model of the teacher as the giver of information and the student as the passive recipient. Multiculturalism's contribution to this movement is the recognition that if schools fail to recognize the diverse needs and abilities of students, they fail to adequately prepare them for the complex world in which they live. Olivet's experience has embodied the model suggested by Barr and Tagg (1995) in which the institution is viewed as a learner itself, going through a process in which it must continuously develop new insights and strategies to produce more and better learning with each entering class.

To do this, Olivet has challenged its faculty to heighten their sensitivity to the various learning styles of students and to discover new ways to facilitate their learning. It has also required them to grow professionally by developing a historically rich and multi-dimensional view of the minority issues that face us. Most of this professional development has been accomplished through in-service seminars or faculty/staff attending regional or national conferences supported by grants. Additionally, Olivet College further embraced the student affairs philosophies of Astin (1993) and Pascarella and Terenzini (1991) by purposefully infusing the student affairs perspective into the institutions structure. One way this was visible was empowering the resident educators (resident directors) with a masters degree with faculty status. The resident educators would not only teach some of our classes, but most importantly would be able to provide critical insights that traditionally would not be heard in faculty meetings when discussions are about our students.

This has not always been an easy process and has raised not only enthusiasm, creativity, and commitment but fear, uncertainty, insecurity, and confusion on the part of a sometimes weary faculty. Dr. Donald Tuski, the Vice President for Academic Affairs and one who has not only been an integral part of this transformation process from its early beginnings, but who has also maintained a critical eye over its progress, reflected on some of the challenges that were present. He shares:

> Some of the challenges that we have faced as an institution during this
> transformation period of eight years have been somewhat philosophical and

political. Diversity and critical pedagogy presented as one of the many solutions for change during that tumultuous time period was greeted by a strong inference of passive skepticism by some of our faculty. Was it a fad? What implications does it have on personal change? Politically, faculty and staff had to be convinced otherwise that this was not a fad . . . . This was accomplished through various mediums such as one-on-one meetings, group meetings, open forums. Communication and demonstrating a strong sense of democracy with decision making became important tools in attempting to empower the faculty. Lots of time was spent on conversing with people on the importance of diversity. It became more challenging when trying to balance with being inclusive and maintaining focus on the goals to be accomplished.

Co-Curricular Initiatives

Since 1992, Olivet has put into place several major co-curricular programs related to diversity issues. One of these was the establishment of the Office of African American Student Development, which, in response to increased enrollment of Chicano students, was redesigned as the Office of Multicultural Affairs. This office provides academic, career, social, and personal counseling and refers students to other campus services. It collaborates with other offices to facilitate leadership development among minority students. For instance, it hosts an annual Multicultural Awards Banquet, a ceremony that recognizes outstanding contributions by minority student leaders during the academic year. This ceremony reinforces the value to the college of their leadership, encourages other students to take on leadership roles, and shares some of the accolades students receive outside of the classroom with invited faculty and administrators. This important office is just one part of the campus-wide program in multiculturalism rather than being solely responsible for it, as is the case on some campuses.

The college also established the African American Cultural Center and the Global Cultural Center, houses in which several students and resident assistants conduct activities that increase understanding and promote the richness of the cultures they represent. Each of these houses has created numerous cultural co-curricular programs in conjunction with the Offices of Residential Life, Student Life, and Multicultural Affairs, such as Kwaanza celebrations and a Taste Fest that features the foods of different countries and cultures represented by Olivet students. In 1997 the College opened a Women's Center to create a supportive environment in which women and men can address issues specific to women and gender relations.

In addition, students have formed several diversity-related student clubs, including the Black Student Union, Olivet College's Gospel Choir, the International Club, MECHA (a Chicano student organization), and Elite, Alpha Phi Kappa, and Nu Gamma XI (African-American fraternities and sororities). These groups give students of color numerous opportunities for intragroup community building, for active roles as campus leaders, and for sharing their cultural heritage with the campus community. These forums create "teachable" moments that entertain as well as educate Olivet students and staff about various cultural heritages.

Another notable co-curricular program is the Group Dialogue Project created in response to President Clinton's call for a national dialogue on race in 1998. Students were trained as mediators to help groups talk with each other about matters of race in an atmosphere of mutual trust and respect. A number of these dialogues were held both inside and outside the classroom and created many powerful learning moments. In her closing remarks at one of the community sessions held in the spring of 1998, higher education consultant Catherine Maddox-Wiley summed up what has been accomplished and what still lies ahead:

> We now realize what the challenges are. It is an on-going process that will require not only the efforts of those senior officers, faculty, staff, and students present here today, but of the rest of the campus community who are absent. Olivet must be willing, patient, and appropriate in taking on these and other challenges to ensure that your institution continues to progress forward.

One measure of the success of these programs is the increase in Olivet's retention rate for students of color, particularly African-American students. During the academic year 1995–1996, Olivet retained 51 percent of its incoming African-American freshmen, compared to 41 percent in 1995–1996. The academic year 1996–1997 showed the college's highest retention rate yet, 66 percent. Especially noteworthy is that this figure was higher than the general student retention rate, which was 58 to 60 percent during that period.

Similar increases are seen in the enrollment rates of all minority students. In 1998, domestic minority students made up 22 percent of Olivet's total student body: 157 African Americans (18.5 percent), 25 Latinos (2 percent), 10 Native Americans (1 percent), and 5 Asian Americans (.5 percent). Sixty-two international students (6.8 percent) were also enrolled. In 1992, Olivet employed no faculty or staff of color; by 1998 the number had increased dramatically to 18, representing 29 percent of the college's faculty and staff. This dramatic shift reflects a conscious and strategic effort on the part of the president, academic vice president, and faculty, an effort that included making clear to potential new faculty that diversity is a major priority in the college's transformation process and that they would be active participants in it.

Gary Wertheimer, current president of the Faculty Senate, points out that it is hard to know if people's feelings and views have changed as a result of these initiatives: "What has changed institutionally is the increased on-going conversations related to issues of diversity within the formal setting such as classes or discussions forums among all students." These discussions, he says, were nonexistent during the late 1980s and the early 1990s and now play an important part in attempting to foster more tolerance and understanding among students.

CONCLUSION

What, then, can we learn from Olivet's example? First, it demonstrates that the purpose of a nurturing and supportive system for all people within higher education is not simply to make it possible for them to survive the process but to build community and create an infrastructure that will limit feelings of alienation and isolation in students, faculty, and staff, whatever their background. Second, it reaffirms the importance of making both the campus assessment and the resulting program development a democratic process that engages all of the campus's constituents—trustees, administrators, faculty, staff, and students. Although visionary leadership and the commitment of key administrators are essential, they are not sufficient by themselves. Lastly, it points out that embracing multiculturalism as a mainstream institutional agenda is an on-going process that requires more than moral scruples and ambitious ideals (Melzer, Weinberger, & Zinman, 1998). It has to be incited institutionally, by consistent and pro-active measures starting from the top. It has to be genuine in its actions as well as its words, and it must be followed by purposeful monitoring of related policies and procedures. It has to be discussed in specific terms and not confounded with vague dialogue. Institutions needs to recognize that there will be no quick solution to these deep-rooted problems that have troubled our institutions of learning for decades even as it they affirm the necessity and transformative potential of the effort.

Altbach and Lomotey (1991) acknowledge that institutions of higher learning should not be viewed as the panacea for all societal problems involving diversity. However, they should play a major role in serving as a model for other societal bureaucracies. In order to move in this direction, colleges and universities must address the facts and stop extending energies on evasion and avoidance. Eight years ago, in response to a troubling racial disturbance on campus, Olivet began a process of analysis where it was forced into reaffirming its commitment to its founding principles. The result was a comprehensive strategy for promoting diversity throughout the institution: in admission, in hiring, in the curriculum, and in virtually every other aspect of daily life in the College community. The results of this newly affirmed commitment have yielded tremendously positive results.

What Olivet attempted to cure is a disturbing American plague that has overcome many institutions of higher learning. Olivet did this by recognizing multiculturalism as not just a matter of deciphering individual prejudices, but as an acknowledging of the "real" issues of inequity and paranoia that accompany this term. It must be understood that numerous challenges remain with this on-going transformation process. These challenges include fear, uncertainty, security and confusion. The transformation experience has been characterized by numerous obstacles that have been compounded by resistance on the part of some faculty, staff and students. But as Olivet's out-going interim president, James Halseth, noted at the 1998 National Minority Student Conference in San Antonio, Texas, the best way to address these challenges has been with more diversity, not only through the programmatic initiatives discussed above but by adding new faculty and staff with a professional interest and background in multiculturalism and empowering them through their participation in faculty and administrative governance. "The vision of institutionalizing diversity must be kept alive and going . . . . We must challenge ourselves to find ways to empower and re-energize this effort, so as to prevent it from stagnating," Halseth said.

Additionally, Olivet understood that multiculturalism can not be implemented in a vacuum, but must be visualized in its historical, social, political and personal context for each group. Multiculturalism should not be used as a ploy to hide or distance real and often uncomfortable issues. A nurturing and supporting system for people of color in higher education is not simply a matter of whether or not they are able to make the necessary transitional progress. A nurturing system involves community, and creating an infrastructure that will limit the feelings of alienation and isolation experienced by students, faculty and staff of color.

In conclusion there are some "general" guidelines which may help institutions begin the process of institutionalizing diversity and multicultural issues within their campuses. The author acknowledges that there are other elements (such as financial status, demographic location) that may make it difficult to embrace some of the following guidelines:

1. *Assessing the institutions current status*—This assessment should be a democratic process that involves all of the campus constituents. Issues that should be probed include: history of the institution, campus decision making processes, the role and structure of faculty governance and the style of current and past administrations. Additionally, existing resources should be looked at. What kind of resources is the institution willing to invest and where will these resources come from?

2. *Develop an appropriate action plan*—An action plan involves looking at strategies for affecting change. What will be the key elements to incorporate? What will the institution intentionally need to do to bring out change? Richardson & Skinner (1991) stress that strategic planning must include coordinated and controlled efforts that go beyond hiring more faculty and staff of color. It should start with the leadership of the president and the faculty. This action plan should include focusing on the following components;

   Institutional: Mission, vision, symbols, traditions, rituals, norms, values— Green (1991) asserts that institutional recognition must include a comprehensive approach toward making multiculturalism a priority. This should be reflected in mission statements, commissions, councils or sub-committees. Welzenbach (1982) sees the mission statement as the general long-term purpose of an institution, which establishes the context and steers the institution's direction. A mission statement that identifies and defines multi-culturalism as a part of its content is an important first step. This sets the direction and highlights the seriousness of this priority to everyone on campus (Lyon, 1993; Pearson, Shavlik, & Touchton, 1989; Roueche & Baker, 1987; Varlotta, 1997).

Organizational: Commissions, committees, councils, forums—Committees are another important way to recognize multiculturalism as a priority through on-going exploration of the various structures such as mission, traditions, norms, and rituals that impact recruitment and retention. Committees should represent senior staff, faculty, student affairs professionals and students for a holistic and diverse perspective. Additionally, the committee must provide Institutional Reports and regular updates. Any attempt to improve the quality of student life must begin with an initial assessment of current services on campus (Smith, 1989).

Educational: Curricular, co-curricular, campus wide-events, training/development/orientation for faculty/staff/students—This area reflects the curricular (content and pedagogy) as well as the co-curricular, campus-wide events, training and development/orientation programs for faculty, staff and students. Appropriate educational interventions, as shared by Wurzel (1988), can help curtail cultural friction and promote the development of multicultural perspectives. As Wurzel states, "Curricular programs can serve to narrow the communication gap in micro and macro-cultural conflict." These learning interventions do not have to be limited to "reactionary," damage control hostile forums. It can take the form of "teachable," non-hostile, proactive, learning moments. Learning moments refer to opportunities in which students, staff or faculty are placed in non-threatening situations conducive to healthy discourse.

Structural: Policies, protocols for responding to incidents, support mechanisms.

Reward System: To recognize and motivate.

3. *Creation of an appropriate assessment process*—How do we know that we are doing the job? Surveys, quantitative as well as qualitative methods, should be in place to keep the constituencies informed on its progress.

Tackling these three areas can be a tedious but fruitful process. Most importantly, these components must be in place for transformation to occur. Factors that may aid or hinder the process include leadership, vision, centralization as opposed to decentralization, communication, data, accountability and commitment.

There are no quick or short term solutions for deep rooted problems that have existed for decades. Institutionalizing multiculturalism, as seen by Dawson (1987), is the greatest challenge that will face universities and colleges. If institutions are to assume a leadership role, they must develop a multi-dimensional view on multiculturalism. They must be willing to grow professionally in gaining both an historical and contemporary perspective on minority issues. Efforts must extend beyond the mere recognition of weeks or months devoted to diversity and as stated earlier in the chapter, they must be dispersed equally top-down across the campus.

REFERENCES

Altbach, P. G., & Lomotey, K. (1991). *The Racial Crisis in American Higher Education.* Albany: State University of New York Press.

Arthur, J., & Shapiro, A. (1995). *Campus Wars: Multiculturalism and the Politics of Difference.* Boulder, Co: Westview Press.

Asante, M. K. (1991). The Afrocentric idea in education. *The Journal of Negro Education, 60*(2), 170–180.

Astin, A. W. (1984). Student involvement: A developmental theory for higher education. *Journal of College Student Development, 26,* 297–308.

Astin, A. W. (1993). *What matters in college: Four critical years revisited.* San Francisco: Jossey-Bass.

Auster, L. (1994, February). Avoiding the issue. *National Review, 46,* 48–54.

Banks, J. A. (Ed.) (1996). *Multicultural Education, Transformative Knowledge, and Action.* New York: Teachers College Press.

Banks, J. A. (1997). *Teaching strategies for ethnic studies* (6th ed.). Boston: Allyn & Bacon.

Barr, R. B., & Tagg, J. (1995 November/December). From teaching to learning: A new paradigm for undergraduate education. *Change.*

Bloom, A. (1987). *The closing of the American mind.* Simon & Schuster

Chavez, L. (1994, February 21). Demystifying Multiculturalism. *National Review,* 26–32.

Crossland, F. E. (1971). *Minority access to college. A Ford Foundation report.* New York: Schocken Books.

Dawson, M. E. (1987, March). *Speech delivered at the 67th Annual Conference of The Association of College Unions International, Boston.*

D'Souza, D. (1991). *Illiberal education: The politics of race and sex on campus.* New York: The Free Press.

Foster, L., & Herzog, P. (1994): *Contemporary philosophical perspectives on pluralism and multiculturalism: Defending diversity.* University of Massachusetts Press, Amherst.

Gates, H. L., Jr. (1992). *Loose canons: Notes on the culture wars.* New York: Oxford University Press.

Gitlin, T. (1995). *The twilight of common dreams: Why America is wracked by culture wars.* New York: Henry Holt.

Glazer, N. (1991; September 2). In defense of multiculturalism. *The New Republic,* 18–21.

Green, M. F. (1989). *Minorities on campus: A handbook for enhancing diversity.* Washington, D. C.: American Council on Education.

Kuh, G. D., & Mackay, K. A. (1989, October). Beyond cultural awareness toward interactive pluralism. *Campus Activities Programming, 22,* 52–58.

Lester, J. S. (1994). *Black issues in higher education: Stages in the diversity process* (pp. 65).

Lester, J. S. (1994). *The future of white men and other diversity dilemmas.* Conari Press.

Melzer, A. M., Weinberger, J., & Zinman, M. R. (1998). *Multiculturalism and the American Democracy.* Location: University Press of Kansas.

National Association of Student Personnel Administrators (NASPA). (1987). *A perspective on student affairs.* A statement issued on the 50th anniversary of the Student Personnel Point of View. Washington, D.C.

Neito, S. (1996). *Affirming diversity: The sociopolitical context of multicultural education.* New York: Longman Publishers.

Neito, S. (1999). The light in their eyes: Creating multicultural learning communities. New York: Teachers College Press.

Pascarella, E., & Terenzini, P. (1991). *How college affect students.* San Francisco: Jossey Bass.

Pearson, C. S., Shavlik, D. L., & Touchton, J. G. (1989). *Educating the majority: Women challenge traditions in higher education* (pp. 25–31). New York: American Council on Education/Macmillan.

Person, D. R. (1990). *The black student culture of Lafayette College* (Doctoral Dissertation, Columbia University, 1990). Dissertation Abstracts International, *51,* 2285.

Rakhsha, G. (1996 Spring). Institutional commitment to multiculturalism. *SAG Newsletter, 18*(2).

Ramsey, P. G. (1998). *Teaching and learning in a diverse world: Multicultural education for young children* (2nd ed.). New York: Teachers College Press.

Richardson, Jr., R. C., & Skinner, E. F. (1991). *Achieving Quality & Diversity. University in a Multicultural Society.* New York: Macmillan Publishing Company.

Roueche, J. E., & Baker, G. A. III. (1987). *Access and excellence.* Washington, DC.: Community College Press.

Schlesinger, A. M., Jr. (1991). *The disuniting of America: Reflections on a multicultural society.* Knoxville, TN: Whittle Direct Books.

Simpson, R. D., & Frost, S. H. (1993). *Who goes to college and why. Inside college: Undergraduate education for the future* (pp. 39–66). New York: Insight Books/Plenum Press.

Sleeter, C, E. (1996). *Multicultural education as social activism.* Albany: State University of New York Press.

Sleeter, C. E., & Grant, C. A. (1993). *Making choices for multicultural education: Five approaches to race, class, and gender* (2nd ed.). New York: Merrill Publishing Company.

Smith, D. G. (1989). *The challenge of diversity: Involvement or alienation in the academy. Report no. 5.* Washington, DC: School of Education and Human Development, The George Washington University.

Tierney, W. G. (1994). *Multiculturalism in higher education: An organizational framework for analysis.* University Park, PA: National Center on Postsecondary Teaching, Learning, and Assessment. ERIC Document Reproduction Service # ED371675.

Torres, C. A. (1998). *Democracy, education, and multiculturalism: Dilemmas of citizenship in a global world.* Maryland: Rowan & Littlefield Publishers, Inc.

Varlotta, L. E. (1997 Winter). Invoking a university's mission statement to promote diversity, civility and free speech. *NASPA Journal, 34,* 123–133.

Walters, E. W. (1996, December). Embracing the spirit of multiculturalism in higher education as a means of Black and Hispanic student retention. *Equity and Excellence in Education, 29*(3).

Welzenbach, L. F. (Ed.). (1982) *College and university business administration.* Washington, DC: National Association for College and University Business Officers.

Wurzel, J. S. (1988). *Toward multiculturalism. A reader in multicultural education.* Yarthmouth, ME: Intercultural Press Inc.

## CHAPTER 12

Five Year Evaluation of the Student Diversity Program: A Retrospective Quasi-Experiment

Vernon R. Padgett and John F. Reid, Jr.

The Student Diversity Program (SDP) initially delivered academic and social support to Black student athletes, but expanded to include a more diverse group of students at risk of disqualification. To assess whether this program increased retention, we examined graduation rates and ending GPAs of students in four SDP cohorts from 1994 and 1995 ($n = 39$), comparing them to matched students who were not in the program ($n = 434$), over five years of academic progress. We matched these comparison students on semester of enrollment in CSUF, ethnic group, sex, age, transfer status (FTF or Transfer), and cumulative GPA at the end of their first semester. SDP students graduated at twice the rate of the comparable students after five years. SDP student's GPA of last record was not however different from that of comparison students. It appears that the Student Diversity Program achieves its goal of delivering academic support, and is effective not only with Black athletes but with a more diverse group of at-risk students as well.

The Mission of the Student Diversity Program (SDP) at Cal State Fullerton is to address the low retention and graduation rates of "at-risk" (at risk of academic disqualification) students by improving their use of campus academic support services, and to enhance student academic development and achievement by providing additional support services tailored to meet students' individual needs.

The SDP began in Summer 1998 after the success of its predecessors, the Black Ombudsman Program (Reid, 1996), which began in 1993, and the Teaching Ombudsman Action Program, which began in 1996. The Student Diversity Program support network, building on the earlier programs, is a multilevel retention program for at risk students. Most of the students in the earlier program cohorts were Black athletes, but later years were characterized by increased ethnic diversity as the program reached out to a broader student base, including non-Blacks and non-athletes. Graduation rates for Black athletes at Cal State Fullerton had been dismal previous to the program. Only three Black basketball players had graduated in the 12 years preceding inauguration of the Black Ombudsman Program. For comparison, the graduation rate is 40.8 percent for nine years across public four-year universities (Peltier, Laden, & Matranga, 1999, p. 358).

The SDP is a large program, and it appears to meet its goals: enrollment of at-risk students doubled from 1997-1998 to 1998-1999, to 361 students, and 93 percent of SDP participants enrolled in the Fall 1998 term were enrolled through the Fall 1999 term (unless they graduated). Fall 2000 SDP student enrollment has soared to 1200. Cost of program in the previous semester was $47 per student, compared to more than $700 for the other major student support service program (calculated as total O&E funds budgeted divided by number of active student participants).

Other Student Support Available

Our campus provides a range of student academic services, including academic tutoring. The campus recently opened a Learning Assistance Center; EOP has provided academic counseling and referrals for many years; our Fullerton First Year program provides a large number of services to selected first time freshmen; and the Dean of Students has a variety of student support programs. Thus, the SDP is one of many programs available to CSUF students.

Goals of SDP

The first goal in the Student Diversity Program has been to provide guidance and retention services to diverse student populations by developing action plans and programs to address academic, social, and cultural needs. The second SDP goal has been to maintain a complex early assessment and reporting system to integrate students into university life. These elements have been shown to correlate with personal and academic success (Ottens, Johnson, & Green, 1996; Sedlacek, 1996; Tracey & Sedlacek, 1987). Factors present in the SDP program are well represented in the set of Out-of-Class Validation Factors given in Holmes, Ebbers, Robinson, and Mugenda's (2000, p. 54) excellent review of variables contributing to the retention and graduation of African-American students.

Description of SDP

Important strategies of the SDP include "catch-back" planning, psychological counseling, faculty mentoring, group counseling, peer mentoring, and multicultural training, all aimed at increasing self-efficacy, self-esteem, mastery, commitment, coping skills, and cultural awareness. The "catch-back" plan uses theories based on building self-esteem, self-efficacy, and mastery through the use of planning, assessment and expectation, and assertiveness training. Key instruments include the Time Management instrument, the Goal Setting Pyramid, and the Art of Mastery instrument (all are available from the second author). The model incorporating the Catch-Back plan and these instruments all aim at moving students' control locus from external to internal, improving academic integration, developing an "information rich" environment, and improving the campus climate for learning. Basic tenets of the SDP are found in Reid (1996, pp. 193-199). The SDP further provides participants with role models, mentors, and advisors via a corps of community leaders who work with the participants on a volunteer basis. The SDP Advisory Council, composed of faculty, staff, and a physician, provides a further communication and support network. Are all parts of the program effective? SDP staff address this concern by conducting evaluations of the program routinely, with staff as well as student participants rating all aspects of the program.

What Program Evaluation Did We Perform

Of the *four* types of Program Evaluation (Needs Assessment, Process Assessment, Outcomes Assessment, and Economic Efficiency Assessment or Cost/Benefit Analysis), we conducted an outcome assessment. This outcome assessment served as a more formal evaluation following two briefer assessments in which SDP Interns provided both quantitative and narrative ratings. These briefer assessments revealed very positive overall evaluations.

What is a "Quasi-Experiment"?

Quasi-experiments attempt to approximate the control features of true experiments "to infer that a given treatment did have its intended effect" and are typically used in program evaluation research (Cozby, 1997, p. 163). This design is classed by Cook and Campbell (1979) as a Nonequivalent Control Group Design (p. 95).

How to Measure Program Success?

As noted earlier, persistence of SDP students exceeded 90 percent on a year-to-year basis, a far higher persistence rate than non-SDP students. Persistence did not seem a suitable dependent measure, however, as persistence data were not obtainable for the university as a whole, and even defining "persistence" precisely and to the satisfaction of all seemed beyond our means. We viewed GPA and graduation rates as "harder" measures, and ones we could obtain.

Research Question and Strategy

Does the Student Diversity Program meet its goals of improving student success? To evaluate the program, we calculated graduation rates and GPAs of students in four early cohorts of the program. We constructed a large comparison group as carefully as we could. We then compared the academic performance of SDP students, on those two measures, to the performance of similar students *not* in the program.

METHOD

Participants and Design

All SDP students from the first two years of the program were studied. There were nine students in the Spring 1994 SDP Cohort, 10 in Fall of 1994, five in Spring of 1995, and 16 in the Fall 1995 Cohort, for a total of 40 SDP students. Demographic characteristics of these students are given in Tables 1 through 5. We eliminated one SDP student from the study because her program enrollment date preceded her university enrollment date (of Spring 1996), allowing her (and her comparison students) less than four years for graduation. Thus, a total of 39 SDP students were studied. The design was a retrospective quasi-experiment.

Table 1. Frequencies of SDP Students
by Ethnicity and Gender,
Spring 1994 Cohort

Black males	8
White females	1
Total students	9

Table 2. Frequencies of SDP Students
by Ethnicity and Gender,
Fall 1994 Cohort

Black males	9
Black females	1
Total students	10

Table 3. SDP Students by Ethnicity
and Gender,
Spring 1995 Cohort

Black males	2
Black females	3
Total students	5

Table 4. Frequencies of SDP Students
by Ethnicity and Gender,
Fall 1995 Cohort

Black (African American) males	2
African male	1
Turkish male	1
African American females	8
Hispanic female	1
Anglo male	1
Asian female	1
Total students	15

Procedure

Extraction from Student Records Database

We extracted data from the CSUF Student Information System (SIS+), on 45 different criteria, on all students enrolled in the university each semester from Fall of 1990 through the following four years. These files included semester-by-semester academic performance through Fall of 1999 (or semester of last enrollment.)

Creation of Comparison Groups

We created comparison groups by matching each SDP student with a group of comparison students taken from the student records database, as follows. First, we selected all students who entered the university the same semester as the SDP student. This involved matching on eight different entering semesters, from Fall of 1990 to Fall of 1995. Next, we sorted the students in an Excel file for the appropriate entering semester, on gender, ethnicity, age, transfer status, and GPA at the end of the first semester of work (nested in that order). We then matched each SDP student with other students who:

Table 5. Frequencies of SDP Students
by Ethnicity and Gender,
All 1994-1995 Cohorts

African American males	21
African male	1
Turkish male	1
African American females	12
Hispanic female	1
Anglo-American females	1
Anglo-American male	1
Asian female	1
Total SDP students	39

- had enrolled in CSUF the same semester,
- were the same ethnic group,
- were the same sex,
- were within two years of the same age,
- were the same transfer status (FTF or Transfer),
- had the same approximate GPA after one semester at CSUF, and
- had enrolled in classes.

This provided a total of seven different matching criteria. For example, we matched one SDP member, a Black male First Time Freshman who entered in Fall of 1990, and was born in April 1972, with a group of students not in the SDP Program. These matching students were male, Black, within ±2 years of the SDP student's age, were also First Time (not Transfer) status, and were within 0.7 G.P.A. units on their GPA after one semester at the university. Each of the 39 students was matched with several non-SDP students. For a single Student Diversity Program member, there were from four to 54 matching students in separate comparison groups. The median number of students across comparison groups was 15. After the selection of comparable students, we removed any students who were also in the SDP program. Finally, these groups were combined and duplications removed.

Most of the members of the SDP were athletes. We were unable to match these students with non-SDP athletes, as nearly all the athletes meeting the matching criteria were already in the Student Diversity Program.

Next, we calculated the final cumulative GPAs and the percentage of students who had graduated in the comparison groups. Ethnicity and gender of the SDP students are shown by cohort in Tables 1 through 4, and combined in Table 5.

RESULTS

Spring 1994 SDP Cohort, N = 9

Of the students who started the SDP in Spring of 1994, five graduated, for a ratio of 5 of 9, or 56 percent, at the time we evaluated the program, which was Spring 2000. The average GPA of last record for these SDP students was 2.11, *sd* =.36. In the comparison group of 95 students, 25 students graduated—a graduation rate of 26.3 percent. The GPA for this comparison group was 2.15, *sd* =.56.

Fall 1994 SDP Cohort, N = 10

For Students in the Fall 1994 SDP cohort, the graduation rate was 3 of 10, or 30 percent. In the comparison group, 25 students graduated. Those comparison students, n = 93, had a graduation rate of 26.8 percent. The graduation rate for the SDP students was about the same as that of the comparison group. The final GPA for the SDP students was 2.53, *sd* = .41. The GPA for the comparison group was 2.20, *sd* = .69.

Spring 1995 SDP Cohort, N = 5

For the Spring 1995 SDP cohort, the graduation rate was 2 of 5, or 40 percent. In the comparison group, 15 students graduated. The comparison group of 51 students had a graduation rate of 29.4 percent. Graduation rate for the SDP students was higher than that of the comparison group. The final GPA for the SDP students was 2.15, *sd* =.30. The GPA for the comparison group was 2.48, *sd* =.61.

Fall 1995 SDP Cohort, N = 15

For the Fall 1995 SDP cohort, the graduation rate was 8 of 15, or 53.3 percent. In the comparison group of 259 students, 52 students graduated. The comparison group had a graduation rate of 20.1 percent. Graduation rate for the SDP students was more than twice that of the comparison group. The final GPA for the SDP students was 2.46, *sd* =.27, compared to a GPA in the comparison group of 2.30, *sd* =.57.

Combined SDP Cohorts

The four comparison groups were combined and duplicate students deleted, leaving 434 comparison students.

Graduation Rates

Overall graduation rate across SDP cohorts is 18 of 39, or 46.2 percent. Overall graduation rate across the combined comparison groups is 102 of 434 or 23.5 percent. The graduation rate for students in the Student Diversity Program was twice that of students in the comparison group. Is the proportion of graduation statistically different among SDP students than among comparison students? The test statistic reveals a highly significant test difference, $\chi^2_{(1)} = 9.70, p < .005$. Less than one time in 200 would we expect to find a difference of this magnitude in the proportion of graduation between these two groups, if the difference was due to chance (see Figure 1).

GPA

Grade point average of last record for the 39 SDP students was 2.36, $sd = 37$, compared to the average GPA of 2.28, $sd = .30$, across comparison student GPAs. This apparent difference was not statistically reliable by Matched Pairs $t(38) = 1.29, p = .11$.

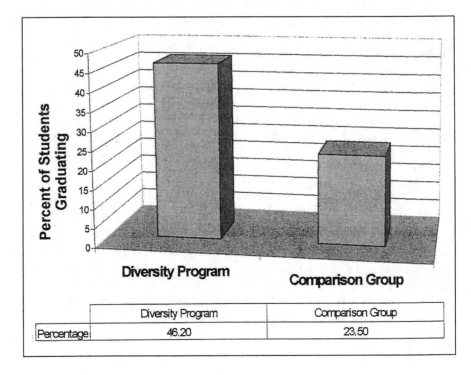

	Diversity Program	Comparison Group
Percentage	46.20	23.50

Figure 1. Graduation rates for student diversity program
vs. comparison students.

DISCUSSION

The 39 students who entered the Student Diversity Program in 1994 and 1995 graduated at twice the rate of comparable students matched on sex, ethnicity, age, transfer status, entering GPA, and on semester they entered the university. The analysis of final GPA showed no statistically significant difference between the two groups, although the average final GPA in the Student Diversity Program appeared slightly higher than that of the comparison students. Further, GPAs from SDP students in the most recent semester did appear to be significantly higher. We attribute this improvement to our earlier intervention with new SDP students who were on academic probation.

What Accounts for SDP Students Graduating at Twice the Rate of Other Students?

Why did the SDP students graduate at a rate double that of comparison students? The most obvious explanation is that the Student Diversity Program is effective in accomplishing its stated goals. Other explanations include the possibility that other local support programs contributed to student success. Further analysis could examine the SDP students on a case-by-case basis to ascertain the extent to which they received support from sources outside the Student Diversity Program. In any case, the data provide support for the general pattern of findings that students who are more involved at their college or university are more likely to graduate (cf. Astin, 1993; Daly & Breegle, 1989; Holmes et al., 2000, p. 54), and that a supportive environment that is culturally relevant fosters persistence (Glorio, 1997).

Selection Bias?

Another explanation is that despite the efforts noted above, the design failed to adequately match students. Although they were matched on the seven factors described above, they were not matched on motivation to do well in college. This is the "selection bias" explanation: a tendency for those more likely to do better in a program to participate in the program, as opposed to participating in the comparison group (cf. Campbell & Stanley, 1963, pp. 12, 15). Volunteers would be more likely to enlist in the treatment program than in the control group, ensuring that more of any effect would occur in the treatment group than the control group, regardless of the efficacy of the treatment (treatment-selection invalidity). Thus, an alternate explanation for the higher graduation rate for SDP students than for comparison group students is that those students who already were more motivated to do well were *both* more likely to graduate, *and* to join a program to help them do so. This is not a criticism of the SDP program; any program is likely to receive participants in accord with participants' interest in that program. The only instance in which selection-treatment invalidity is not an alternate explanation for a treatment effect is when participants are randomly assigned to groups, or possibly when two equally desirable, but different programs are available. A method to rule out treatment-selection invalidity with respect to the Student Diversity Program (short of randomly assigning future participants) is to evaluate SDP students against students in a comparable volunteer program. In that case the selection bias would be removed to some extent, although that extent cannot be measured.

Improvements for Future Research: Matching on Cumulative G.P.A.

Matching on cumulative grade point average should be done at the point of entry to the SDP Program, not at the end of the first semester of university work. Specifically, a student who enters the university in Fall 1993 enters the SDP Program in Fall of 1995 might have a 2.05 when she finishes one semester of university and have a 1.85 two years later when she enters the SDP Program. In this research, we have matched on GPA at the end of the first semester (GPA = 2.05 in the example) not at the point of entry to the SDP Program (1.85 in the example). The difference may not be great in contrasting GPA at end of first semester and at entry to the SDP program. For now, we have made the assumption that GPA at end of first semester is not significantly different from GPA at entry to the SDP program. That assumption should be tested by tracking student GPA change over time, and replicating the study with GPA matching as outlined above. In an informal test of GPAs at end of first semester versus entry to the SDP program, we found little difference.

Other Ways to Evaluate the SDP Program

There are other ways to evaluate academic support programs; for example, the criteria for success could have been other than the criteria used in these studies: GPA, graduation rates, and academic standing. We could have examined positive attitudes towards learning, or other outcome measures. Another approach, as introduced above, is to select a different treatment group rather than a no-treatment group to serve as the comparison group. Instead of students not in the SDP, we could have selected students in a different academic support program, and then contrasted the relative effectiveness of the two programs by comparing them on final GPA and graduation rates, or on other outcome measures. A third approach would involve comparing SDP students to matched students at another university where there is no such support program, or where there is a different type of support program. This would allow matching of athletes with other athletes, unlike in the current study, in which all or nearly all the athletes were already in the "treatment" group.

ACKNOWLEDGMENTS

We thank Dr. Cherine Trombley for data handling and calculations, and Farhan Abassi, Jeff Herzog, and Susan Kachner for extensive programming to provide extractions from the student records database. We also thank Carole Jones, Sabrina Sanders, Deborah Corey, and Jerry Moore for helpful comments.

REFERENCES

Astin, A. (1993). *What matters in college: Four critical years revisited.* San Francisco: Jossey-Bass.

Campbell, D. T., & Stanley, J. C. (1963). *Experimental and quasi-experimental designs for research.* Chicago: Rand McNally.

Cook, T., & Campbell, D. (1979). *Quasi-experimentation: Design & analysis issues for field settings.* Chicago: Rand McNally.

Cozby, P. C. (1997). *Methods in behavioral research.* Mountain View, CA: Mayfield.

Daly, B., & Breegle, G. (1989). Retention in higher education: A statewide perspective. Paper read at Association for Institutional Research, Baltimore. (From *Higher Education Abstracts, 1989, 25*(1)u, Abstract No. 0231-25).

Glorio, A. (1997). Chicana academic persistency: Creating a university-based community. *Education and Urban Society, 30,* 107-121.

Holmes, S., Ebbers, L., Robinson, D., & Mugenda, A. (2000). Validating African American students at predominantly white institutions. *Journal of College Student Retention, 2*(1), 41-58.

Ottens, A., Johnson, I., & Green, J. (1996). Summary and additional resources (promoting academic success for students of color). *New Directions for Student Services, 74,* 93-98.

Peltier, G., Laden, R., & Matranga, M. (1999). Student persistence in college: A Review of the research. *Journal of College Student Retention, 1*(4), 357-375.

Reld, J. (1996). Black Ombudsman Program Model. In C. Ford (Ed.), *Student Retention Models in Higher Education* (pp. 193-200). Tallahassee: CNJ Associates.

Sedlacek, W. (1996). Employing noncognitive variables in admitting students of color. *New Directions for Student Services,* No. 74, pp. 79-84, cited in *Leveling the Playing Field: Promoting Academic Success for Students of Color.* San Francisco: Jossey-Bass.

Tracey, T., & Sedlacek, W. (1987). Prediction of college graduation using noncognitive variables by race. *Measurement and Evaluation in Counseling and Development, 19,* 177-184.

CHAPTER 13

Fitting In By Race/Ethnicity: The Social and Academic Integration of Diverse Students at a Large Predominantly White University

Kathleen M. Morley

This study examined the influence of racial/ethnic dynamics on the process of social and academic integration. Students of diverse racial/ethnic and academic backgrounds were interviewed throughout their first-year and again at the beginning of their sophomore year about their pre-college and in-college experiences. Results yielded a qualitative description of the process of integration and indicated the importance of peer culture and institutional environment. Racial/ethnic accountability, the pervasiveness of White culture, and the pursuit of a color-blind society led to differences in integration by race/ethnicity. These dynamics, in addition to differences in pre-college learning opportunities, challenged the social and academic integration of minority students, particularly African-American and Latino/a students, into campus life.

African-American and Latino/a students are significantly less likely to graduate than Asian-American or White students in predominantly White institutions of higher education (Harvey, 2001; Kroc, Woodard, Howard, & Hull, 1995; National Collegiate Athletic Association, 2001). These students who are less likely to graduate from college have historically faced disadvantages in the American educational system. African-American and Latino/a students are largely over-represented in the lower socioeconomic stratum and, as such, often come from primary and secondary school systems that offer limited learning opportunities due to limited educational resources (Trent et al., 2000). Many African-American and Latino/a students do not attend college for this reason. Those who do go on to college are more likely to arrive with weaker academic backgrounds as compared to their Asian-American or White counterparts (Hu & St. John, 2001; Johnson, 1990; Mingle, 1987; Mow & Nettles, 1990; Nettles, 1990). Studies have linked academic preparation (i.e., college preparatory courses, high school grade point averages, and SAT scores) to persistence, as defined either by one-year retention or six-year college completion rates at the same institution of initial enrollment (Adelman, 1999; Hu & St. John, 2001; Smith, 1990). Tinto (1993) argued that, in addition to the social and educational backgrounds of entering students, the college experience influences the likelihood of remaining in college. The literature on African-American, Latino/a, Asian, and Native-American persistence indicates that there are unique experiences that minority students face at predominantly White institutions that hinder the persistence of these students, particularly those of African-American and Latino/a descent. In light of the argument that the college experience can have an influence independent of academic preparation on minority student persistence, this study examined the influence of racial/ethnic dynamics on the process of social and academic integration described in Tinto's model of institutional departure.

Twenty-three students of diverse racial/ethnic and academic backgrounds were interviewed throughout their first year and again at the beginning of their sophomore year about their pre-college and in-college experiences at the University of Massachusetts Amherst, a public, four-year, predominantly White institution. Questions were designed to examine the importance of racial/ethnic dynamics in the process of becoming a part of the social and academic realms of campus life. Numerous studies have found evidence to support the relationship between social and academic integration and persistence (Bean, 1980; Cabrera, Castaneda, Nora, & Hengstler, 1992; Hinderlie & Kenny, 2002; Hurtado, Carter, & Spuler, 1996; Nora, Cabrera, Hagedorn, & Pascarella, 1996; Pascarella & Terenzini, 1991; Stoecker, Pascarella, & Wolfle, 1988; Tinto, 1975, 1989, 1993). This study was unique in that it focused on the relationship between race/ethnicity and the process of integration. In addition, it differed from the numerous quantitative studies in retention analysis that measured race/ethnicity categorically in that it examined race/ethnicity in terms of racial/ethnic dynamics in student interactions. Results yielded a qualitative description of the process of integration that illustrated the impact of specific racial/ethnic dynamics on the process of becoming a part of campus life.

LITERATURE REVIEW

While African-American, Latino/a and American-Indian students have lower college retention and graduation rates than Asian-American and White students, this study focused on African-American and Latino/a students because of the small numbers of American-Indian students at the institution in this study. The explanation for the lower retention and graduation rates for African-American and Latino/a students must begin with an understanding of the context in which African-American and Latino/a students receive their education. As reported in *One-Third of a Nation* (American Council on Education, 1988), African Americans and Latinos/as in the United States face serious disadvantages in the areas of "education, employment, income, health, longevity, and other basic measures of individual and social well-being" (p. vii). Current statistics indicate that African Americans and Latinos/as continue to face the disadvantages reported in the 1988 American Council on Education report. African Americans and Latinos/as are less likely than Whites or Asian Americans to reap the benefits of college. In 2000, four-year college completion rates for individuals 25 years or older were as follows: 17% for African Americans, 11% for Latinos/as, 26% for Whites, and 44% for Asian Americans (United States Census Bureau, 2001a). In the same year, the median household income was $30,439 for African Americans (non-Hispanic), $33,447 for Latinos/as, $55,521 for Asian, and $45,904 for Whites (non-Hispanic) (United States Census Bureau, 2001b). African Americans and Latinos/as are also more likely to face unemployment than Whites. Eight percent of African Americans, 6% of Latinos/as, and 4% of Whites were unemployed in 2000—the corresponding total for Asians is not available in this source (United States Census Bureau, 2001c). Finally, African Americans and Latinos/as are also more likely to experience the hardships of poverty as compared to Whites and Asian Americans. In 2000, 22% of African Americans, 21% of Latinos/as, 8% of Whites, and 11% of Asian Americans had incomes below poverty level (United States Census Bureau, 2001d).

Trent et al. (2000) linked high poverty rates with racial segregation in educational school districts. For example, in 1990 school districts with 25% or more of school-age children living in poverty were 57% African American and Latino/a. In contrast, school districts with less than 5% of school-age children living in poverty were 88% White. High poverty rates translate into weaker tax bases and lower quality educational resources. Limited resources lead to limited learning opportunities and, not surprisingly, result in weaker academic performance as measured by standardized tests. Trent et al. reported, for example, that African Americans and Latino/as scored substantially below those of Whites for each age group (9, 13, and 17) on the 1996 National Assessment of Educational Progress reading proficiency exams. African-American and Latino/a students are more likely to face educational disadvantages due to economic disparity than Asian-American and White students. Trent et al. added that these disadvantages not only begin early in students' educational career, but are also cumulative as students are tracked into different educational programs.

African-American and Latino/a students are likely to begin college with weaker academic backgrounds than White and Asian-American students (Hu & St. John, 2001; Johnson, 1990; Mingle, 1987; Mow & Nettles, 1990; Nettles, 1990). Differences in high school curriculum account for a significant amount of this variation in academic preparation (Adelman, 1999; Hu & St. John, 2001; Mow & Nettles, 1990; Nettles, 1990). While there are a number of studies that describe the negative effect of low socioeconomic status on persistence (Crosson, 1988; Hu & St. John, 2001; Madrazo-Peterson & Rodriguez, 1978; Mingle, 1987; Smith, Edminster, & Sullivan, 2001), others have found that much of the influence of socioeconomic status is mediated by both academic preparation (Astin, 1982; Fleming, 2002; Mow & Nettles, 1990; Nettles & Johnson, 1987) and the distribution of financial aid (Hu & St. John, 2001; Murdock, 1990; Nora & Horath, 1989; St. John, Kirshstein, & Noell, 1991). Lower socioeconomic students who have acquired sufficient academic preparation and who have received sufficient financial aid tend to do well.

The retention literature clearly links differences in academic preparation with differences in persistence rates (Adelman, 1999; Astin, 1982, 1993; Crosson, 1988; Fleming, 2002; Hu & St. John, 2001; Kennedy & Sheckley, 1999; Mow & Nettles, 1990; Noel, 1978; Opportunity for Postsecondary Education, 1996, 2000). However, as Smith (1990) found, such studies often do not account for large amounts of variation in retention or graduation rates. Smith (1990) reported that the combined variables of socioeconomic status, parental education, high school grades, and Scholastic Aptitude Test scores accounted for only 10 to 12% of the variance in either attrition or college grades. In a more recent study using the national High School and Beyond/Sophomore cohort files collected by the National Center for Education Statistics, Adelman (1999) was able to account for 43% of the variance in bachelor's degree completion. He reported that the most significant variable was the academic resources index variable, a composite variable that included a senior year test ("a mini, enhanced SAT"—Scholastic Aptitude Test), class rank/grade point average, and academic curriculum. He found that academic resources accounted for 17% of the variation in bachelor's degree, and that attendance patterns (11.5%), course-taking behavior (8.5%), college grade point average (4%), having children at a young age (1%), socioeconomic status (1%), and student employment (<1%) accounted for the remaining 26% of the explained variance. Even in Adelman's comprehensive national study, academic preparation only accounted for 17% of the variation in college completion rates. These results indicate that there is still a significant amount of variation in college completion that cannot be explained by academic preparation alone.

While rates of minority college participation have vastly improved, the gaps in college graduation rates by race/ethnicity have persisted. The American Council on Education reported the following six-year graduation rates for full-time, first-year students entering college in Fall 1992 in its *2000-2001 Eighteenth Annual Status Report on Minorities in Higher Education* (Harvey, 2001): 66% for Asian-American students, 59% for White students, 48% for Latino/a students, 37% for African-American students, and 37% for American-Indian students. According to the same report, this trend of fewer Latino/a, African-American, and American-Indian students graduating within six years at four-year public and private colleges and universities, as compared to Asian-American or White students, has been consistent for at least the last six years.

The American Council on Education figures noted above represent the graduation rates for the estimated 300 National Collegiate Athletic Association Division I institutions that returned the graduation rate disclosure form each year. While National Collegiate Athletic Association data only represent a subset of four-year post-secondary institutions, they are repeatedly used because they are readily available, known to be reliable, and represent a large number of institutions. The National Collegiate Athletic Association Division I Graduation Rate Report (2001) further delineates graduation rate statistics by institutional type. The six-year graduation rates for full-time, first-year students at public National Collegiate Athletic Association Division I institutions ($n = 210$) were 62% for Asian Americans, 55% Whites, 42% Latino/as, 35% African Americans, and 35% American Indians. While these totals indicate a trend particular to large public National Collegiate Athletic Association Division I institutions, they reveal a similar trend to that found in the American Council on Education data, i.e., a trend of American-Indian, African-American, and Latino/a students having lower six-year graduation rates than Asian-American and White students. As will be discussed below, this same trend occurs at the University of Massachusetts Amherst.

The University of Massachusetts Amherst is a four-year, public land-grant institution that offers undergraduate and graduate degrees. At the time of this study (Fall 1995), the University of Massachusetts Amherst enrolled nearly 24,000 students, 18,000 of whom were undergraduates. Of the undergraduate population, 73% were in-state residents, 6% were part-time students, and 58% lived on campus. Most of the students living on campus were first-year or sophomore students, since undergraduates were, and continue to be, required to live on campus through their sophomore year. Excluding international or non-resident alien and non-reporting students, 15% of the undergraduates identified themselves as having an minority background. Using the most recent graduation rates, 59% of the full-time, first-year students who entered in Fall 1995 graduated within six years (Office of Institutional Research, 2002a), a rate comparable to the average rate of its peer institutions (63%). Consistent with national trends, campus graduation rates reveal differences by race/ethnicity. While 60% of the White and 58% of the Asian-American full-time, first-year students entering the university in Fall 1995 graduated within six years, 52% of the African-American, and only

51% of the Latino/a students completed their baccalaureate degree in the same time-frame (Office of Institutional Research, 2002).

The one-year retention rates for this Fall 1995 entering cohort were not consistent with the overall pattern of White and Asian students persisting at higher rates than Black and Hispanic students (Office of Institutional Research, 2002). While 79% of the White (Non-Hispanic) and 78% of the Asian/Pacific Islander students returned for their sophomore year, 80% of the Black (Non-Hispanic) and only 70% of the Hispanic students did the same. The retention rate of Black students in this year was one of only three times in the past 10 years in which the retention rate of Black students was equal to or better than retention rates for White and Asian students.

Table 1 examines attrition rates of full-time, first-year students who entered the University of Massachusetts Amherst in Fall 1995. This table shows where the loss of students occurs over time. Between 33% and 100% of the attrition occurred during the first year for each of the racial/ethnic groups in the Fall 1995 entering cohort. Given these totals, it is important to examine what dynamics are leading students to leave during their first year.

Table 2 examines University of Massachusetts Amherst one-year retention rates by race/ethnicity while holding academic preparation constant (Office of

Table 1. UMass Amherst Attrition Rates of Fall 1995 Full-Time
First-Year Students by Race/Ethnicity

Race/Ethnicity	Number entering	One-year attrition	Six-year attrition	Percentage of attrition occurring in first-year
White, Non-Hispanic	3,069	21%	40%	51%
Asian/Pacific Islander	251	22%	42%	50%
Black, Non-Hispanic	188	20%	48%	41%
Hispanic	188	31%	50%	60%
American Indian/ Alaskan Native	7	29%	29%	100%
Non-resident alien	23	4%	13%	33%
Non-reporting	87	21%	51%	80%
Total	3,813	22%	41%	52%

Table 2. UMass Amherst One-Year Retention Rates by Race/Ethnicity
and Academic Background for Full-Time First-Year Students
Entering Fall 1995-Fall 1997

	Fall 1995	Fall 1996	Fall 1997	Three-year average
Strong	86%	87%	88%	87%
White	86%	88%	87%	87%
Asian	83%	89%	92%	88%
Black	88%	**80%**	100%	85%
Latino/a	**75%**	**75%**	100%	**80%**
Average	78%	78%	79%	78%
White	78%	77%	79%	78%
Asian	83%	77%	76%	78%
Black	86%	83%	**71%**	80%
Latino/a	**68%**	81%	**72%**	74%
Weak	69%	71%	68%	69%
White	69%	79%	74%	73%
Asian	57%	73%	66%	66%
Black	74%	**63%**	**69%**	**68%**
Latino/a	71%	**65%**	**59%**	**65%**
Total	78%	79%	79%	79%
White	79%	80%	81%	80%
Asian	78%	78%	76%	77%
Black	81%	**72%**	**73%**	**74%**
Latino/a	**70%**	76%	**69%**	**71%**

Note: Items in **bold** show at least a 5-point lower retention rate for Black and Latino/a students as compared to the rate for White students.

Institutional Research, 2000b). Academic preparation was measured by using University Admissions Ratings. In the Fall 1995 admissions cycle, the University Admissions Office assigned applicants an admissions rating from one to six which categorized student potential to succeed. The admissions ratings were based on objective and subjective criteria, which included Scholastic Assessment Test scores, high school rank, letters of recommendation, high school grade point average, essay, and extracurricular activities. Indications of self-initiative, willingness to seek out enriching opportunities, motivation to succeed, and an ability to identify personal strengths and weaknesses were just some of the subjective criteria also used to sort students. Ratings were used in the admissions process and were used to identify students who may have needed academic support. For the purpose of Table 2, the Admissions Ratings of one through six were condensed into three categories. The categories of one and two, three and four, and five and six were assigned to the categories of strong, average, and weak academic background, respectively.

Table 2 illustrates year-to-year variability in one-year retention rates by race/ethnicity when holding academic preparation constant. If academic preparation explained differences in one-year retention rates by race/ethnicity, the expectation would be not to find differences in rates by race/ethnicity after holding constant academic preparation. In the three-year rolling average, strong Latino/a students and weak Black and Latino/a students continued to have lower one-year retention rates despite holding academic preparation constant. In the comprehensive study of national High School and Beyond/Sophomore cohort files collected by the National Center for Education Statistics, Adelman (1999) examined the significance of race/ethnicity in college completion rates and found no significance in either multivariate or logistic regression models. However, he noted that the High School and Beyond/Sophomore cohort files did not capture measures of social or academic integration. He added that while these measures may be important, students in the database often attended two or three institutions, and as such it would not be possible to decipher the unique impact of students' experiences at each of the various institutions. This analysis used qualitative methods to capture what the High School and Beyond/Sophomore cohort files could not, i.e., the impact of race/ethnicity on the process of social and academic integration.

METHODS

In this study, the process of integration was defined as the series of social and academic adjustments new students needed to make in order to feel a sufficient sense of belonging to want to stay enrolled. Time-series interviews, supplemented with limited ethnographic observation, were used to identify both how diverse students at the University of Massachusetts Amherst progressed through college adjustments throughout their first year, and in what ways the dynamics of race/ethnicity influenced these adjustments. First-year students were studied because the first year has been identified as a crucial time period in which students become involved in campus life (Elkins, Braxton, & James, 2000; Malaney & Shively, 1995; Tinto, 1987; Upcraft & Gardner, 1989). In addition, as illustrated in Table 1, depending on the racial/ethnic group, between 37% and 71% of the attrition that occurred at the University of Massachusetts Amherst within a six-year period occurred within the first year of attendance.

The research design of this study entailed interviewing 24 full-time, first-year diverse students. The sample was stratified by gender, race/ethnicity, and academic preparation. A male and a female from an academically strong, average, and weak background from each of four racial/ethnic backgrounds were interviewed—three times throughout their first year and one time at the beginning of their sophomore year—about their high school and college experiences. Students of varied academic backgrounds were included so that differences in race/ethnicity could be examined without the confounded effects of academic preparation. The purpose of stratifying the sample by gender was to have a balanced sample. This study was designed to examine racial/ethnic differences and did not specifically examine differences by academic background or gender. The 2 × 3 × 4 matrix of gender, academic background, and race/ethnicity was completed with the exception of not being able to get a Black, academically strong, female student to participate. Table 3 has the basic characteristics of participants in the study.

One benefit of doing a qualitative analysis is the ability to understand the context of the racial identity of the participants. Racial/ethnic classifications often limit people who are identifying their racial/ethnic identity to one category. Table 3 shows that three of the minority students in this study had mixed racial/ ethnic backgrounds, two others were adopted at birth by white, European-American parents, and yet another two grew up in a racially/ethnically mixed neighborhood, but attended a predominantly white school through a special program. It is likely that the complexity of racial/ethnic experiences of students at other institutions of higher education is hidden by simple racial/ethnic classifi-cations. Interviews were helpful in unraveling this complexity. A total of 76 interviews were done with 23 first-time, first-year students who enrolled at the University of Massachusetts Amherst in Fall 1995.

Class observations were done in addition to the time-series interviews. A subset of students were asked at the end of the first interview if they would be willing to allow the author to attend some of their classes with them. Since the majority of students entered the University as academically average students, the students asked were also primarily average students. The author observed 30 classes in the company of eight students in the fall. After the second interview, the same group of students were asked if the author could accompany them to their best and worst class. The author observed 10 additional classes in the spring. Class observations increased rapport with students, added to the understanding of how they described their classroom experiences, and offered select views of both the physical and academic settings in which students were expected to learn.

RESULTS AND DISCUSSION

Social and Academic Integration

The analysis in this study started with the premise in the literature that social and academic integration influences student persistence. The more integrated students are, the more likely they are to remain in college. The process of integration began with the initial adjustment to college in which students needed to learn the social and academic landscapes of the university. When they began college, students

Table 3. Selected Characteristics of Study Participants*

Name	Race	Ethnicity	Academic rating	Where from	High school diversity
Maria	Latina	Puerto Rican	Strong	New Jersey	Black, working-class city school
Craig	Latino and White	Brazilian/Russian/Ukrainian	Strong	Western Massachusetts	White, middle-class, prep school
Linda	Latina and White	Italian, adopted by White/Latino parents	Average	Northeast of Boston	White, middle-class, suburban school
Richard	Latino	Guatemalan	Average	Southeast of Boston	White, working-class suburban school
Angie	Latina	Puerto Rican	Weak	Central Massachusetts	Racially/Ethnically mixed, city school
John	Latino	Puerto Rican	Weak	Worcester	Racially/Ethnically mixed, city school
Martin	Black	Nigerian/Cape Verdean	Strong	Massachusetts Cape	White, middle-cass suburban school
Nicole	Black	African American	Average	Boston	White, upper-middle-cass suburban school through METCO
Jason	Black and White	African American/German	Average	South of Boston	White, middle-cass suburban school
Tamar	Black	African American	Weak	Boston	White, middle-class city school
Louis	Black	Haitian	Weak	Boston	White, upper-middle-class suburban school through METCO
Pamela	Asian	Indian	Strong	North of Boston	White, middle-class suburban school

Ken	Asian	Korean, adopted by White parents	Strong	Southeast of Boston	White, middle-cass suburban school
Lorrie	Asian	Korean, adopted by White parents	Average	Massachusetts Cape	White, middle-class suburban school
Rohit	Asian	Indian	Average	Eastern Massachusetts	White, upper-middle-class suburban school
Amanda	Asian	Indian	Weak	East of Boston	White, upper-middle-class suburban school
Alex	Asian	Chinese	Weak	East of Boston	White, upper-middle-class suburban school
Melissa	White	German/Irish	Strong	Springfield	Racially/Ethnically mixed, city school
Peter	White	English/Scottish/Portuguese/Spanish	Strong	Southeast Massachusetts	White, middle-class suburban school
Tracey	White	Did not know	Average	Vermont	White, upper-middle-class suburban school
Brian	White	Irish/French	Average	Southeast of Boston	White, middle-class suburban school
Stephanie	White	English/German	Weak	Outside of Boston	White, working-class suburban school
Steven	White	German/English/Native American/Norwegian	Weak	Southeast Massachusetts	White, middle-class suburban school

* Names are pseudonyms.

were anxious to develop new relationships, they missed the comforts of home, they lost the status they had gained as veteran high school students, and they faced new responsibilities as they became increasingly independent. The university size made it particularly challenging for new students to map the social geography of campus life. Linda, a White student of Italian descent who entered as an academically average student, was concerned that the size of the University of Massachusetts Amherst would make it difficult to become a part of the University, as she described in the following:

> It's so big. It's huge. At first, it was hard to find my way around. I was like, oh, my God, it's so big. . . . I kept finding places . . . like this is still part of UMass (University of Massachusetts Amherst) . . . when I heard that there were like thirty-thousand students, I was like I'm not going to meet anyone here. I thought I was just going to be a number. That's one thing that scared me because I was not used to be being a just . . . a number—everyone knew who I was, everyone knew my name.

Linda was concerned about how she would fit into the social landscape of a school so large. Like many of the other students, she was accustomed to being a part of a closed community in which most everyone knew everyone else. Before developing a sense of belonging, students felt like a number, i.e., they felt that they belonged to the University of Massachusetts Amherst because they registered, but not because of meaningful relationships that connected them to a community.

The difficulty of adjusting to a university the size of the University of Massachusetts Amherst was that it took time to acquire local knowledge about the numerous social groups on campus. Orientation did not assist students in this endeavor. Instead, students reported that they were overwhelmed and bored by the information they received during orientation. Students relied primarily on word-of-mouth and trial-and-error to discover what circumstances best matched their social interests.

New students initially overcame feelings of normlessness by conforming to the patterns of behaviors set by their dormitory peers. Dorm-life frequently entailed late nights, lack of sleep, loud music, and loud people. It entailed frequent socializing, romantic interludes, floor parties, drinking, and drug-use. The acceptance of dormitory norms often made it very difficult for students to pay attention in, or even make it to, early morning classes. For some, dormitory activities bonded them to their peers. For others, who did not share a strong interest in alcohol or drug-use or who preferred to focus more on academics than socializing, dormitory norms made them feel out of place. The degree to which drinking and drug-use dominated dorm-culture varied by residential area, but many new students did not know this since students did not have an informal map of the campus' social geography. Those students who did not fit in with their peers relied heavily on family member encouragement to remain enrolled. Family members offered students both respite and assurance that in time their social circumstances would improve.

In the academic realm, new students needed to adjust to an academic environment, or context, that significantly differed from their high school classroom experiences. There were differences in academic responsibility, instruction, class preparation, and evaluation. Select majors, such as Engineering, Art, and Music, and learning communities, such as the Talent Advancement Program—a program through which students live together, take classes together, and share a special seminar designed to introduce faculty within that major—fostered the transition from high school to college academics. These academic programs were unique in that they reduced the circles within which students were obligated to interact. They placed students within the academic landscape, involved them in academic life by overlapping social and academic realms, and outlined steps for students to take to meet their academic goals.

The adjustment of new students to college academics was made more challenging by the University's large-school, collegiate or highly social, and vocational environments. The size of the University required the scheduling of large lectures that made it difficult to employ interactive learning techniques, made it difficult to develop close student/faculty relationships, and made it difficult to provide personal advising. This resulted in new students feeling academically isolated rather than integrated into an academic community. The collegiate and vocational environments also undermined a sense of academic community by reinforcing social and vocational interests over academic ones. Students made their academic adjustment in an environment in which they had a fair amount of free time, socializing and partying were emphasized, there was a lack of excitement in students' prior academic experiences, and students' main objective in college was to secure a good job. This environment reinforced a culture of student disengagement from intellectual development, from the learning process, and from the academic realm of college life. Weak students were particularly predisposed to the negative influences of large-school and collegiate/vocational environments on academic integration.

Peer culture, i.e., the normative attitudes and values of students on campus, primarily encouraged students to put social interests over academic ones. However, this changed when new students began to see their peers academically suspended. For example, Peter, a White student of English/Scottish/Portuguese/Spanish descent, who entered as an academically strong student, noted that about half of the first-year Engineering students on his floor were no longer at the University. He and his remaining peers decided that they needed to start attending more classes. In a symbolic gesture toward this end, they had a contest to see who would last the longest before missing a class. Such peer support was important in sustaining changes in academic routines.

The social adjustment to college was also influenced by the university's environment and peer culture. As a large institution, the University of Massachusetts was highly bureaucratic, and this frequently made students feel like a number rather than a member of a campus community. Bureaucratic dynamics reinforced student identification with individual peer groups rather than the university as a whole. Similarly, as a large institution, the University had few social activities that involved the majority of students. Unlike many small colleges, the University did not have a unifying identity or purpose. Consequently, the social realm of campus life was both complex and informally arranged. This structure allowed for the development of numerous diverse peer groups that gave students a wide range of social options. However, it also delayed social integration because students needed time, often a full semester, to assess the range of social options.

Student culture at the University of Massachusetts was also dominated by a party-school environment. Such an environment was instrumental in social integration. Several students described how drinking and drug-use at parties served as a social lubricant. However, the party-school environment was associated primarily with White-student, rather than minority-student, socializing. Outside the predominant presence of White social circles, there were clusters of Black and Latino/a students, clusters of Indian students, and clusters of Chinese students who came together through common housing or through racial/ethnic student organizations. These clusters tended to sponsor separate student parties and these parties tended to serve different social and cultural interests. Jason, a Black and White student of African-American and German descent, gave the following description of how these parties differed:

> . . . they're generally two different types of parties. Like most of like the parties, like Jeans and T-Shirt, and X-Center . . . it's mostly like the ALANA (African American, Latino/a, Asian and Native American) groups, the Blacks, the Latinos, a lot of people like that, and where the frat parties, it's the majority just, you know, White, you know, White people. . . . Whereas, I mean, I go to both of them a lot, you know, and it's like at a lot of the frat parties, it's mostly like so many people there just . . . just drinking, just wanting to drink, get trashed. Whereas the other parties, like people might drink before they go there, but they want to go and they want to dance, and have a good time dancing, and . . . and just hanging out with people, and . . . and a lot of people don't drink there, too, you know. They just go; they like to dance, and be around people and have a good time that way.

Jason described how fraternity parties sponsored and attended by primarily White students tended to emphasize binge drinking while parties sponsored and attended by primarily Black and Latino/a students tended to emphasize socializing over the use of drugs or alcohol. The dominance of the party-culture at the University of Massachusetts Amherst caused some minority students to feel left out. For example, Alex, an Asian student of Chinese descent who entered as an academically weak student, felt that he was in the minority because he chose not to drink or do drugs. He added that he was considering transferring to a private institution, where he felt students would take academics more seriously.

Differences in Integration by Race/Ethnicity

Both White and minority students felt that the campus social life was clustered around racial/ethnic groups, and that outside the classroom there was a lack of interracial interaction. Differences in the process of social and academic integration by race/ethnicity help explain this racial/ethnic clustering. Differences by race/ethnicity began with the initial adjustment to college. In the students' descriptions of what it was like to leave home, there was a pattern among minority students of noting how they missed their families when they came to college. The minority students described a closeness with their families from which they did not want to be away and a closeness they took active steps to maintain.

For example, Angie, a Latina student of Puerto Rican descent, explained that she was particularly close to her parents and siblings, and that she postponed going away to college for one year because she found it too difficult to leave them. Despite the tension of leaving home, she did make the decision to go to college after working for one year. She came to college in part because of her parents' encouragement and in part because she wanted more from a job than she could get with a high school degree. On the day she moved to campus, she did not want her parents to join her because she felt that it would be too emotional for her, as she described in the following:

> My parents weren't working that particular day, but I didn't want them to come up here. I didn't want to have to say good-bye to them here. I cried all day, just like from the time I woke up to the time I got all the way up here. I'm so sensitive. It definitely has gotten better, but at the same time I've been home like four weekends in a row, and I'm going home this weekend because I have a concert to go to.

Angie dealt with missing her family by making frequent trips home.

In contrast, White students spoke of the independence they would have, how they missed a girlfriend or boyfriend, how they missed the comforts of home, or how their families missed *them*. For example, Melissa, a White student of Irish and German descent, mentioned in the following that she did not think it would be hard to leave home: "Not really, I was kind of happy because everything was going kind of crazy at my house. My mom was kind of strict about things. She gets overprotective, so I was excited to be on my own. I wouldn't have to worry about that any more." Melissa was looking forward to the freedom associated with going away to college. There was a cultural difference at play here. For minority students, family included grandparents, aunts and uncles, and cousins. In contrast, White students defined family as the nuclear family unit. For the minority students, the transition to college forced a compromise of family-life and community values as they moved away from close-knit family and community networks. In contrast, White students defined the transition to college as a transition to independence and adulthood.

The institutional structure that separated students from family life while they pursued their higher education degree caused role strain for students who were expected and/or wanted to continue participating in family and community activities. Role strain is not unique to minority students. Part-time and older White students tend to face this tension as well (Pascarella & Terenzini, 1991; Tinto, 1993), but the students in this study were all full-time students who—with one exception—came to college within a year or two of high school. The traditional White students in this study did not experience role strain with regards to family ties, while in contrast several of the minority students did.

Another difference in both the initial and social adjustment of minority vs. White students was the means by which students were placed socially by race/ethnicity. When minority students came to the University of Massachusetts Amherst, others placed them socially by their apparent racial/ethnic background. If they did not obviously fit within a particular racial/ethnic category, they were frequently asked to explain or account for their backgrounds. For example, Ken, an Asian student of Korean descent, was adopted at birth by White European-American parents and did not think of himself as Asian. However, he mentioned in the following how he considered joining an Asian student group at the University of Massachusetts Amherst despite his lack of identification with Asian culture:

> I did become just somewhat just curious about at least some of the Asian groups. I don't know where that arose from. It's just . . . I don't know, I just started to look around and see everyone, and it just seems that here people tend to belong somewhere, and it was just kind of . . . just kind of a period where I was trying to figure out where I belonged.

As he explained in the following, Ken later came to the conclusion that his interest in Asian groups on campus had more to do with how others perceived him than with how he perceived himself:

> It was more trying to find a place that I'd feel totally comfortable in and not feel threatened or intimidated by anyone. . . . I've been finding that people, at least a lot of people, don't really care about your ethnic background. It's simpler than that. I think a lot of people really only care what you look like. . . . I don't know, it always seems that (being at a predominantly White school) there's maybe something against you or something. Not really in the like more political sense as most people think of it, but as kind of a . . . you definitely stand out more, and the way here it is at UMass (the University of Massachusetts Amherst) here, I don't know, ethnic groups get together and that's how most of the student body sees them, so they immediately make that connection with anyone they see fitting that description.

Ken found that, because of his Asian appearance, he stood out and that others assumed he belonged to Asian student groups. He decided not to join an Asian student group because he felt that his only connection to such a group was a shared physical appearance and that that was not enough to share a sense of belonging with other Asian students.

Students sought to identify the racial/ethnic background of others as a means of gauging social interactions. Once categorized, they were then expected to fit the role of someone from that particular background. They were also expected to socialize within their own racial/ethnic circles. Being placed socially by race/ethnicity caused several minority students, particularly students who had been previously immersed in White culture, to rethink their racial/ethnic identity and question where they fit in. The assumption that they were a part of a social group to which they did not feel an affiliation often undermined their sense of belonging.

A related difference in the social adjustment of minority vs. White students was that, unlike White students, minority students faced racial/ethnic accountability that undermined their sense of belonging. Racial/ethnic accountability refers to how people respond to others on the basis of preconceived notions and then hold them accountable to those notions (West & Fenstermaker, 1995). The preconceived notions to which minority students were held accountable reinforced the theme that in one way or another minority students were either not as good as White students or did not belong to White social circles. For example, Linda, a middle-class White student of Italian descent who identified herself as Latina on her University of Massachusetts Amherst application because her adoptive father was Puerto Rican, explained her reluctance to associate herself with Spanish culture with the statement that "I know a lot of people who look down on it."

The preconceived nations to which students were held were consistent with the overall racial/ethnic hierarchy in society. White students were presumed to be judgmental of non-Whites, snobbish, and pretentious with regards to wealth. Asians were presumed to be foreigners, therefore less knowledgeable about American culture, as well as quiet and passive. These notions about Asians referred to less powerful characteristics than the preconceived notions about Whites. However, they were not as damaging to social integration as the preconceived notions about Blacks and Latinos/as. Blacks and Latinos/as were presumed to have been admitted through special admissions, to be less intelligent than Asian and Whites, and less likely to succeed in college than Asians or Whites.

For example, Angie, a Latina student of Puerto Rican descent who entered as an academically weak student, gave the following response to the question of whether or not being Puerto Rican had affected her first-year experience:

> Sometimes . . . in the way that people expect . . . not expect, but sometimes think that you're going to do worse. Like, we're not as smart or yeah, she's here this year—it's her freshman year, but is she going to be back? . . . just sometimes people not knowing that you're (Puerto Rican) . . . and then they might say something about . . . maybe not yours, but like they might say something about African Americans, and to me that still hurts

because it's still a minority, and . . . so it's like, okay, is that what you think of me? But, you don't want to say that because I happened to be standing next to you, you know?

Angie was offended by the generalization that Black and Latino/a students were not as smart as Asian or White students and that they were expected to fail out of college. Consistent with findings of other researchers (Fries-Britt & Turner, 2001, 2002), this generalization undermined Angie's confidence as she struggled to adjust to college academics. She regained her confidence when changes in how she managed her time helped her to substantially raise her grades, but prior to doing so, she considered leaving college.

Black students and Latino/a students also described how they were not fully accepted because of their racial/ethnic background. For instance, Jason, a Black and White student of African-American and German descent, found it difficult to be fully accepted by either Black or White students, as he described in the following:

> . . . I don't fit in to any particular group, and sometimes it's kind of . . . it's good in some ways, but sometimes it's kind of . . . you know, you just feel like an outcast, so to speak, because you don't fit in with this group or that group, or whatever . . . there's like a lot of White people who'll look at me, and they think . . . they say I'm Black, label me Black, whatever, based on, you know, the music I listen to, or whatever . . . but then a lot of Blacks look at me and where I'm light skinned and I have blue eyes, or whatever, and if I'm not from the inner-city or something, they see, oh, I have a car, they think I'm a rich White person or something, and so I'm kind of left in the dark by them, you know, so that kind of leaves me in the middle.

Jason felt like an outcast because neither White students nor Black students included him in their social circles. He explained that many White students labeled him Black because of the music he played and consequently opted not to socialize with him, and that many Black students labeled him as White because he did not appear to be working-class, i.e., they held him accountable to the racial/ethnic categorization of Whites as rich suburbanites who would not understand the challenges faced by inner-city, working-class Blacks. These dynamics undermined his sense of belonging and caused him to question whether or not he should transfer to another school.

In addition to racial/ethnic accountability, minority students were confronted with two more racial/ethnic dynamics that challenged their social adjustment to campus life. These included the pervasiveness of White culture and the pursuit of a color-blind society. The pervasiveness of White culture overshadowed the social and cultural interests of some minority students, leaving several to feel that they were outside the dominant campus culture. Of particular importance was the difference in musical tastes by race/ethnicity. Music is often used, especially by adolescents, to demarcate social and personal identities (Gonzalez, 2002; Perry,

1997), as the following scenario illustrates. When Jason, a Black and White student of African-American and German descent, was asked if there were any people who made it difficult to adjust to college, he gave the following response:

> No . . . (pause) there was one incident where I met this girl once, a friend of someone on the floor, and she asked if we would drive her and her friend into town. They were putting down my music and they wouldn't stop. It turned into a fight and I pulled the car over and told them if they couldn't deal with the music, they could walk. Her boyfriend later called me up and threatened me and insisted that I apologize. I didn't think I did anything wrong, although I did call her a name, so I apologized for that, but I felt she owed me an apology for being so disrespectful, which she did do. I get along with her now, although I'm not that crazy about her.

Jason liked to listen to Rap, Hip-Hop, and Rhythm and Blues. It was not the musical choice within the dominant culture, and it was likely that his music was put down for that reason. Jason explained that people identified him as African American partially because of his taste in music. He felt that someone being disrespectful toward his music amounted to showing disrespect for who he was as an African American. This strong association between music and identity became important in a predominantly White, racially/ethnically clustered campus environment. Students were associated with racial/ethnic clusters on the basis of their musical tastes. The act of making fun of non-dominant tastes in music implied not only that the music was not as good as the dominant cultural form, but that the racial/ethnic groups associated with that music were not as good as Whites. The tension over musical tastes revealed the underlying tension with a racial/ethnic hierarchy that accepted Whites as the dominant cultural group.

The pursuit of a color-blind society functioned as a pattern of students seeking to downplay the social significance of race/ethnicity. Behind this pattern was the assumption that less attention to race/ethnicity would result in less racial/ethnic tension. Students believed that the pursuit of a color-blind society would lead to a more just society. However, this pursuit of a color-blind society did not account for power differences by race/ethnicity, as became evident in student discussions on Affirmative Action and reverse discrimination. White students, in particular, welcomed racial/ethnic diversity, but objected to any special measures—e.g., the recruitment of minority students—to increase the likelihood of that diversity. They perceived Affirmative Action measures as removing resources from White individuals and transferring them to minority, namely Black, individuals.

For example, Peter, a White student of English/Scottish and Portuguese/Spanish descent, was concerned about the use of Affirmative Action in employment, as he explained in the following discussion:

> . . . you know, we have all this stuff, Affirmative Action, in place and things to get more students of color into . . . well, you know, into upper-level jobs and stuff like that, but right now, it's obvious . . . I mean, for now, there will be

more White people in jobs, just because there are more White people in the country . . . you know, I guess that's the idea right now, that they think that's wrong that there's too many White people in the job, so put more Black people in the school, but I mean as long as you're not stepping on anybody's feet, or on . . . as long as you're not stepping on anybody's feet, then it's okay, I think.

Peter concluded that the lack of people of color in upper-level jobs was due to the representation of people of color nationwide—Peter did not understand that minority representation in upper-level jobs was not only small, but also nationally under-representative. He explained that he did not object to Affirmative Action measures as long as "you're not stepping on anybody's feet," i.e., as long as the improved access to schools and quality jobs for Blacks did not affect the academic and employment opportunities for Whites.

Unlike other social categorizations, such as gender, sexual orientation, or class, race/ethnicity was a salient social characteristic along which students felt the need to compete for resources. White students objected to the denial of resources on the basis of being White. However, they did so without recognizing the social, political, and economic advantages that have been historically structured to place them at the top of the racial/ethnic hierarchy. Minority students were acutely aware of these advantages. The pursuit of a color-blind society reinforced White dominance. It implied that minority students were unwelcome if they did not already have educational advantages equivalent to those of White students.

Racial/ethnic clusters offered some minority students reprieve from negative racial/ethnic dynamics. These mainstream minority subgroups developed through shared housing, student organizations, and informal social networking. They offered many minority students the opportunity to socialize with others who shared their social and cultural interests, and to have communities in which they could be among others who experienced similar day-to-day racial/ethnic dynamics. However, each racial/ethnic cluster had its own peer group identity and norms. In an effort to form group identity and loyalty, racial/ethnic clusters were particular about who was socially accepted. As was the case with any student peer group, students interested in participating in a given cluster were expected to follow particular norms, and ultimately, some minority students who sought acceptance within a cluster did not find it. For example, Amanda, an upper-middle class Asian student of Indian descent, noted in her February interview that she had some interest in joining the South Asian Club because she had done an Indian dance performance with them. However, in her May interview, as she described below, she lost interest in the South Asian Club since she was not fitting in with the other members:

I've been dancing every night for three hours for the past three weeks with dancers from the South Asian Club. It was tiring, but fun. I don't go to the meetings. I don't have any interest in it. They talk about what it's like to be Asian on this campus, which I think is helpful, but other than that they just try to get things together and they just can't because they are so disorganized. I

> feel like the Indian people here are gossipy. Plus, a lot of the Indian women were born in India and still have an accent . . . and I'm kind of like different, you know, and my roommate is too, and they like kind of like shun us for that, so I don't like it, and I don't think it's fair for them to do that because we didn't grow up there and so we're not going to be like that, you know. Just, so, there's like the cliqueyness, and all that, and it's just bad. And I hate it.

Amanda felt a lack of acceptance from the other South Asian Club members because she was raised in America rather than in India. The students who dominated this particular racial/ethnic cluster grew up in India, had Indian accents, and apparently socialized together to the exclusion of the Indian students raised in America. Amanda and her roommate did not feel welcome.

Only six of the 18 minority students in this study socialized within a racial/ethnic cluster. Similarly, in a September 1995 survey of minority students on campus, only one-third of the minority students belonged to Registered Student Organizations, which served as the locus of many racial/ethnic clusters on campus (Student Affairs Research, Information, & Systems, 1995). Because the racial/ethnic clusters were relatively small, they could not meet the needs of the heterogeneous interests and backgrounds of students within any given racial/ethnic group. In particular, there was no cluster for minority students who had mixed cultural values. Consistent with other findings (Smith & Moore, 2000), students who had a minority racial/ethnic background and were raised with White cultural values did not have a social support network within the racial/ethnic clusters on campus. The racial/ethnic subgroups on campus needed to be more sizeable and diverse in order for the benefits of racial/ethnic clustering to reach more minority students.

The role of racial/ethnic dynamics functioned differently in academic adjustment as compared to how it functioned in initial and social adjustment. While the racial/ethnic dynamics of being socially placed by race/ethnicity, racial/ethnic accountability, the pervasiveness of White culture, and the pursuit of a color-blind society directly affected the initial and social integration of minority students, racial/ethnic dynamics affected the academic integration of minority students indirectly. Minority students did not identify race/ethnicity itself as influential in their adjustment to college academics. They did not raise racial/ethnic concerns when discussing their experiences with faculty, the University's problems, the challenges of being at a predominantly White school, or how they felt their racial/ethnic background affected their first-year experience. However, this finding is tentative since direct questions about the role of race/ethnicity in minority student relationships with faculty and staff were not asked.

Despite this, it was evident that race/ethnicity influenced the academic integration of minority students in that minority students, particularly Black and Latino/a students, were over-represented among those who entered the University as academically weak students. Weak students were more prone to have difficulties with learning course material, to have weak study habits, and to be more negatively impacted academically by the failure to balance social and academic demands. In addition, because minority students were over-represented in the lower socioeconomic stratum, they were more likely than White students to face the need for academic validation. Society's racial/ethnic hierarchy has led to minority students, particularly Black and Latino/a students, being over-represented in the lower socioeconomic stratum. This results in the limiting of educational opportunities, which in turn weaken academic preparation for college. Improvement in minority, particular Black and Latino/a student, academic preparation for college would enhance minority academic integration into campus life. This would help reduce the impact of society's racial/ethnic hierarchy on minority student persistence at predominantly White universities.

CONCLUSION

This analysis revealed six racial/ethnic dynamics that hindered the social and academic integration of minority, particularly Black and Latino/a, students at a large predominantly White institution. These included the following: the role of family life; being placed socially by race/ethnicity; racial/ethnic accountability; the pervasiveness of White culture; the pursuit of a color-blind society; and the overrepresentation of minority, particularly Black and Latino/a, students among weaker students. This study illustrated how these dynamics weakened social integration, i.e., the completion of social adjustments needed to feel a sufficient sense of belonging to want to stay enrolled. Given weaker social integration, one would expect that the minority students at the University of Massachusetts Amherst, particularly Black and Latino/a students, would have left the University at greater rates than their White peers. However, almost three-fourths of Black and Latino/a students return for their sophomore year, as can be seen in the three-year rolling average reported in Table 2. Why do substantial numbers of Black and Latino/a students remain enrolled for a second year if differences in academic preparation (primarily high school grade point averages and SAT scores) are driving one-year attrition (i.e., the percent of entering full-time first-year students who do not return to the same institution a year later)? We can see in Table 2 that six-year attrition rates are consistent with the findings of this study, but one-year attrition rates for Black and Latino/a students are lower than findings in this study would indicate.

This contradiction leads to two further questions. First, why do minority students leave when they do, i.e., with increasing numbers over time? Second, are the reasons for leaving related to the racial/ethnic dynamics found in this study or do the minority students, particularly Black and Latino/a students, persist despite them, but then leave as a consequence of weaker academic preparation? Adelman (1999) would likely say that it is a consequence of academic preparation (college preparatory courses, high school grade point average, and SAT scores), but then why does the loss continue over time? Why is it that weaker students are not weeded out immediately? This study suggests that racial/ethnic dynamics in social and academic integration help explain continued attrition.

Minority students in this study considered leaving because they felt a lack of social integration, because the mainstream party-culture did not appeal to them, because they were expected to socialize where they did not think they would fit in, and for Black and Latino/a students, because they were under constant suspicion that they were not intelligent enough to stay. Yet, they returned for their sophomore year. They returned because one year did not seem long enough to make the judgment to leave, and because the same racial/ethnic dynamics were likely to be elsewhere. These dynamics may not be the same at predominantly Black or Latino/a schools. However, students indicated that they did not want to attend such schools because they wanted to learn how to adjust to being in predominantly White environments. Finally, they returned because they did not want to start all over again so soon. It is possible that minority students are giving up over time or deciding that in time things are bad enough to try again elsewhere. In addition, retention efforts are focused on keeping students enrolled during the first year and often do not address later years.

This study did find a relationship between race/ethnicity and integration. The students' experiences in this study illustrated how society's racial/ethnic hierarchy shapes day-to-day experiences in general, and in-college experiences in particular. The racial/ethnic dynamics identified in this study influenced where students fit in and the degree to which they felt a sense of belonging. They undermined or reinforced academic confidence depending on the student's racial/ethnic background. They defined the environment as segregated and unequal. They reinforced the identification of Whiteness as the norm.

Racial/ethnic clusters challenged these dynamics, but served too few students and hindered interracial interaction. Change should begin with greater academic preparation for Black and Latino/a students in particular, so that the playing field can be made equal. Efforts need to be made to insure that disadvantaged students have a core curriculum known to affect persistence rates (Adelman, 1999). Efforts to certify that teachers are qualified to teach in specific subject areas are to be applauded. Recent legal challenges to the Affirmative Action programs in Admissions have led to changes in admissions procedures that could assist in leveling the academic playing field for minority and non-minority students. Institutions that were employing less stringent admissions criteria for minority students than for non-minority students were effectively reinforcing the racial/ethnic hierarchy by placing some minority students in a position to be less successful than their White counterparts, while at the same time reinforcing the notion that all minority, particularly Black and Latino/a, students did not need the same academic backgrounds as White students to be accepted. Current efforts that redefine merit to acknowledge a student's ability to overcome disadvantages can benefit Black and Latino students without reinforcing the racial/ethnic hierarchy. Beyond academic preparation, an effort should be made to increase interracial interactions, but with the care of minimizing if not removing the dynamics that reify the racial/ethnic hierarchy. Programming that focuses on inter-group dialogue among diverse students can raise consciousness about the role of racial/ethnic stereotyping in reinforcing power differences.

The conclusions of this study need to put in the context of its limitations. There were two important limitations to this study. First, the qualitative methods of ongoing interviewing and occasional in-class visits with participants likely resulted in the Hawthorne effect, i.e., data collection methods may have influenced the dynamics under study. Some students made reference to the how participation in the study helped them with the adjustment to college life. In fact, 74% of the 23 participants in this study graduated within six years, in contrast to 54% for minority students and 60% for White students who entered in Fall 1995. This outcome suggests that the researcher's interactions with students may have assisted with their integration into college life. Despite this outcome, the experiences of students in this study illustrate how racial/ethnic dynamics enacted on college campuses reinforce a racial/ethnic hierarchy that challenges the integration of minority, particularly Black and Latino/a students, into campus life.

A second limitation to this study is that a White interviewer of English/Irish descent completed the interviews. It is likely that this resulted in limited access to the opinions and experiences of some of the minority participants. During the first interview with Nicole, a Black student of African-American descent, Nicole described the White female middle-class students in her high school as snotty and intolerant, and then apologized to the interviewer, presumably because Nicole thought the interviewer would identify with this group and be offended by her characterization. Clearly, the interviewer was not a neutral observer in Nicole's eyes. Nicole concluded this first interview by saying it was not as bad as she expected it to be, but she later withdrew from the study. The one other participant who withdrew from the study, Louis, was also African American. Neither Nicole nor Louis graduated from the university, yet only elements of their stories were available for this study.

In addition to these limitations, as a qualitative study of 23 students, the extent to which results can be generalized to the overall campus and beyond is limited. However, while the experiences of this small population could be unique, participants addressed overall campus dynamics that were consistent with other campus studies, e.g., focus group interviews in the 2000 Diverse Democracy study (Office of Institutional Research, 2001). Beyond campus, the dynamics of racial/ethnic accountability, the pervasiveness of White culture, and the pursuit of a color-blind society are well documented in the sociological literature (Frankenberg, 1993; Omi & Winant, 1994; Perry, 1997; Schofield, 1982; West & Fenstermaker, 1995). The minority student experiences of alienation and social isolation are well documented in the minority retention literature (Fries-Britt, 2001; 2002; Gonzalez, 2002; Grant & Breese, 1997; Hughes, 1987; Malaney & Shively, 1995; Mow & Nettles, 1990; Suen, 1983). This study takes well-known racial/ethnic dynamics occurring in society at-large and links them to minority experiences at a predominantly White university, While the experiences of the students in one particular large state university could be unique, they are consistent with dynamics in the wider society.

Future research should examine why Black and Latino/a students leave college when they do. An informative follow-up to this study would be one that followed the progress of Black and Latino/a students of diverse academic backgrounds from the time they entered an institution to the time they left it. Given the difficulties of getting responses from non-returning students, a qualitative approach may be the best way to retain contact with participants. Interviewing and ethnographic methods allow a rapport to develop between the researcher and participant in a way that would increase the likely of getting data over time. Long-term tracking of academic performance and racial/ethnic experiences once in college would help us better understand why Black and Latino/a students are more likely than White or Asian students to leave college with increased rates over time.

Note—Presented at the Association for Institutional Research's 41st Annual Forum, Long Beach, California, June 2001.

REFERENCES

Adelman, C. (1999). *Short Web-based version of answers in the toolbox: Academic intensity, attendance patterns, and bachelor's degree attainment.* Retrieved March 28, 2000 (http://www.ed.gov./pubs/Toolbox/toolbox.html).

American Council on Education and Commission on the States Commission on Minority Participation in Education and American Life (1988). *One-third a nation.* Washington: American Council on Education.

Astin, A. W. (1993). *What matters in college? Four critical years revisited.* San Francisco: Jossey-Bass Inc., Publications.

Astin, A. W. (1982). *Minorities in American higher education: Recent trends, current prospects, and recommendations.* San Francisco: Jossey-Basss, Inc., Publications.

Bean, J. (1980). Dropouts and turnover: The synthesis and test of a causal model of student retention. *Research in Higher Education, 12*(2), 155-187.

Cabrera, A. F., Castaneda, M. B., Nora, A., & Hengstler, D. (1992). The convergence between two theories of college persistence. *Journal of Higher Education, 63*(2), 143-164.

Crosson, P. H. (1988). Four-year college and university environments for minority degree achievement. *The Review of Higher Education, 11,* 365-382.

Elkins, S. A., Braxton, J. M., & James, G. W. (2000). Tinto's separation stage and its influence on first-semester college student persistence. *Research in Higher Education, 41*(2), 251-268.

Fleming, J. (2002). Who will succeed in college? When the SAT predicts Black students' performance. *The Review of Higher Education, 25*(3), 281-296.

Frankenberg, R. (1993). *White women, race matters: The social construction of whiteness.* Minneapolis: University of Minnesota Press.

Fries-Britt, S., & Turner, B. (2001). Facing stereotypes: A case study of black students on a white campus. *Journal of College Student Development, 42*(5), 420-429.

Fries-Britt, S., & Turner, B. (2002). Uneven stories: Successful black collegians at a black and a white campus. *The Review of Higher Education, 25*(3), 315-330.

Gonzalez, K. P. (2002). Campus culture and the experiences of Chicano students in a predominantly white university. *Urban Education, 37*(2), 193-218.

Grant, G. K., & Breese, J. R. (1997). Marginality theory and the African American student. *Sociology of Education, 70*(July), 192-205.

Harvey, W. B. (2001). *Minorities in higher education 2000-2001: Eighteenth annual status report.* Washington, DC: American Council on Education.

Hinderlie, H. H., & Kenny, M. (2002). Attachment, social support, and college adjustment among black students at predominantly white universities. *Journal of College Student Development, 43*(3), 327-339.

Hu, S., & St. John, E. P. (2001). Student persistence in a public higher education system: Understanding racial and ethnic differences. *The Journal of Higher Education, 72*(3), 265-286.

Hughes, M. S. (1987). Black students' participation in higher education. *Journal of College Student Personnel,* (November), 532-545.

Hurtado, S., Carter, D. F., & Spuler, A. (1996). Latino student transition to college: Assessing difficulties and factors in successful college adjustment. *Research in Higher Education, 37*(2), 135-157.

Johnson, J. (1990). How prepared are our minority students for college-level mathematics? In M. T. Nettles (Ed.), *The effect of assessment on minority student participation, no. 65: New directions for institutional research* (pp. 83-97). San Francisco: Jossey-Bass Inc., Publishers.

Kennedy, P., & Sheckley, B. G. (1999). *Attrition and persistence in higher education: A review of the literature.* Paper presented at the North East Association for Institutional Research annual meeting, November, Cincinnati, OH.

Kroc, R., Woodard, D., Howard, R., & Hull, P. (1995, May). *Predicting graduation rates: A study of land grant, research I and AAU universities.* Paper presented at the annual meeting of the Association for Institutional Research Forum, Boston, MA.

Madrazo-Peterson, R., & Rodriguez, M. (1978). Minority students' perceptions of a university environment. *Journal of College Student Personnel, 19,* 259-263.

Malaney, G. D., & Shively, M. (1995). Academic and social expectations and experiences of first-year students of color. *National Association of Student Personnel Administrators Journal, 32*(1), 3-18.

Mingle, J. (1987). *Trends in higher education participation and success.* Denver, CO: Education Commission of the States and State Higher Education Executive Officers.

Mow, S. L., & Nettles, M. T. (1990). Minority student access to, and persistence and performance in, college: A review of the trends and research literature. In J. C. Smart (Ed.), *Higher education: Handbook of theory and research* (Vol. VI, pp. 35-105). New York: Agathon Press.

Murdock, T. A. (1990). Financial aid and persistence: An integrative review of the literature. *National Association of Student Personnel Administrators Journal, 27*(3).

National Collegiate Athletic Association (2001). *2001 NCAA Division I graduation-rates report.* Indianapolis, IN: The National Collegiate Athletic Association.

Nettles, M. T. (1990). Editor's notes. In M. T. Nettles (Ed.), *The effect of assessment on minority student participation, no. 65: New directions for institutional research* (pp. 1-6). San Francisco: Jossey-Bass Inc., Publishers.

Nettles, M. T., & Johnson, J. R. (1987). Race, sex and other factors as determinants of college students' socialization. *Journal of College Student Personnel, 28*(6), 512-524.

Noel, L. (1978). *Reducing the dropout rate, no. 3: New directions for student services.* San Francisco, Washington, & London: Jossey-Bass Inc., Publishers.

Nora, A., Cabrera, A. F., Hagedorn, L. S., & Pascarella, E. (1996). Differential impacts of academic and social experiences on college-related behavioral outcomes across different ethnic and gender groups at four-year institutions. *Research in Higher Education, 37*(4), 427-451.

Nora, A., & Horvath, F. (1989). Financial assistance: Minority enrollments and persistence. *Education and Urban Society, 21*(3).

Office of Institutional Research (2001). *Diversity democracy qualitative data report.* University of Massachusetts, Amherst, MA.

Office of Institutional Research (2002a). *Factbook updates.* University of Massachusetts, Amherst, MA.

Office of Institutional Research (2002b). *Retention census file and longitudinal student database.* University of Massachusetts, Amherst, MA.

Omi, M., & Winant, H. (1994). *Racial formations in the United States: From the 1960s to the 1990s.* New York and London: Routledge.

Opportunity for Postsecondary Education (1996, December). Institutional graduation rates by pre-college academic records. *Postsecondary Education Opportunity: The Mortenson Research Seminar on Public Policy Analysis of Opportunity for Post-Secondary Education, 54,* 1-4.

Opportunity for Postsecondary Education (2000, February). Academic preparation for college by gender, race and family income, 1983 to 1999. *Postsecondary Education Opportunity: The Mortenson Research Seminar on Public Policy Analysis of Opportunity for Post-Secondary Education, 92.*

Pascarella, E. T., & Terenzini, P. T. (1991). *How college affects students.* San Francisco: Jossey-Bass Inc., Publishers.

Perry, P. (1997, August). *White by any other name: Youth cultures and "white" racial identity in comparative focus.* Paper presented at the annual meeting of the American Sociological Association, Toronto, Canada.

Schofield, J. W. (1982). *Black and white in school: Trust, tension, or tolerance?* United States of America: Praeger Scientific.

Smith, D. G. (1990). The challenge of diversity: Implications for institutional research. In M. T. Nettles (Ed.), *The effect of assessment on minority student participation, no. 65: New directions for institutional research.* San Francisco: Jossey-Bass Inc., Publishers.

Smith, S. S., & Moore, M. R. (2000). Intraracial diversity and relations among African-Americans: Closeness among black students at a predominantly white university. *American Journal of Sociology, 106*(1), 1-39.

Smither, W. R., Edminster, J. H., & Sullivan, K. M. (2001). Factors influencing graduation rates at Mississippi's public universities. *College and University Journal, 76*(3), 11-16.

St. John, E. P., Kirshstein, R. J., & Noell, J. (1991). The effects of student financial aid on persistence: A sequential analysis. *The Review of Higher Education, 14*(3), 383-406.

Stoecker, J., Pascarella, E. T., & Wolfle, L. M. (1988, May). Persistence in higher education: A nine-year test of a theoretical model. *Journal of College Student Development, 29,* 196-209.

Student Affairs Research, Information, & Systems (SARIS) (1995). *Survey of ALANA students (F95-C), September 1996.* Amherst, MA: University of Massachusetts Amherst.

Suen, H. K. (1983). Alienation and attrition of black college students on a predominantly white campus. *Journal of College Students Personnel, 24*(2), 117-121.

Tinto, V. (1975). Dropout from higher education: A theoretical synthesis of recent research. *Review of Educational Research, 45*(1), 89-125.

Tinto, V. (1987). *Leaving college: Rethinking the causes and cures of student attrition.* Chicago and London: The University of Chicago Press.

Tinto, V. (1993). *Leaving college: Rethinking the causes and cures of student attrition* (2nd ed.). Chicago and London: The University of Chicago Press.

Trent, W., Owens-Nicholson, D., Eatman, T. K., Burke, M., Daugherty, N., & Norman, K. (2000). Justice, equality of educational opportunity and affirmative action in higher education. In M. Chang, D. Witt, J. Jones, & K. Hakuta (Eds.), *Compelling interest: Examining the evidence on racial dynamics in higher education* (A report of the American Educational Research Association (AERA) Panel on Racial Dynamics in Colleges and Universities). Retrieved February 27, 2000
(http://www.Stanford.edu/~hakuta/RaceInHigherEducation.html).

United States Census Bureau (2001a). No 215. Educational attainment, by race and Hispanic origin: 1960 to 2000. *Statistical Abstract of the United States.* Washington, DC: United States Census Bureau.

United States Census Bureau (2001b). Table A. Comparison of summary measures of income by selected characteristics: 1993, 1999, and 2000. *Current population survey, March 2001.* Washington, DC: United States Census Bureau.

United States Census Bureau (2001c). No. 569. Employment status of the civilian population: 1970 to 2000. *Statistical abstract of the United States.* Washington, DC: United States Census Bureau.

United States Census Bureau (2001d). Table A. People and families in poverty by selected characteristics: 1999 and 2000. *Current population survey, March 2001.* Washington, DC: United States Census Bureau.

Upcraft, M. L., Gardner, J. N., & Associates (1989). *The freshman year experience.* San Francisco and London: Jossey-Bass Publishers.

West, C., & Fenstermaker, S. (1995). Doing difference. *Gender and Society, 9*(1), 8-37.

## CHAPTER 14

Sociolinguistic Challenges to Minority Collegiate Success: Entering the Discourse Community of the College

John Wesley White

A significant body of research has examined the reasons behind high minority collegiate attrition. All of this work has contributed to our understanding of the unique challenges minority and first generation college students face in the difficult transition to the often new culture that is the college experience. One area that has gone virtually ignored in the literature, however, is the relationship of language, discourse, and literacy to collegiate success. Because the university comprises its own "discourse community"—with its own "ways with words"— those wishing to help minority students in their transition to college should not ignore students' levels of academic literacy. Rather, differences in language use contribute to many students' feelings of alienation from the academic and social culture of the academy. Fortunately, results from this study support the thesis that students lacking academic literacy may be able to learn it—and have a better chance at academic success—through the efforts of college-preparatory programs, college-level student academic services programs, pre-collegiate "bridge" programs, and college mentoring programs.

RATIONALE AND CONCEPTUAL FRAMEWORK

An abundance of studies has demonstrated that minority students face many obstacles in addition to those faced by other students entering the university

(Allen, Epps, & Haniff, 1987; Chavous, 2000; Gloria & Rodriguez, 2000; Johnson, 1986; Pancer, Hunsberger, Pratt, & Alisat, 2000; Rodriguez, 1994; Rowley, 2000; Tinto, 1987). High attrition rates for minority students would seem to add credence to the belief that these students face a far more difficult transition to college life than do their majority peers (Gonzales, 1999; Tinto, 1999; Zea, Reisen, Biel, & Caplan, 1997). Statistics from the site of this research study confirm that minority enrollment and retention are highly problematic. The University of Colorado at Boulder, like many other large public universities, has a large but fairly homogeneous undergraduate student body. In 1999, for example, 4,521 freshmen enrolled at CU Boulder. Of this total number, only 602 (14%) were minorities/students of color (7% Asian, 6% Hispanic/Latino, 2% African American, and 1% Native American) University of Coloardo at Boulder (2001).

Similarly, though the University of Colorado claims as one of its goals to foster learning through an academically and socially diverse student body, it also faces the common and persistent problem of high minority student attrition. Thus, countering efforts to recruit, enroll, and graduate a large number of minority students for its Boulder campus is the fact that a disproportionately high number of minority and nontraditional students tend to leave campus before earning a degree (see Table 1). Thus, the University of Colorado at Boulder—the site for this research study—faces a problem endemic to many large, public universities: enrolling and maintaining a diverse student body.

Many plausible reasons have been put forth to help explain why minority students face a more difficult transition to college (and therefore why many of

Table 1. Graduation Rates by Race/Ethnicity, University of Colorado at Boulder

	Graduate by 4th summer (1995)*	Graduate by 6th summer (1996)*
All	35%	64%
Students of color	21%	49%
Other	37%	67%
Asian American	26%	54%
African American	13%	46%
Hispanic/Chicano	19%	47%
Native American	16%	32%
White	37%	67%
Other	39%	70%
International	40%	45%

University of Colorado at Boulder (2001) www.colorado.edu/pba/records/gradrate.htm.

them leave college prematurely) than other students. Some of the most commonly cited reasons for high minority collegiate attrition are: that many minority students are academically unprepared for the challenges of college (Anyon, 1990; Kozol, 1991; Oakes, 1990; Oakes & Keating, 1988), that minority students may perceive that predominantly white college campuses are unwelcoming or even hostile to them (Allen, 1981; Bennett & Okinaka, 1989; Fleming, 1981; Just, 1999), and that the families of minority students—because many had not themselves experienced college—offer less practical and emotional support for these students (ACT Policy Report, 2002; Crump, Roy, & Recupero, 1992; Nettles & Perna, 1997). Research suggests—both directly and indirectly—that the transition from high school to college is, for most freshmen, a significant cultural transition. Yet, when entering large mainstream universities, minority students are, in many ways, entering a society modeled upon a white, western tradition (Fitzgerald, 1993; Tyack, 1976). Their transition to the university is, therefore, complicated by the fact that they must adapt to a foreign culture (and one that represents a part of society that has historically demonstrated significant hostility toward minorities).

Though the research cited above has helped educators understand many of the unique challenges minority students face when trying to find social and academic success at mainstream universities, it has largely ignored an important aspect of cultural transitions: differences in discursive styles. This is important because sociolinguistic theory suggests that culture and cultural identity are closely associated with specific uses of language (Gee, 1990, 1998; Vygotsky, 1999; Wertsch, 1991). Changes in cultures often bring with them—or require— changes in discursive and literate practices (Gee, 1998; Lave & Wenger, 1991). There can be little doubt that when they enter the university, many minority students are under-prepared in a strict academic sense. What should not be ignored, though, is that many minority students are not familiar with the linguistic styles or "academic discourse" required by the university. The university, like many other cultures, has its own unique and specialized discursive practices; as such, it is a "discourse community" (Bizzell, 1982, p. 7). As a discourse community, it is a place that "has its own language, its own forms and devices for that language, and its own specific laws for the ideological refraction of a common reality" (Medvedev & Bakhtin, 1978, p. 87). Thus, to be accepted as a member of this community—or any unique discourse community—one must both know and practice the kinds of discursive characteristics expected therein (Lave & Wenger, 1991; Street, 1984).

While sociolinguistic and cultural difference theorists have put forth ample evidence showing that minority students bring with them their own linguistic styles to their K-12 experiences—and that these socioculturally based linguistic styles often clash with those expected within schools (Au, 1980, 1986, 1991; Heath, 1983; Snow, 1990, 1991a, 1991b, 1993)—they ignore the fact that these linguistic styles do not merely disappear during a student's K-12 schooling.

Rather, cultural reproduction theory (Willis, 1977) suggests that the opposite is the case: students propagate and perpetuate specific linguistic styles throughout their schooling (Au, 1986, 1991; Ogbu & Wilson, 1990). Thus, the same linguistic challenges that some minority students face when entering the K-12 educational system may, this research suggests, add to these students' difficulties when trying to make the transition from high school (and their respective home cultures) to the college. In short, because some minority students come to college lacking literacy in academic discourse, they also lack the "codes of power" (Delpit, 1995, p. xvi) that they need to be "full participants" (Lave & Wenger, 1991, p. 105) in the academic discourse community.

Thus, this study expands upon the research on minority collegiate attrition by examining how language plays a part in the transition to college. It also examines how mediation—specifically in the form of instruction in specific academic practices and habits—may help traditionally under-served college students attain higher levels of college level academic success. The cases presented in the following pages provide evidence on the efficacy of attempts to mediate, in the form of instruction in academic literacy and "study skills," minority students' transition to the academic environment and culture.

METHODOLOGY

Evidence for the study was collected from students at the Student Academic Services Center (SASC), a part of the University of Colorado at Boulder's Student Services. All of the four study participants were first-generation, minority students from lower-middle class backgrounds. Students selected for the study were those who stood to benefit most from instruction in academic literacy and "skills" mediation. Academic need was determined through the SASC database,[1] through consultation with the Intake Coordinators (who work directly with students), and through consultation with the student her/himself.

In order to provide the specific context of each student and our work together, I employed case study methodology. Case study methodology lends itself to answering the contextual nature of the research questions and allows for multiple methods of data collection and analysis (Merriam, 1988; Stake, 1981; Yin, 1984). Similarly, because the goal of a case study is to examine an instance of some concern, issue, or hypothesis, selectivity (rather than random sampling) of study participants is warranted (Merriam, 1988).

---

[1] The database provides for all registered students' current grade point averages (GPA), previous and current class schedule(s) and course grades, demographic information, and staff comments on students' academic strengths and weaknesses as determined through individual meetings/consultations with the student(s).

In this study I acted as a participant observer—in Spradley's "active" sense of the term (Spradley, 1980, p. 58)—while working individually with the study participants as a tutor. More specifically, because I had extensive experience in the area of academic literacy and "Study Skills" assessment and instruction, as I collected data I also used the knowledge I had gained from these experiences to provide each study participant with instruction in academic literacy, study skills, and other related academic areas.[2] Through individual tutoring sessions that took place on a weekly basis, I collected data from the students about their experiences while I worked with them on academic literacy and study skills-related issues. Detailed fieldnotes, including verbatim student accounts of their activities, thoughts and behaviors, were collected during individual meetings. I supplemented the information I gathered in these meetings through formal pre- and post-study interviews. Similarly, periodically throughout the course of data collection I reviewed with each student their written work, their test results, their class notes, and any other pertinent information for the classes/topics in which they were having difficulties. When appropriate—and with the student's permission—I photocopied said materials for further review and for inclusion in this study. Throughout the data collection process, I also asked students to keep a personal journal in which they described the nature of the academic difficulties they encountered, their feelings about being students at the university and about the work they were required to do therein, and their reaction to academic mediation and the effects they witnessed from this instruction.

To analyze the data collected through the means above, I employed James Spradley's (1980) models of Domain Analysis and Componential Analysis. I reported the data in the form of vignettes and "realistic tales" (Van Maanen, 1988). Drawing from both the information gathered through domain and componential analyses as well as from an ongoing review of fieldnotes and interview transcripts, I included in the "write-up" particular information and examples that add credence to the topic at hand. To present the material in a readable fashion, I transformed the data into a narrative form.

THE CASE[3]

"Simon"

Simon was an 18-year-old Native American male and first-generation college student from a large Navajo reservation in central New Mexico. Simon had, during his first semester, earned a 1.65 Grade Point Average (GPA) on a 4-point

[2] I worked for two years as the Study Skills Specialist at the University of Colorado.
[3] All names are pseudonyms and various aspects of their personal histories have been changed to protect their identity.

scale. He was on academic probation and therefore facing a possible dismissal notice if he failed to bring his GPA to a 2.0 or better in his second semester. Similarly, he was threatened with the loss of his reservation scholarships, which provided his only real hope of being able to afford a college degree. In our first meetings, Simon repeatedly complained both that he felt like an outsider in his classes and that he lacked the knowledge and skills it would take for him to be a good college student. Because of his previous academic experiences and his cultural heritage, Simon had never learned to value the kinds of verbal displays of knowledge that in many ways define the collegiate academic setting; he was not literate in the discursive traditions common to most mainstream freshmen. As a result, he felt lost—like an "outsider"—in the academy.

"Alex"

Alex was a lower-middle class 18-year-old Hispanic freshman from a large city in Texas who came to the study needing help bringing up his GPA. Like Simon, Alex had been placed on academic probation following his first semester as a college student (he had earned a 1.9 GPA in 13 credit hours of what he called "easy classes" and was facing dismissal from the University if he failed to bring his GPA up to the minimum level (2.0). Like Simon, Alex felt that his own discursive practices did not match well with those expected in his classes. He mentioned on numerous occasions that "I just don't talk like them [his peers]" and that, at least in part because of language differences, he felt like an outsider on the campus. He seldom participated in any of his classes and even made efforts to avoid contact with his fellow students and professors because, he said, "I worry that they'll judge me because of how I talk." Adding to Alex's feelings of alienation from his college peers was the fact that he was a homosexual on a campus that he said "talks a lot about diversity, but is really pretty conservative." Not surprisingly, Alex admitted that he preferred to "stay to himself" both in classes and socially.

"Maria"

Maria was an 18-year-old middle-class Hispanic freshman from a small industrial city in southern Colorado. She explained to me that she was at the university largely because "my parents expected me to go to college" rather than out of choice. During her first semester, she had attempted 12 credit hours (four courses) and had earned a GPA of only .33. She therefore had one semester to reverse completely her academic performance and bring up her GPA before she would be dismissed from the university. Maria was a commuter student— she lived in a neighboring town—and seldom associated with her university peers. Rather, she chose to spend most of her time "partying" with her room- mate and other friends from home. She did so, she said, because with her friends she could "talk like I normally do . . . we can be all ethnic and stuff."

When on campus (or at college social events), on the other hand, Maria complained that she had to "act all smart . . . you know, use big words." Maria felt that success in the university required that she talk like her peers. This she equated with "acting white," which for a number of cultural reasons was highly problematic for her.

"Latricia"

Latricia, a 19-year-old lower-class African American, was a third-semester freshman from a large mid-western metropolitan area. Like all of the other students with whom I worked in the study, Latricia was on academic probation and in danger of being dismissed from the university. Like Simon, she was also in danger of losing her "full ride" scholarship. She had, in only 13 hours in her first year, earned a GPA of 1.5. Though Latricia had done well in high school—she was on the honor roll every term and was a member of the National Honor Society—she had come from an inner-city school in which her peers "didn't take school seriously" and in which her courses were "not as demanding as they probably should've been." Upon arriving at the university she was surprised to discover that she was "not prepared for the kind of work they make you do here." Part of her academic difficulties were—like they were for the other students in the study—a result of differences in language use and a lack of understanding of the university system.

DISCOVERING AREAS OF ACADEMIC WEAKNESS

To determine the topics we would work on throughout the semester, I asked each student to describe areas in which he or she wished to improve. The issues they mentioned ranged from doing better on tests (Alex and Maria) to being able to take better notes (Simon, Alex, Latricia), to reading academic texts more efficiently (Simon and Alex), to becoming more comfortable speaking in class (Alex, Simon, Latricia and Maria).[4] The latter was the focus of much of the work I did with each student, in part because it is so closely associated with discourse and academic literacy. Nonetheless, all of these issues had, I found through my work with each of these students, affected their academic performance. They were also areas that were, at least tangentially, related to academic literacy and discourse; all of the academic areas above involved literate practices specific to the university setting.

---

[4] This is not an exhaustive list. Rather, they are the areas that were, generally, common to all of the study participants. For a more detailed description of each student's weaknesses, their work in specific areas, etc., please see White, 2003.

Though all of the study participants admitted to having specific problems that they wished to work on during our time together, I quickly learned that discovering students' areas of academic weakness—and more specifically their problems with academic literacy—is a task complicated by a number of factors. Most notable was the fact that though all of the study participants were—to varying degrees—aware of the fact that they had academic weaknesses that needed attention, it was also apparent to me that each had academic weaknesses of which he or she was not even aware. Coming from an environment that is in most ways quite dissimilar from the culture of the college, they had no way of knowing that they needed help in various other areas if they wished to improve academically. For example, each student had trouble maintaining a schedule and studying wisely and efficiently. This, in turn, affected their class attendance, their understanding of the topics discussed in class, and their ability to stay focused on academic issues. Time management and study skills were topics we would tackle early on in our work together. These are also, research suggests, the basic foundations on which academic literacy—and subsequently success in the academic discourse community—are based (National Association of Student Personnel Administrators, 2000).

Finally, early in my work with these students it also became apparent that they lacked a basic understanding of the very workings—a kind of institutional literacy if you will—of the university system. They were all caught up in a bureaucracy they did not fully understand. Similarly, they did not know how to navigate the diverse discursive spaces and the corresponding ways of talking and being common to the university community. Simon's comment in many ways represents the feelings of all of the students in the study. He said, "You know, I'm still wet behind the ears and I don't know much, man. I came from a place where I hardly even knew that this system [the university bureaucracy and its corresponding discourses] existed" (interview). The students described in this study came to college unaware of the shared intellectual, linguistic, and social conventions that define the discourse community of the university system (Walvoord & McCarthy, 1990). Lacking this understanding of the operation of the university system—a kind of basic academic literacy—had caused and continued to cause these students significant problems and frustrations. For them to find success on a large university campus, they first needed to know the basics of how that system operated and how they were expected to interact with it. Thus, not only did Simon, Latricia, Alex, and Maria need assistance developing a proficiency in specific academic areas, they also needed help understanding the most basic levels of academic literacy and discourse—how the system works and how to operate (and communicate) effectively within it. Developing academic literacy was, I discovered, highly contingent upon students first having a more basic institutional literacy. There are, in other words, auxiliary literacies that are associated with and requisite for academic literacy.

FINDINGS

Basic Academic Literacy

As suggested above, I found early on in our work together that many of Simon, Alex, Maria, and Latricia's problems in adjusting to the university and to college classes came from a misunderstanding of the workings of a college campus and college classes. In this sense, these students lacked some of the most important information and skills—a kind of basic academic literacy—that they needed for success at the school. Like many minority students (ACT, 2002; Young, 2003)—and in contrast to most of their mainstream peers—these students had not been taught (by teachers, counselors or family) the basic skills they needed to succeed within the collegiate academic setting. Collectively, their experiences demonstrate, in many ways, that important kinds of literacies "remain hidden" to those not traditionally included within specific discourse communities (Street, 1984). Ironically, because the academy is itself so imbued with white western culture and therefore has a corresponding discursive tradition (Elbow, 1998), as an outsider to that culture these students were not even aware that they lacked the requisite literacy they needed for survival in the system. Each student was, in other words, unaware of his or her illiteracy in the academic discursive tradition. As such, they had no way of knowing that they needed—or any reason to advocate for—learning these skills and thereby becoming more academically literate. Rather, the discourse community of the university expected them to possess this kind of literacy—to know the rules of participation—prior to their entry into this system.

When these students entered the study, none had a conceptual understanding of their respective academic situations. For example, though Simon, Alex, and Maria all knew that they had not performed at a very high academic level and that this was the reason for their respective probationary status, none of them knew how to compute or predict grade point averages. As a result, they misunderstood what specifically it would take for them to get off of probation. Simon complained that "I never really know where I stand, like, grade wise" (meeting) while Maria had set for herself a goal for the semester—"nothing lower than a B" (interview)—that would fall far short of her getting off of probation. In short, because these students did not know how to compute a GPA, they were not fully empowered to take the steps necessary to get off probation.

Similarly, each student showed weaknesses in other areas that are crucial to success at the university level. For example, even after a completed semester Simon did not adequately understand how to use email. Similarly, Latricia "hated computers" (meeting) and was unaware of how to use the internet (she was, for example, unable to find the site for one of her classes, on which the professor had put assignment descriptions, sample tests, and his lecture outlines). Not knowing some of the more practical uses of their computers, these students were, therefore, lacking an increasingly important academic tool and resource (Eisenberg & Johnson, 2002; Shelley, 1998). Similarly, Alex and Simon did not know to whom to turn for advice on getting student loans and neither knew where to go to get help when they each felt "stressed out" by their personal situations. Just as importantly, none of these students knew about the policy of grade forgiveness or how it might affect their respective GPAs or their academic record. Similarly, Maria, Latricia, and Simon all misunderstood the registration system (including how courses and course sections are listed). During his first semester, Simon had even mistakenly registered for—and was taking—two sections of the same course. In addition—and in spite of the fact that each student was in danger of being dismissed from the university following the semester—none of them were aware of the Continuing Education program and how, through it, they might both remain students and improve their GPAs so that they might re-enroll as matriculated students at a later date.

This lack of a basic understanding of the university system—a lack of a basic academic literacy and with it all of its ways of talking, working, valuing, and being—led to numerous and significant problems during each student's first semester. Because they did not understand the workings of the university system—they lacked this "auxiliary" or basic academic literacy—they did not know how to navigate their way successfully through it. They did not have the tools they needed to "take charge" of their academic situations. Thus, soon after our first few meetings, we began to address these more basic areas of academic literacy.

Before we could address issues more traditionally associated with literacy and academic success (National Association of Student Personnel Administrators, 2000), each student first needed to gain a better understanding of the university system and his or her respective place within it. Thus, we began our work by examining each of the issues above. In addition, I talked with the students—as appropriate—about the various resources available to them on campus. This proved to be especially useful to Simon and Alex, who were suffering from extreme stress and other psychological issues.[5] All of these were lessons that seemed to provide each student with a means for taking control of his or her academic situation. Said Simon, ". . . at least now I can figure out what I gotta do to stay here" (meeting). Similarly, Alex said in our final interview that, without

---

[5] Alex felt "alone" (meeting) as a homosexual on a campus that he felt was hostile toward gays and lesbians. He did not know, prior to our work together, about the Gay/Lesbian/Transgendered Center on campus, the possibility of getting a mentor through them, or the services and support groups available to him at the psychiatric/psychology center at the Student Health Center. Similarly, Simon was suffering from extreme anxiety, so much so that he was having problems sleeping and concentrating. Yet, being a relative outsider to the university community, he did not realize (again, prior to our work together) that such feelings were abnormal or that he needed to get help for them. Once he did seek out help, he was diagnosed with chronic depression and anxiety disorder. With medication and therapy, he showed remarkable improvement.

having this knowledge and finding the resources available to him, he would "probably have been out of here [the university] by now." By learning more about the university system, and each student's respective place within that system, Alex, Simon, Maria, and Latricia were in better stead to take charge of their academic futures. Instruction in this basic or "auxiliary" literacy helped these students improve their respective situations dramatically.

Similarly, it was apparently from a number of data sources—students' grades, formal interviews, students' journal entries, and from repeated and informal contacts with them—that all of the students in this study needed to change their respective study habits dramatically if they wished to improve academically. In this sense, they needed to develop an understanding—a literacy—of beneficial academic habits and also where and why they were making mistakes in their own practices. None of these students were studying well; rather, they studied only when it was most convenient to them, such as late in the night, early in the morning, and—when they failed to finish individual assignments before its due date—even during classes or class time. Like many freshmen (Fisher & Hood, 1987; Margolis, 1976; Sadava and Park, 1993), Maria, Alex, and Latricia were often and unwisely scheduling their study time around socializing rather than the other way around.[6] In addition, and contrary to what Latricia, Maria, and Alex had claimed during the interview, it was also apparent that they were not studying often or for any duration. Thus, in our first few meetings, I discussed with each student effective study habits and attempted to get each to adopt a reasonable daily schedule (which included study time).[7] Managing time—which includes studying at good times and for proper intervals—is, research suggests, highly correlated with success in any intellectual endeavor, including academic success (Barkley, 1998). It is one of the often "hidden" skills (Street, 1984) associated with academic literacy.

In summary, each student was, by the completion of the study, much more literate in the ways in which the university operated. Through learning basic academic literacy, each had added "yet another style" (Kutz, 1998, p. 41) of discourse to his or her existing repertoire, which is, many researchers suggest, a requisite for success in the academic community (Elbow, 1998; Street, 1984). Able to appropriate a new form of literacy, Simon, Latricia, Alex, and Maria were better equipped to become participating members of the discourse community in which they now found themselves. By learning and then beginning to appropriate

---

[6] Simon was not suffering from a lack of studying. Unlike the other students, he was studying too much, albeit ineffectively. He was, he said "burning myself out" (meeting) because he was working so hard with very little noticeable progress. Nonetheless, he too needed to learn effective study habits/techniques in order to improve academically.

[7] We discussed, in our first set of meetings, effective study habits as determined through research in this field (National Association of Student Personnel Administrators, 2000), from psychological and "learning" research (Barkley, 1998) and from my own experiences both as a student and, more importantly, as an academic "skills" specialist and tutor.

a new kind of literacy—basic academic discourse in this case—these students were better prepared for the demands that they would face in the academic community; each was slowly gaining the knowledge and skills required to be a discursive insider in the discourse community of the university.

Academic Literacy: Reading, Writing and Speaking in the Academic Discourse Community

Though an important part of the work these students and I did together focused on more basic aspects of academic life and literacy, the majority of our work focused on areas more traditionally associated with academic literacy—reading, writing, and speaking—and academic success in their more traditional senses. Even though Simon, Latricia, Alex, and Maria had come to college with their own unique discursive styles (all of which were culturally based and had cultural and personal importance to them), they were not truly familiar with the discursive practices expected of them at the university. More specifically, I found in my research that each student had problems reading academic texts, taking "essay" tests in their classes, and—most importantly—speaking in their classes. As a result of linguistic differences between their own respective cultures and those expected in the university setting, each of these students had distinct problems understanding what was expected of them, understanding the texts they were expected to read, and each showed a palpable fear of speaking/participating in their classes. This, in turn, affected both their academic performance and their feelings of alienation from their peers.

Reading

Via discussions with these students, it became apparent that—as a whole—they approached the reading of academic textbooks largely as they did reading novels. They had, therefore, come to college lacking an important part of academic discourse: they were unaware that for academic texts they needed to read in a different way from that of everyday practice (Street, 1984). Rather, each student saw no distinction in the ways in which he/she should approach the two different kinds of text. Said Alex, "well, it's all just reading . . . you just gotta do it I guess" (interview). A common complaint of all of these students was that "it's [the reading assignments] just too much to do and remember all of it" (Simon, meeting). In an effort to help the students with their reading, we first discussed the difference in "academic" books and works of literature. This was a distinction that all caught on to quite quickly. Comparing their different courses and their requisite reading assignments, each come to see that different texts had different purposes and that they were consequently written in different ways. We then discussed how each student's reading style should differ for the different kinds of texts. They should, we discussed, learn how to select what they need for particular purposes; they needed to learn to read in a way common to academics, which includes going "from different parts of the text, using the contents page, index, chapter headings, etc. and moving backwards and forwards within that text and to other texts" (Street, 1984). We discussed "skimming" the text for important clues, we highlighted important concepts, looked for bolded or italicized terms, and examined the margins and photo captions for information. Reading textbooks need not, each student found through these discussions, be approached in the same way as reading a novel. The important information in the former could be found more efficiently often by *not* reading it word for word.

Just as importantly, these students and I discussed the importance of taking notes on the text. I felt it very important to convince each student that trying to read and "remember" everything that he/she read was an impossible task. A common problem I discovered when discussing each student's respective academic difficulties was that each felt that he/she needed to read and "remember" everything that they had read. This proved problematic because: a) the amount of materials they were to read for their classes was largely beyond memorization; and b) professors did not expect their students to "know" everything that was assigned to them. These students were, in other words, misinterpreting their reading assignments and the very nature of academic reading. They assumed that because it was assigned, they were to "know it all" (Alex, meeting). Thus, early in our work together, I worked with these students on the nature of academic reading. Using myself as an example, I told them that though I had read a great deal of material in my many years of being a student, I certainly could not remember many specific details of individual texts. Rather, I explained, I took notes while reading both so that I could use them to study for tests and so that I could refer to them later if necessary. I then had each student take notes—in an outline format—of a chapter he or she was to read for upcoming classes. Through this exercise, the students came to understand that—by note-taking—they could more efficiently cover more material. They also found, much to their surprise, that future studying would prove to be easier when they could refer to their notes. They no longer had to go back and "reread everything for the tests" (Maria, interview 1) as they had been doing.

Test Taking

In a lesson similar to that described above, these students and I worked on test taking strategies. Alex, Simon, Maria, and Latricia had all complained in our first meetings that they were having problems taking tests. Generally—and again similar to their problems with reading—they claimed to have problems remembering and "knowing" all the materials required for answering test questions property. Said Alex:

> . . . the exams here are like almost all short answer and essays, where you have to write on whatever they tell you. In high school, they'd give you multiple choice tests, stuff that wasn't so, I don't know, like general, like um,

asking anything from the readings and class. They, professors, expect you to give certain kinds of answers to readings and stuff, but they don't like really tell you before what to look for, what they want. So, it's more confusing here. You don't always know what to answer. (interview 1)

A large part of these students' problems with test taking was, we learned early in our time together, from their problems taking notes. As suggested above, each student was having problems discerning important information from that which was either used to support a main idea or that was relatively superfluous. As a result, their notes provided little information which would prove useful for upcoming tests. Correspondingly, when studying for exams, they did not know the more important areas to study. Rather, they would attempt to "know it all" rather than focusing on the more important points discussed in readings and in class. Similarly, when writing essays or short answers for tests, each student found himself or herself failing to focus on the specific points/topics referred to in the questions. Not surprisingly, this problem seemed to resolve itself once these students became more proficient at taking notes (and when they had other people's notes from which to study).[8] When studying for finals, for example, each student (with the exception of Maria) had an abundance of detailed notes from which to study. These students' improvement in taking notes corresponded with an improvement in their respective test results.

Nonetheless, when examining each student's returned tests early in our work together, I found a significant problem with the way that they answered written test questions. For example, they would take the implied directions for answering "short answer" test sections too literally. Not being versed in the discourse of the university, they had no way of knowing specifically what "short answer" meant; they did not understand the irony that short answer questions often require somewhat extended answers. Though most of their answers to test questions would be technically correct, they consistently failed to answer the question as fully as necessary. Alex, for example, answered an identification question about the culture of the Anasazi people of southwestern Colorado with "Ancestral Pueblo people, lived around 1300 AD and they grew squash, beans and corn" (Alex, blue book test). Though there was nothing in his answer that was not correct, Alex did not provide enough details on the Anasazi people, their importance, the mystery surrounding their disappearance, or their major contributions to the History of Colorado. As a result, his professor gave him only six of ten points possible. Similarly, on his essay answers, Simon provided correct but brief answers. He too was losing points by not writing enough. His professor commented on his answer that it was, "overall OK, but brief" (Simon, blue book test). Each student was—to differing degrees—suffering from the fact that

---

[8] I had suggested to each that, as an exercise in taking notes, they borrow and photocopy friends' class notes. From these, they could see how other students took notes, they could learn to emulate this practice and they would have additional information to help them prepare for their tests.

many of the rules—the "hidden skills" (Street, 1984)—associated with test taking had never been discussed. These rules were yet another part of academic literacy that had not been, either in their previous academic experiences or in college, taught to them.

I suggested to each student during our meetings that the answer to this problem was quite simple and required two things. First, they would need to know as many facts as possible for answering these questions properly. If they had good notes from readings and from class, they should have enough information to answer the question fully and correctly. All they would need to do is study and "know" their notes. As their note taking improved, so would their ability to focus on important facts for exams. Seldom, I said, do professors test students on information that they have not covered in class. Just as importantly, professors often give both overt and hidden clues as to what will be "on the test." With practice listening and taking notes—and by reviewing other's notes—each student would, I insisted, learn to pick up on these clues. Second, Simon, Alex, Maria, and Latricia needed to change the manner in which he or she answered questions. Just as they had learned to adjust their reading for academic texts, they needed to transfer many of these same skills to answering test questions. I encouraged each student to write more details and to elaborate on his or her answers with facts, dates, and if possible, connections to the theme of the class. One way of doing this, I suggested, was for them to write as much as they possibly could, in the time permitted. I even suggested that, from my own "insider's perspective" as a student and instructor, it was not a bad idea to write down facts that were only tangentially related to the topic (especially when the student felt that he or she was weak in answering the particular question). The more information that each student wrote down as answers, the more possible points she or he might receive. Lastly, I suggested that, when thinking about answering the question, they write down in the margins all of the facts, connections, and ideas they remembered so that, during the stress of the test, they did not forget important information.

By the end of the semester, each student was attempting to use the information and lessons we had discussed. When "prepping for exams," for example, Alex said that his strategy for answering short answer and essay questions was to "study my ass off . . . and really know the notes" and just as importantly to "try to write everything I know on it [the topic]" (meeting). Adopting this strategy paid off for these students in a number of ways. First, three of the four were able to do well on their finals. Just as importantly, though, this new knowledge also helped to boost these students' respective levels of confidence about their academic abilities. Armed with more test-taking knowledge, each felt better about himself or herself as a student. This is reflected in Simon's statement "I still struggle sometimes [with tests], but once I study, I can do good" (Simon, interview 2). Becoming literate in a few of the "tricks" for better test taking helped these students significantly, both immediately and for the future.

Learning this part of academic literacy—strategies and rules for taking tests—empowered each of the students in the study. Armed with a better understanding of this unique discursive practice, these students began to both improve academically and with it to feel more confident in their academic abilities. Said Simon, "learning how to get ready for tests and to take them . . . was something no one had ever shown me. I just didn't know what I was supposed to be doing" (interview 2). Mediation—through direct instruction in this form of academic literacy—enabled each of these students to grow academically.

Overcoming Fears of Speaking in Class

I learned early in my work with these students that all of them were reluctant to speak in their classes, even though participation grades affected their overall grades and therefore affected their status as college students. All of the students expressed to me their fear that, by speaking in class—using their own native voices/discursive styles and therefore in a different manner than did their peers—they would be judged in a negative manner. Said Alex, "I just don't want to [participate] . . . because I don't want to be judged . . . I guess if I was more confident, like in how I talked, if I felt safer, I would talk more" (interview 1). Yet, because of their fears of appearing "stupid" (Maria, meeting) or "ignorant" (Simon, interview 1) by talking in class, each student had done his or her best to remain quiet throughout the semester (even though each was aware that remaining silent in classes was damaging them academically). These students were unanimous in their preference for large lecture classes— in which they all admitted they had more trouble taking notes, concentrating, and in which they basically disliked the content—to smaller classes because in smaller classes there was a far greater chance that they would be expected to speak and participate. Alex explained, "I like bigger classes, 'cause you get picked on in smaller classes. I don't like getting picked on" (interview 1). When asked to define what he meant by "getting picked on," Alex responded with, "Picked on like . . . ask me questions and expect me to answer. They [professors] want you to talk in front of class, to answer stuff. I don't like being singled out or asked to talk like that" (interview 1). I found it both interesting and representative of these student's true feelings that they referred to either being called on or encouraged to speak in class "getting picked on," a term which carries with it an obvious punitive sense.

In our first interviews and early meetings, these students cited many reasons for their respective reluctance to participate in their classes (which included feelings of racism from their peers and expectations that they be the "token" minority in their classes). Yet most important for the purposes of this study, each student complained that, as Alex put it, they did not ". . . have the language, you know, the vocabulary" to be able to speak in class (interview 1). Rather, they felt that they did not have the linguistic skills—including the proper lexicon—to express themselves to their peers in the manner expected of university students. All of these students feared that their respective lack of "college-like talk" (Maria, meeting) would cause their peers to "look down on [them] as stupid," (Alex, interview 1), thereby adding to their sense of inferiority and alienation. Such a fear of being judged as a cultural and/or linguistic minority on mainstream campuses is, research suggests, quite pervasive and often leads to a silencing of minority voices (Gonzales, 1999; Just, 1999; Wallace, 2002). The collective experiences of these students demonstrate how the college classroom serves as a distinct "discourse community." As a discourse community, there are specific yet unspoken "rules" for participation in class discussions. The most important of these rules is knowing and employing a specific kind of language and vocabulary. Alex and Maria each termed the use of this knowledge and ability as "college talk," which they described as using "big words" (Maria, meeting) and "high language" (Alex, meeting) to discuss both topics of importance and "even simple stuff" in class (Alex, meeting). These students easily recognized that "exclusionary language" (Elbow, 1998) was a part of academic discourse. Unfortunately, they did not trust that they knew the language of academics; rather, they thought that they lacked the ability to engage in college talk. Thus, they remained silent.

In order to help these students feel more comfortable talking in class—and to impress upon them the need for class participation—we repeatedly came back to class participation in our weekly meetings. With each student I consistently attempted to reinforce the importance of speaking in class; they had come to our work together, I realized, not fully understanding the reasons why many professors grade students on participation or how significantly their grades could be affected by a lack of participation. Therefore, together we went through their respective syllabuses to determine how much participation counted in their course grades. Through these discussions, each student came to see that a large part (generally a minimum of 15% of their grade) was determined through class participation. Improving enough to stay at the university was, each saw, dependent at least in part upon each student making attempts at participation. This seemed to give each additional reason for making an attempt to become more integrated in their classes. They felt an added pressure to make attempts to participate. This was, I felt, the first step toward their becoming more comfortable as participants. Learning through practice is, research suggests, "an integral and inseparable aspect of social practice" (Lave & Wenger, 1991, p. 31) that is the first step toward "full participant" (Lave & Wenger, 1991, p. 29) in any discursive community. By making a conscious effort to say a few things occasionally, these students could, therefore, begin to practice some of the discursive practices common to the academic community and by doing so, start to integrate themselves into this community. Interestingly, having realized the importance speaking in class had on their very academic futures, each student

began—judging from our conversations and students' mid-term reports[9]—
attempting to participate more often in their classes.

To help these students better understand academic discourse—and thereby be
better able to appropriate it for their own uses—we spent the better part of some
of our early meetings discussing some of the components of academic discourse.
We examined, one by one, many of the discursive characteristics that his peers
used when talking in class. By examining each one, I hoped that Alex, Simon,
Latricia, and Maria might see how their peers' use of "big words" and "exclusionary language" did not necessarily equate with superior content knowledge.
These students' peers were simply versed in a discursive style that intimates
knowledge, whether or not such knowledge actually exists. Rather, they came
to see through a breakdown of academic discourse—as it is generally used in
college classrooms—that it was through the manner in which their colleagues
expressed their ideas that they conveyed the image that they were knowledgeable.
They commonly used "exclusionary language" (Elbow, 1998), "author
evacuated" (Geertz, 1973) statements, and "big words" to state their ideas. Their
ideas, whether based in fact or simply personal opinions, took on an air of
authority because they were stated using a specific discursive style. This style,
moreover, was one that—with practice and conscious effort—each of my students
could appropriate for his or her own needs.

Together, over the course of the semester, these students and I discussed
how they might employ this form of academic discourse when speaking in class.
Going over some of their respective ideas about various topics, we attempted
the process of "style shifting" (Kutz, 1998) from vernacular—or what Alex
called "normal, everyday speech" (meeting)—to academic discourse. Again, I
hoped that through their work with me—by having them act as an "apprentice"
in the learning and practice of academic discourse (Lave & Wenger, 1991)—
they might begin to appropriate some of its "norms" for their own use. During
these meetings (and following frequent reminders from me) each student
began the practice of translating ideas from his or her own—often self-
doubting—manner of speaking to the more authoritative style of academic
discourse. Most commonly, I would "remind" each student when he or she
would say things in a doubting tone. A common trait of all of these students
was that they would often put disclaimers around their statements ("I'm not
sure, but" or "I don't know if I'm right, but . . ."). With time and practice,
however, each seemed to become more comfortable making statements in a
more assertive manner. With some encouragement from me—as well as from
the suggestions I gave on how to alter specific statements—they began to become
more versed in and comfortable using the conventions of academic discourse.

---

[9] SASC solicits from professors mid-term reports on its students. These reports include grades as
well as professors' comments on students' attendance, participation, and motivation.

This, in turn, led to greater participation in class. Alex explained how these lessons affected his feelings about speaking in class:

> Well, now it's like I can, I don't know, I know better how to say things differently than before. It's not like what I'm saying is different, it's more like how I say it. I guess I'm a little more, I don't know, maybe confident, you know? I can say stuff and not be so worried if it's not exactly right. . . . I can say what I'm thinking. I don't have to know it all. (interview 2)

By apprenticing with me—a discursive insider in the academic community— these students began to learn how to "code switch" their own thoughts into a discursive style that was appropriate for classroom use. At the same time, they seemed to grow more confident in their respective abilities to speak in class. No longer were they self-censoring their ideas because of a fear of appearing stupid by the ways they expressed themselves. Rather, they were becoming a more integral part of their classes by using some of the linguistic tools common to academic discourse.

CONCLUSIONS AND DISCUSSION: RESULTS OF LEARNING ACADEMIC LITERACY

Each of the students in this study changed dramatically over the course of a semester. All of them improved academically and subsequently; they all seemed to grow more confident in their abilities as students. They were studying more efficiently and therefore had more time to do the social activities common to college students. Most importantly thought, after learning academic discourse, they are all better prepared for lives as college students.

The most immediate and tangible effect of learning academic literacy—and with it the "skills" associated with and requisite for this literacy—was a change in academic performance. Alex and Simon both reached their primary goal of getting off of academic probation. At the conclusion of our work together, Alex was able to report a 2.92 GPA for the semester. His GPA had, in one semester, improved slightly more than an entire grade point. Alex's cumulative GPA had risen to a 2.45. Not only had Alex done well enough to get off of academic probation, he had earned enough grade points to insure that, absent a major catastrophe, he would not fall back into probationary status. By learning academic literacy and by subsequently changing some of his academic habits, Alex had earned more personal and academic freedom. Alex's improvement was also a large step toward his reaching "a good overall GPA, like a 3.0 or above" (interview 2). Simon's grades also improved over the course of a semester. His GPA went from a 1.75 the previous semester to a 2.55 for the current semester. Simon's performance during the spring semester brought his cumulative GPA to a 2.1, thereby taking him off academic probation. Simon no longer faced the threat of being ejected from the university based on academic performance and he was able to move beyond the stigma and shame he felt from being on academic probation. He stated in our final interview that "now it's over [the semester and academic probation] I can go home proud" (interview, 5/20/02). Simon even took a job— in the University's Upward Bound Program—in which he used his new-found knowledge to assist future entering Native American freshmen in their transition to the university. He was using his new literacy to help other students from backgrounds similar to his own.

Maria and Latricia also showed academic improvement, though they did not improve enough to be removed from academic probation. Nevertheless, Maria improved exponentially. Her GPA went from a .33 after her first semester to a 1.71 GPA. Had Maria attempted and succeeded in getting an Incomplete in one of her courses rather than giving up on the course completely (she did not even sit for the final), her GPA for the semester would have been significantly higher at a 2.13. Similarly, had Maria not "given up" (meeting) in her Spanish class at the end of the semester (and therefore earned a D+), her GPA would likely have been high enough to warrant a reprieve from suspension.

Latricia also performed noticeably better while working in the study. She began the semester with a 1.51 GPA and had only 14 credit hours. She had, in her first semester, only completed five hours. Yet while working in the study, Latricia successfully completed 12 hours in which she earned a 2.15 for the semester. She improved her overall GPA to a 1.75. Had she applied for a reprieve from suspension, her improvement may have allowed her to have another semester during which she could improve her GPA further.

Though Maria and Latricia were both dismissed from the university, the lessons they learned in this study nonetheless helped them academically. Both students were, in part thanks to becoming more literate in the workings of the academy, working in the Continuing Education Program to stay in school and improve their GPAs (learning about Continuing Education as an option allowed each student to remain in school). Furthermore, both Maria and Latricia expressed to me their hopes that they might, through this program, continue to bring up their respective grades enough to be readmitted at a later date. Similarly, Maria and Latricia claimed—at the conclusion of our semester working together—that they were better equipped for the academic demands they were facing. In short, they were both employing many of the lessons they learned in the study to grow stronger as students.

By learning and "deconstructing" (Derrida, 1978) some of the most common components of academic literacy, Simon, Maria, Latricia, and Alex were each able to become more fully functioning members of the academic community in which they found themselves. Moreover, by learning these literary conventions, they all grew more confident in and more comfortable with being in this environment. The results of this study support the theses on which it is based. First, many minority students face additional challenges in their transition to the university because of differences in language use. The culturally-imbued language patterns of students' home culture often clash with those expected within the academic discourse community. This leads to feelings of alienation from the academic community (as well as feelings that the cultural/linguistic heritage of each is not respected within this supposedly liberal community). Issues of difference in language and discursive styles are, this study shows, a major factor for many students in their attempts to find collegiate success. Second, the experiences of the students in this study show that mediation in academic literacy—both broadly and traditionally defined—may enhance some students' chances at finding academic success (and increased feelings of inclusion) in the college community. This has implications for pre-collegiate programs, college preparatory programs, and college-level mediation programs. Being versed in academic literacy is, obviously, an important part of being academically successful. It is an area that should not be ignored, especially in efforts at collegiate-level mediation.

Finally, results from this study demonstrate that connected with academic literacy is an associated "auxiliary" literacy: knowing and using specific academic or study skills in the college environment. Though knowing academic literacy—in its traditional sense—is highly correlated with academic success, such literacy is undercut (and difficult to learn) without students first having a strong skills foundation on which to build. Fortunately, the experiences of the cases presented in this chapter show that many of these skills can be taught. This, too, has implications for mediation services. Program directors, tutors, etc. should not assume that students entering the university have the kind of academic literacy and associated skills that they need for success therein. Rather, building a foundation—based on study skills and academic habits—may be a prudent place to being work with many students (especially those who were not likely to have received such instruction prior to entering the college community).

FINAL THOUGHTS: A CAVEAT

The work that these students did while in this study goes far beyond the description as presented here. What appears above is, in many ways, an accurate but simplistic account of their semester. The work we did together would, if described in detail, comprise far too long a study for the parameters of this chapter. For a more detailed account, please refer to White (2003; the research study from which this chapter originated). Similarly, the students in this study deserve a great deal of credit both for the work that they did to improve academically through this study as well as for their courage in attempting to make changes that were, for many of them, tantamount to cultural changes. Though I was able—as an "insider" in the workings and literacy of the academic community—to help them in their transition to this community, their success is due in great measure to their own efforts and their desire to succeed academically. Finally, with changes in discursive practices come many cultural and personal conflicts.

Changing their "ways with words" (Heath, 1983) was for these students no simple feat. Rather, Simon, Latricia, Maria, and Alex each had to confront a myriad of conflicts (many of them cultural in nature) in their attempts to become more successful as college students. Asking students to change their discursive habits—even temporarily—is complicated by the relationship of language/discourse to cultural identity. Again, these are issues that must be taken into account in efforts at mediation (they are also issues that are discussed at length in the study from which this chapter comes).

REFERENCES

ACT Policy Report. (2002). *School relationships foster success for African American students*. (Report Number 050802040). Iowa City, Iowa: George Wimberly.

Allen, W. (1981). Correlates of black student adjustment, achievement, and aspirations at a predominantly white southern university. In G. Thomas (Ed.), *Black students in higher education: Conditions and experiences in the 1970's* (pp. 126-141). Westport, CT: Greenwood Press.

Allen, W., Epps, E., & Haniff, N. (1984). *Undergraduate survey of black undergraduate students attending predominantly white, state-supported universities*. (ERIC Document Reproduction Service No. 252 615.)

Anyon, J. (1990). Social class and the hidden curriculum of work. *Journal of Education*, *162*(1), 67-92.

Au, K. (1980). Participation structures in a reading lesson with Hawaiian children: Analysis of a culturally appropriate instructional event. *Anthropology and Education Quarterly*, *11*(2), 91-115.

Au, K. (1986). Encouraging reading and language development in cultural minority children. *Topics in Language Disorders*, *6*(2), 71-80.

Au, K. (1991). Culture and ownership: Schooling minority students. *Childhood Education*, *67*(5), 280-284.

Barkley, R. (1998). *Attention deficit hyperactivity disorder: A handbook for diagnosis and treatment* (2nd ed.). New York: The Guilford Press.

Bennett, C., & Okinaka, A. (1989). *Factors related to persistence among Asian, Black, Hispanic, and White undergraduates at a predominantly White university: Comparisons between first and fourth year cohorts*. Paper presented at the annual meeting of the American Educational Research Association, San Francisco, March 1989.

Bizzell, P. (1982). Cognition, convention, and certainty: What we need to know about writing. *PRE/TEXT*, *3*, 213-243.

Chavous, T. (2000). The relationship among racial identity, perceived ethnic fit, and organizational involvement for African American students at predominantly white universities. *Journal of Black Psychology*, *26*(1), 79-100.

Crump, S., Roy, F., & Recupero, C. (1992). *Racial attitudes of white college students: Yesterday, today and tomorrow*. Paper presented at the Centennial Convention of the American Psychological Association, Washington, D.C.

Delpit, L. (1995). *Other people's children: Cultural conflict in the classroom*. New York: The New Press.

Derrida, J. (1978). *Writing and difference*. Chicago: University of Chicago Press.

Eisenberg, M., & Johnson, D. (2002). Learning and teaching information technology—Computer skills in context. *ERIC Digest*. (ERIC Document Reproduction Service No. ED 465 377.)

Elbow, P. (1998). Reflections on academic discourse: How it relates to freshmen and colleagues. In V. Zamel & R. Spack (Eds.), *Negotiating academic literacies: Teaching and learning across languages and cultures* (pp. 145-169). Mahwah, NJ: Lawrence Erlbaum Associates, Publishers.

Fisher, S., & Hood, B. (1987). the stress of the transition to university: A longitudinal study of psychological disturbance, absent-mindedness and vulnerability to homesickness. *British Journal of Psychology, 78*, 425-442.

Fitzgerald, J. (1993). Views on bilingualism in the United States. A selective historical review. *Bilingual Research Journal, 17*, (1&2), 35-56.

Fleming, J. (1981). Special needs of blacks and other minorities. In A. W. Chickering & Associates (Eds.), *The modern American college: Responding to the new realities of diverse students and a changing society* (pp. 279-295). San Francisco: Jossey-Bass.

Gee, J. (1990). *Social linguistics and literacies: Ideology in discourses*. Brighton, England: Falmer Press.

Gee, J. (1998). What is literacy? In V. Zamel & R. Spack (Eds.), *Negotiating academic literacies: Teaching and learning across languages and cultures* (pp. 52-59). Mahwah, NJ: Lawrence Erlbaum Associates, Publishers.

Geertz, C. (1973). *The interpretation of cultures*. New York: Basic Books, Inc.

Gloria, A., & Rodriguez, E. (2000). Counseling Latino university students: Psycho-sociocultural issues for consideration. *Journal of Counseling & Development, 78*(2), 145-154.

Gonzales, K. (1999). *Campus culture and the experiences of Chicano students in predominantly white colleges and universities*. Paper presented at the Annual Meeting of the Association for the Study of Higher Education, San Antonio, TX, November 18-21, 1999. (ERIC Document Reproduction Service No. ED 437-873.)

Heath, S. B. (1983). *Ways with words: Language, life and work in communities and classrooms*. Cambridge, England: Cambridge University Press.

Hymes, D. (1971). Competence and performance in linguistic theory. In R. Huxley & E. Ingram (Eds.), *Language acquisition: Models and methods* (pp. 3-28). New York: Academic Press.

Johnson, I. (1986). *Minorities orientation science seminar at Purdue University: A counseling/mentoring approach*. Paper presented at the Annual Convention of the American Association for Counseling and Development, Los Angeles.

Just, H. (1999). Minority retention in predominantly white universities and colleges: The importance of creating a good "fit." (ERIC Document Reproduction Service No. ED 439 641.)

Kozol, J. (1991). *Savage inequities: Children in America's schools*. New York: Crown Publishers.

Kutz, E. (1998). Between students' language and academic discourse: Interlanguage as middle ground. In V. Zamel & R. Spack (Eds.), *Negotiating academic literacies. Teaching and learning across cultures* (pp. 37-50). Mahwah, NJ: Lawrence Erlbaum Associates, Publishers.

Lave, J., & Wenger, E. (1991). *Situated learning: Legitimate peripheral participation.* Cambridge, England: Cambridge University Press.

Margolis, G. (1976). *Pushing the freshman first semester panic button: Some perspectives on counseling anxious freshmen the first weeks of school.* (ERIC Document Reproduction service No. ED 126-406.)

Medvedev, P., & Bakhtin, M. (1978). *The formal method in literary scholarship: A critical introduction to sociological poetics.* Baltimore: The Johns Hopkins University Press.

Merriam, S. (1988). *Case study research in education: A qualitative approach.* San Francisco: Jossey-Bass Publishers.

National Association of Student Personnel Administrators. (2000). *Bridges to student success. Exemplary programs, 2000.* (ERIC Document Reproduction Service, No. ED 445 307.)

Nettles, M., & Perna, L. (1997). *The African American education data book. Volume I: Higher and adult education. Executive summary.* Fairfax, VA: College Fund/UNCF. (ERIC Document Reproduction Service No. ED 406 807.)

Oakes, J. (1990). *Multiplying inequalities: The effects of race, social class, and tracking on opportunities to learn math and science.* Santa Monica, CA: Rand Corporation.

Oakes, J., & Keating, P. (1988). *Access to knowledge: Breaking down school barriers to learning.* A paper prepared for The College Board (New York) and The Education Commission of the States (Denver), August 1998. ED 305407.

Ogbu, J., & Wilson, J. (1990). *Mentoring minority youth: A framework.* Columbia University Institute for Urban and Minority Education. (ERIC Document Reproduction Service, No. ED 354 293.)

Pancer, S., Hunsberger, B., Pratt, M., & Alisat, S. (2000). Cognitive complexity of expectations and adjustment to university in the first year. *Journal of Adolescent Research, 15*(1), 38-57.

Prior, P. (1998). *Writing/Disciplinarity? A sociohistoric account of literate activity in the academy.* Mahwah, NJ: Lawrence Erlbaum Associates, Publishers.

Rodriguez, E. (1994). *The role of psychosocial separation, ethnic identity, and world view in college adjustment.* Unpublished doctoral dissertation, Arizona State University, Tempe.

Rowley, S. (2000). Profiles of African American college students' educational utility and performance: A cluster analysis. *Journal of Black Psychology, 26*(1), 3-26.

Savada, S., & Park, A. (1993). Stress-related problem drinking and alcohol problems: A longitudinal study and extension of Marlatt's model. *Canadian Journal of Behavioural Science, 25*, 446-464.

Shelley, J. (1998). *Incorporating computer literacy into the composition classroom.* (ERIC Document Reproduction Service No. ED 422 584.)

Snow, C. (1990). The development of definitional skill. *Child Language, 17*, 697-710.

Snow, C. (1991a). Language proficiency: Towards a definition. In H. Dechert & G. Appel (Eds.), *A case for psycholinguistic cases.* Amsterdam: John Benjamins.

Snow, C. (1991b). The theoretical basis for relationships between language and literacy in development. *Journal of Research in Childhood Education, 6*, 5-10.

Snow, C. (1993). Families as social contexts for literacy development. *New Directions for Child Development, 61*, 11-24.

Spradley, J. (1980). *Participant observation.* Fort Worth: Harcourt Brace.

Stake, R. (1981). Case study methodology: An epistemological advocacy. In W. Welsh (Ed.), *Case study methodology in educational evaluation*. Proceedings of the 1981 Minnesota Evaluation Conference, Minneapolis: Minneapolis Research and Evaluation Center.

Street, B. (1984). *Literacy in theory and practice*. Cambridge: Cambridge University Press.

Tinto, V. (1987). *Leaving college*. Chicago: University of Chicago Press.

Tinto, V. (1993). *Leaving college: Rethinking the causes and cures of student attrition* (2nd ed.). Chicago: University of Chicago Press.

Tinto, V. (1999). Taking retention seriously: Rethinking the first year of college. *NACADA Journal, 19*, (2), 5-9.

Tyack, D. (1976). Ways of seeing: An essay on the history of compulsory schooling. *Harvard Educational Review, 46*(3), 355-389.

University of Colorado at Boulder. (2004). *Graduation Rates by Race/Ethnicity*. Retrieved November 1, 2001 from www.colorado.edu/pba/records/gradrate.htm.

Van Maanen, J. (1988). *Tales from the field: On writing ethnography*. Chicago: University of Chicago Press.

Vygotsky, L. (1999). *Thought and language*. Cambridge, MA: MIT Press.

University of Colorado. (2001). *Graduation rates by race/ethnicity*. Retrieved November 1, 2001 from www.colorado.edu/pba/records/gradrate/htm

Wallace, D. (2002). Out in the academy: Heterosexism, invisibility, and double consciousness. *College English, 65*, 53-66.

Walvoord, B., & McCarthy, L. (1990). *Thinking and writing in college: A naturalistic study of students in four disciplines*. Urbana, IL: National Council of Teachers of English.

Wertsch, J. (1991). *Voices of the mind: A sociocultural approach to mediated action*. Cambridge, MA: Harvard University Press.

White, J. (2003). *Sociolinguistic challenges to minority collegiate success: Entering the discourse community of the college*. Unpublished doctoral dissertation, University of Colorado at Boulder.

Willis, P. (1977). *Learning to labour: How working class kids get working class jobs*. Farnborough, England: Saxon House.

Wintre, M., & Yaffe, M. (2000). First-year students' adjustment to university life as a function of relationships with parents. *Journal of Adolescent Research, 15*(1), 9-37.

Yin, R. (1984). *Case study research: Design and methods*. Beverly Hills, CA: Sage Publications.

Young, J. (2003). Black students have fewer mentors in schools than white students, study finds. *Chronicle of Higher Education* [On-line]. Available: http://chronicle.com/daily/2003/01/2003012301n.htm

Zea, M., Reisen, C., Biel, C., & Caplan, R. (1997). Predicting intention to remain in college among ethnic minority and nonminority students. *Journal of Social Psychology, 137*(2), 149-160.

Contributors

I was thrilled at the response of my colleagues when I approached them to help me select the "best of the best" articles on minority college student retention that appeared in the *Journal of College Student Retention: Research, Theory & Practice.* They all enthusiastically took on this challenge and worked hard to complete the task in a timely manner. For this I am thankful and recognize their enormous contribution by introducing them.

David H. Buchanan

Dr. David H. Buchanan became the Provost and Vice President for Academic Affairs at Salisbury University on July 1, 2001. He served for seven years as Dean of the College of Arts and Sciences at West Chester University of Pennsylvania. While Dean he also served one year as the Chief Information Technology Officer for the institution.

At West Chester he worked closely with local businesses, industry, and arts organizations. A result of these collaborations was the development of a B.S. degree in Pharmaceutical Product Development, named by the Eastern Technology Council as the Best New Educational Program of the Year in the Greater Philadelphia region. The College of Arts and Sciences also developed two other new degrees during his tenure, both firsts for the Pennsylvania State System: the B.A. in Women's Studies and an M.A. in Holocaust and Genocide Studies.

Prior to West Chester he was chemistry professor and department chair at Eastern Illinois University. Extensively published, particularly in the field of coal research, he earned his B.S. degree in Chemistry from Case Institute of Technology and Ph.D. degree in Organic Chemistry from the University of Wisconsin, Madison. He was an NIH Postdoctoral fellow at the University of California, Berkeley and Visiting Scientist at SRI International. He is a 1999 graduate of the Harvard Graduate School of Education, Institute for Educational Management.

Wesley R. Habley

Wesley R. Habley has held numerous positions at ACT, Inc. and is currently the Principal Associate and Coordinator of ACT's Office of State Organizations. He received his B.S. in music education and M.Ed. in student personnel from the University of Illinois-Urbana/Champaign, and his Ed.D. from Illinois State University in educational administration. Prior to joining ACT, Habley served first as an academic advisor and later as the Director of the Academic Advisement Center at Illinois State. Habley also served as the Director of Academic and Career Advising at the University of Wisconsin-Eau Claire.

Habley recently published a series of four reports based on ACT's national retention study, *What Works in Student Retention?* Along with Virginia Gordon, Habley edited *Academic Advising: A Comprehensive Handbook.* He is the editor of the monograph on ACT's third, and author of monographs on ACT's fourth, fifth, and sixth National Surveys of Academic Advising. He contributed chapters to *Developmental Academic Advising* and *Faculty Advising Examined.* Additional published material has appeared in the *NACADA Journal, The Journal of College Student Personnel, NASPA Journal, NACADA Monograph Series,* the Jossey-Bass New Directions Series, and several monographs published by the First Year Experience Program at the University of South Carolina.

Habley has served as a consultant or workshop leader at more than 125 colleges in the United States, the Middle East, and Canada. He originated the NACADA Summer Institute on Academic Advising in 1987 and continues to serve on the faculty and as chairperson of the Advisory Board.

Habley is a charter member, past board member, past president, and past treasurer of the National Academic Advising Association (NACADA) and is the recipient of NACADA's awards for Outstanding Contributions to the Field of Academic Advising and Service to NACADA.

Linda Serra Hagedorn

Linda Serra Hagedorn is Professor and Chair of the Educational Administration and Policy Department at the College of Education–University of Florida. She is also the director of the Institute for Higher Education. She is the director of the Transfer and Retention of Urban Community College Students Project (TRUCCS). Prior to coming to Florida in Fall of 2005, Hagedorn was the Associate Director of the Center for Higher Education Policy Analysis at the Rossier School of Education at the University of Southern California and the co-director of the Higher Education/Community College Leadership concentration of the Ed.D. Program.

Dr. Hagedorn's research focuses on community college issues, college retention of underrepresented student groups, and equity. She is currently serving as the Division J (Postsecondary) Vice President of the American Educational Research

Association (AERA). Included in her more recent publications are: *An Investigation of Critical Mass: The Role of Latino Representation in the Retention of Urban Community College Students* (2005); *Hispanic Community College Students and the Transfer Game: Strikes, Misses, and Grand Slam Experiences* (2005); and *Serving Los Angeles: Urban Community Colleges and Educational Success among Latino Students* (2004).

David Kalsbeek

David H. Kalsbeek currently serves as Vice President for Enrollment Management at DePaul University in Chicago, Illinois. In that capacity he leads the marketing and enrollment development strategies for the nation's largest and fastest-growing Catholic university enrolling 24,000 students in nine colleges and seven campuses throughout the greater Chicago region. His responsibilities at DePaul encompass enrollment management, alumni relations, career center and employment relations, university and media relations, and marketing communications.

The innovative models he has developed at DePaul have been highlighted by CASE, by The Associate of Governing Boards, and by The American Marketing Association Symposium and Marketing of Higher Education. Prior to joining DePaul in 1997, Dr. Kalsbeek served as the senior enrollment management administrator at Xavier University in Cincinnati, Ohio and before that at Saint Louis University in St. Louis, Missouri.

Dr. Kalsbeek is a frequent speaker on issues related to strategic enrollment management and marketing, net revenue planning, assessment and learning organizations. He has been a plenary speaker or presenter at nine of AACRAO's eleven Strategic Enrollment Management conferences, as well as NASPA, NACUBO, AAHE, AIR, ACT, AACSB, and AMA conferences. He currently serves on the Editorial Board of the *Journal of College Student Retention: Research, Theory & Practice* and previously served as Feature Editor for *About Campus* magazine. He has been a consultant to over 25 colleges, universities, and associations on issues related to strategic enrollment management.

Dr. Kalsbeek holds a Ph.D. in Public Policy Analysis from Saint Louis University. He earned his master's degree in higher education administration at Ohio State University and a B.A. from Muskingum College in Ohio where he graduated summa cum laude with a major in Philosophy.

Ernest Pascarella

Ernest Pascarella is the Mary Louis Petersen Chair in Higher Education and co-director of the Center for Research on Undergraduate Education at the University of Iowa. Previously he was professor of higher education at the University of Illinois at Chicago. Pascarella has focused his research and writing on the impact of college on students and student persistence in higher education. He has authored over 150 journal articles on these topics, and is coauthor (with Patrick T. Terenzini) of the 1991 Jossey-Bass book *How College Affects Students*, a synthesis of over 2,600 studies on the impact of college. *How College Affects Students* received the 1991 Research Achievement Award from the Association for the Study of Higher Education. An updated volume of the book was published in 2005.

Pascarella has also received a number of other national awards for research. These include the 1981 Albert J. Harris Award from the International Reading Association, the 1987 Sidney Suslow Award, and the 1990 and 1995 Forum Best Paper Awards from the Association for Institutional Research, the 1998 Outstanding Contributions to Research Award from the National Association of Student Personnel Administrators, the 1989 Distinguished Research Award from Division J of the American Educational Research Association, the 1992 Contribution to Knowledge Award from the American College Personnel Association, and the 1997 Assessment Research Award from Commission IX of the American College Personnel Association. In 1989-90, he served as president of the Association for the Study of Higher Education, and in 2003 received the Howard R. Bowen Distinguished Career Award from ASHE.

Pascarella's research has been supported by the National Institute of Education, the National Science Foundation, the Office of Educational Research and Improvement, the American College Personnel Association, the National Association of Student Personnel Administrators, the Mellon and Spencer Foundations, and the Wabash College Center of Inquiry in the Liberal Arts. From 1990-95, he directed the National Study of Student Learning, which was supported by the federally-funded National Center on Postsecondary Teaching, Learning, and Assessment. He is currently co-directing a study of the impact on liberal arts colleges and liberal arts education on student intellectual and personal development.

Thomas R. Phillips

Tom R. Phillips is the Director of Soutenir Ltd., an international consultancy that serves universities, higher education organizations, government agencies, and professional societies. His background includes 17 years in university student services, including admissions, advising, orientation, and international student programs. He served as staff consultant and project officer at the Accreditation Board for Engineering & Technology (ABET). Mr. Phillips researched and wrote the *ABET/Exxon Student Achievement Profile*, a major study of performance and retention among minority and non-minority students in MSE fields.

For over a decade he has been involved in international comparative education research and consulting projects. Mr. Phillips was the ABET Project Manager for the ABET/CHEPS comparative study of 21 European university engineering programs. He has served as a consultant and program evaluator for the IIE

North American RAMP Program, and for two European/American engineering exchange consortia. Mr. Phillip authored the *North American Engineering Exchange Guide,* and *International Perspectives: Engineering Education in Europe, North America, and the Asia-Pacific Region* (FIPSE/ABET, 1997, 1998). He write, edited, and collaborated in the design of the 1998 ASME/Sloan Foundation CD-ROM on mechanical engineering careers.

Between 1997 and 2004 he served as an advisor to the Rector of a European technical university, as a board member for CESAER, and as a consultant at the Center for Higher Education Policy Studies. At present Mr. Phillips is developing criteria, procedures, and evaluator training materials for QUESTE, an EU-funded assessment and improvement program for European engineering institutions.

John H. Schuh

John H. Schuh is Distinguished Professor of Educational Leadership and Policy Studies at Iowa State University. Previously he held administrative and faculty assignments at Arizona State University, Indiana University, and Wichita State University. He is the author, co-author, or editor of over 200 publications including 24 books and monographs. Schuh has held several editorial positions and is the current editor of the *New Directions for Student Services* sourcebook series. He has been recognized for his scholarship, service, and teaching by various professional organizations.

Alan Seidman

Alan Seidman is the Executive Director of the Center for the Study of College Student Retention (www.cscsr.org). The Center provides retention resources to individuals and educational institutions including the *Journal of College Student Retention: Research, Theory & Practice* which Dr. Seidman founded and edits. It is the only scholarly journal devoted exclusively to college student retention issues. The Center also hosts a retention discussion list with over 1,000 members worldwide, a retention reference list with over 1,300 retention references, slide shows, issues, and consulting services.

Dr. Seidman's book, *College Student Retention: Formula for Student Success,* was published in 2005 by ACE/Praeger Press as was his book chapter "Minority Student Retention: Resources for Practitioners" in *Minority Retention: What Works?* He has also published articles in scholarly journals in the areas of retention and attrition, student services, enrollment management, and has given presentations on these topics at local, state, regional, national, and international conferences. Dr. Seidman appeared on *Fox News Live Weekend* to talk about college student retention.

Dr. Seidman has over 30 years of experience in education as a college administrator, educational consultant, and elementary school teacher and earned his B.A. and M.A. from Glassboro State College, New Jersey and his Ed.D. from Syracuse University, New York.

Index